Devolution and power in the United Kingdom

MANCHESTER
1824

Manchester University Press

DEVOLUTION series
series editor Charlie Jeffrey

Devolution has established new political institutions in Scotland, Wales, Northern Ireland, London and the other English regions since 1997. These devolution reforms have far-reaching implications for the politics, policy and society of the UK. Radical institutional change, combined with a fuller capacity to express the UK's distinctive territorial identities, is reshaping the way the UK is governed and opening up new directions of public policy. These are the biggest changes to UK politics for at least 150 years.

The *Devolution* series brings together the best research in the UK on devolution and its implications. It draws together the best analysis from the Economic and Social Research Council's research programme on Devolution and Constitutional Change. The series will have three central themes, each of which are vital components in understanding the changes devolution has set in train.

1 **Delivering public policy after devolution**: **diverging from Westminster**: Does devolution result in the provision of different standards of public service in health or education, or in widening economic disparities from one part of the UK to another? If so, does it matter?

2 **The political institutions of devolution**: How well do the new devolved institutions work? How effectively are devolved and UK-level matters coordinated? How have political organisations which have traditionally operated UK-wide – political parties, interest groups – responded to multi-level politics?

3 **Public attitudes, devolution and national identity**: How do people in different parts of the UK assess the performance of the new devolved institutions? Do people identify themselves differently as a result of devolution? Does a common sense of Britishness still unite people from different parts of the UK?

already published

Devolution and constitutional change in Northern Ireland
Paul Carmichael, Colin Knox and Bob Osborne (eds)

Beyond devolution and decentralisation
Alistair Cole

Between two Unions
Europeanisation and Scottish devolution
Paolo Dardanelli

Territorial politics and health policy
UK health policy in comparative perspective
Scott L. Greer

The English Question
Robert Hazell

Devolution and electoral politics
Dan Hough and Charlie Jeffery (eds)

Debating nationhood and government in Britain, 1885–1939
Perspectives from the 'four nations'
Duncan Tanner, Chris Williams, Wil Griffith and Andrew Edwards (eds)

Devolution and power in the United Kingdom

Edited by
Alan Trench

Manchester University Press
Manchester and New York

distributed exclusively in the USA by Palgrave

Published by Manchester University Press
Oxford Road, Manchester M13 9NR, UK
and Room 400, 175 Fifth Avenue, New York, NY 10010, USA
www.manchesteruniversitypress.co.uk

Distributed exclusively in the USA by
Palgrave, 175 Fifth Avenue, New York,
NY 10010, USA

Distributed exclusively in Canada by
UBC Press, University of British Columbia, 2029 West Mall,
Vancouver, BC, Canada V6T 1Z2

British Library Cataloguing-in-Publication Data
A catalogue record for this book is available from the British Library

Library of Congress Cataloging-in-Publication Data applied for

ISBN 978 07 190 7575 9 *hardback*

First published 2007

16 15 14 13 12 11 10 09 08 07   10 9 8 7 6 5 4 3 2 1

Typeset by Servis Filmsetting Ltd, Manchester
Printed in Great Britain
by Biddles, King's Lynn

Contents

List of figures and tables

Figures

Tables

List of contributors

David Bell is Professor of Economics at the University of Stirling and Co-director of the Scottish Economic Policy Network. He has carried out research on the Barnett formula as part of the Leverhulme Trust's programme on 'Nations and regions: the dynamics of devolution' and was recently a member of the Care Development Group which looked into Long-Term Care of the Elderly in Scotland.

Alex Christie is a Research Fellow with the Centre for Public Policy for Regions and the Fraser of Allander Institute at the University of Strathclyde. His research interests lie in the field of public finance and multi-level governance. He has written on the nature and future of the Scottish budget process and the future of territorial funding in the UK.

Scott Greer, a political scientist and member of the Constitution Unit, is Assistant Professor of Health Management and Policy at the University of Michigan School of Public Health. His books include *Territorial Politics and Health Policy: UK health policy in comparative perspective* (2004), the edited *Territory, Democracy and Justice: Regionalism and federalism in Western democracies* (2006), and *Nationalism and Self-Government: The politics of autonomy in Scotland and Catalonia* (forthcoming).

Holly Jarman is a doctoral student at the London School of Economics. She previously worked in Parliament at Westminster and for the Department of Health.

Charlie Jeffery is Professor of Politics in the School of Social and Political Studies at the University of Edinburgh and Director of the Economic and Social Research Council's research programme on 'Devolution and Constitutional Change'.

Martin Laffin is Professor of Public Policy and Management and Director of the University Centre for Public Policy at Durham University. He recently completed a project on 'The Role of the Parties in Inter-Governmental Relations after Devolution' as part of the Economic and Social Research Council Devolution and Constitutional Change Programme.

James Mitchell is Professor of Politics at Strathclyde University and headed the Scottish Devolution Monitoring team between 2001 and 2005. He is the author of numerous books and articles on Scottish and UK politics and devolution, most recently *Governing Scotland: The invention of administrative devolution* published by Palgrave in 2003.

Dr Rosanne Palmer is a Lecturer in European Studies in the School of European Studies at Cardiff University. Prior to this appointment, she worked as a Research Fellow at the University of Birmingham on projects examining multi-level governance in the EU. Her main teaching and research interests include European politics, UK devolution and comparative territorial politics.

Eric Shaw is a Senior Lecturer in the Department of Politics at Stirling University. Prior to entering academic life, he worked as a researcher for the Labour Party. He has written three books plus numerous other publications on the Labour Party and is at present working on a study of New Labour and the Blair Government.

Gerald Taylor is Lecturer in Politics and Media Studies in the School of Humanities and Social Sciences at the University of Glamorgan. His research interests include intergovernmental relations and party governance, the Labour Party and Welsh Politics. His publications include the forthcoming book *Welsh Politics Today*.

Alan Trench was a Senior Research Fellow at the Constitution Unit between 2001 and 2005, working on devolution and intergovernmental relations in the United Kingdom and comparative intergovernmental relations in federal systems. He remains an honorary Senior Research Fellow there. A solicitor by profession, he was specialist adviser to the House of Lords Select Committee on the Constitution for their inquiry into *Devolution: Inter-institutional Relations in the United Kingdom* in 2001–03.

Ronald Watts is Principal Emeritus, Professor Emeritus of Political Studies and Fellow of the Institute of Intergovernmental Relations at Queen's University, Ontario, where he has been a member of the academic staff since 1955. He was Principal and Vice-Chancellor of Queen's University 1974–1984. From 1988 to 1993, he was Director of the Institute of Intergovernmental Relations at Queen's University. He is a Companion of the Order of Canada, a Fellow of the Royal Society of Canada, and a member of the board of directors of the Forum of Federations.

Acknowledgements

This book is principally a product of the research programme on 'Nations and Regions: the dynamics of devolution' based at the Constitution Unit, University College London, between 2001 and 2005. The programme was generously funded by the Leverhulme Trust, and the Unit and I personally are hugely grateful to the Trust and its directors, Professors Barry Supple and Richard Brook, for their support of this work.

The book has also drawn on work carried out as part of the Economic and Social Research Council's 'Devolution and Constitutional Change' research programme, which funded the work behind chapter 9 and some of that behind chapter 2. That programme also enabled Professor Ron Watts to spend two months as a research visitor at the Constitution Unit in May and June 2003 and see the UK's experience of devolution at first hand. That visit enabled Professor Watts to prepare chapter 11, as well as enabling those of us at the Unit to share his huge expertise on the working of federal systems across the world. We are grateful to the ESRC and particularly to the programme's director, Professor Charlie Jeffery, for facilitating that visit, and for all their and his other help and support.

As editor, I should like to record my personal thanks to a number of people whose work has contributed greatly to this book. First, to Akash Paun, for his meticulous work in helping prepare chapters for submission and otherwise keeping the editor to the mark, and his limitless tolerance and good humour in doing so. Second, to two colleagues at the Constitution Unit – Professor Robert Hazell CBE, the Unit's Director, for all his help and support, and Scott Greer, with whom many of the ideas in the book were aired before being committed to paper. Third, to the contributors to this book, for their ideas, enthusiasm and forbearance, both in preparing drafts of their contributions and in coping with the editor's requests for changes to them. I am also grateful to the contributors and Robert Hazell for taking part in a number of seminars in 2003–04 to discuss drafts of chapters; I hope that process of discussion has helped ensure that the book has a common and consistent point of view. Fourth, to the administrative staff at the Constitution Unit past and present, particularly Helen Daines and Matthew Butt, who helped with organisational matters in the earlier stages of work. Fifth, to numerous, necessarily anonymous civil servants (and others involved in devolution) for their cooperation in the research on which this book was based. We are grateful to them for finding time to be interviewed, and for their candour and helpfulness when interviewed. We are equally grateful to the officials who attended a 'Chatham House rule' seminar at Dover House to discuss a number of draft chapters for the book in June 2004. Sixth, to Dr Bill Lawton and the Academic Relations branch of the Canadian High Commission in London, who offered us splendid accommodation at Canada House for one of our meetings when UCL had run out of rooms. Seventh, to David Crawley, then Head of the Scotland Office, and to the Secretary of State for Scotland for making rooms at Dover House available for the June 2004 seminar. Eighth, to Tony Mason and his colleagues at Manchester University Press, for their help in producing the book and forbearance in the editor's delays in supplying it to them. I am also grateful to the Press's reviewer for a number of helpful comments. And ninth, but by no means least, to my mother and stepfather and my late father, for all their intellectual stimulation and personal support over many years.

Editor's note

Work on the manuscript of this book finished in December 2005. It therefore does not take account of subsequent developments, or books published after that date. In particular, it does not consider the results of the St Andrew's agreement regarding Northern Ireland of October 2006, the March 2007 elections there or the subsequent agreement for the restoration of devolution, or the May 2007 elections in Scotland and Wales.

Probably the most notable developments in Great Britain relate to the powers of the National Assembly for Wales. With the passing of the Government of Wales Act 2006, from May 2007 the Assembly will acquire legislative powers as well as be legally separated from the Welsh Assembly Government.

Chapter 11 was prepared before the rejection by referendum in Italy in June 2006 of proposals to extend significantly the powers of the Italian regions.

Except where otherwise stated, URLs for websites were verified in November 2005.

1
Introduction: territory, devolution and power in the United Kingdom

Alan Trench

This is a book about the system of intergovernmental relations that has developed in the United Kingdom since devolution to Scotland, Wales and Northern Ireland took effect in 1999.[1] It understands intergovernmental relations as meaning principally the relationships between the various administrations or executives that are now responsible for government within the UK – the UK Government and the devolved administrations for Scotland, Wales and (intermittently) Northern Ireland. It seeks to understand what the system of relations that has developed since devolution is, how it works, how it has influenced the making of policy, and to assess more broadly the impact of devolution on the working of the UK constitution.[2] In doing so, it seeks to understand the post-devolution territorial politics of the UK in a broader historical and comparative context. It also seeks to examine the implications of major constitutional and institutional change for UK institutions, and looks at the way the British state has responded to that change in its organisation and ways of working. Underlying all this is the question of where power now lies in the devolved United Kingdom.

Its approach is therefore rather different from many of the books about devolution that have appeared so far. It is about the impact of devolution on the United Kingdom as a whole, rather than one specific part of the UK and

1 The year 1999 is used to indicate the start of devolution, as that was when powers were transferred to the Scottish Parliament and Executive, the National Assembly for Wales and (somewhat later in the year) the Northern Ireland Assembly and Executive.
2 There have been a number of previous general discussions of intergovernmental relations in the UK. See in particular House of Lords Select Committee on the Constitution, *Devolution: Inter-institutional Relations in the United Kingdom*, Session 2002–03 2nd Report, HL 28 (London: The Stationery Office, 2003); Trench, A., 'The More Things Change the More They Stay the Same: Intergovernmental relations four years on' in Trench, A. (ed.), *Has Devolution Made a Difference: The State of the Nations 2004* (Exeter: Imprint Academic, 2004).

its politics. In other words, it takes a system-wide approach to the working of devolution. It is also concerned with the implications of large-scale institutional change on those power relations – how the creation of elected legislatures or assemblies, with territorial governments accountable to those elected bodies – affects the territorial distribution of power. However, its interest is primarily in what the executives do in relation to each other, rather than in relations between legislatures and other elected bodies.

Forming a view of this is not a straightforward task. This book uses materials and approaches not just from the study of politics, but also from history, economics, law, policy studies and public administration to try to come to a rounded view of the nature of territorial power in the United Kingdom after devolution. Moreover, it incorporates a comparative element, which both puts the impact of constitutional change in the UK in a broader context, and will help overseas readers to understand that impact better.

The background: territorial politics in the United Kingdom

The United Kingdom, as is well known, is a territorially complex state. The political project of 'Great Britain' was a goal of James VI and I when, already King of Scotland, he became King of England in 1603. England itself had been built into a single unit from a number of competing Saxon Kingdoms following the Norman invasion in 1066. During the early middle ages it conquered Wales by military force, and established dominance over Ireland, again through military power. Only under the Tudors did 'England' come to be a unified political entity, and one that also absorbed Wales. By 1603 the lands under the rule of the English Crown were ruled in varied ways.[3] The seventeenth century saw, however, a transformation in this pattern of rule, in which three factors were vital. First was the accession of James to the English as well as the Scottish throne, and his project of a broader British union. From the outset, the Union of the Crowns had broader objects of political union than a mere personal union of the monarch's realms.[4] Second were the

---

3   For historical discussions of these parts of the United Kingdom and their relationship with England, see Kearney, H., *The British Isles* (Cambridge: Cambridge University Press, 1989); Foster, R., *Modern Ireland 1600–1972* (Harmondsworth: Penguin, 1990); Davies, J., *A History of Wales* (Harmondsworth: Penguin, 1994); Lynch, M., *Scotland: A new history* (London: Pimlico, 1992).

4   This can be contrasted with the attitude towards the Electorate and later Kingdom of Hanover after 1714 – a purely personal union with no political or economic integration at all, emphasised by Hanover's retention of a different law of succession that resulted in the union being broken in 1837.

experiences of the whole archipelago during the (English) civil wars, with English military power established as the dominant force in Scotland and Ireland as well as England under the Commonwealth and English political ambitions to dominate it made plain.[5] This use of bloody brute force underlined English concerns with both dominating and maintaining the safety of the British Isles – and England was plainly the overwhelming military force within those islands. Third were the problems Scotland increasingly faced come the end of the century in exercising any meaningful autonomy under the shared Crown. It found its overseas trade obstructed by English merchants, leading to the embrace of the Darien venture and the seriously damaging consequences of its collapse. Come the crisis of Stuart rule in 1687–88 and the arrival of William and Mary it was politically impossible for the Scots to make any alternative choice of monarch.[6]

At the start of the eighteenth century, therefore, the choice for Scotland was between incorporation into a United Kingdom, with the prospect of sharing the advantages that brought particularly for trade within the British isles and the broader empire, or a continued relationship of dependence on England with little freedom of manoeuvre. Neither was particularly promising for Scotland. Notwithstanding the widespread evidence of fraud and corruption surrounding the passing of the Act of Union in Scotland, a real political choice was made by Scots in 1706–07, which had advantages and disadvantages for Scotland. Scotland chose to be in. And following the Union, Scotland was still able to exercise significant and meaningful autonomy, even though some Scottish institutions (such as the Scottish Privy Council) were dismantled within a short time.[7] Yet uprisings such as the '15 and the '45 underlined the vulnerability of that Union and the real threats to it – while brutality such as that exhibited at Culloden, Glencoe or during the Highland Clearances was bound to fuel resentment in Scotland, and to create a firm foundation for a myth of national martyrdom.

During the eighteenth century somewhat similar issues developed in Ireland – a country in a greater state of subjugation to England to start with, which asserted its independence to an increasing degree and in 1782 attained a form of legislative autonomy that bears some striking resemblances to that

---

5 See Kishlansky, M., *A Monarchy Transformed: Britain 1603–1714* (Harmondsworth: Penguin, 1996), particularly chap. 8; and Kearney, *The British Isles*, chap. 7.
6 See Trevelyan, G. M., *The English Revolution 1688–1689* (London: Oxford University Press, 1938).
7 See Murdoch, A., 'Scottish Sovereignty in the Eighteenth Century', in Dickinson, H. T. and Lynch, M. (eds), *The Challenge to Westminster: Sovereignty, devolution and independence* (East Linton: Tuckwell Press, 2000).

of Scotland today.[8] Yet that autonomy came to constitute a sufficient threat to the United Kingdom (after the attempted French invasion of 1796 and the Great Rebellion of 1798) that a legislative union became an attractive option for London, and was achieved in 1801 – with the effect of reinforcing Protestant (meaning Anglican, and Ascendancy) dominance of politics in Ireland, disenfranchising the Catholic and Presbyterian populations. This created the basis for political nationalism that, in the absence of Home Rule (and despite that issue dominating UK politics in the late nineteenth and early twentieth centuries), led to the twenty-six counties declaring their independence in 1921, rather than accepting a limited measure of autonomy within the UK (and under the British Crown).

After Ireland's independence, political debate about territorial matters in the United Kingdom largely ceased until the 1970s. A large part of the reason for this was the emergence of class-based party politics, and (especially after the Second World War) the importance of the welfare state.[9] Regional inequalities were treated as cases of uneven distribution needing action from the centre, rather than as reflecting the distribution of power across the UK's various territories. Northern Ireland experienced devolution to the Stormont Parliament, which took Northern Ireland off the UK's political agenda, and territory was otherwise treated as a politically unimportant issue until the rise of Scottish and Welsh nationalism in the 1960s and 1970s, and its emergence as a threat to the Britain-wide political parties. A fairly typical mid-twentieth-century writer (presumably English) could recognise the multi-national character of the United Kingdom but deny it any political importance:

> The development in Britain of vocal and enthusiastic Welsh and Scots Nationalist groups is an unwelcome illustration of the continued strength and growth of Nationalism. No one wishes to deny to the Scots or the Welsh their national pride and their national peculiarities. But to break up the unity of a community which has learned through centuries of struggle and difficulty to become a real community on the basis of toleration of differences would be a retrograde step of the most serious nature. Britain is an example of the possibility of another basis than Nationalism for a healthy and civilized State; to break it into fragments by Home Rule movements of its various constituent parts would not only be foolish; it would be criminal. There is no real parallel with the Irish movement; no one thinks of claiming that Scotland has ever been conquered; and the 'conquest' of

8 No-one has expressly compared the powers of the Scottish Parliament since 1999 with that of the Irish Parliament between 1782 and 1800, but see Bartlett, T., 'Ireland: From legislative independence to legislative union', in Dickinson and Lynch (eds), *The Challenge to Westminster*; Foster, *Modern Ireland*.

9 See chapter 2 by James Mitchell, and McEwen, N., 'State Welfare Nationalism: The territorial impact of welfare state development in Scotland', *Regional and Federal Studies*, 12:1 (2002), 66–90.

Wales was a feudal affair which affected the real life of the Welsh very little. All these movements for fragmentation are based on the delusion that only a national group is suitable for a stable State.[10]

However, the practice of management of the UK state always reflected its variety, as James Mitchell shows in chapter 2. Even looked at from the most systematic unionist view (exemplified in the writings of A. V. Dicey), the UK acknowledged territorial differences, and found ways of reflecting these whether in the extent of administrative devolution to Scotland from 1885 or the 'leeway' granted to Stormont after 1921, and more tenuously for Wales. Yet as Mitchell notes, no-one ever succeeded in working out what the UK was *for*. Consequently, when the ability of central institutions to reflect territorial difference became questionable, so the transfer of power from the centre to the periphery came onto the agenda.[11]

The study of territorial politics in the UK began in the 1960s with work on Scottish and Northern Irish politics, but developed and broadened its approach from the 1970s onward. Its starting points were the emergence of political nationalism from the 1920s in both Scotland and Wales, and the complexities that developed regarding Northern Ireland and its relations with the Republic of Ireland and the UK, both during the period of devolution to the Northern Ireland Parliament at Stormont until 1972, and with the start of the Troubles in 1969. Scottish and Welsh nationalism had of course produced the push toward devolution in the later 1970s, which after much debate within the Labour Party and at Westminster eventually produced the Scotland Act 1978 and Wales Act 1978. The former would have given Scotland an elected legislature, with functions in a significant number of defined areas and use of those powers subject to the approval of the Secretary of State, who would have acquired some of the functions of a governor-general as a result. The latter would have given Wales an elected assembly with executive powers working through committees, rather like a county council of the time writ large. The workability of each scheme is highly questionable.[12] That question is however moot, as in neither case did the Act secure the necessary level of approval in a referendum – failing in Wales by a

10 Featherstone, H. L., *A Century of Nationalism* (London: Thomas Nelson, 1939), 191–2.
11 This happened despite over-representation for both Scotland and Wales at Westminster, at least after 1944; see McLean, I., 'Are Scotland and Wales Over-represented in the House of Commons?', *Political Quarterly*, 66 (1995), 250–68.
12 For discussion of the 1978 Acts, see Bogdanor, V., *Devolution* (Oxford: Oxford University Press, 1979). Rose, R., *The Territorial Dimension* in *Government: Understanding the United Kingdom* (Chatham, NJ: Chatham, 1982), 199–203, emphasises the limited powers of assemblies established under the 1978 legislation.

substantial majority, and in Scotland securing a plurality of votes but failing to reach the threshold of 40 per cent of the whole electorate set as an obstructing tactic by opponents of legislation in Parliament. Thus the issue of devolution disappeared from the Westminster agenda (if not from that in Scotland or Wales) for over a decade.

A second consequence of the devolution debates concerning Scotland and Wales, and the Troubles in Northern Ireland, was the generation of sizable academic literatures (in the case of Northern Ireland a huge one). There is not space properly to summarise let alone analyse those literatures here, but it is worth discussing some features of them.[13] One key division in the literature was between those works concerned with the United Kingdom as a whole, and those primarily interested in the periphery and how Scotland, Wales and Ireland or Northern Ireland related to an English-dominated whole. Much therefore belongs properly to the category of Scottish or Welsh rather than UK politics, and was concerned with the background and growth of political nationalism, or with the extent to which a particular territory constituted a distinct political system.[14] Tom Nairn combined political nationalism with Marxism in an almost messianic portrayal of the impending demise of the United Kingdom, to find small-nation (e.g. Scottish) nationalism not merely purged of the vices of big-country nationalism but as capable of serving as a way of achieving a Marxist transformation of state and society.[15] Michael Hechter, a sociologist, used dependency theory to emphasise the economic as well as political exploitation of the Celtic periphery by the English heartland, going so far as to characterise the phenomenon as 'internal colonialism'.[16] This view has been widely criticised, however, and is shared by few.

That part of the territorial politics literature concerned with the UK as a whole sought to make sense of the territorial complexity of the United Kingdom, developing the concept of 'union state' (rather than a unitary one)

13 For a magisterial if now somewhat dated guide to the Northern Ireland literature, see Whyte, J., *Interpreting Northern Ireland* (Oxford: Clarendon, 1991). See also O'Leary, B. and McGarry, J., *The Politics of Antagonism: Understanding Northern Ireland* (London: Athlone Press, 2nd edn, 1996).
14 For example, Kellas, J., *The Scottish Political System* (Cambridge: Cambridge University Press, 1973); Harvie, C., *Scotland and Nationalism* (London: George Allen & Unwin, 1977); Butt Philip, A., *The Welsh Question: Nationalism in Welsh politics 1945–1970* (Cardiff: University of Wales Press, 1975).
15 Nairn, T., *The Break-Up of Britain* (London: Verso, 1981). See also Nairn, T., *After Britain: New Labour and the return of Scotland* (London: Granta Books, 2000).
16 Hechter, M., *Internal Colonialism: The Celtic fringe in British national development 1536–1966* (London: Routledge & Kegan Paul, 1975).

to do so. (As James Mitchell shows in chapter 2, this concept is now in need of further revision.) Thus it examined political institutions, including the role of Westminster and representation in Parliament; election studies, particularly for Scotland and Wales; and detailed examination of the working of the UK's administrative apparatus for Scotland and Wales, the Scottish and Welsh Offices, and sometimes related this to studies of local government, urban politics and central–local relations.[17] Richard Rose emphasised the degree to which the United Kingdom was the product of a sequence of unplanned historical events, 'an agglomeration created by the expansion and contraction of territorial power in the course of a thousand years', and characterised by a set of political institutions rather than a sense of common British identity.[18] It was characterised by a widely shared but largely unconscious public support, and by significant territorial variations in services and policies, which were seldom articulated let alone justified. Jim Bulpitt took these approaches rather further in his *Territory and Power in the United Kingdom*.[19] Bulpitt sought to explain territorial power relations in the UK by using the idea of a 'dual polity', in which the UK state at the centre (or in his terminology the Centre) was principally concerned to assure itself of control over 'high politics' matters such as defence, foreign affairs or the economy, but was willing to allow local control of 'low politics' ones – the bread-and-butter staples of the services that governments provide every day, whether that be administering markets and weights and measures in the eighteenth century, or provision of health and housing in the twentieth. This dual polity had functioned after the 1920s but had broken down in the 1960s, with the result that many 'low politics' matters became matters of concern to the Centre – local government finance because of its impact on macroeconomic policy, for example. Consequently the Centre lost its autonomy from such concerns, and was hampered in its ability to act regarding 'high politics' matters. Bulpitt saw the 1970s devolution proposals as an attempt to reassert the Centre's autonomy, as powers to be devolved were limited and did not threaten the Centre's sovereignty, the losers were the Scottish and Welsh Offices rather than the Centre properly speaking, and England and Northern Ireland were wholly excluded. Writing a little later, and reviewing most of this phase of research, R. A. W. Rhodes drew on Bulpitt's concepts of the dual polity and Centre autonomy, but found

17 A good example, reflecting many of these trends, is Madgwick, P. and Rose, R. (eds), *The Territorial Dimension in United Kingdom Politics* (London: Macmillan, 1982). See also Rhodes, R. A. W., *Beyond Westminster and Whitehall: The sub-central governments of Britain* (London: Unwin Hyman, 1988).

18 Rose, *The Territorial Dimension*, 37.

19 Bulpitt, J., *Territory and Power in the United Kingdom* (Manchester: Manchester University Press, 1983).

the best explanatory concepts to be 'policy networks', which emphasised the relationship between sub-central government and central government (rather than local autonomy), and the 'differentiated polity' in which different levels of government assumed different functional responsibilities.

Devolution research: how this book came about

Devolution was a response to a variety of political factors in the late 1990s. In particular it was a response to years of Conservative government of Scotland (and Wales) despite the Tories winning little representation at Westminster from those nations. It was also a response to both a continuing challenge from nationalist parties to the UK state, and (on the part of Tony Blair and New Labour) to the inherited commitment made by John Smith as party leader (and supported by most Scottish Labour politicians, notably Gordon Brown and Donald Dewar) to establish a Scottish Parliament. What it introduced was, without doubt, a significant shift in constitutional and territorial power. Elected political institutions responsible for a wide range of executive matters, and endowed in Northern Ireland and Scotland with legislative powers, were established. While these institutions owed a great deal to the administrative apparatuses that preceded them (an issue that is explored in detail through-out this book), the fact that elected, autonomous institutions were put in place for the first time was a major change.[20] The question is quite how major a change it is.

Making sense of that change has been a major task for the last few years. It is one that has been supported by the Leverhulme Trust-funded 'Nations and Regions: The dynamics of devolution' research programmes based at University College London and the University of Edinburgh, and by the larger Devolution and Constitutional Change programme funded by the Economic and Social Research Council. Both have been large-scale multi-disciplinary (and interdisciplinary) efforts, which have already influenced practical as well as academic debates about devolution. Yet much, if by no means all, of the earlier discussion of devolution was dominated by two approaches. One emphasised devolution as a national phenomenon in Scotland or Wales, and was concerned with its impact on those nations.[21] In

20 For the importance of the fact that territorial variation took place within a single government, see Rose, *The Territorial Dimension*, and Rhodes, *Beyond Westminster and Whitehall*, especially 143–53.

21 For examples of the former, see Taylor, B. and Thomson, K. (eds), *Scotland and Wales: Nations again?* (Cardiff: University of Wales Press, 1999); Jones, J. B. and Balsom, D. (eds), *The Road to the National Assembly for Wales* (Cardiff: University

contrast to that approach, this book takes a UK-wide perspective on devolution, and seeks to assess its impact on the system of the UK as a whole, rather than on one or more of its component parts. This approach involves close scrutiny of what the devolved administrations do as well as of the centre.

The second approach looked at devolution as a UK-wide phenomenon, and tried to understand it in terms that were often related to or borrowed from the study of federal systems.[22] This approach has a long pedigree, and federal ideas have influenced UK constitutional debates for a long time – most notably in the context of seeking solutions for Ireland and for Britain's relations with further-flung parts of the Empire, in the nineteenth century, and more recently in the context of the UK's membership of the European Community and European Union.[23] The early arguments were largely forecasts, based on expectations of how devolution would develop. This book re-examines those parallels in a sustained way for the first time since devolution. This is an opportunity to re-assess how far those predictions have been justified in the light of experience of how devolution actually works. Its broader perspective on devolution can also be seen in the inclusion of a comparative chapter by the doyen of students of comparative federalism, Ronald Watts. The view presented also pays close attention to the role of the European Union, both in how it affects the devolved administrations and how they affect (or seek to affect) it.

Although it is an edited volume, this book is not simply a collection of conference or seminar papers. It draws on original research to present what we hope is a coherent view of intergovernmental relations in the UK after devolution from a variety of perspectives, in subject matter as well as in the disciplines of the contributors, and the contributors met on a number of occasions to discuss their work and how it related to the argument of the book. The research was mostly conducted as part of the Leverhulme-funded

of Wales Press, 2000); Lynch, P., *Scottish Government and Politics: An introduction* (Edinburgh: Edinburgh University Press, 2001); Rawlings, R., *Delineating Wales: Constitutional, legal and administrative aspects of national devolution* (Cardiff: University of Wales Press, 2003); Keating, M., *The Government of Scotland: Public policy making after devolution* (Edinburgh: Edinburgh University Press, 2005).

22 For examples of the latter, see Burrows, N., *Devolution* (London: Sweet & Maxwell, 2000); Bogdanor, V., *Devolution in the United Kingdom* (Oxford: Oxford University Press, 2nd edn, 2001); and Hazell, R. (ed.), *Constitutional Futures: A history of the next ten years* (Oxford: Oxford University Press, 1999).

23 See Kendle, J., *Federal Britain: A history* (London: Routledge, 1997); Burgess, M., *The British Tradition of Federalism* (London: Leicester University Press, 1995); and (for one of the more recent arguments in favour of federalism in the UK) Banks, J. C., *Federal Britain? The case for regionalism* (London: George Harrap & Co., 1971).

'Nations and Regions' programme based at the Constitution Unit at University College London. It has also drawn on research carried out as part of the ESRC's Devolution and Constitutional Change programme. Much of this research (notably that used in chapters 3 and 5–10) was interview-based. Except for chapter 9, the interviewees were generally serving or retired civil servants or others involved in the administration of public services affected by devolution. In these cases (and subject to exceptions noted in the chapters) interviews were semi-structured and conducted on the basis that the interviewees would not be named or publicly identified, to avoid the risk of personal and professional embarrassment and to enable them to speak freely. Where possible, the contributors have referred to published sources or documents to support their reasoning; that does not diminish the value of our interviews in helping us understand the realities of government after devolution. The contribution of our interviewees is noted in the acknowledgements to this book but bears repeating here. This work would not have been possible without them, and we are hugely grateful to them for all their assistance.

It is worth saying something at this point about the treatment of Northern Ireland in this book. Northern Ireland is at present a part of the United Kingdom, and before 1999 was the only part of it to have experienced devolution in modern times. One legacy of devolution to the Northern Irish Parliament between 1922 and 1972 was the establishment of a separate administrative structure for Northern Ireland (discussed further by James Mitchell in chapter 2), which itself has affected government there during periods of direct rule from Westminster as well. Since 1999 Northern Ireland has experienced intermittent spells of devolved government, meaning the devolved Assembly and Executive established under Strand 1 of the Belfast or Good Friday Agreement.[24] It has also experienced rather longer periods during which devolution has been suspended and direct rule has been restored instead. This creates a problem for this book, which is about the relationship between devolved institutions and power in the United Kingdom. The approach we have taken is to include consideration of Northern Ireland, when the experience of devolution there has something to say about the broader cross-UK phenomenon of intergovernmental relations after devolution. Equally, however, this is not a book about Northern Ireland, or territorial variations in policy and policy-making more generally, and it does not consider the broader issues of the peace process or policy development

24 *An Agreement Reached at the Multi-Party Talks on Northern Ireland*, Cm 3883 (London: The Stationery Office, 1998). For a discussion, see Wilford, R. (ed.), *Aspects of the Belfast Agreement* (Oxford: Oxford University Press, 2001), especially chapters 5 (Brigid Hadfield), 6 (Rick Wilford) and 7 (Graham Walker).

there. By the same token, it does not comprehensively assess the working of Strands 2 and 3 of the Good Friday Agreement (the north–south and east–west aspects), but it does discuss them in the context of their impact on UK matters.

This book's basic argument

As well as reconsidering the extent to which the UK after devolution can be considered in some sense, or to some degree, a federal system, this book's main argument is to consider the working of the UK's post-devolution system. In particular, it seeks to address a significant paradox about the working of the UK. That paradox relates to the nature of the autonomy that the devolved administrations can exercise. As Agranoff has noted, intergovernmental relations is a characteristic if not ubiquitous feature of all devolved systems of government, and of great importance for them: 'Autonomy must also rest on a foundation of supportive intergovernmental relations'.[25] (It is also now widely accepted as a characteristic of all federal systems, but for perhaps somewhat different reasons.) The importance of intergovernmental relations for such systems means that a key issue for maximising devolved autonomy is ensuring that the constituent (or sub-state) units are strong enough to have meaningful bargaining power in relation to the central or national government. That is especially the case in the UK. Many of those involved in creating devolution have been keen to say that 'devolution is not federalism', by which they appear to mean classical dual federalism involving separate but co-ordinate governments (an ideal type now not to be found anywhere, if it ever was). One official involved in European Union affairs regarded this area of activity as *intra*-governmental relations, not intergovernmental relations (which is what he practised, in relation to other EU member states).[26] What devolution is, exactly, is something few are keen to specify.

The paradox is this. On one hand, intergovernmental relations in the devolved UK have not developed by happenstance; they are an integral part of the institutional framework of devolution (an argument developed more fully by Alan Trench in chapter 3). An analysis of the power of the devolved administrations in intergovernmental matters strongly suggests that they are significantly weaker than the UK Government, which in most respects is able

25 Agranoff, R., 'Autonomy, Devolution and Intergovernmental Relations', *Regional and Federal Studies*, 14:1 (2004), 26–65, at 30.
26 In similar vein, the chapter of Noreen Burrows's book concerned with this subject matter addresses itself to 'intra-governmental relations'; Burrows, *Devolution*, chap. 5.

to out-manoeuvre, overwhelm or even countermand them. Their powers are contingent, dependent on the passive restraint and non-opposition of the UK Government or its active cooperation. This means that devolved autonomy is contingent and the devolved administrations' position in intergovernmental relations fundamentally weak. The safeguards the devolved administrations have, by contrast, are much more limited in scope and likely effect, or are essentially incapable of being measured. This applies equally to their formal constitutional powers (see chapter 3), their financial position (which David Bell and Alex Christie analyse from an economic point of view in chapter 4, and Alan Trench examines from a political one in chapter 5), and to the practice of intergovernmental relations in relation particularly to UK legislation and the resolution of disputes (assessed by Alan Trench in chapter 8). The problem is all the more serious because intergovernmental relations are in fact built into the fabric of devolution by both its legal structure (discussed in chapter 3) and its administrative precursors (illustrated by James Mitchell in chapter 2, as well as in chapters 3, 5 and 8). Intergovernmental relations may be ubiquitous in federal states, but as a practical necessity rather than something built into the fabric of the arrangements for government from the outset.

On the other hand, the fact that devolved autonomy is at best limited and constrained does not alter its reality. The devolved administrations have been able to use their powers to follow their own path and develop their own policies to a very significant degree. Their autonomy may be contingent, but it is also real. They have been able to develop their own policies and actions in a range of areas, surveyed by Alan Trench and Holly Jarman in chapter 6 and examined in one area (health) in detail by Scott Greer in chapter 7. The devolved administrations are also able to exercise considerable practical influence on relevant areas of EU policy, despite their limited formal power (explained by Charlie Jeffery and Rosanne Palmer in chapter 10). To the extent the devolved administrations are constrained, it is not by their formal powers or the actions of the UK Government and its reserve powers. Rather, it is by factors such as their policy inheritances, the political and policy-making environments in which they operate, their overall financial resources, and to an extent the impact of UK Government decisions as government for England.

Explaining how, and why, this situation has arisen is not straightforward. A conventional assumption has developed that it is due to the Labour Party's dominance of politics across Great Britain; it has formed the government in London since 1997, and in Wales and Scotland since 1999, albeit in coalition in Scotland throughout and in Wales between 2000 and 2003. Martin Laffin, Eric Shaw and Gerald Taylor show (in chapter 9) that this assumption is wrong, and that the effect of Labour's dominance is rather different in practice. Labour has sought to maximise its electoral advantage (for both UK and devolved elections), but not to use party loyalty or party mechanisms as a back-channel for the conduct of intergovernmental relations, and the high level of cooperation is due to the party continuing to operate as a national (Britain-wide) party, not as a centralised organisation driven from party head-quarters. As chapters 8 and 10 taken together show, the practice of intergovernmental relations does not merely rely on informal cooperation and operate outside formal frameworks and mechanisms, it rests upon a set of assumptions of common interest and mutual goodwill between administrations that is highly vulnerable. Not only would the nature of intergovernmental relations change if different parties were in government in Cardiff or Edinburgh and London, but even if the existing conditions were to change (for example, by serious cleavages developing within the Labour Party). To quote the title of Scott Greer's chapter, what has been created is a fragile divergence machine. At present, it creates conditions of maximal autonomy for policy divergence – but it could easily be upset by one of a number of circumstances that would emphasise the importance of the UK Government in relation to the devolved administrations.

Using the concept of power

Trying to assess the power of actors in a political or organisational system is never an easy task. Power is a highly contested concept, and has been the subject of voluminous discussion over many decades (indeed centuries).[27] This book does not seek to advance the theoretical debate on this subject but rather to address empirical issues. However, we do need a conceptually grounded definition of power if we are to address properly the issue of what sort of changes devolution has caused in the territorial distribution of power within the UK. Likewise, we need to clarify what we understand by autonomy for the purpose of this undertaking.

This is not a straightforward task. A conventional definition might conceive of power as 'the ability to deliver a desired outcome'. However, this raises serious problems. First, it does not address the question of whether that outcome can actually be achieved. A US state legislature once famously considered declaring the value of the mathematical constant pi (π) to be 3.2. If enacted, no clock in the state would have told accurate time and many bridges would have fallen down. The state's formal power to alter the value

---

27 For a brief but concise discussion of existing approaches and their shortcomings, see Lukes, S., *Power: A radical view* (London: Macmillan, 1974).

of pi bore little relation to the practicalities or physics of the real world.[28] Second, less absurdly, it takes little account of the context in which power is exercised, and what a particular actor has the means to do. Sheer practical constraints impact on the devolved institutions (as they do on Westminster). Suggestions that Parliament can repeal the Statute of Westminster of 1931 (by which the Dominions gained their autonomy) or the European Communities Act 1972 have an air of unreality and abstraction about them; such actions would in the former case be impossible (the former Dominions are now independent) and in the latter at least gravely difficult. Other actions may be possible legally but politically inconceivable, such as abolishing the National Health Service, given its totemic significance. Is the Scottish Parliament powerless because it cannot enable Scotland to withdraw from the European Union? That is not a power that was ever on offer to a Scottish Parliament through devolution. Using this as a measure of power does not assist us for our present purpose at all.

A related problem is the question of how one might measure power when the nature of the relationship is one that involves a good deal of bargaining. The nature of such a process means neither party is likely to secure its desired outcome (or at least its formally stated one), but to reach a compromise solution in the context of an ongoing relationship which is both an adequate compromise in relation to the immediate issue and which sustains that broader relationship. (This is one reason why autonomy needs to be regarded as an element of power in the intergovernmental context.[29]) And this formulation presents serious empirical problems as well; it is far easier to look at the allocation of power in retrospect. With hindsight one can look at a particular situation or sequence of events, and determine power in the light of the circumstances surrounding that situation or sequence. That does not help our purpose as we are concerned with a developing set of relations, however, and the trends immanent in them. Moreover, as the UK's experience of devolution is comparatively short (only five years and a half at the time of writing) this gives us relatively little material to use. Consequently we cannot permit ourselves the luxury of such an approach.

The most suitable definition of power for our purposes is therefore one that treats power in a broader context and uses measurable criteria to do so. The easiest way to do this is to regard power as a function of the resources available to the parties (a resource-dependency model). Such an approach was suggested by Rhodes in the context of UK central–local relations, a situation

28 For details, see www.agecon.purdue.edu/crd/Localgov/Second%20Level%20pages/Indiana_Pi_Story.htm.
29 This point is emphasised by Agranoff, 'Autonomy, Devolution and Intergovernmental Relations'.

that resembles in a number of key respects the relationship between the UK Government and Parliament and the devolved institutions.[30] These resemblances include the discharge of specified functions by multi-purpose agencies which owe their existence and constitution to the UK level (as they are created by Act of Parliament), but which are themselves elected and can therefore claim democratic legitimacy and a mandate for the pursuit of distinct goals from those of the UK level.[31] A further resemblance is the allocation of functions between the two levels, which remains relatively unclear in legal terms and dependent on political negotiation and goodwill to make it work.[32] If neither party in fact has control in the sense that it can block any action of the other of which it disapproves, one needs a more sensitive and subtle means of identifying power, which can reflect changing balances of power over time and also differing balances of power in particular areas of relations (such as policy arenas) at the same time. Rhodes's basic approach has the further great advantage that it enables us to draw up a list of key elements of power which can be considered in a variety of contexts (and by people working in a number of disciplines). It is appropriate for the study of relations between different governmental organisations operating within a single state. It also enables us to consider the nature of power relations not just at specific points in the past but as they are at present and as they are likely to develop over the coming few years. It is therefore suitable for empirical work in a way other approaches are not.[33]

30 Rhodes, R. A. W., *Control and Power in Central–Local Government Relations* (Aldershot: Gower, 1981), especially chap. 5. It is worth noting that both Bulpitt's and Rose's understanding of power embraced a resource-dependency approach; see *Territory and Power*, 63–4 and 157–60, and *The Territorial Dimension*, 167–71.

31 A note on terminology: it is now common in the study of some federal systems to refer to 'orders' rather than 'levels' of government, to emphasise that neither is at least formally dependent on the other in the exercise of its functions. In the UK context this seems inappropriate, given the dominance of the UK Government and the unrestricted sovereignty of the Westminster Parliament. An alternative approach, adopted in South Africa, is to refer to 'spheres' of government. Neither of these terms reflects adequately the nature of the UK state following devolution. For these reasons, the term 'level' will be preferred.

32 For the importance of goodwill in intergovernmental relations in the UK, see House of Lords Select Committee on the Constitution, *Devolution: Inter-Institutional Relations in the United Kingdom*, especially chap. 1.

33 It needs to be noted that Rhodes himself later came to the view that there were better approaches to the study of central–local relations, by developing the concept of policy networks within which the various parties deployed their resources as they 'played the game': see Rhodes, R. A. W., ' "Power Dependence". Theories of central–local relations: A critical – reassessment', in Goldsmith, M. (ed.), *New Research in Central–Local Relations* (Aldershot: Gower, 1986), 33, and Rhodes, *Beyond Westminster and Whitehall*.

This approach is not without problems, which are best addressed at the outset. First, great care needs to be taken with the resources which one takes into account as elements of power. For example, Rhodes himself notes that control of agendas (in particular, what items do not become the subject of discussion or action between the various governmental agencies) is a problem with his approach.[34] To an extent this can be dealt with by looking at resources in a broad sense that includes control of agendas as one of the resources available to the parties, but even so this is not wholly adequate. Indeed, careful consideration of what constitutes resources would serve to resolve many of the criticisms of the approach that Rhodes himself discusses in his later work.[35] This does not resolve the issue of whether resources are an instrument used in the process of intergovernmental negotiation or the result of that process (a 'weapon' or a 'prize', in Gyford and James's formulation).[36] Again, this requires sensitivity in use of the understanding of resources in practice, as the same resource can be both. It may change its status over time, according to the context (the issue or policy arena) in which it is deployed, or even serve as both simultaneously. Drawing a firm distinction between them is likely to prove impossible.

A second problem is that looking at resources (or autonomy) tells one little about the aggregate amount of power in a system. It is quite possible for both sets of political institutions to become stronger by means that this measure does not necessarily identify, because it is looking at the relative balance of power between the two levels and not the total amount of power exercisable by them in relation to other bodies (such as lobby groups or governments in other states). For example, the activities internationally and on the European Union stage of the devolved administrations can be viewed as a way by which the devolved administrations become more effective actors on a wider stage, which may give them access to a broader range of allies (and so resources) to deal with the UK Government. But there is also some evidence (to be discussed in chapter 3 below) that these activities can also serve as means by which the UK Government gains information or influence internationally as well. Power is not necessarily a zero-sum game, and we need to be conscious that a measure that treats power as such a game in relation to a limited number of levels creates a tendency to disregard a growth in the sum of power available to those actors in other settings.

But the greatest problem with a resource-dependency approach is that it does not in fact measure power, but rather elements of power. It is a measure

34 Rhodes, *Control and Power in Central–Local Government Relations*, 122–3.
35 See Rhodes, 'Power Dependence'.
36 Quoted in *ibid.*, 7.

of power by using the proxy of resources, but not of power itself. This objection is true to a considerable degree, but it can be answered in three ways. The first is that this is in fact a rather good proxy for power, provided the identification of resources is an accurate one, has been done with sufficient care and takes into account the underlying nature of the relationship (the 'ground' of interaction as well as the 'figures' of it, to adopt Rhodes's terminology). The control of resources is certainly a necessary condition for the possession of power. In many cases it will also be a sufficient condition. Thus, even if this measure is only a second-hand reading of power, at worst it tells us with a high degree of probability of accuracy who is likely to possess power in a particular setting. Second, for our purposes it is hard to identify a better empirical measure of power. While this one may not correspond entirely with power by an abstract definition, in the absence of perfect historical knowledge it is hard to formulate a better one to serve the purposes of this book. Third, used in the extended form identified above it avoids the problem that studying power by studying observable behaviour means one cannot study the background to that behaviour – the context within which individuals, groups or institutions behave. In particular, looking only at observable behaviour presents the attendant difficulty of being unable to look at the question of agenda-setting and latent interests and conflicts, rather than ones which manifest themselves in a tangible way, particularly in the absence of conflict.[37] While this formulation therefore involves a number of intellectual compromises, these are fewer and less serious than alternative measures would involve.

A related and secondary concept is that of autonomy. This is similarly not straightforward, although in the context of UK devolution it is also less important. This is largely due to the structure of devolution and the understanding of what devolution means held by those who created it, a topic discussed in detail in chapter 3. Autonomy can be formulated in a number of ways, and for present purposes it will be treated as closely related to the concept of power and dependent on that. A party possesses autonomy if it is able to exercise power in relation to its functions and its own existence without requiring the assent or assistance of the other party in doing so. Thus if a devolved administration can introduce and implement its own policies without needing any consent of the UK Government, and without the UK Government being able to hinder it from doing so, it can be said to be autonomous. This is complicated partly by the extent to which the structure of the devolution settlements compels the two levels of government to take each other's views into account in a wide range of situations (a subject further discussed in chapter 3).

---

37 This therefore provides a way of looking at power in, to use Lukes's terminology, a three-dimensional way.

We need, then, to identify those resources that constitute power.[38] The key areas in which it is necessary for a level of government to possess resources appear to be the following:

1 Constitutional resources

These take three forms, all reflecting the fundamental legitimacy of each order of government. First is the allocation of functions of sufficient breadth and importance to enable the government to exercise meaningful powers over significant areas of government activity, and for these to be protected from interference by another level acting unilaterally.[39] Local government in Great Britain has been at a disadvantage (at least since the 1980s) because its powers have been limited to functions of limited importance, and have been subject to extensive direction and control by central government, for example. Second is the entitlement to be informed and consulted about (if not to veto) actions of another level of government which affect those functions. Third is the power of one level of government to alter internal constitutional arrangements (such as the relationship between executive and legislative) without reference to another level of government.

2 Legal and hierarchical resources

These take two forms. First, the ability of a level of government to command the legal instruments (that is, to pass legislation) to exercise the functions allocated to it in an autonomous way. Second, the ability of that level of government to implement its policies (for example by issuing advice or guidance) which is not legally binding, but which has sufficient authority that it nonetheless impels compliance by bodies subordinate to it. Taken together, these resources amount to the ability to make and implement policy.

3 Financial resources

This means, first, the possession of sufficient finance to discharge a level of government's functions (whether derived from tax revenue or borrowing);

38 This list of resources is developed from those identified in Rhodes, *Control and Power in Central–Local Government Relations*, 100–1. See also Rhodes, *Beyond Westminster and Whitehall*, 90–1.

39 A major problem with Rhodes's work is that it was written immediately before the wholesale changes to central–local relations and the working of local government during the Conservative governments of the 1980s and 1990s, effected both by statute and particularly by what has been called the process of 'juridification' of central–local relations. See Loughlin, M., *Legality and Locality: The role of law in central–local government relations* (Oxford: Oxford University Press, 1996); and more generally, Young, K. and Rao, N., *Local Government since 1945* (Oxford: Blackwell, 1997).

second, the ability to allocate finance freely to accommodate the priorities of the devolved administration; and third, the ability to control the amount of income as a means of implementing policy in the areas of functions allocated.

4 Organisational resources

This entails the possession of sufficient staff with sufficient skill and expertise to enable the administration to manage its functions, including developing and implementing policy (and changes to policy), and the ability to have such other resources (buildings and premises, information technology and so on) for those purposes. It also includes the ability to adjust the resources available and the use made of them in the light of changing circumstances or priorities, which may involve the desire to use its own organisation as a means of affecting policy in the territory concerned (for example by the use of pay or recruitment policies).

5 Lobbying resources

This means the ability to take part in, and shape, debates about matters which affect the level of government's functions or more generally its territory. In a UK context, it includes the ability of one government to have the other governments take into account its views on matters beyond its direct control but which influence it. Thus it means the ability of a devolved administration to have the UK Government consider its views on non-devolved matters, for example on the implications of a UK-wide policy on devolved functions in Scotland or Wales, or of the UK Government to influence social exclusion policies in the devolved territories. It also includes the ability to shape the agenda for what issues are the subject of political or policy discussion and debate, such as reform of financial arrangements under the Barnett formula or the pursuit of policies by a devolved administration which the UK Government wishes to obstruct, both by getting some subjects considered in such debate and by excluding others from attention.

6 Informational resources

This means the possession of information about what is going on within other governments which may affect the administration in question, and the professional and other skills necessary to make use of that information.

These resources need to work in combination with one another. There is little point in being able to shape the agenda for financial matters if an administration does not have the staff or professional skills to be able to respond and make an effective case for its own position, or the range of functions to mean that it can make use of a changed system for allocating finance if that were to be the result of creating a debate about the issue. There is moreover an inherent assumption about the constitutional nature of the regime in which these resources are applied: that each party has legal rights to use the resources available to it, including access to courts that will determine any legal disputes impartially and whose judgments will be respected and if need be enforced.

The structure of this book

The argument sketched above is developed throughout this book. Chapter 2, by James Mitchell, explains the general historical background to the recent development of the UK state, and its approach to territorial power as that developed during the nineteenth and twentieth centuries. Chapter 3, by Alan Trench, examines the formal and legal framework of devolution, and examines the implications of that framework for intergovernmental relations. Chapter 4, by David Bell and Alex Christie, considers the financial implications of the Barnett formula and the other arrangements for financing the devolved administrations, and chapter 5, by Alan Trench, examines the power of the Treasury in the devolved UK as a consequence of the way the Barnett formula works. These chapters therefore emphasise the power of the centre and the constraints that devolution places on the devolved institutions. The next chapters look at what has happened in policy terms following devolution. Chapter 6, by Alan Trench and Holly Jarman, is an overview of the implications of devolution for policy divergence. Chapter 7, by Scott Greer, is a more detailed examination of how health policy has developed across the UK as a result of devolution. The next chapters assess the working of intergovernmental relations in practice. Chapter 8, by Alan Trench, looks at how the various forms of interaction between formal institutions (governments, parliaments and assemblies) within the UK work. Chapter 9, by Martin Laffin, Eric Shaw and Gerald Taylor, considers the role of the political parties, with an emphasis on Labour and the Liberal Democrats. In chapter 10 Charlie Jeffery and Rosanne Palmer consider the impact of the European Union on the devolved administrations and how the devolved administrations interact with the EU. Ron Watts, in chapter 11, considers the UK's system of intergovernmental relations comparatively, putting it into the context of a variety of federal, regionalised and decentralised unitary states around the world. Finally, in the conclusion, Alan Trench assesses the UK's system of intergovernmental relations in the context of the resource-dependency framework set out above, and seeks to identify the nature of the shifts of power that devolution has brought about.

Table 1.1. Chronology of key events affecting intergovernmental relations, 1997–2005

Date	Event
May 1997	Election of Labour government with 179 seat majority in House of Commons. No Conservative MPs elected from Scotland or Wales. Donald Dewar becomes Secretary of State for Scotland, Ron Davies Secretary of State for Wales and Mo Mowlam Secretary of State for Northern Ireland.
July 1997	UK Government publishes white papers on devolution for Scotland and Wales: *Scotland's Parliament* and *A Voice for Wales*.
September 1997	Referendums on devolution in Scotland and Wales. Devolution endorsed in Scotland by 74.1 per cent (63.5 per cent also supporting a tax-varying power) and in Wales by 50.3 per cent of the vote.
December 1997	Scotland and Government of Wales bills introduced into Parliament at Westminister.
April 1998	Belfast/Good Friday Agreement signed in Northern Ireland.
July 1998	Northern Ireland Bill introduced into Parliament.
July 1998	Comprehensive Spending Review published.
July 1998	Scotland Act and Government of Wales Act receive Royal Assent.
November 1998	Following resignation of Ron Davies as Secretary of State for Wales, an election to choose a leader for Labour in Wales results in Alun Michael defeating Rhodri Morgan, thanks to support from the UK Labour leadership. Michael becomes Secretary of State for Wales.
November 1998	Northern Ireland Act receives Royal Assent.
May 1999	Elections for Scottish Parliament and National Assembly for Wales.
May 1999	Opening of National Assembly for Wales and transfer of functions to it. Alun Michael is First Secretary, at head of a Labour minority cabinet.
June 1999	Royal opening of the Scottish Parliament. Transfer of functions to Scottish Parliament and Executive, with Donald Dewar as First Minister and coalition government between Labour and the Liberal Democrats. Dr John Reid becomes Secretary of State for Scotland, Paul Murphy Secretary of State for Wales. Mo Mowlam remains Secretary of State for Northern Ireland.

Table 1.1. (continued)

Date	Event
October 1999	Memorandum of Understanding (published as Cm 4444) signed by UK Government, Scottish Executive and National Assembly for Wales.
October 1999	UK Cabinet reshuffle: Peter Mandelson becomes Secretary of State for Northern Ireland, replacing Mo Mowlam.
December 1999	Northern Ireland Assembly assumes its functions.
July 2000	2000 Spending Review published.
September 2000	First meeting of plenary Joint Ministerial Committee. JMC adopts a new version of the Memorandum of Understanding, including the Northern Ireland Executive.
October 2000	Labour form coalition with the Liberal Democrats in Wales. Coalition 'partnership agreement' includes commitment to establish a commission to consider the powers and electoral arrangements of the National Assembly.
October 2000	Following death of Donald Dewar, Henry McLeish becomes First Minister of Scotland.
January 2001	Following Peter Mandelson's resignation from the UK Government, Dr John Reid becomes Secretary of State for Northern Ireland. Helen Liddell succeeds Reid as Secretary of State for Scotland.
May 2001	UK general election returns Labour government with 167 seat majority. In post-election reshuffle, Helen Liddell remains Secretary of State for Scotland. Paul Murphy Secretary of State for Wales.
September 2001	Alun Michael resigns as First Secretary of National Assembly for Wales, to be succeeded by Rhodri Morgan.
October 2001	Second meeting of plenary Joint Ministerial Committee. Meeting adopts slightly revised version of Memorandum of Understanding (published as Cm 5240).
November 2001	Following resignation of Henry McLeish, Jack McConnell becomes Scottish First Minister.
May–June 2002	Lords Select Committee on the Constitution takes evidence in Scotland, Wales and Northern Ireland.
July 2002	2002 Spending Review published, preceded by announcements of matching funding for Objective 1 in Wales and 'Reinvestment and Reform' initiative in Northern Ireland.

September 2002	First meeting of the Commission on the National Assembly for Wales's powers and electoral arrangements, chaired by Lord Richard of Ammanford.
October 2002	Third meeting of Joint Ministerial Committee.
October 2002	Paul Murphy becomes Secretary of State for Northern Ireland. Peter Hain becomes Secretary of State for Wales, and remains the UK Government's representative on the Giscard Convention on the European Constitution.
January 2003	Lords Select Committee on the Constitution publishes report on *Devolution: Inter-Institutional Relations in the United Kingdom*.
March 2003	Commons Welsh Affairs Committee publishes report on *The Primary Legislative Process as it Affects Wales*.
May 2003	Elections for Scottish Parliament and National Assembly for Wales. Labour and Liberal Democrats remain in coalition in Scotland. Labour forms government with 30 seats out of 60 in Wales.
June 2003	UK Cabinet reshuffle: Alistair Darling becomes Secretary of State for Scotland (while retaining Transport portfolio); Peter Hain becomes Leader of the House as well as Secretary of State for Wales, Paul Murphy remains Northern Ireland Secretary, Lord Irvine leaves government, and Lord Falconer becomes Secretary of State for Constitutional Affairs and Lord Chancellor.
April 2004	Richard Commission publishes its report on the powers and electoral arrangements of the National Assembly for Wales.
July 2004	2004 Spending Review published.
May 2005	UK general election returns Labour to office with a reduced majority. Labour loses its majority in National Assembly for Wales, after Peter Law stands as an independent for Westminster. In post-election Cabinet reshuffle, Paul Murphy leaves government. Peter Hain becomes Secretary of State for Wales and Northern Ireland.
June 2005	Wales Office publishes white paper *Better Governance for Wales*.
July 2005	HM Treasury announces change in arrangements for next spending review: it is postponed a year, to 2007, and expanded in scope to become a Comprehensive Spending Review.
December 2005	Wales Bill (implementing *Better Governance for Wales*) laid before Parliament.

2

The United Kingdom as a state of unions: unity of government, equality of political rights and diversity of institutions

James Mitchell[1]

Introduction

This chapter sets out to place today's territorial politics in a historical setting. It is not an account of the unions that created the modern state nor is it concerned with constitutional arrangements at various stages in the past unless this helps us understand politics today. It is not, therefore, a piece of political or administrative history. Neither is it an attempt to look at the past through the prism of modern times, not, that is, Whiggish history. But it recognises the importance of history. It is commonly asserted that history matters and this informs the chapter. It matters in the context of this chapter in three respects. Whatever kind of constitution a state has, it will be informed by ideas and practice drawn from the past. These ideas may not be explicit or found in formal written documents. Indeed, these ideas and practices may contradict the formal position. Thomas Grey famously noted that the US Constitution had been interpreted not only on the basis of the written document but also on the basis of 'basic national ideals of individual liberty and fair treatment, even when the content of these ideals is not expressed as a matter of positive law in the written Constitution'.[2] It seems even more important to identify those 'basic national ideals', noting the shifts in their balance, that have informed the UK's territorial constitution. Second, history matters because it allows us an opportunity to see the extent to which change has occurred. There are many new formal institutions associated with devolution but considering these without setting them in context may lead to an exaggerated

1 The author wishes to acknowledge the support of the ESRC (Devolution and the Centre Grant no. L219252026) as well as the Leverhulme 'Nations and Regions' programme, for supporting the research on which this chapter is based.
2 Grey, T., 'Do We Have an Unwritten Constitution?', *Stanford Law Review*, 27 (1975), 706.

view of change. Continuities that exist below the surface in the early days of new institutions have a habit of reasserting themselves. We should not be surprised that much of the commentary on territorial politics since 1997 stressing its newness has been ahistorical, given the number of social science researchers attracted by the lure of research grants aplenty as well as much comment from journalists and politicians stressing novelty. Third, the past is not a foreign place but remains with us. Decisions made in the past reverberate within the politics of the new institutions. Anyone expecting to understand territorial finance who fails to understand the origins and development of the Barnett formula and who fails to appreciate that policies create interests more often than the other way around will fail to note just how embedded some policies and practices have become.

Territorial power viewed historically

Power is a contested concept, as Steven Lukes demonstrated in his celebrated book.[3] Discussion of the territorial distribution of power should be expected to provoke controversy too. That controversy concerns not only where power resides but where it should reside. It has become almost a standard starting point of discussions of devolution and constitutional change in the UK to note the significant changes that have been brought about since New Labour came to power in 1997, but this is contestable. It is also often noted in discussions of new public management, governance and regulatory politics that the UK has undergone considerable changes in the relationship and boundaries between the state, society and economy over the last quarter century. These changes are an important backdrop, though they are rarely incorporated into discussions of devolution through having no obvious part in the political movements pressing for devolution. The nature of the state, its reach and its form, are significant in any attempt to trace the evolution of the distribution of territorial power in the UK and are important in helping us understand the UK's devolved polity today.

Much more so than is generally appreciated, today's devolved polity is deeply rooted in the past. All too often, 'Year Zero' assumptions are implicit in writings on devolution.[4] Year Zero assumptions involve the mistaken belief that devolution wiped the slate clean and ushered in an era of 'new politics'. This is not to deny that considerable change has occurred – and much more

3 Lukes, S., *Power: A radical view* (London: Macmillan, 1974), 9.
4 Mike Watson, formerly an MSP, even entitled his book on the first year of the Scottish Parliament *Year Zero* though that was partly ironic.

is likely – only that a useful way of understanding devolution, most obviously measuring how much change it involved, requires an account of the past.

To avoid falling into the trap of British exceptionalism, it is useful to recognise the value of comparative tools. Comparative analysis need not involve the study of more than one case. Serious study of one case can be informed by concepts and ideas drawn from comparative work. Reflecting both the importance of the past and the need to draw on comparative work, this chapter draws heavily on historical social science. In other words, social science methods are applied in a historical setting. The typology offered by Rokkan and Urwin to distinguish between different state formations in Europe offers an obvious starting point.[5]

> The unitary system is built up around one unambiguous centre enjoying economic dominance and pursuing an undeviating policy of administrative standardisation: all areas of the state are treated alike and all institutions are directly under the control of the centre.
> The union state does not enjoy direct political control everywhere. Incorporation of parts of its territory has been achieved through treaty or agreement; consequently integration is less than perfect. While administrative standardisation prevails over most of the territory, the union structure entails the survival in some areas of variations based on pre-union rights and institutional infrastructures.[6]

This distinction was drawn to describe state formation. Notably, Rokkan's work with S. M. Lipset on social cleavages is frequently cited as an example of historical institutionalism, meaning essentially that these cleavages set at the times of the two historic 'revolutions', national and industrial, became embedded and continued to be evident in electoral politics in the twentieth century.[7] Rokkan and Urwin's work on state formation might equally be seen in the historical institutionalist genre though it is rarely expressed as such. It has been argued that the UK continued to show the characteristics of a union state well into the twentieth century despite the common tendency to describe it as a unitary state and that how it was perceived – union or unitary – had an impact on constitutional debates in the twentieth century.[8] Those

---

5 Particularly obvious in my own work perhaps. I initially adopted the framework many years ago and continue to find it fruitful.

6 Rokkan, S. and Urwin, D., *Economy, Territory, Identity: The politics of West European peripheries* (London: Sage, 1983), 181.

7 Lipset, S. M. and Rokkan, S.,'Cleavage Structures, Party Systems and Voter Alignments', in Lipset, S. M. and Rokkan, S. (eds), *Party Systems and Voter Alignments: Cross-national perspectives* (New York: Free Press, 1967).

8 See for example Mitchell, J., 'Conceptual Lenses and Territorial Government in Britain', in Jordan, U. and Kaiser, W. (eds), *Political Reform in Britain, 1886–1996* (Bochum: Brockmeyer, 1997).

wedded to the view that the UK was or is a unitary state had difficulty accommodating devolution. The power of how we conceive the political world is acknowledged in this analysis.[9]

The notion that the UK was a unitary state, as defined by Rokkan and Urwin, was more than simply a description of the territorial constitution of the UK.[10] It had ideological overtones. Edmund Morgan expressed this well in his study of popular sovereignty in England and America:

> Government requires make-believe. Make believe that the king is divine, make believe that he can do no wrong or make believe that the voice of the people is the voice of God. Make believe that the people have a voice or make believe that the representatives of the people are the people. Make believe that governors are the servants of the people. Make believe that all men are equal or make believe that they are not.[11]

The 'make believe' is necessary because 'we cannot live without them, we often take pains to prevent their collapse by moving the facts to fit the fiction, by making our world conform more closely to what we want it to be. We

9 This notion was most notable in Allison's study of the Cuban Missile Crisis in which he notes the importance of the 'conceptual lenses' which tell us what is relevant and important and, consequently, what is irrelevant and unimportant (Allison, G., *Essence of Decision: Explaining the Cuban Missile Crisis* (Boston: Little, Brown and Company, 1971), 251). The updated study largely provides further empirical evidence and adds little to ideas about conceptual lenses (Allison, G. and Zelikov, P., *Essence of Decision* (Harlow: Longman, 1999)). More eloquently, Doris Lessing has published a series of essays entitled *Prisons We Choose to Live Inside*. In the conclusion of the first, entitled 'When in the Future They Look Back on Us', Lessing argues, 'There is no such thing as my being right, my side being in the right, because within a generation or two my present way of thinking is bound to be found perhaps faintly ludicrous, perhaps quite outmoded by new development – at the best, something that has been changed, all passion spent, into a small part of a great process, a development.' Lessing, D., *Prisons We Choose to Live Inside* (London: HarperCollins, 1994), 17.

10 Territorial politics was defined by Jim Bulpitt, '. . .as that arena of political activity concerned with the relations between the central political institutions in the capital city and those interests, communities, political organisations and governmental bodies outside the central institutional complex, but within the accepted boundaries of the state, which possess, or are commonly perceived to possess, a significant geographical or local/regional character' (Bulpitt, J., *Territory and Power in the United Kingdom* (Manchester: Manchester University Press, 1983), 1). By 'territorial constitution' I refer to the constitutional aspect of territorial politics. That branch of political science concerned with these matters has come to be known as 'territorial politics'. This has taken institutional form in the Territorial Politics Group of the Political Studies Association which succeeded the old UK Politics Group.

11 Morgan, E. S., *Inventing the People: The rise of popular sovereignty in England and America* (New York: W. W. Norton & Company, 1988), 13.

sometimes call it, quite appropriately, reform or reformation, when the fiction takes command and reshapes reality.'[12] In the case of the UK, the unitary state fiction has been especially significant and within that has been the notion of Parliamentary sovereignty.

Rokkan and Urwin did not argue that the UK was founded as a federal state and their definition of a union state was one that recognised a strong centre. Bulpitt defined the 'centre' broadly as the 'central government, above all the central bureaucratic departments, in the capital city'.[13] The related but more precise definition of the 'core executive' focuses on functions performed by parts of the government machine.[14] In a devolved polity, these functions remain important, perhaps become more important. What arises in debates on devolved government are which policy areas, as well as which functions, should be retained by the centre or the core executive. Whether referred to as the centre or the core executive, the institutions associated with them have a privileged position in UK politics. This privilege has amounted to a form of constitutional entrenchment usually referred to as Parliamentary sovereignty. In twentieth century debates, the works of the late nineteenth/early twentieth century legal theorist Albert Venn Dicey have been important in the ideology of Parliamentary sovereignty though, of course, the central idea dates from well before Dicey.[15] Dicey was less a 'founding father' in the sense associated with those described as such in the US, not least because the UK was not 'founded' in the same way, and his role might more properly be seen as analogous to Alexis de Tocqueville.[16]

Parliamentary sovereignty was never as simplistic in Dicey's work as subsequent Diceyians suggest nor was his conception of the territorial state one

---

12 *Ibid.*, 14.

13 Bulpitt, *Territory and Power in the United Kingdom*, 60.

14 Rhodes, R. A. W. and Dunleavy, P. (eds), *Prime Minister, Cabinet and Core Executive* (Basingstoke: Macmillan, 1995); Smith, M., *The Core Executive in Britain* (Basingstoke: Macmillan, 1999).

15 Dicey's work is more often cited than read and he approached the territorial politics of the UK with greater subtlety than is often suggested. See Mitchell, James, 'Re-inventing the Union: Dicey, devolution, and the Union', in Miller, William (ed.), *Anglo-Scottish Relations from 1900 to Devolution* (Oxford: The British Academy/Oxford University Press, 2005), 35–61.

16 In a recent introduction to *Democracy in America*, Kramnick writes, 'If the number of times an individual is cited by politicians, journalists, and scholars is a measure of their influence, Alexis de Tocqueville – not Jefferson, Madison, or Lincoln – is America's public philosopher' (Kramnick, I., 'Introduction' to Alexis de Tocqueville, *Democracy in America* (London: Penguin, 2003), ix). Perhaps even more pertinent was Kramnick's reference to the *New York Times* columnist who noted that 'of all the great unread writers I believe Tocqueville to be the most widely quoted' (Russell Baker in Kramnick, 'Introduction', xi).

that conformed with an undifferentiated unitary state. Nonetheless, the centre assumed a significant role in his thinking and in its simplified caricature form it has informed constitutional debate in the UK with particular reference to devolution (and Europe). Dicey enunciated three constitutional 'watchwords' in his works on Irish home rule. These were:

- unity of government;
- equality of political rights;
- diversity of institutions.[17]

These watchwords have significance today and relate to the role of the centre or core executive. From a Diceyian perspective, unity of government and equality of political rights would be associated with central government while diversity of institutions would be associated with extra-central institutions. In the days of the nightwatchman state, at least the state that Dicey believed that existed in his day,[18] unity of (limited) government and equality of political rights within a highly restricted franchise were much easier to achieve than they would be in the days of an expanded state and a fuller franchise. Even John Morley, taking an opposed view, saw merit in Dicey's argument. Morley wrote to Dicey after the publication of the latter's 1886 anti-home-rule book, 'full of admiration' at the 'exhaustive completeness' and 'faultless' argument. 'I don't know another instance where the subject of passionate and burning controversy has been so honestly dealt with.'[19] Morley conceded that Dicey's work would be a 'great armoury for my opponents' but was still glad it had been written. No other informed polemic was produced of this quality and vitality, especially none by home rulers and, in this respect, it can probably be compared with Keynes's *Economic Consequences of the Peace*.

Lord Bryce, friend of Dicey, put forward an alternative view of territorial politics. Dicey reviewed Bryce's 'masterly work', the *American Commonwealth*,

---

17 Dicey, A. V., *England's Case Against Home Rule* (London: John Murray, 1886), 30–1. In addition to numerous articles, Dicey wrote four books against Irish home rule (1886, 1887, 1893 and 1913). The second was a collection of essays that had originally appeared in the *Spectator* magazine. The other two were, as the first, responses to Liberal government measures of home rule and each followed the first in essentials.

18 Dicey's conception of the growth of the state in the nineteenth century has been roundly criticised as historically inaccurate, but leaving aside its historical inaccuracy, its influence remained (Parris, H., *Constitutional Bureaucracy: The development of British central administration since the eighteenth century* (London: George Allen & Unwin, 1969), 258–9).

19 Dicey Papers, Glasgow University: MS Gen508 (52–4).

which he compared with Tocqueville's *Democracy in America*.[20] However, Dicey could see little relevance in Bryce's work to debates on home rule. Neither home rulers nor Unionists would gain from the arguments in the book and, indeed, the wider relevance of the book and many works like it over time appear to have been lost on audiences in the UK. Dicey's point of comparison illustrates a point that has been accepted as part of the UK's informal constitution:

> The most obvious difference between the position of Scotland and that, say, of Pennsylvania is that Scotland possesses no theoretical independence. The less obvious but more important difference is that modern Scotland is the outcome of a national history. The essential point of likeness is that the understandings of the unwritten British constitution secure to Scotland, as the articles of the written United States Constitution secure to Pennsylvania, that the people of the country shall be governed under local law, and enjoy local institutions.[21]

Alternative understandings of the territorial constitution emerged but never attained anything like the status of Dicey's thinking. In the event, devolution came about not because an alternative federalist paradigm was developed but in response to pressures from below, notably sub-state nationalism in Scotland and Northern Ireland's 'Troubles'. English regional administrative matters and other issues, including the developing Welsh Question, were carried along in the wake of these matters.

The Royal Commission on the Constitution set up by Prime Minister Harold Wilson in 1969 (latterly chaired by Lord Kilbrandon) reported in November 1973 and identified some elements of UK constitutional thinking. Constitutional change comes slowly in the UK. There have been major upheavals, such as over Ireland or extending the franchise, but there has never been anything like a revolution which resulted in a completely new constitutional order. The incremental development of the UK constitution has left asymmetries, anomalies and loose ends. This background has informed constitutional debate. Grand masterplans for constitutional change are presented by opponents as alien to the 'British' way of doing things. In its report in 1973, the Royal Commission maintained that a constitution should 'suit both the character of the people and the times in which they are living. It should reflect the people's history, traditions and social attitudes in such a way that it will be accepted as a natural development out of what has gone before.'[22] Accordingly, the Commissioners rejected laying down a complete

20 Dicey, A. V., 'The American Commonwealth', *Edinburgh Review*, 169 (1889), 481.
21 *Ibid.*, 494.
22 Kilbrandon, Lord, *Report of the Royal Commission on the Constitution*, Cmnd 5460 (London: HMSO, 1973), 121, para. 390.

blueprint for the future or a written constitution. Their task necessitated taking account of the 'deep-rooted national traditions and of the proven value of existing institutions', most notably Parliament as the 'supreme authority'. Any innovations, they maintained, should be 'grafted on to our existing institutions' otherwise, they warned, any proposals would be unlikely to win acceptance.[23] They also noted the 'deep-rooted British tradition' of pragmatism and compromise, looking to practice rather than theory.

The Commissioners described the UK as a 'unitary state' but understood its territorial complexity well:

> The United Kingdom is a unitary state in economic as well as in political terms. It has, for example, a single currency and a banking system responsible to a single central bank. Its people enjoy a right of freedom of movement of trade, labour and capital and of settlement and establishment anywhere within the Kingdom (though there is an exception in Northern Ireland in a restriction on employment imposed in the interests of Northern Ireland workers). Similarly, all citizens are free to participate in trading and other concessions obtained by the United Kingdom abroad.[24]

Despite this, the Royal Commission recommended devolution throughout the UK. However, in describing the state as unitary, Kilbrandon was establishing parameters beyond which constitutional change, despite its recommendations, would be inconsistent. It might be argued that these were self-imposed parameters – conceptual prisons – but there were reasons why the Commission adopted them. The perception that constitutional change in the UK comes gradually, the importance of Parliamentary sovereignty and the fact that the UK is asymmetrical informed their conclusions as they have many other reformers. Others have set out a programme of constitutional reform which amounts to a radical transformation of the UK constitution.[25]

Arch-defenders of the constitutional *status quo ante* argued that radical change, especially altering the status of Parliament, would run contrary to British or English tradition. Enoch Powell told a French audience in 1971 that the creation of assemblies or parliaments elsewhere in Europe was the

23 *Ibid.*, 122, para. 395.
24 *Ibid.*, 19, para. 57. What makes this definition interesting in contemporary politics is its application to debates on the future of the European Union. The notion that a polity with a single currency and various freedoms of movement, even allowing for exceptions (opt-outs), constitutes a unitary state would raise serious questions about the nature of the European Union. An alternative view, however, is that this is an inadequate definition of a unitary state.
25 Best known among these is Charter 88. See its website at www.charter88.org.uk. See also Institute of Public Policy Research, *A Written Constitution for the UK* (London: Mansell, 1991).

result of recent and deliberate political acts and that the notion that a new sovereign body can be created is as 'familiar to you as it is repugnant, not to say unimaginable, to us'.[26] British nationalist rhetoric surrounds constitutional debate leaving supporters of radical change appearing to be in some sense alien and unBritish. This British nationalist ideology has been one of the most enduring and powerful impediments in the way of reform. Tam Dalyell, Labour MP and leading opponent of home rule, similarly made a telling point in Parliament in 1977: 'Would it not be more honest to admit that it is impossible to have an Assembly [for Scotland or Wales] – especially any kind of subordinate Parliament – that is part, though only part, of a unitary state?'[27] The point is valid only if one accepts the premise on which the question is asked. Other contributions, including Enoch Powell's, were along the same lines and particularly laid stress on Parliamentary sovereignty. They very much followed the line set down a century before by Dicey. Dalyell's own book published in 1977 is a more vulgar version of Dicey's argument.[28]

This is not to suggest that adopting a union state perspective leads to support for constitutional change. In his study of *Territory and Power in the United Kingdom*, Jim Bulpitt argued that it was hard not to conclude that 'the terms confederation, federation and unitary system should be pensioned off and left to the second oldest profession, the lawyers, to play with'.[29] Bulpitt was anything other than a supporter of elected devolved government in the United Kingdom and represented the kind of unionist in the Diceyian tradition, accepting territorial diversity while supporting a strong centre.

In the context of discussing Scotland, it has long been argued that the UK is a union state and that the union with Ireland had the characteristics of a union state.[30] However, taking the UK as a whole, a more complex picture emerges. It is difficult to characterise the Anglo-Welsh union as involving the creation of a union state. It had more of the characteristics of a unitary state, a military conquest given legal form centuries later. Even more certainly, the union which created England brought into being the rudiments of a unitary state. These four unions – the unions of territories creating England, England's union with Wales, the subsequent union with Scotland and finally that with Ireland – tell us much, though not everything, about the fundamentals of territorial politics in the UK today. In this sense the UK is a state of unions rather than a union state. Two initial observations are offered: the chronologies of these unions are

26 Powell, E., 'Britain and Europe', in Holmes, M. (ed.), *The Eurosceptical Reader* (Houndmills: Macmillan, 1996), 85.
27 HC Deb, 14 November 1977, cols. 78–9.
28 Dalyell, T., *Devolution: The End of Britain?* (London: Jonathan Cape, 1977).
29 Bulpitt, *Territory and Power in the United Kingdom*, 19.
30 Mitchell, 'Conceptual Lenses and Territorial Government in Britain'.

relevant to understanding processes of integration or assimilation; and while a Whiggish interpretation of the past is tempting, it must be guarded against. By the time the National Assembly for Wales had been established, Wales's position within the union could be characterised as suggesting that it had been founded on a union, not a unitary state basis.

The state performs different functions and these changes have been the most significant explanations for changes in its institutional structures. The Kilbrandon Royal Commission noted the very different functions performed by the state a century before it reported in 1973:

> The individual a hundred years ago hardly needed to know that the central government existed. His birth, marriage and death would be registered, and he might be conscious of the safeguards for his security provided by the forces of law and order and of imperial defence; but, except for the very limited provisions of the poor law and factory legislation, his welfare and progress were matters for which he alone bore the responsibility. By the turn of the century the position was not much changed. Today, however, the individual citizen submits himself to the guidance of the state at all times. His schooling is enforced; his physical well-being can be looked after in a comprehensive health service; he may be helped by government agencies to find and train for a job; he is obliged while in employment to insure against sickness, accident and unemployment; his house may be let to him by a public authority or he may be assisted in its purchase or improvement; he can avail himself of a wide range of government welfare allowances and services; and he draws a state pension in his retirement. In these and many other ways unknown to his counterpart of a century ago, he is brought into close and regular contact with government and its agencies.[31]

In the thirty years since, much has changed. Industries have been privatised, European Union policies affect our daily lives and a new 'regulatory state' has arisen.[32] These changes not only affect what services the state delivers but how its services are delivered. The establishment of the welfare state required not only machinery of government in London in the shape of Whitehall departments but also machinery beyond the centre. This extra-Whitehall machinery was necessary both to deliver policy on the ground and to make policy. The notion that policy-making was done in London and then implemented in the localities was as mythical as the classical distinction that policy was made by ministers and Parliament while civil servants put it into effect. Indeed, these myths were inter-related. Implementation has long been recognised as equipping 'street level bureaucrats' with resources allowing them scope for interpretation and policy-making.[33]

31 Kilbrandon, *Report of the Royal Commission on the Constitution*, 76, para. 232.
32 Moran, M., *The British Regulatory State: High modernism and hyper-innovation* (Oxford: Oxford University Press, 2003).
33 Lipsky, M., *Street Level Bureaucrats* (New York: Russell Sage Foundation, 1980).

England: creating the prototypical unitary state

England is important as the largest part of the state. Often, to the irritation of the rest of the state, what passes for the United Kingdom really only refers to England. This seems to have been the case with respect to constitutional development. The old argument as to whether English constitutional traditions continued to be relevant after unions with other parts of the state or whether these traditions were superseded has been well rehearsed in Scotland. The 1953 legal case of *MacCormick v. Lord Advocate*[34] entered Scottish nationalist folklore when the Lord President of the Court of Session concluded:

> The principle of the unlimited Sovereignty of Parliament is a distinctively English principle which has no counterpart in Scottish constitutional law. It derives its origins from Coke and Blackstone, and was widely popularised during the eighteenth century by Bagehot and Dicey, the latter having stated the doctrine in its classic form in his *Constitutional Law*.[35]

But the principle of Parliamentary sovereignty, as thus outlined, is a deeply engrained part of the ideology of union in England. It has had significant consequences for territorial politics within England. This is not to suggest that an alternative popular conception of sovereignty did not exist, only that it did not take hold in England in the twentieth century.

By the 1840s, local government in England was always seen as a 'creature of statute', as so commonly described in numerous textbooks. By that was simply meant that local self-government was a limited notion, limited by Parliament at Westminster. However, local government assumed a significant role for itself over time. Corruption led Parliament to take a keener interest in the activities of local government combined with the fact that Parliamentary subventions became an increasing source of local authority finance in the nineteenth century. English local government developed from below but was always regulated and controlled and partly financed from above to create what one authority described as a 'chaos of areas, bodies, and rates' with a plethora of Town Councils and Vestries, Boards of Guardians, Commissioners of Sewers, Improvement Commissioners, Lighting Inspectors, Turnpike Trustees, Highway Boards, Nuisance Commissioners, Local Boards of Health, River Conservancy Boards, Port Sanitary Authorities, Burial Boards and School Boards.[36] It was hardly any surprise, therefore, that against this

---

34   *MacCormick v. Lord Advocate*, [1953] SC 396.
35   Cited in: MacCormick, J., *The Flag in the Wind: The story of the national movement in Scotland* (London: Victor Gollancz, 1955), 216.
36   Clarke, J., *The Local Government of the United Kingdom* (London: Sir Isaac Pitman & Sons Ltd, 14th edn, 1948), 54.

backdrop any alternative territorial arrangement which might have involved creating competing authorities in territories lying somewhere between local government and Westminster would find few friends. The Eurosceptic claim that the tradition of federalism is alien has at least some roots in this domestic constitutional ideology.

England has proved least complex and often over-looked in debates on territorial politics. But this simplicity masks an important truth: as the largest component of the UK, England's position carries weight and cannot be ignored. Westminster is both the UK's and England's Parliament and the prospects at this stage of regional government across England look very limited. The tradition of making allowances for constitutional anomalies appears less true when England is considered on its own. The challenge for the UK in the twenty-first century remains the reconciliation of the unitary state basis of its largest component alongside an even more entrenched union state form of the other unions that created the United Kingdom.

Administrative devolution: putting on a kilt

The past, even if occasionally 'modernised', provided the continuance of diverse institutions to exist within the UK. The paradoxical notion of modernisation of the past refers to those changes which were deemed necessary to maintain the essential features of a union state. The union state entailed 'the survival in some areas of variations based on pre-union rights and institutional infrastructures'[37] but these were not necessarily the same rights and institutions. The causes of union have been much debated as have the extent of corruption, benefits and costs from a Scottish perspective (though less often from an English perspective). More significant was the nature of the union that was established. The Church of Scotland, for example, had been retained under the terms of union but declined in significance from the middle of the nineteenth century. Its decline was in part due to internal divisions but also the rise of the secular state. The state took over many of the functions previously performed by the Church, most notably in the field of education. However, while the Church declined, a distinctive educational administration developed. Diverse institutions lived on, though not always in the form that had existed at state formation.

'Administrative devolution' was the main means through which diverse institutions existed in the twentieth century in Scotland. Administrative devolution was a term invented by a civil servant in the Scottish Office asked to

37 Rokkan and Urwin, *Economy, Territory, Identity*, 181.

write a paper responding to early nationalist agitation and administrative needs.[38] Central government in the UK was primarily organised along functional lines but the Scottish Office, established in 1885, was an exception.[39] Its remit was primarily territorial – Scotland – rather than functional. Its functional remit grew over time from being responsible for education (apart from the universities) and local government at its foundation to include law and order within a few years, agriculture after 1912, health (including housing) after 1919 and piecemeal additions thereafter, including some economic and planning functions in the 1960s. Special Parliamentary procedures were established to accommodate the territorial department to deal with separate Scottish legislation and scrutiny of the Scottish Office (for example, through the Scottish Grand Committee).

The Scottish Office had no responsibility for redistributive policies, policies involving redistribution between classes of people, most notably taxation and welfare payments. It did, however, have competence over many allocative policies. It also had some competence for stabilisation policies. Initially, its role was largely concerned with the market failure end of allocative policies but as state spending on welfare services increased, its role in allocating public expenditure grew. The public spending dimension became important given the range of policies for which it had responsibility.

Administrative devolution allowed a degree of administrative autonomy but this was constrained in a number of ways. First, there were financial constraints. The funding arrangements were technically complex but straightforward in effect.[40] The situation by the 1960s was described by John Mackintosh:

> The expenditure for the Scottish Office is not voted as a single sum leaving Scottish Ministers free to move money from roads to schools or to industrial development as they feel priorities require. The investment in school building is worked out as part of a national policy on this subject, and the money for hospitals is negotiated between English and Scottish Departments of Health acting together and the Treasury. Thus there are financial, administrative and heavy political pressures brought to bear on St Andrew's House to make it operate in a manner and according to priorities which are as close as possible to those of Whitehall. It is scarcely surprising that as a result few can distinguish between Scottish and English patterns of action. . . ..The great pride of the civil service is not that it has developed special methods or a different emphasis in Scotland, but rather that no gap can be found between Edinburgh and London methods so that no politically awkward questions can be raised.[41]

38 Mitchell, J., *Governing Scotland* (Basingstoke: Palgrave Macmillan, 2003), 124–32.
39 For an account of its establishment and development see *ibid.*
40 See *ibid.*, 149–81.
41 Mackintosh, J. P., *The Devolution of Power* (London: Penguin, 1968), 132.

This permitted little autonomous action. Mackintosh's solution was devolution. A democratically elected body would have the 'positive incentive to be different, to take local needs into consideration rather than to struggle to be the same'.[42] But his arguments did not find favour among Treasury officials, as contemporary records show.

Second, the ministerial complement running the Scottish Office was appointed by the Prime Minister regardless of the results of elections in Scotland. The manifestos on which policies were based were either common across Britain as a whole or else differed only in detail. The ideological cohesion provided by the governing party was significant. Third, Scottish Office civil servants were part of a unified British civil service.

As a result, where differences existed they were usually a consequence of some basic differences between Scotland and England. In moving the second reading of the National Health Service (Scotland) Bill in the Commons, Joe Westwood, Secretary of State for Scotland, had explained the need for separate legislation:

> Scotland has her own legal system, her own traditions, and her own system of local government. The geographical distribution of her population is different. It is necessary, therefore, to adjust the application of general principles to suit Scotland's particular circumstances and need.[43]

The particular circumstances and needs were listed towards the end of his speech. These included different administrative arrangements for the ambulance services which would be under the Scottish Office rather than local health authorities as in England. In addition, teaching hospitals would be taken out of the 'regional ambit'. This was because while Scotland had 10 per cent of hospital beds, one third of all of the UK's medical students were trained in Scotland. Endowments to hospitals would also be dealt with differently.[44]

One of the policy areas of difference was in housing (arguably more so than in education, which is often cited). By 1979, Scotland's public sector housing as a proportion of its total housing stock was greater than in parts of eastern or central Europe. This was mainly the result of two factors: differences in the regulation of land and property as a consequence of a distinct legal and local administrative apparatus; and generous subsidies from central government for building public sector housing due to the poorer quality of Scottish housing and greater need. Though never articulated as such, the policy which was pursued was similar to 'leeway' that existed in Northern

42 *Ibid.*, 133.
43 HC Deb, 10 December 1946, col. 1003.
44 *Ibid.*, cols. 1007, 1010.

Ireland under Stormont between 1922 and 1972 (see below). This allowed for differences to allow a part of the state to make up for an underprivileged position.

The perverse consequence of the combination of different regulatory regimes and favourable central government grants (paid to local authorities through the Scottish Office) was the growth of a substantial public sector in housing. This had considerable social and economic consequences, as labour mobility was reduced and in some cases ghettos were created. Not all council housing estates were ghettos, however, and indeed one of the positive dimensions of such a substantial public sector in housing was that it lacked the stigma found elsewhere. Another feature of public sector housing was subsidised rents. These dated from the First World War when central government intervened to prevent rent strikes in the private sector after landlords attempted to take advantage of the shortage of housing to push up rents. This was to spread over into the newly developing public sector. This had the twin effects of increasing reliance on central government grants and promoting under-investment. It became almost totemic for the Labour Party to support low-rent mass council housing in Scotland. It also had an electoral dimension by creating large predominantly Labour-voting areas.

In the 1960s, partly in response to the rise of nationalism and partly due to pressure from the newly established Welsh Office, debate occurred inside central government as to whether the territorial departments should be allowed the power of virement in their spending. The Welsh Office, without the same historical development (and consequently an education system more integrated with England's and a much smaller public housing sector), pressed for greater autonomy, while the Scottish Office argued for the status quo. In a letter to a Treasury colleague, the Scottish Office Permanent Secretary Douglas Haddow argued that it was rarely possible to depart from the English pattern except, for example, in housing as Scotland had a larger public sector. The reason given was that the Scottish Secretary found it difficult coping with complaints from those using services who 'drew unfavourable comparisons between Scottish and English programmes of trends'.[45] The phrase that was used in much of the correspondence was that Scotland might wish to 'shade the allocations a little differently from England' but in essentials the desire was to follow English spending patterns.

These views were echoed strongly by Willie Ross, Secretary of State for Scotland throughout the years Harold Wilson was Prime Minister (1964–70 and 1974–76). In a letter to Judith Hart, a Scottish Labour MP and Cabinet

45 Letter from Haddow to Peter Vinter, Treasury, 12 December 1968, PRO CAB 151/45.

colleague, Ross argued that there was no benefit presentationally or practically in a system under which Scotland received a total allocation and was left to distribute it as it wished, and opposed a 'major official exercise on this'. He argued that Scottish needs 'should be, and should be seen to be, the basis for Scottish allocations'.[46] Ross cited the allocation for public housing and feared that the alternative system would require the Scottish Office to find 'off-setting reductions in other sectors'. Ross could see no advantage in gaining greater autonomy to prioritise according to Scottish needs when, as he saw it, this was already evident in the generous housing budget which also provided Scotland with a total spending advantage. Ross was determined to maintain Scotland's spending advantage and his own control over this even if, for most items, he followed English spending patterns.

Administrative devolution still provided the centre with a considerable role. It allowed for Scottish shading of UK Government policies rather than substantial Scottish autonomy. Over time, incremental shading could make for real differences and these were guarded jealously. Innovation was rare. The pejorative expression used by Parliamentary draftsmen in the House of Commons when taking account of such Scottish shadings was 'putting a kilt on' existing policy designed for England, the rest of Britain or the UK.

As noted above, redistributive matters – taxation and welfare benefits – were never the prerogative of the Scottish Office. While policies pursued through the Scottish Office – including those relating to housing, health and education – had some redistributive consequences, those were long-term consequences. No immediate method of redistributing wealth existed other than through policies held elsewhere in Whitehall. The consequence of diverse institutions in the UK taking the institutional shape of the Scottish Office was that there were differences in important respects between allocative policies across the state while redistributive policies remained the prerogative of all-Britain or all-UK departments.

Many problems with administrative devolution stemmed from its hybrid nature – part devolution, part field administration. Smith defined 'field administration' by distinguishing it from devolution in three ways: bureaucratic rather than political authority is delegated; field administrators are usually civil servants; and administrative requirements rather than local community functions delimit areas in which field officers operate.[47] The Scottish Office was not a form of field administration but had some of its characteristics. Though a ministerial team was accountable to Parliament, the array of

46 Letter from Ross to Hart, 13 February 1969, PRO CAB 151/45.
47 Smith, B. C., *Decentralisation: The territorial dimension of the state* (London: George Allen & Unwin, 1985), 142–3.

functional responsibilities and the distance which the main headquarters were from the rest of Whitehall, the Cabinet and Westminster, meant that considerable delegation to civil servants was inevitable. Lord Alness, who as Robert Munro had been Scottish Secretary between 1916 and 1922, expressed this well:

> A Secretary for Scotland must put a severe curb upon his personal predilections, and endeavour to deal with those branches of his activities, whatever they may be, that call for immediate attention. He cannot, being merely human, expand habitually to the width such a catalogue would demand. He has to live from day to day, to attend Cabinets, to think of Upper Silesia as well as, let us say, Auchtermuchty.[48]

However, the scope for autonomous decision-making was circumscribed by the funding regime. The Scottish Office was a relatively weak Whitehall department and had to have a strong case to win battles for additional resources which might provoke calls for similar treatment in the rest of the UK.

Legislative devolution in practice: parity and leeway

The one part of the United Kingdom that had experienced devolved government before 1999 was Northern Ireland, that part which had been most staunchly hostile to devolution. The irony of this has frequently been noted but the consequences for the nature of devolution less often appreciated. Devolution came to Northern Ireland as part of central government's response to pressure for Irish home rule.[49] The built-in Unionist majority had no desire to sever the link with London. Unionism's central idea was expressed by its very name; the rulers of the devolved state from 1922 until Stormont's prorogue were not members of the Ulster Devolutionist Party.[50] There were,

---

48 Munro, R., *Looking Back: Fugitive writings and sayings* (London: Thomas Nelson, 1930), 282.

49 This has been covered in numerous works. See O'Day, A., *Irish Home Rule, 1867–1921* (Manchester: Manchester University Press, 1998) for the background; Mansergh, N., *The Unresolved Question: The Anglo-Irish settlement and its undoing, 1912–72* (New Haven and London: Yale University Press, 1991) for an excellent account of its operation; and Jackson, A., *Home Rule: An Irish history, 1800–2000* (London: Weidenfeld and Nicolson, 2003) for the best recent treatment of the subject that places home rule into a wider framework. Relations between Stormont and London viewed from four different perspectives – constitutionalist, intergovernmentalist, community conflict and policy-making – are discussed in a paper by the author at: www.devolution.ac.uk/Mitchell_Stormont_London_paper.pdf.

50 The bizarre nature of Northern Ireland home rule was captured by Jackson: 'in 1936 a liberal of southern Unionist extraction, Nicholas Mansergh, presented an

nevertheless, tensions within the party which became obvious after 1972 between integrationists and devolutionists. Enoch Powell's political re-emergence as an Ulster Unionist MP considerably increased the integrationist view. This view was adopted by James Molyneaux, party leader until 1995 (when David Trimble, from the devolutionist wing of the party, became leader). The tension between assimilationist and devolutionist unionisms in recent times is historically rooted. The nature of Ireland's union with Britain has, in some senses, been inherited by Northern Ireland. The extent to which union should entail integration and assimilation against allowing for diversity was central to debates on the union. Indeed, notions of independence came rather late in Irish home rule politics.

The financial dependence of Stormont on the centre and the principles of parity and leeway which informed relations ensured that it was a truncated form of devolution. Terence O'Neill, Northern Ireland Prime Minister 1963–69, was a supporter of home rule for Scotland. In 1947, he argued for Scottish home rule in his constituency[51] and was again to lend it support in the 1960s. In a speech at Edinburgh University on 'Devolution for Scotland' in 1969 he argued for Scottish devolution modelled on Stormont but his conception of devolution was limited and typically Unionist:

> When Northern Ireland was set up it was originally conceived that she would continue with an Irish standard of living and a fixed sum for an Imperial Contribution. But before long she fought for and won parity in her social services which eventually led to the full post-war British Welfare State. She couldn't possibly have afforded to pay for this herself and I venture to suggest that this would also not be within Scotland's own resources. Who will form the first Scottish Government which is prepared to lower the social services by reducing the amount spent on Health, Welfare and Education and find it impossible to finance a Development Area as generously as the English? I certainly wouldn't be prepared to take on the task . . . I hope I will live to see a Scottish Parliament in Edinburgh. . .Not necessarily spending more money than the English on a particular service, but doing it more intelligently, or in a way particularly suited to Scotland.[52]

eloquent case for devolution on the basis of a sharp critique of the Northern Ireland regime; while thirty years on, in 1965, R. J. Lawrence, writing with some Unionist sympathies, presented an argument against devolution on the basis of a more generous portrayal of the same administration. More recently and convincingly, the American political scientist, Alan J. Ward, has suggested that Northern Ireland, for all its manifold failings, presents a good case for devolution, but a bad case for Gladstonian Home Rule' (Jackson, *Home Rule: An Irish history*, 236).

51 Mulholland, M., *Northern Ireland at the Crossroads: Ulster Unionism in the O'Neill years, 1960–9* (London: Macmillan, 2000), 14.
52 PRO HO221/161.

Legally, devolved matters were defined broadly, expressed with the goal of securing 'peace, order and good government'.[53] This wide definition of powers was, however, not a true reflection on how it operated. Northern Ireland's rulers chose to pursue parallel policies with the rest of the UK.[54]

Parity was established as a principle governing arrangements after 1938. As the Imperial Contribution had fallen to a low level in the 1930s a new arrangement was agreed. The Treasury would make up any deficit to ensure that Northern Ireland enjoyed the same standard of social services that existed in Britain. This applied so long as the deficit was not the result of higher social expenditure in Northern Ireland nor the result of lower taxation compared with Britain. This was confirmation that the revenue financing system was dead. The 1938 agreement was merely the crystallisation of a process that had already been taking place and would continue to evolve. As Kilbrandon remarked, 'in practice parity was a vague and flexible concept, and it was being developed all the time'.[55] Problems in defining parity inevitably arose as a consequence of the nature of the UK as a state of unions. Policy across a wide range of policies associated with the welfare state, including social services, lacked uniformity across the state. It would prove difficult to make meaningful comparisons across the state in efforts to achieve parity. Nonetheless, the broad principle was established and was only occasionally challenged.

Leeway was a principle related to parity. This principle recognised different starting points in the provision of new services and the need to make up 'leeway'. Under the principle of parity, the establishment of the National Health Service in Britain necessitated similar legislation for Northern Ireland. Complex financial resourcing was the subject of discussion between the Treasury and Stormont. A passage from a letter from an official in Stormont's Ministry of Finance to a Treasury official on the Northern Ireland Health Services Bill of 1948 encapsulated the issues:

> This element of 'leeway' which I mentioned is one which has frequently been taken into account in the past in discussion on the relationship between Northern Ireland and United Kingdom expenditure on particular Services. It is, of course, unrealistic to attempt to build a new Service on exact parity principles of expenditure when the existing foundations are at different levels. In the past

53 The 'POGG' clause is found in the Government of Ireland Act 1920, section 4 (1) but has many antecedents in British Imperial history; see for example section 91 of the British North America Act 1867 (now the Constitution Act (Canada) 1867), or sections 51 and 52 of the Constitution of the Commonwealth of Australia, part of the Commonwealth of Australia (Constitution) Act 1901.
54 Mitchell, 'Undignified and Inefficient'.
55 Kilbrandon, *Report of the Royal Commission on the Constitution*, 387, para. 1288.

the Treasury has shown a generous realisation of this factor in numerous instances.[56]

This had come in response to a request from the Treasury for 'an analysis of any departure from the principle of parity of services and expenditure involved in your proposals' which acknowledged 'fundamental differences in the two schemes'.[57] Fundamental differences could exist within a system that was governed by the principle of parity despite provision of welfare having different roots in the different parts of the UK. When, in 1955, Newark listed the 'more important English (sic) Acts of the past twenty-five years', he noted that these had been 'immediately or shortly followed by parallel Northern Ireland legislation'.[58] The key term here is 'parallel', as the legislation passed by Stormont was not entirely a replication of Westminster legislation. This often required considerable discussions with the centre. Pursuing parallel policies, as against uniform ones, suggests that parity would be a contentious notion. What was 'parallel' was a far less precise idea and would be interpreted differently in London and Stormont.

Legislative devolution as practised in Northern Ireland between 1922 and 1972, most notably with respect to welfare politics, conformed with the characteristics of a union state. The only peculiarity in respect of a union state was that 'pre-union rights and institutional infrastructures' could not be said to have survived as there never was a pre-existing Northern Ireland territorial entity.[59] Northern Ireland inherited the attributes of a union state from Ireland's accession to union in the sense that it would be treated as a distinct entity within the United Kingdom. But the centre remained important and policy autonomy was severely constrained. Differences in policy certainly existed but, once more, these can be accounted for in much the same way as differences between Scotland and England. There were shadings and differences that had accumulated over time. Northern Ireland's

---

56 PRO T 233/170, Letter from G. C. Cox, Finance Ministry, Stormont to I. De L. Radice, Treasury, 23 September 1947.
57 PRO T 233/170, Letter from I. De L. Radice, Treasury to G. C. Cox, Finance Ministry, Stormont.
58 Newark, F. H., 'The Law and the Constitution', in Wilson, T. (ed.), *Ulster Under Home Rule: A study of the political and economic problems of Northern Ireland* (Oxford: Oxford University Press, 1955), 52, n.1.
59 That is not to say that an entity called Ulster did not exist and the historic antecedents of Ulster have, of course, been symbolically important for Unionists. As is well known, Ulster's boundaries and those of Northern Ireland do not conform with each other. Stewart, A. T. Q., *The Narrow Ground: Aspects of Ulster, 1609–1969* (London: Faber and Faber, 1977) remains a classic work on the background to the establishment of Northern Ireland.

politicians and civil servants would inevitably attempt to make the case for more resources for the area and would, where it suited this purpose, stress differences. But the differences were generally those of scale rather than fundamentally different policy prescriptions, meaning, in effect, asking for more of the same.

Ironically, Dicey's strictures concerning equality of rights were taken seriously across the state in the form of parity but internally rights were not applied uniformly. While there remains debate as to the extent to which Stormont discriminated against its minority community, there is little doubt that in a number of significant respects its people were treated differently. While striving to maintain equality of rights across the UK, Stormont was less concerned with equality within the polity, creating the problems which ultimately removed its legitimacy and led to its demise.

Wales: in Scotland's wake

The union of Wales and England differed in two important respects from the Anglo-Scottish Union or union with Ireland: it came much earlier and it had more of the characteristics of a unitary state. Consequently, Wales was more integrated with England than either Scotland or Ireland at the start of the twentieth century. Nonetheless, there was a Welsh administrative dimension, often related to Welsh language, especially in education. A Welsh Department within the Board of Education had been set up in 1907 under the Liberals. It has been argued that this 'formally began the process of departmental decentralisation which eventually led, over half a century later, to the establishment of a Secretary of State for Wales with direct responsibility for a range of Welsh affairs'.[60] In 1911, Lloyd George agreed to 'defer to sentiment' in allowing a Scottish Insurance Commission to be set up when legislating for national insurance and extended this to Wales also.[61] This set a pattern for future developments.

In 1945 a committee chaired by Herbert Morrison, Lord President of the Council in Prime Minister Attlee's post-war government, rejected proposals for a Welsh Office modelled on the Scottish Office. Morrison maintained that 'the proper remedy for Wales, as for Scotland, is to ensure that they both form part of a single economic plan for the whole country and are not thrown back

60 Randall, P. J., *The Development of Administrative Decentralisation in Wales from the Establishment of the Welsh Department of Education in 1907 to the Creation of the Post of Secretary of State for Wales in October 1964* (Unpublished MSc. Econ. Thesis, University of Wales, 1969), 2.
61 HC Deb, 13 November 1911, col. 60.

on their sectional resources'.[62] When Welsh MPs again requested the establishment of a Welsh Office in 1946, it was once more rejected. Attlee explained his thinking, refuting comparisons with Scotland and repeating Morrison's argument:

> Scotland, unlike Wales, had codes of civil and criminal law and a system of administration which are different in important respects from those of England. Moreover all who have the welfare of Wales at heart are particularly concerned with differences in the economic sphere, and it is in just this sphere that there is no separate Scottish administration. Economic matters for Britain as a whole have been handled, as they must be, by departments covering the whole country.[63]

Attlee was alluding to the differing types of union that had brought Wales and Scotland together with England. Stafford Cripps, President of the Board of Trade, warned against establishing a Welsh Office, arguing that it would place Wales at an economic disadvantage and Nye Bevan, Minister of Health and Welsh MP, maintained that the Welsh Secretary would be 'nothing but a Welsh messenger boy'.[64] An Advisory Council on Wales and Monmouthshire was established in 1948 to report on a wide range of matters. It appeared a small concession to Welsh sentiment at the time, but small concessions can grow.

Matters progressed in the 1950s in what at first sight appears the opposite way in Wales from that of Scotland. The fact that the Conservatives had few Welsh MPs played a part in Welsh Labour coming to favour a Welsh Office. Playing the Welsh card in opposition, Labour moved towards support for a Welsh Office. It was aided in this by the third memorandum of the Advisory Council on Wales and Monmouthshire on 'Government and Administration in Wales', which argued for a Secretary of State for Wales with a seat in the Cabinet.[65] It would be the 'most remarkable contribution the Council made'.[66] The small concession of 1948 was about to bite. In 1959, in a further memorandum, the Advisory Council issued a further report in which it argued:

> Wales was a separate nation and not just a region, province or appendage of England. Time and again we were made to realise that the problems of administration in certain fields were different from those in England and that there was

---

62 Quoted in Morgan, K. O., *Wales: Rebirth of a nation, 1880–1980* (Oxford: Oxford University Press, 1982), 377.

63 Quoted in Gibson, E. L., *A Study of the Council for Wales and Monmouthshire, 1948–1966* (Unpublished LLB Thesis, University College of Wales, Aberystwyth, 1968, 13).

64 HC Deb, 28 October 1946, Cripps at cols. 310–17 and Bevan at col. 315.

65 Council of Wales and Monmouthshire, *Third Memorandum on its Activities*, Cm 53 (London: HMSO, 1957).

66 Gowan, I., *Government in Wales*, Inaugural Lecture as Professor of Political Science (University College Wales, Aberystwyth December 1965).

therefore a clear and unmistakable need to secure for Wales a different system of administrative arrangements to deal with these special problems.[67]

The previous October, the Chairman of the Council, Huw Edwards, had resigned when MacMillan's Conservative government had refused to accept administrative changes. In office, Labour became more firmly committed to administrative devolution. Jim Callaghan, Cardiff MP and later Labour Prime Minister, came to support a Welsh Office having witnessed the way the Scottish Office had successfully campaigned within government for a road bridge over the River Forth, a major infrastructure project.[68] Among their other functions, the Welsh and Scottish Offices were institutionalised and influential pressure groups for Scotland and Wales at the heart of government.

The more integrated arrangements that existed in Wales compared with Scotland meant that the new Welsh Office was more likely to press for greater autonomy simply because a degree of difference was already allowed for in Scotland. Over time, the responsibilities of the Welsh Office also grew but always remained behind those of the Scottish Office. Its form mirrored the Scottish Office. Administrative devolution existed in two parts of the state until in 1972 Stormont was prorogued and 'direct rule' was imposed on Northern Ireland. Thereafter the arrangements for governing Northern Ireland (with the existing Northern Ireland departments working to UK ministers and retaining their separate existence) were, in many respects, the same as those for Scotland and Wales but the starting point was markedly different. Hence, the Northern Ireland Office was termed 'direct rule' while Scottish and Welsh Offices were examples of 'administrative devolution'. There was, of course, an added difference. Ministers heading the Northern Ireland Office never represented constituencies in Northern Ireland whereas Scottish Office ministers were invariably either MPs with Scottish constituencies or were members of the Lords with some Scottish connection. For the most part Welsh Office ministers came from Wales but in the later years of Conservative rule, when there were very few Welsh Conservative MPs, the Welsh Office was headed by MPs with English constituencies. As much as anything, the past has determined the language of territorial government.

The post-devolution polity and devolved competences

The constitutional reform programme of the New Labour government elected in 1997 has been described as 'wider than that of any political party taking office

---

67 Council of Wales and Monmouthshire, *Fourth Memorandum on Government Administration in Wales*, Cmnd 631 (London: HMSO, 1959), para. 13.

68 Morgan, K. O., *Callaghan: A life* (Oxford: Oxford University Press, 1997), 197.

this century'.[69] Without necessarily disputing this claim, devolution has deep roots in existing constitutional traditions. The starting points for devolved government in Scotland, Wales and Northern Ireland were the three territorial offices. It would, therefore, be wrong to ignore the nature of administrative devolution while acknowledging the differences between it and legislative devolution. The key difference has been the democratisation of administrative devolution. In place of territorial departments accountable to Parliament at Westminster as a whole, devolved government involves accountability to locally, directly elected chambers in Scotland, Wales and Northern Ireland.

The continuities that are evident post-devolution are notably in the kinds of policies which have been retained at the centre. The tax-varying power of the Scottish Parliament is merely symbolic. Redistributive policies remain concentrated in London. Distributive policies have been devolved as they had been under administrative and legislative devolution before. Any efforts to redistribute wealth, to create social democratic or socialist celtic polities will prove illusory so long as the centre continues to pursue an alternative type of polity across the state. However, incremental changes will kick in and very different rights are likely across the state. Institutions matter.

The United Kingdom has had its Tocqueville in the shape of Dicey but it has never had its Madison. It never produced anything equivalent to the *Federalist Papers* and consequent debates, and its constitutional evolution has emerged piecemeal. The move towards a devolved polity has been no different from previous changes. These changes have been accommodated within existing statutes and frameworks. The consequence has been that devolution owes a great deal more to the past, both in the historical working of the Union and in the ways the UK at the centre managed its various constituent parts, than is generally appreciated. The UK was and remains a state of unions. Devolution underlines the variety of forms this union takes, and in part it was recognition that the UK never was a unitary state, at least not in the sense meant by Rokkan and Urwin, that opened up possibilities for constitutional reform. One source of thinking about these problems is the arch-Unionist Dicey, who did outline the bones of ideas that might be seen to inform thinking about territorial politics. His three watchwords – equality of political rights, diversity of institutions and unity of government – perhaps cannot offer principles to guide future constitutional arrangements, or underpin existing ones. However, they can offer choices that remain highly relevant.

---

69 Blackburn, R. and Plant, R. (eds), *Constitutional Reform: The Labour Government's constitutional reform agenda* (London: Longman, 1999), 1.

3
The framework of devolution: the formal structure of devolved power
Alan Trench*

This chapter will examine the institutional and legal framework of devolution, and assess where, in formal terms, power lies after devolution – what legal constraints devolution imposes on the UK Government and Parliament and on the devolved institutions, and what effect they are capable of having in practice. It has two main concerns: first, to explain why intergovernmental relations are integral to the structure of UK devolution as a whole, and second to show how and why structural features of devolution in general and the arrangements put in place for intergovernmental relations in particular place the devolved administrations at a systematic disadvantage in intergovernmental relations. In a nutshell, it will explain why the devolved administrations are compelled to play a game in which the cards are always stacked against them.

To make sense of this, one needs to recognise that from an institutional point of view, devolution has three limbs. First are the constitutions of the devolved bodies themselves, set out in the Scotland Act 1998, Northern Ireland Act 1998 and Government of Wales Act 1998. These pieces of legislation define the powers of the devolved bodies, and so create what legal autonomy they have. They also create constraints on the devolved bodies that can be exercised by the UK Government and other bodies. Second, there is a framework of intergovernmental agreements (the Memorandum of Understanding and the specific concordats) defining how the UK's four governments relate to each other.[1] Third, there are the financial arrangements

* I am grateful to Robert Hazell, Ron Watts, Scott Greer and other contributors to this book for their comments on earlier drafts of this chapter. I am of course solely responsible for any mistakes or errors of judgment that remain. Like my other chapters in this book, it draws on extensive interviewing of UK Government and devolved administration officials and politicians involved in various aspects of devolution, as well as the published sources noted in the footnotes. When my source for information not otherwise in the public domain is interviews, I have indicated this in the text.
1 *Memorandum of Understanding and Supplementary Agreements between the United Kingdom Government, Scottish Ministers, the Cabinet of the National Assembly for*

set out by HM Treasury, which are not discussed here but are discussed further in chapters 4 and 5.[2] Devolution takes effect partly through Acts of the Westminster Parliament, which in theory are open to modification at Westminster like any other Act of Parliament, partly through intergovernmental agreements and partly through a statement of what the Treasury proposes to do. A complete picture of the structure of the relationship between the four governments can only be found by taking all three into account.

The constitution of devolution

One of the ironies of devolution is that intergovernmental relations appear to have been something of an afterthought in its construction, despite their importance. The main thrust of devolution, and of government activity in 1997–99, was with creating the devolved institutions themselves. This meant framing white papers, arranging for referendums, drafting legislation and securing its passage through Parliament and then making administrative arrangements for the new institutions to take up their work. In the case of Scotland, the starting point was the work of the Scottish Constitutional Convention; in the case of Wales, debate appears to have been largely within the Labour Party, split between supporters and opponents of devolution.[3] The devolution white papers are notably silent about issues of intergovernmental

Wales and the Northern Ireland Executive Committee, Cm 5240 (London: The Stationery Office, 2001) (henceforth 'Memorandum of Understanding'). There have been three versions of the Memorandum of Understanding: one published in 1999, a second in 2000 (which included the Northern Ireland Executive) and the third in 2001 (which dealt with the Cabinet of the National Assembly, to reflect developments in Wales).

2 Those arrangements are set out in HM Treasury, *Funding the Scottish Parliament, National Assembly for Wales and Northern Ireland Assembly: A statement of funding policy* (London: HM Treasury, 3rd edn, 2002). The Statement also first appeared in 1999 and was reissued in 2000 and 2002, following the Treasury's Comprehensive Spending Review. These reissues have not involved changes to the principles set out in the Statement.

3 See Scottish Constitutional Convention, *Scotland's Parliament, Scotland's Right* (Edinburgh: Scottish Constitutional Convention, 1995); Jones, J. B. and Balsom, D. (eds), *The Road to the National Assembly for Wales* (Cardiff: University of Wales Press, 2000), chaps 3 and 4. Intergovernmental relations were paid more attention in the Constitution Unit's reports: *Scotland's Parliament: Fundamentals for a new Scotland Act* (London: The Constitution Unit, 1996) and *An Assembly for Wales* (London: The Constitution Unit, 1996), which appear to have been widely read in Whitehall.

relations, finance excepted.[4] So far as one can tell from interviewing, the main concern of the officials involved was with making sure that those new institutions could work. Implicit to this was the belief that they would function (but only function) within the spheres of autonomy granted to them. Only once the bills had been introduced into Parliament did officials' minds turn to how these new bodies would work with the UK institutions, and the impact that each might have on the other. This led, for example, to the development of the Sewel convention about Westminster legislation affecting devolved matters, first enunciated during the Committee stage in the Lords' consideration of the Scotland Bill in July 1998.[5] It also led to officials drafting the first version of what became the Memorandum of Understanding, the principal intergovernmental agreement, and formulating the idea of 'concordats' between devolved administrations and UK Government departments to govern the conduct of relations between them.

With the benefit of hindsight, it is clear that what was being created was a system in which intergovernmental relations would be central to carrying on any government business. They are, in fact, essential to the system that was being established. The slowness with which this was appreciated may owe a great deal to the pressures under which the officials involved were working (perhaps aided by the relative inexperience in office of their new ministers). It may also derive from officials taking for granted the assumption that devolution would accentuate the existing autonomy of the territorial departments. Nor were they alone in this approach – a number of the earlier academic discussions of devolution downplay the importance of intergovernmental relations as well.[6] Without even looking to issues of party politics and the working of the party system (or systems) after devolution, it is possible to identify a number of reasons why intergovernmental relations were to be central to the United Kingdom after devolution, however. Some of these are essentially legal in character, and some essentially administrative.

On the legal side, what powers are allocated to the devolved institutions or retained by UK ones is highly important. As is well known, the powers of the Scottish Parliament (and Northern Ireland Assembly) are framed so that all matters are within their legislative competence except for those that are reserved to the UK (in Scotland) or excepted or reserved (in the case of

---

4 Scottish Office, *Scotland's Parliament,* Cm 3658 (London: The Stationery Office, 1997); Welsh Office, *A Voice for Wales: The Government's proposals for a Welsh Assembly,* Cm 3718 (London: The Stationery Office, 1997).

5 HL Deb, 21 July 1998, col. 791.

6 See for example Burrows, N., *Devolution* (London: Sweet & Maxwell, 2000); Bogdanor, V., *Devolution in the United Kingdom* (Oxford: Oxford University Press, 1999).

Northern Ireland).[7] Therefore, they can do anything except what is expressly forbidden. In particular, they are not subject to any sort of control over the merits of devolved legislation; the only challenge possible is one that relates to the legal competence of the legislation. (The procedural checks on this are discussed in detail later in this chapter.)

Making sense of the structure of reserved and devolved matters is not straightforward. A good starting point for all three sets of arrangements is that for Scotland, where the general pattern of reserved matters is as follows:

- **The constitution of the UK** – meaning the Union of Scotland and England itself, the Crown, the UK Parliament, the law of treason and the structure of the Scottish judicial system. Also protected are key provisions of the European Communities Act 1972, the Human Rights Act 1998, the status of the Home Civil Service and the regulation of political parties and elections.
- **The conduct of foreign affairs and defence**, including the military and arms control.
- **Macro-economic management**: fiscal, economic and monetary policy and the currency.
- **The demand side of the economy**, so that the UK is maintained as a single economic unit. This includes banking, insurance and financial services regulation, company law, business associations and corporate insolvency (but not personal bankruptcy), consumer protection, weights and measures, intellectual property, competition law and employment law. This heading arguably also includes regulation of a number of professions (such as architects, auditors and medical professions), the regulation of medicines, and reservations relating to the Private Legislation Procedure (Scotland) Act 1936 and powers to designate enterprise zones under the Local Government, Planning and Land Act 1980.
- **The infrastructure of the UK**, including transport by air, sea and rail (although the last has subsequently been extensively devolved), telecommunications, broadcasting regulation, the BBC, the post office, university research and outer space.
- **Natural resources**, particularly oil, gas, coal and nuclear energy.

---

7 Scotland Act 1998, s. 29; Northern Ireland Act 1998, s. 6. For discussions, see Burrows, *Devolution*, especially chaps 3 and 4; Himsworth, C. M. G. and O'Neill, C. M., *Scotland's Constitution: Law and practice* (Edinburgh and London: Lexis Nexis, 2003); and Hadfield, B., 'Seeing it Through? The multifaceted implementation of the Belfast Agreement', in Wilford, R. (ed.), *Aspects of the Belfast Agreement* (Oxford: Oxford University Press, 2001).

- **Home affairs matters**, including emergency powers, national security (including the intelligence services), immigration and nationality.
- **Matters relating to 'social citizenship'**, again so that persons retain equal entitlements across the UK. This covers social security, pensions and child support, data protection and equal opportunities.
- **Other areas** where allowing Scotland to legislate would either run the risk of different rules applying across the UK and so create anomalies (e.g. xeno-transplantation – the transplantation of animal organs into humans) or would be politically controversial in Scotland (abortion).[8]

While the broad outlines of this list are straightforward, it also contains some reservations that are harder to explain and which appear to have been included either because of political whim or for some obscure administrative reason. The structure of the list (split between two Schedules to the Act, with provisions in Schedule 5 being capable of being amended but those in Schedule 4 not) is even odder.

For Northern Ireland, the structure of non-devolved functions is largely similar. However, as it distinguishes between 'reserved' functions (which could be transferred to the Assembly at some future date by order in council) and 'excepted' ones (which cannot), it is somewhat more complex.[9] The lists of reserved and excepted matters bear a family resemblance to reserved matters in Scotland but with some significant differences; postal services are reserved not excepted, for example, so could be transferred at some point, while on the formal level social security is devolved.[10] However, the major difference is the reservations relating to criminal law, prosecutions, public order and policing.

Executive devolution is somewhat different from legislative devolution. It applies also to Wales as well as Scotland (and intermittently Northern Ireland).[11]

---

8 See Scotland Act 1998, Schedules 4 and 5.
9 See Northern Ireland Act 1998, Schedules 2 and 3.
10 So far as social security is concerned, section 87 of the Northern Ireland Act 1998 (complemented by sections 88–9) provides for parity between Northern Ireland's system of social security and that of the rest of the UK.
11 Rawlings has argued that devolution to Wales should be regarded as 'quasi-legislative' and not simply executive, because the powers conferred on the National Assembly enable it to make a wide range of secondary legislation which is broader than the scope of powers that Secretaries of State within the UK Government have. See Rawlings, R., 'Quasi-legislative Devolution: Powers and principles', *Northern Ireland Legal Quarterly*, 52 (2001), 54–81. That is correct from an internal point of view as far as Wales is concerned, but from a technical (and UK-oriented) perspective, what Wales has remains executive devolution because it remains limited to executive functions and because of the exclusive competence the Assembly has for most of its functions as a result.

In the case of Scotland and Northern Ireland, its starting point is legislative devolution: the Scottish ministers (the statutory term for the Scottish Executive) and Northern Ireland ministers have executive powers for matters that are legislatively devolved in each case.[12] Additional powers – relating to matters which are reserved for legislative purposes – can be devolved as well.[13] For Wales, the Assembly has functions transferred to it by or under the Government of Wales Act 1998 or conferred on it under other Westminster Acts.[14] The list of devolved functions is set out with mind-numbing exactness in secondary legislation made under the Government of Wales Act 1998 (particularly the main transfer of functions order made in 1999), or in Acts of the Westminster Parliament made since 1998. These functions are in areas comparable to those devolved to Scotland or Northern Ireland set out above (and indicated in Schedule 2 to the Government of Wales Act 1998), but the general powers of the Assembly are nowhere set out in its founding legislation.[15] Being a statutory body, the Assembly can only act in the areas where it expressly has powers to do so. Because it needs to be able to identify an express power for any action it takes, the system that arises is complex and full of anomalies, and has led to much legal confusion and widespread academic criticism.[16] (The 1999 jumbo transfer of functions order runs to 31 closely printed pages in the HMSO printed version, citing numerous Acts under which some or all functions pass to the Assembly. A measure of its complexity is that the Assembly's internal working version, which sets out what these powers are item by item with a single-line

12 Scotland Act 1998, s. 53; Northern Ireland Act 1998, s. 23.
13 For Scotland, powers may be transferred by order under s. 63 of the Scotland Act 1998 or by agreement under s. 55. For Northern Ireland, agency arrangements between the UK and Northern Ireland may be made under s. 28 of the Northern Ireland Act 1998.
14 Government of Wales Act 1998, s. 21. For a discussion of the institutional characteristics of devolution to Wales, see Patchett, K., 'The New Welsh Constitution: The Government of Wales Act 1998', in Jones and Balsom (eds), *The Road to the National Assembly for Wales.*
15 The starting point to establish them was the 'jumbo' transfer of functions order: The National Assembly for Wales (Transfer of Functions) Order 1999, SI 1999 no. 672. Subsequent orders include SI 1999 no. 2787, SI 2000 no. 253, SI 2000 no. 1829, SI 2000 no. 1830, SI 2001 no. 3679, SI 2004 no. 3044 and SI 2005 no. 1958. The 1998 Act does set out some specific powers for the Assembly, for reorganisation of health authorities and a wide range of public bodies (quangos).
16 For examples, see Rawlings, R., 'Quasi-legislative Devolution' and 'Towards a Parliament: Three faces of the National Assembly for Wales', *Contemporary Wales*, 15 (2003), 1–19; Lambert, D. and Miers, D., 'Law-making in Wales: Wales-legislation online', *Public Law* (2002), 663–9. On Wales generally, see Rawlings, R., *Delineating Wales: Constitutional, legal and administrative aspects of national devolution* (Cardiff: University of Wales Press, 2003).

explanation of each power's effect, runs to over 500 pages.) One important feature, though (for all three territories) is that executive devolution – unlike legislative devolution – is exclusive. Subject to a number of express exceptions, where joint action by the devolved administration and a UK Secretary of State is needed, the devolved administrations are wholly autonomous in the exercise of executive functions.[17] Thus there is no analogue to the Sewel convention for executive matters, nor any need for one.

What these arrangements for transferring powers (or not) leave the devolved institutions remains extensive. By implication, devolved powers in all three parts of the UK include the following areas:

- education, both in schools and colleges or universities;
- the health service and public health;
- local government, housing and planning, and personal social services;
- the environment (though heavily subject to EU regulation);
- agriculture and fisheries (likewise heavily regulated by the EU);
- public transport and roads (with substantial control over local railway services devolved subsequently);
- cultural matters (including the Welsh language for Wales, and other minority languages);
- the courts and the legal system generally (in Scotland);
- criminal law, prosecutions and policing (in Scotland).

Even these areas remain subject to the possibility of Westminster legislating for them. Such legislation would be governed by the Sewel convention, that Westminster would not normally legislate for a devolved matter without the consent of the devolved legislature. Thus, on the formal level devolution creates a system of concurrent legislative powers, even if functional competences are separate.

These sorts of functions can be characterised in various ways. Sharpe dubs them 'SHEW' (social, health, education, welfare) ones, and notes that they are commonly devolved to meso levels of government across Europe, because their externalities are too great for local government.[18] Mitchell, adopting a framework from Lowi, identifies them as distributive or regulatory, but

17 UK ministers retain powers over a range of matters set out in ss. 56–57 Scotland Act 1998 concurrently with Scottish Ministers. The areas affected include a number of powers to make grants, and powers to implement UN Security Council resolutions, to prevent breach of international obligations by Scottish Ministers, and to implement EU obligations under the European Communities Act 1972.

18 Sharpe, L. J., 'The European Meso: An appraisal', in Sharpe, L. J. (ed.), *The Rise of Meso Government in Europe* (London: Sage, 1993), 10–11.

generally not redistributive.[19] These generalisations are helpful analytically or comparatively, but may also mask the complexity that lies under such broad-brush terms. For those who have to apply them in practice, the various definitions of what is or is not devolved are complex and uneven; one official interviewed considered the line between devolved and non-devolved matters to be a 'jagged edge', while another compared it to a jigsaw, extending in different ways in more than two dimensions.

How these functions came to be identified is also important. The starting point was the existing pattern of administrative devolution, so the functions to be transferred were generally those already exercised by the Scottish or Welsh Offices or Northern Ireland departments. In the cases of Scotland and Wales, this only provided the first outline of what was to be transferred, which was subject to a process of consideration within government and a good deal of interdepartmental horse trading, in which (interviewing confirms) some departments were supportive of the process and others (notably the former Department for the Environment, Transport and the Regions and the Department of Trade and Industry) were unhelpful. In the case of Northern Ireland, the commitment in the Belfast Agreement to transfer functions exercised by the existing Northern Ireland departments trumped resistance from some parts of Whitehall, notably over social security.[20] The historical inheritance has therefore played a large role here, with existing transfers of powers for administrative purposes used as the basis for the next step of elected political control.

Constitutional arrangements and intergovernmental relations

The implications of this set of arrangements are several. First, it is very hard to generalise about what devolution means. It is different for each of Scotland, Wales and Northern Ireland, in many important respects. The devolution arrangements as a whole are profoundly asymmetric. The implications of this will be discussed further below, and indeed in many other parts of this book.

Second, it is very hard to take any action in respect of devolved functions without having some effect on non-devolved ones. This can arise for a number of reasons. There may be significant knock-on effects, so policy for

19 Mitchell, J., 'Scotland: Expectations, policy types and devolution', in Trench, A. (ed.), *Has Devolution Made a Difference? The State of the Nations 2004* (Exeter: Imprint Academic, 2004).

20 *An Agreement Reached at the Multi-Party Talks on Northern Ireland*, Cm 3883 (London: The Stationery Office, 1998), Strand One, para. 3.

a devolved matter has an effect on policy for a non-devolved matter. An example is the effect of the Scottish policy of free long-term care for the elderly, which affected the eligibility of residents of Scotland for attendance allowance (a social security benefit). While higher education is devolved, the Research Councils are reserved matters and subject to direction from the UK Government. This means that universities in the devolved territories receive a substantial amount of their funding from a UK source and not the devolved funding councils, are assessed for their research (but not their teaching) by a UK body, and consequently may find it hard to respond to devolved priorities or policies. Sometimes, the issue is to work out whether a particular policy (and the legislation to implement it) falls within a devolved or non-devolved area. The problems this presents may be practical but may also be conceptual, forcing governments to decide what legislation is 'about'. For example, legislation to repeal the prohibition on the 'promotion of homosexuality in schools' in Scotland (the notorious 'section 28' of the Local Government Act 1988, amending section 2A of the Local Government Act 1986) caused an internal discussion about whether it related to education or local government (in which case it was devolved) or to equal opportunities, which would mean it was reserved.[21] (This is made worse by the fact that many reservations in Schedule 5 to the Scotland Act refer to the 'subject matter' of another Act, although it can be hard to work out exactly what the subject matter is.) Many other activities may raise issues of compliance with European Union obligations, or the European Convention on Human Rights, in which case the action will similarly be beyond competence. The effect of the settlement is to mean there will be similar debate in a wide range of instances.

Third, many reserved matters similarly have significant implications for devolved matters. The UK Government's policies to house asylum-seekers outside London, particularly in vacant housing in Glasgow and south Wales, have led to major tensions with both devolved administrations – whether because of the direct payments to local authorities for this, or the costs imposed on devolved services such as health from having significant numbers of extra users of services located in their territories.

Fourth, many areas of reserved competence are hugely important for the devolved administrations. Scotland, facing a shrinking population, has sought to find ways to increase it from abroad – whether by attracting immigrants to

---

21 See Ethical Standards in Public Life (Scotland) Act 2000, s. 34. For a discussion of issues relating to the repeal, see Armstrong, K., 'Contesting Government, Producing Devolution: The repeal of "section 28" in Scotland', *Legal Studies*, 23:2 (2003), 205–28.

Scotland or by persuading overseas students to stay there after graduating. Broadcasting is another example, whether it be through arguments before devolution about coverage of Scottish news on the BBC, or provisions of minority language television services (highly significant in Wales). The strong Scottish presence in the UK's armed forces, particularly the Army, is outside the Parliament's powers. Energy and natural resources are another area of high importance, given the size of the North Sea oil fields serviced from Aberdeen and the Shetland islands. Part of the logic of devolution appears to have been to strengthen the voice of Scotland and Wales (more than Northern Ireland) within the Union, increasing the importance of ensuring that that voice can be heard.[22]

A further aspect of this is that many of the areas of traditional Scottish distinctiveness, which have underpinned Scottish autonomy within the Union state, are in fact reserved rather than devolved.[23] While the legal system and most aspects of Scots law are devolved, the framework of the court structure protected by the Treaty of Union is in fact reserved. Similarly, although the Scottish banking system has long been distinct, and the larger Scottish banks retain the privilege of issuing their own banknotes, both banking and currency are reserved matters. Differences in company and partnership law may exist between Scots law and that of England and Wales (or Northern Ireland), but these too are reserved matters.

Fifth, the areas retained by the UK include the devolution legislation, and so the constitution of the devolved bodies. Except for relatively minor matters (such as the enactment of standing orders), none of the Scottish Parliament, National Assembly for Wales or Northern Ireland Assembly can alter the terms of devolution, even for internal matters. Issues such as the number of members of the legislatures, the electoral system used, the nature of executive power and its relation to the legislature are outside devolved competence. Thus the UK Government and Parliament retain a central role in decisions about the development of devolution. Since 2000 this has included:

- Deciding that the number of MSPs should remain at 129, although the number of Scottish MPs at Westminster was reduced to 59 (from 72)

22 See Curtice, J., 'Public Opinion and the Future of Devolution', in Trench, A. (ed.), *The Dynamics of Devolution: The State of the Nations 2005* (Exeter: Imprint Academic, 2005) for a discussion of the importance of this to public opinion.

23 See Kellas, J., *The Scottish Political System* (Cambridge: Cambridge University Press, 3rd edn, 1984); Paterson, L., *The Autonomy of Modern Scotland* (Edinburgh: Edinburgh University Press, 1994).

which, under the Scotland Act, should have triggered a similar reduction at Holyrood.[24]

- Reconsidering the arrangements for Wales following the report of the Richard Commission, including the number of Assembly Members, the electoral arrangements, the 'single body corporate' structure for the Assembly and its legislative powers, with a bill introduced into Parliament in December 2005.[25]

- Passing legislation at Westminster to enable devolution in Northern Ireland to be suspended, used on a number of occasions in 2001 and notably in October 2002, since when direct rule has been in place.[26]

- Passing further Westminster legislation to create an Independent Monitoring Commission to monitor paramilitary ceasefires in Northern Ireland.[27]

The UK's continuing role in these matters does not simply mean that the agreement of the UK is needed for any significant change to the devolution arrangements put in place in 1997–98. That agreement may present problems, as it gives the UK Government a veto over the constitutional development of each part of the United Kingdom. It also imposes practical constraints, notably in the need to secure Parliamentary time as well as legislative support for any changes sought by the devolved institutions. The case of the size of the Scottish Parliament, noted above, is one example, with the change strongly supported by practically every interest connected with the Scottish Parliament and with opposition coming mainly from Scottish MPs, especially Labour ones, whose own futures would be adversely affected by the change. A similar consideration applies to the proposed changes to the National Assembly for Wales in 2004–05. Opposition to the Richard Commission proposals has chiefly come from within the Welsh Labour Party and to a degree from the Welsh Conservatives, both of which are internally split over the question – and particularly from among the Welsh Labour MPs whose position (like the Scottish MPs) might be undermined if the changes

---

24 See Scotland Office, *The Size of the Scottish Parliament: A consultation* (December 2001); Scotland Office Press Release, 'Liddell Announces Decision on MSP Numbers' (18 December 2002); and the Scottish Parliament (Constituencies) Act 2004.

25 See Commission on the Powers and Electoral Arrangements of the National Assembly for Wales, *Report of the Richard Commission* (Cardiff: National Assembly for Wales, 2004); Wales Office, *Better Governance for Wales*, Cm 6582 (London: The Stationery Office, 2005).

26 Northern Ireland Act 2000.

27 Northern Ireland (Monitoring Commission etc.) Act 2003.

are approved.[28] In contexts such as these, the devolved constitutions figure as much as an issue of intergovernmental relations as its 'ground', in the terminology used in chapter 1.

A further aspect of 'constitutional' control is that the devolution arrangements contain a number of mechanisms for transferring additional functions to the devolved institutions (or away from them).[29] These mechanisms do require the consent of the devolved institutions affected (as well as the UK Parliament), so only work where there is agreement between the two governments, but (as discussed in chapter 8) they have proved valuable mechanisms in practice, both for extending the scope of devolved powers and for negotiating the complex boundary between devolved and non-devolved matters. In some cases, this has enabled the resolution of matters without the need for litigation that in other systems have been considered by the courts.

These formal aspects alone would make intergovernmental relations an essential part of governing the UK after devolution. However, their importance is increased by various administrative factors. First, the process of devolution is a form of 'spinning out' of various policy functions. Many of the functions devolved relate to the welfare state to some degree. All were formerly functions of a single government, albeit one that allowed there to be variations in their operation for Scotland, Wales or Northern Ireland, and they are closely related to non-devolved functions (notably social security). This means that devolved functions remain closely related politically and administratively to similar functions retained by the UK Government for the UK as a whole, or for England and perhaps other parts of the UK, and they start from a platform of considerable similarity in both working and objective. There will be an interaction between devolved and non-devolved parts of the UK as a result.

Second, as James Mitchell shows in chapter 2, the UK has a long history of territorial administration. Many features of that set of administrative arrangements moved across into the devolved administrations. Many of the civil service

---

28 The Welsh Labour Party's response to the Richard Report was *Better Governance for Wales: A Welsh Labour policy document* (Cardiff: Wales Labour Party, 2004).

29 For legislative matters, see Scotland Act 1998, ss. 104 and 107. In addition, s. 30 enables matters to be added or removed to the lists of 'reserved' matters in Schedule 5. Devolution Guidance Note 14 provides guidance to Whitehall departments about the making of such orders. For Northern Ireland, see Northern Ireland Act 1998, s. 80 (power to remedy ultra vires acts) and s. 4 (2) (power to make reserved matters transferred matters). The key powers for executive devolution to Scotland are Scotland Act 1998, ss. 63, 106 and 108. For Wales, the principal power is the general power to transfer functions under s. 22 of the Government of Wales Act 1998; see note 15 above.

staff were the same, at least initially, and for all the dramatic impact of devolution on the civil service much civil service culture has persisted, although it has had to adapt to the new circumstances.[30] As already noted, the existing framework of devolved administration was the basis for transferring functions to the new institutions. Despite substantial and long-standing autonomy for the territorial departments within UK Government, they had to function as part of UK Government. The administrative starting point for devolution has therefore been patterns of behaviour built up in a single government, with a need to coordinate policy with (non-territorial) UK departments, particularly through the machinery of Cabinet, Cabinet committees and interdepartmental (official) committees such as the Wednesday morning meetings of permanent secretaries, underpinned by the doctrine of Cabinet collective responsibility. Coordination of government has been part of UK experience for a long time, and devolution has started against the backdrop of this behaviour.

While intergovernmental relations may have been an integral part of the devolution arrangements from the outset, the impact of such relations varies from territory to territory.

Scotland's long tradition of distinctiveness in both policy and institutions, accompanied by the autonomy devolution has provided, mean that intergovernmental relations are a concern for Scotland, but it is something that the Scottish Executive does as part of the business of governing Scotland. Similar considerations applied to devolved government in Northern Ireland. For Wales, however, the system created has involved an extremely close relationship with the UK Government.[31] One might say that while devolution for Scotland and Northern Ireland involves intergovernmental relations, for Wales it *is* intergovernmental relations.

The strength of the UK Government in intergovernmental relations

Having shown how important intergovernmental relations are in the UK's devolved system of government, it is necessary to consider why and how that system, from the outset, has put the UK Government at an advantage. It is not particularly surprising that this is the case – even in the most decentralised

30 See Parry, R., 'Devolution, Integration and Modernisation in the United Kingdom's Civil Service', *Public Policy and Administration*, 16:3 (2001), 53–67; and Rhodes, R. A. W., Carmichael, P., McMillan, J. and Massey, A., *Decentralizing the Civil Service: From unitary state to differentiated polity in the United Kingdom* (Buckingham: Open University Press, 2003).

31 For a detailed discussion see Rawlings, *Delineating Wales*, especially chaps 2 and 12–14.

of federal systems, the state-wide government generally has the upper hand. What is notable in the case of the UK is the extent of this.

One feature is apparent from the discussion of the institutional structure of devolution above. That is the fundamental asymmetry of the UK's devolution arrangements. This asymmetry arises first from the fact that devolution is limited to Scotland, Wales and Northern Ireland; second, from the different arrangements for devolution to each territory, creating a different set of constitutional issues for each of them; and third, from the significant differences that exist in the functions exercised by each devolved administration and its Parliament or Assembly. The last is compounded by differences in the issues that most concern each administration; fishing is for example a pressing issue for Scotland but not Wales or Northern Ireland, while hill-farming is a major concern for Wales, and pastoral agriculture for Northern Ireland. This means that each devolved territory has concerns with the UK Government that will largely be unique to it, not shared with the other devolved territories. It follows that each territory has little reason to develop its relations or make common cause with institutions from the other devolved territories, because its concerns are for the most part specific to that territory, not shared, and there is only limited scope for forming a common front with the other devolved institutions.

This creates a situation where intergovernmental relations are mainly bilateral ones between one devolved administration and the UK Government (usually a single department). This is how the framework for intergovernmental relations expects issues to arise, and in which it envisages most of them being resolved; the Memorandum of Understanding assumes that business will be conducted through 'normal administrative channels' and that only 'where a dispute cannot be resolved bilaterally or through the good offices of the relevant territorial Secretary of State' will other machinery such as the Joint Ministerial Committee be involved.[32] Equally, interviewing has shown how strong this expectation was among the officials concerned with establishing devolution.

The Memorandum of Understanding and concordats

Discussion of the framework for intergovernmental relations in the UK has to focus on the Memorandum of Understanding, the overarching master agreement between the UK Government and the devolved administrations.[33] As noted above, the Memorandum of Understanding was drafted by officials

32 Memorandum of Understanding, paras 24–25.
33 For discussion of the Memorandum of Understanding, see Rawlings, R., 'Concordats of the Constitution', *Law Quarterly Review*, 116 (2000), 257–86; and Poirier, J., 'The Functions of Intergovernmental Agreements: Post-devolution concordats in a comparative perspective', *Public Law* (2001), 134–57.

towards the end of the Parliamentary passage of the devolution legislation, though not published until after the elections to the devolved bodies. But it was not a document that the devolved institutions as such could shape. While the negotiations that produced it involved officials at the Scottish and Welsh Offices or in the Northern Ireland Civil Service who would later work for the devolved administrations, they were not working for those institutions at the time and the politicians directing them were not at that stage elected to a devolved body either (though many later were).[34] To approach the Memorandum of Understanding as an agreement between distinct governments is therefore wrong; it reflects officials' understanding of what was likely to be needed, driven by experience of working in UK Government and largely reflecting the priorities of the UK Government.[35]

The Memorandum of Understanding is a curious document, which undertakes several quite different tasks at the same time and often in the same paragraph. It purports to be an agreement between governments, but also to be a statement of political intent 'binding in honour only' and not creating legal obligations.[36] Some of its provisions set out administrative practice for running government after devolution, for handling matters such as Parliamentary questions and other (non-legislative) business, or correspondence. Some of it restates basic understandings of matters already dealt with in the devolution legislation, such as obligations for implementing EU, international and European Convention on Human Rights obligations, or the role of the UK Government in non-devolved matters, or the possible role of the courts in determining competence issues.[37] These are effectively redundant. More important are those parts setting out general principles for the conduct of government, which are in the nature of soft law. These provisions include those embodying the Sewel convention, stating arrangements for involving the devolved administrations in formulating EU policy, establishing the Joint Ministerial Committee and making the 'four Cs' (communication, consultation, cooperation and confidentiality) the basis for day-to-day relations.[38] Certainly they lack any sort of enforcement mechanism.

34 Publication of the Memorandum of Understanding was in fact postponed until June 1999, so that it could be 'agreed' by the newly elected devolved governments. It had already been finalised through inter-departmental negotiations, however.
35 One curious feature of it is that the text finally agreed reflected politicians' desires for a shorter and less categorical document than the earlier drafts presented to them by officials.
36 Memorandum of Understanding, Part I, para 2.
37 Ibid., Part I, paras 20–1 and 26.
38 Ibid., Part I, paras. 4–11 (4 Cs), 14 (Sewel convention), 19 (EU policy; see also the Concordat on the Co-ordination of European Union Policy Issues, Annex B

A small number of provisions are of real legal effect, if only between governments. The most notable case is a single sentence in paragraph 20 regarding EU matters, which provides, 'It is agreed by all four administrations that, to the extent financial penalties are imposed on the UK as a result of any failure of implementation or enforcement, or any damages or costs arise as a result, responsibility for meeting them will be borne by the administration(s) responsible for the failure'. This amounts to an indemnity to the UK Government for (inter alia) any fine imposed by the European Court of Justice should devolved actions lead to the UK being held to be in breach of EU law, and for any successful claim against the UK (rather than the devolved administration directly) for 'Francovich' damages for loss following failure to comply with EU law – a powerful sanction, and a remarkable provision to impose on the devolved administrations as a price for their autonomy (especially as the UK, being the member state, would have conduct of any proceedings before the European Court of Justice).

Generally speaking, the provisions of the Memorandum of Understanding embody two underlying assumptions. One, sometimes made explicit, is that relations would be underpinned by the principle of 'no surprises'. Each would ensure that the other (or others) were informed in advance of developments that would affect them. Many of the stickier moments in intergovernmental relations since have been due to a belief that this principle had not been complied with. The second assumption, which is unstated but implicit in what many officials have said in interview, is that the existing 'operating code' for managing relations between Whitehall departments (or between Whitehall and the territorial offices) would continue to apply. While devolution may have created different governments accountable to different elected bodies, the relations between them would still work in much the same way as they had when all were part of a single government accountable to Westminster.

The Memorandum of Understanding appears to impose largely equal obligations on all the parties to it, the UK Government as much as the devolved administrations. To the extent it does not, it appears to be an even-handed and reasonable document, creating practicable and workable ways to deal with a variety of situations considered likely at the time of devolution with minimal disruption to the governmental machine. In one memorable phrase, the Memorandum (and other concordats) are 'roadmaps for bureaucrats'.[39] The same applies to the so-called 'bilateral concordats' – those between particular Whitehall departments and devolved administrations,

to the Memorandum of Understanding), 22–5 (JMC; see also Agreement on the Joint Ministerial Committee, Annex A).

39 See SP Official Report, 7 October 1999, col. 1099 (Donald Dewar).

intended to deal with the practicalities of relations between those particular parties.

This impression is somewhat misleading, however. Many of the 'soft law' provisions of the Memorandum of Understanding (and the bilateral concordats) work to the benefit of the UK Government far more than they do to that of the devolved administrations. In large part this is due to the difficulties of seeking to enforce these obligations, when the UK Government already holds so many resources (whether staff, information, money, or ability to drive policy agendas or develop policy). The obligation of confidentiality serves as a good example. Breach of this would lead to the other party being denied access to confidential information in future, notably about policy developments and proposed developments. If the UK Government were to lose access to such information from Wales or Scotland, it might suffer occasional embarrassment or inconvenience, but nothing more. For a devolved administration, however, losing access to information from the UK Government could be very serious. It would be uninformed about policy developments that might have a great impact on its own activities, potentially making those activities irrelevant or unworkable. If taken publicly, such a step would also involve considerable embarrassment for the devolved administration. This inequality leaves the devolved administrations in a disadvantaged position. On rare occasions, the lack of any means of enforcement works to devolved advantage. The refusal of the National Assembly for Wales to comply with the Concordat on Financial Assistance to Industry (annexed to the Memorandum of Understanding) might cause annoyance in Whitehall, but (interviewing suggests) has not led to any action as it does not cause any major *practical* problem – because there is little inward investment into the UK at present (and if there were, this would affect other devolved administrations as much or more than the UK Government).

Devolved and UK legislation

The devolution legislation creates a complex set of rules to govern devolved legislation. These rules vary somewhat between the various sets of devolution arrangements, but have certain elements in common. The questions are what exactly those rules mean and what mechanisms exist to make them work.

The general rule is that devolved legislation is valid provided it is within the legislature's legislative competence. As the competence of the Scottish Parliament and Northern Ireland Assembly is general, but subject to reservations (and exceptions, for Northern Ireland), any challenge to their powers needs to be based on what the reservations (and exceptions) provide. The devolved legislatures have the benefit of the doubt and competence over matters that have not been expressly kept from them. However, legislation that does fall outside their powers is void. So: what means that a particular piece of legislation is outside their powers?

The first set of exclusions is a general set of protections for certain UK obligations – European Union and European Convention on Human Rights ones, in particular, but also for international legal obligations. Thus devolved legislation (whether an Act of the Scottish Parliament or Northern Ireland Assembly, secondary legislation made by a Scottish or Northern Ireland minister, or legislation made by the National Assembly for Wales) will be beyond that body's legal competence, and void, if it is in breach of those obligations.[40]

Second, as discussed above, legislation will also be void for dealing with reserved (Scotland or Northern Ireland) or excepted (Northern Ireland) matters, and with non-devolved ones (Wales). Quite what that means varies; the ultra vires rule applies strictly to Wales, fairly strictly to Northern Ireland and not particularly strictly to Scotland, thanks to a number of provisions in the Scotland Act to protect Holyrood legislation. Thus section 29(3) of the Scotland Act provides that the test of whether a measure is within legislative competence is not whether it affects a reserved matter, but its effect 'in all the circumstances'. Legislation that affects reserved matters indirectly, while its main thrust relates to devolved ones, will therefore be valid. (This is a form of the pith-and-substance test developed by the Judicial Committee of the Privy Council in deciding Canadian federalism cases from the 1880s to the 1930s, and adopted by the House of Lords for devolution to Northern Ireland under the Government of Ireland Act 1920.[41]) Section 101 of the Act provides that, where Scottish legislation could be read so as to be outside competence, it should be read as narrowly as is required for it to be within competence if such reading is possible. In legal terms, this is a form of a blue-pencil rule to preserve legislation which might otherwise be beyond the Parliament's competence.[42] Taken together, these provide a considerable cushion for the

---

40 For Scotland, see Scotland Act 1998, s. 29 (2) for primary legislation and s. 54 for administrative Acts (including subordinate legislation). For Northern Ireland, see Northern Ireland Act 1998, s. 7 (1) and s. 24. For Wales, see ss. 106–8 Government of Wales Act 1998. There are also express powers (in s. 58 Scotland Act 1998 and s. 26 Northern Ireland Act 1998) for UK ministers to intervene if a devolved minister acts or proposes to act in a way inconsistent with the UK's international obligations.

41 *Gallagher v. Lynn* [1936] AC 863, House of Lords.

42 A blue-pencil rule is a lawyer's term for deleting such words or clauses as are necessary to make an otherwise unlawful provision lawful, but without adding anything new.

Scottish Parliament to legislate in a way that may touch on reserved matters without making the legislation wholly void.[43] A further cushion is the power under section 107 for secondary legislation (made by UK ministers, with consent of Scottish ministers) to extend the legislative competence of the Scottish Parliament if the Parliament has exceeded that. For legislation enacted by the Northern Ireland Assembly, the test to determine whether devolved legislation has become ultra vires by straying into excepted or reserved matters is somewhat stricter. If Northern Ireland legislation merely 'deals with' excepted matters or reserved ones without the Secretary of State having given his consent, it is invalid unless that is merely 'ancillary' or incidental to the excepted or reserved matters.[44] This is appreciably more stringent a test than that for Scottish legislation, and the Act contains no provision akin to s. 101 of the Scotland Act directing the courts about issues of interpretation. The National Assembly for Wales simply gets a version of the old (and notably weak) protection local government got for ultra vires acts.[45]

Thus, at the margins of its competence, there are numerous ways to seek to save devolved legislation which by mischance is ultra vires. However, all these depend on the cooperation of UK authorities. For Scotland they need either the Government and Parliament (to make an order extending jurisdiction) or the courts, notably the Judicial Committee of the Privy Council, to determine that the matter is within competence, in the light of the interpretative clauses in the Act. For Northern Ireland, the key requirement is the consent of the Secretary of State.[46] For Wales, there would be no UK executive power to cure an ultra vires act, so the only option would be to seek legislation to protect the act retrospectively at Westminster. Given the time and embarrassment this would involve as well as the difficulty of securing legislative time, this is unlikely ever to be practicable.

It is worth noting that the new legislative powers for Wales, proposed by the UK Government as the third stage for extending the National Assembly's

---

43 There are also provisions to enable the Parliament to legislate in a way that affects reserved matters if it is modifying Scots criminal or private (civil) law, and does not solely affect reserved matters in doing so: Scotland Act 1998, s. 29 (4).

44 Northern Ireland Act 1998, s. 6 (2) (b) and s. 8 (Secretary of State's consent).

45 Government of Wales Act 1998, s. 40, mirrors s. 111 of the Local Government Act 1972 and authorises it to do anything 'which is calculated to facilitate, or is conducive or incidental to, the exercise of any of its functions'. For the failings of this in its local government context, see Sharland, J., *A Practical Approach to Local Government Law* (London: Blackstone Press, 1997), chap. 7; Bailey, S., *Cross on Principles of Local Government Law* (London: Sweet & Maxwell, 1992), chap. 1.

46 In certain circumstances, this will also need the consent of the Westminster Parliament as an order in council.

powers in its 2005 white paper *Better Governance for Wales*, would not give it these advantages.[47] What is proposed for Wales appears to be the transfer only of powers to deal with certain defined matters, such as health or education, not the generality of legislative power subject to reservations as for Scotland or Northern Ireland. This was the model for devolution to Scotland proposed in the Scotland Act 1978, and is significantly inferior in its effects to what the 1998 Act achieved.[48]

Moreover, there is a big unanswered question: if legislation of both legislatures is within their legal competence, and it conflicts, which takes precedence? Federal systems commonly establish some sort of rule giving paramountcy to federal legislation in such circumstances. The UK has no rule whatever; while there may be a belief that Westminster could oust devolved legislation on the ground that it is a species of secondary legislation, that has little legal basis.[49] (One answer may be that the doctrine of implied repeal would apply – meaning that the last legislation to be passed would take precedence. That is a recipe for legislative ping-pong, likely only to be avoided by the pressure of other priorities on scarce legislative time, particularly at Westminster.)

Procedurally, there is an array of controls to prevent the devolved legislatures exceeding powers. Some exist in the general law: legislation or executive acts which were ultra vires would be void in accordance with normal legal principles, and could be challenged in the courts by ordinary proceedings or by judicial review. But there are other routes of challenge as well. Most Scottish and Northern Irish legislation must be certified twice to be within competence – once by the Executive on its introduction to the legislature (assuming the bill is an Executive one), and once by the Presiding Officer or Speaker.[50] In addition the UK Government may submit the issue of whether a bill is within competence to the Judicial Committee of the Privy Council,

---

47 Wales Office, *Better Governance for Wales*, paras 3.22–3.29. See also the Government of Wales bill introduced into Parliament in December 2005, in particular clause 107 and Schedule 7.

48 For a discussion of the white paper and particularly its proposals on legislation, see Trench, A., *Better Governance for Wales: An analysis of the white paper on devolution for Wales* (ESRC Devolution and Constitutional Change programme, Devolution Policy Paper, no. 13, August 2005). For the Scotland Act 1978, see Bogdanor, V., *Devolution* (Oxford: Oxford University Press, 1979).

49 See Winetrobe, B., 'Scottish Devolved Legislation and the Courts', *Public Law* (2002), 31–8.

50 Scotland Act 1998, s. 31; Northern Ireland Act 1998, ss. 9 and 10. Committee and private members' bills are only certified once, by the Presiding Officer, although no doubt the Executive would form its own view about their legislative competence.

after it has completed its progress through the Parliament or Assembly but before the bill receives Royal Assent.[51]

The existence of these powers may not be unusual in itself, but their use is. These powers were not used between 1999 and 2005, but are not simply theoretical constraints either. They provide the impetus and rationale for detailed scrutiny of all devolved legislation, not just within the devolved institutions themselves but also within the UK Government. This generates a large amount of work for government lawyers generally and particularly the UK Government's legal advisers on Scottish law, the Office of the Solicitor to the Advocate General, for whom checking all Scottish Parliament legislation is a substantial area of work.[52] This acts as a powerful constraint on legislation by the devolved Parliament and Assemblies and their administrations, as they have to scrutinise any legislative proposals with care to ensure that they do not exceed their legal competences. They are, in effect, denied the option of deciding to take a chance that something is lawful, or if unlawful will not be challenged, by the proliferation and regular use of such internal scrutiny.

The civil service

It will be apparent from this chapter that the constraints on the devolved administrations mean that in many ways they are not masters in their own houses. That is reinforced by the position of the Home Civil Service (so far as Scotland and Wales are concerned; once again, Northern Ireland is different). Devolution has not altered the position of the civil service and its operation as a single civil service is preserved.[53] Staff working for the Scottish Executive and National Assembly for Wales are part of the Home Civil Service in the same way as staff of any Whitehall department, even though they serve quite different political masters.[54] That is tempered in practice by two

51 Scotland Act 1998, s. 33 and s. 35; Northern Ireland Act 1998, s. 11. In each case the UK Government acts through its law officers. In the case of s. 35 Scotland Act, the challenge may relate to a bill breaching the UK's international obligations or undermining defence or national security, even if otherwise it is within competence.
52 See Trench, A., 'Whitehall and the Process of Legislation after Devolution', in Hazell, R. and Rawlings, R. (eds), *Devolution, Law Making and the Constitution* (Exeter: Imprint Academic, 2005), 165–92; and chapter 8 below.
53 For discussion of the adaptation of the civil service and its role since devolution, see Parry, 'Devolution, Integration and Modernisation in the United Kingdom's Civil Service', and Rhodes et al. *Decentralizing the Civil Service*.
54 Scotland Act 1998, s. 51 and Schedule 5, para. 8; Government of Wales Act 1998, s. 34. For Northern Ireland, the separate Northern Ireland Civil Service is protected from political interference by making the functions and procedures

changes. First, individual departments (including the devolved administrations) have considerable autonomy for matters including grading structures, staffing and pay levels.[55] This has given the devolved administrations considerable flexibility to reshape their internal organisational arrangements and pay and staffing structures to support them, in a way that does not undermine the unity of the Home Civil Service. They have used this, for example, to expand the pool of potential recruits by increasing the range and seniority of posts that are openly advertised. Second, the Civil Service Code was amended in 1999 to provide that officials owe their loyalty to the administration in which they serve, not a single UK Government, though what that means has never been put to the test publicly. Moreover, accountability within the civil service and its professional leadership still ends in Whitehall, with the Cabinet Secretary in his or her capacity as Head of the Home Civil Service, and the UK Prime Minister as Minister for the Civil Service. Consequently, disciplinary issues, staffing levels and other matters (at least at the highest levels) are beyond the control of devolved ministers, and their officials look to Whitehall not their immediate political masters for guidance. This can lead to rows behind the scenes over staffing matters, such as those involving Muir Russell and Jack McConnell in Scotland in 2003.[56] Nonetheless, the extent of devolved control is considerable, to the point at which the Home Civil Service therefore starts to resemble a brand and a set of safeguards for integrity, impartiality and independence.

of the Civil Service Commissioners for Northern Ireland a reserved matter: Northern Ireland Act 1998, Schedule 3, para. 16. The Northern Ireland Assembly can therefore only legislate on the subject with the consent of the Secretary of State.

55 This was done under the Civil Service (Management Functions) Act 1992. The delegations to the National Assembly, Scottish Executive and Whitehall departments can be found at www.civilservice.gov.uk/management_of_the_civil_service/ management_ guidance/delegation/index.asp (visited November 2005). At the same time, the higher grades of the civil service (the former grade 5 and above) became part of the senior civil service, and their pay and numbers are controlled centrally not by departments.

56 McConnell was reportedly angered on learning through newspaper advertisements of staff recruitment at a time when the Executive was supposed to be reducing its spending. He had not been consulted about the proposed appointments by his Permanent Secretary. In fact almost all the posts advertised were existing ones, not new creations. See Trench, A., 'Intergovernmental Relations: Officialdom still in control?' in Hazell, R. (ed.), *The State of the Nations 2003: The third year of devolution in the United Kingdom* (Exeter: Imprint Academic, 2003), 155.

Conclusion: the UK Government's structural dominance of intergovernmental relations

The above discussion has identified the main elements that combine to give the UK Government a structural advantage in the conduct of intergovernmental relations. This advantage can itself be viewed as one of the key resources possessed by the UK Government in intergovernmental relations, although it is itself composed of a number of resources.

One starting point for this advantage is the continued entanglement of the UK Government and devolved administrations with each other. While the outlines of devolution may be reasonably clear, a closer examination shows that there remains a close relationship between devolved and reserved or non-devolved functions. This entanglement is both legal and administrative in nature, reflecting the fact that the UK was until recently a state with a single government, albeit one with separate territorial arrangements for Scotland, Wales and Northern Ireland. Thus devolved governments can do little without affecting non-devolved functions, non-devolved matters have a huge impact on devolved territories in general and devolved matters in particular, and even for devolved matters what the UK Government does in or for England will have a major impact on the devolved administrations. This entanglement also reflects the clear view among those who designed devolution's institutional framework (shown in interviews) that what they were devising was not a federal system, by which they understand a clear distinction of functions and governments.[57] Devolution is a relationship that is considerably closer than a federal one, in this view. This integration of functions and administration was desired, if not consciously designed, and the nature of the task facing devolution's engineers would have made it hard to act differently.

A second starting point is the institutional superiority of the UK Government. Two factors are key: the size of England within the UK and the continued supremacy of the Westminster Parliament. England accounts for 85 per cent of the population of the UK, and for its richest parts. Whatever happens in England has a profound impact on the devolved territories. With the stalling of moves towards elected regional government after the referendum in the North East in October 2004, any change in that is extremely

---

57 An illustration of this was the spat between London and Edinburgh in 2001 over the suggestion that the Scottish Executive should be known as the Government of Scotland – resisted by Alistair Campbell, in particular, as the UK retained a major role in relation to Scotland. By contrast, there was no sign of demur from London when the executive parts of the National Assembly became known as the Welsh Assembly Government in March 2002.

unlikely.[58] For the foreseeable future, the devolved administrations will have to deal with a UK Government responsible for all matters in England. The role of Westminster after devolution is a curious one, but its sovereignty remains untouched.[59] It can (and as shown in chapter 8 does) legislate for all parts of the UK, for devolved as well as non-devolved matters. The restraint imposed by the Sewel convention has had an effect, but only a limited one. The fact that Westminster can legislate for all parts of the UK, and that both the framing of legislation and the availability of Parliamentary time are largely in the control of the UK Government, gives it significant advantages even if such legislation needs devolved consent. This combines with the various checks and controls over devolved legislation. Notwithstanding the safeguards for Scottish legislation, in particular, to bring it within competence, the fact that devolved legislation can be (and is) scrutinised with such care is a significant source of control for the UK Government. (The fact that there are no parallel mechanisms for UK legislation only reinforces this.)

A third starting point is the asymmetry of the devolution arrangements. Asymmetry means that the devolved territories have little in common, whether in institutional arrangements or policy matters. It is therefore hard for them to combine with each other. It also means that the UK Government needs to deal with the administrations individually, because their specific circumstances are so different from each other. While the engineers of devolution may have had a wish to see relations conducted and managed largely bilaterally, asymmetry has helped ensure that this becomes reality. Once that is the case, it also considerably strengthens the position of the UK Government, which can marshal greater resources than the devolved administrations in terms of staff or information (as well as finance).

Asymmetry also affects how the neutral-seeming Memorandum of Understanding works. Not only was this drawn up to reflect UK Government concerns and priorities more than devolved ones, but the lack of sanctions for breach of this mean that it is hard for the devolved administrations to seek recourse if the UK Government breaches it. (A notable case of this, which is discussed further in chapter 8, is the failure of the Joint Ministerial Committee's plenary form to meet every twelve months, to keep the Memorandum and intergovernmental arrangements generally under review,

58 See further Hazell, R. (ed.), *The English Question* (Manchester: Manchester University Press, 2006).
59 See Lodge, G., Russell, M. and Gay, O., 'The Impact of Devolution on Westminster: If not now, when?', in Trench, A. (ed.), *Has Devolution Made a Difference? The State of the Nations 2004* (Exeter: Imprint Academic, 2004), 193–216.

as the Memorandum expressly requires; the last meeting took place in October 2002, so at the time of writing it had failed to meet for more than three years.) Similar concerns apply to bilateral concordats, which serve the priorities of Whitehall departments far more than their devolved counterparts, and whose most useful function with hindsight seems to be that drafting them forced Whitehall to think about the implications of devolution and to adjust their working practices and expectations as a result.[60]

What this means is that the UK Government enjoys three key advantages in intergovernmental relations. First, it has significant constitutional resources, far greater than those of the devolved administrations. These relate notably to legislation and to intergovernmental arrangements (the Memorandum of Understanding and the Joint Ministerial Committee). Devolved autonomy is real, but can be constrained at a variety of points by the UK Government (or other UK agencies). Second, the UK Government controls much of the agenda for intergovernmental relations, because of the need of the devolved administrations to take account of UK Government policies (whether for devolved matters, because of its role in England, or because of the entanglement of devolved and non-devolved matters). One might add that its ability to drive the news agenda is also greater than the devolved administrations', though perhaps not as great as many UK politicians might wish. It is much harder for the devolved administrations to make the agenda. Third, the UK is able to derive significant advantages from being able to conduct bilateral relations with the devolved administrations, rather than have to approach them as a group. This significantly reduces the challenge that the UK faces from them.

These advantages are, however, theoretical ones. This picture of the structure of devolution and its implications for intergovernmental relations is only that. To see what impact these advantages have in reality, we need to look at the practice of government in the devolved United Kingdom, in a number of areas.

---

60 In order to maximise this advantage, which is now long past, the Lords Select Committee on the Constitution recommended that such concordats should expire after five years and be re-drafted so that both their wording and the experience of putting them in place were current: House of Lords Select Committee on the Constitution, Session 2002–03 2nd Report, *Devolution: Inter-institutional Relations in the United Kingdom*, HL 28 (London: The Stationery Office, 2003), paras 38–45. The UK Government rejected this recommendation in its response to the Report, and has never acted on it.

4

Funding devolution: the power of money

David Bell and Alex Christie

The issue of how devolution is funded in the UK has never been far from the headlines during the last few years. The funding mechanism has been roundly attacked by all shades of political opinion, both in the centre and the periphery, but the UK Government has steadfastly refused to countenance change, despite a stream of complaints within the Labour Party, particularly among MPs from the north of England. An uneasy truce has descended, but unless this issue can be satisfactorily resolved, the tensions caused by the perceived unfairness of the system of allocating resources between the constituent parts of the UK will undermine the legitimacy of devolution.

The funding arrangement in question is, of course, the Barnett formula, the mechanism by which financial resources have been allocated by HM Treasury to Scotland, Wales and Northern Ireland for the last two decades. The formula was named after the Chief Secretary to the Treasury, Joel Barnett, in the Callaghan Government, but has direct antecedents that can be traced back to the 'Goschen' formula of 1888, when the Chancellor of the day, George Goschen, used a similar mechanism to allocate revenues to local government.

But even with this long history, the Barnett formula is now almost without friends. Even Joel Barnett, its originator, has disowned it. This chapter investigates some of the reasons why politicians have grown increasingly disenchanted with the formula over the recent past. It concentrates on three main issues:

1   The first concerns the complaint that the formula does not allocate a fair *level* of spending among the component parts of the UK.
2   The second concerns the growing unease that the formula is putting the system of devolved government in the UK under strain.
3   The final argument is concerned with the difficulties arising from the relationship between the Barnett formula and the rest of the UK's fiscal structure.

But before addressing the reasons why there has been a growing clamour for change to the Barnett formula, we must first explain a little of its background and how it has suited successive UK Governments and in particular the Treasury that it should survive.

The Barnett formula

The Barnett formula determines the *changes* in resources available to the Scottish Parliament, the National Assembly for Wales and the Northern Ireland Assembly based on a fixed share of any *changes* agreed between the Treasury and departments that operate in England (or in some cases England and Wales) in the value of 'comparable programmes'. Northern Ireland's allocation is based on GB expenditures. The share, which is updated regularly, is based on the size of the population in the relevant devolved authority as a percentage of that in England (or England and Wales, or Great Britain).

The 'comparability percentage' of each spending programme under the control of Westminster is assessed as part of each Spending Review. The percentages are dependent on whether the spending programme covers reserved or non-reserved matters. For example, comparability percentages for social security are 0 per cent in Scotland and Wales, but 100 per cent in Northern Ireland. This is because social security is a reserved issue as far as the Scottish Parliament and the National Assembly are concerned. This is not the case in Northern Ireland, where (as discussed in chapter 3) the Assembly/Office controls social security spending, at least in theory. Though this is an important difference in principle, in practice social security benefits in Northern Ireland are paid at the same rates as in Great Britain and the Treasury retains the right to amend the assigned budget should the Assembly/Office choose to vary the rates paid relative to Great Britain.[1]

For most spending programmes relating to education, the comparability percentage is 100 per cent for each of the devolved administrations. For example, the budget of the Higher Education Funding Council for England is 100 per cent comparable. It was allocated a budget of £5.9 billion in 2003–04. If this increased by, say, £100 million in financial year 2004/05, then the increase in the assigned budgets would be as shown in table 4.1. Thus, a commitment to increase spending on higher education by £100 million in England translates into a total financial commitment of around £120 million for the UK as a whole. It is important to note that the Barnett

---

1 There are also of course statutory requirements to maintain parity between the social security systems in Great Britain and Northern Ireland.

Table 4.1. Barnett-determined increases in assigned budgets resulting from
£100m increase in funding to HEFCE

Devolved administration	Comparability percentage	Population/ population of England	Barnett-determined increase in budget
Scotland	100	0.102	£10.2m
Wales	100	0.0589	£5.89m
Northern Ireland	100	0.0342	£3.42m[a]

Note:
[a] The budget assigned to Northern Ireland is reduced by a further 2.5 per cent to reflect the differential treatment of VAT in Northern Ireland. VAT payments made by Northern Ireland Departments are refunded by Customs and Excise. In the rest of the UK, this is not the case and therefore Departments require provision to meet their VAT commitments.

Source: HM Treasury, *Funding the Scottish Parliament, National Assembly for Wales and Northern Ireland Assembly: A statement of funding policy* (London: HM Treasury, 4th edn, 2004).

formula, though dependent on the changes in spending programmes in England (or GB in the case of Northern Ireland), does not place any obligation on the devolved administrations to spend the increases in the same way as in England (or GB). This is not a new feature brought about by devolution – the Secretaries of State for Northern Ireland, Scotland and Wales have always been free to reflect the spending priorities of their territories. The relationship between HM Treasury and the devolved administrations was codified in *Funding the Scottish Parliament, National Assembly for Wales and Northern Ireland Assembly: A statement of funding policy.*[2]

The fact that the Barnett mechanism has survived the significant constitutional changes associated with devolution is testament to the strength of the Treasury and its determination to control the key macroeconomic variables in the UK economy. Principal among these are the fiscal stance – the balance of government spending and taxation – and the extent of public borrowing. The Treasury's determination to control government debt led to the denial of significant borrowing powers to any of the devolved authorities. Instead, capital spending is either funded from the current budget or from Public Private Partnerships. And Treasury determination to control taxation and public spending is evident from the extent to which the arrangements for devolution reflect its determination to micro-manage the UK fiscal

2 HM Treasury, *Funding the Scottish Parliament, National Assembly for Wales and Northern Ireland Assembly: statement of funding policy* (London: HM Treasury, 4th edn, 2004), www.hm-treasury.gov.uk/media/CB2/3C/Funding_the_ Scottish_Parliament_National_Assembly_for_Wales(296kb).pdf.

stance. Take, for example, the regulations relating to local council spending in Scotland:

> Should self-financed expenditure start to rise steeply, the Scottish Parliament would clearly come under pressure from council tax payers in Scotland to exercise its powers. If growth relative to England were excessive and were such as to threaten targets set for public expenditure as part of the management of the UK economy, and the Scottish Parliament nevertheless chose not to exercise its powers, it would be open to the UK Government to take the excess into account in considering the level of their support for expenditure in Scotland.[3]

There is clearly an implicit threat that if the Scottish Parliament fails to curb 'excessive' council spending, then the Treasury will penalise the Parliament by reducing the size of the assigned budget.

Tight control by central government has the benefit of producing 'fiscal clarity'. One authority is in charge of determining the allocation of spending. The situation in the UK, where such matters are resolved by UK ministers or the Joint Ministerial Committee (as discussed in chapters 5 and 8), is in marked contrast to federal states or states where devolved government has significant fiscal authority, which often require legal mechanisms to resolve disputes between central and devolved governments. For example, in both Germany and Spain, the constitutional courts are charged with this duty. Disputes are frequently complex and lengthy, and thus inimical to detailed fiscal management. There are no parallel legal arrangements in the UK, where disputes are principally a matter for Treasury ministers (see further chapter 5). This may be good for fiscal clarity at the macro level, but makes life difficult for devolved administrations that are keen to differentiate their policies from those of the centre.

This issue is addressed by Iain McLean.[4] He argues that the perceived unfairness of the Barnett formula, the asymmetrical nature of devolution and the lack of any significant taxation powers in the devolved administrations suggest that the UK requires a 'fiscal constitution'. His preferred model is Australia, where the third party which weighs the respective claims of the state governments is the Commonwealth Grants Commission. It stands at arm's length from the federal government and allocates revenues between the states using the principle of fiscal equalisation, which broadly implies that each state should be given resources to supply services of the same standard, if they make the same effort to raise taxes and operate at the same level of efficiency.

---

3 Scottish Office, *Scotland's Parliament*, Cm 3658 (London: The Stationery Office, 1997), para. 7.24.
4 McLean, I., 'A Fiscal Constitution for the UK', in Chen, S. and Wright, T. (eds), *The English Question* (London: The Fabian Society, 2000, 80–95).

From an economist's point of view, the Barnett formula is part of a political process that allows the centre to retain tight control over the resources available to the devolved administrations and thus the extent to which they can differentiate their policies. The devolved authorities each have a cake that they can divide however they choose, but other than at the margin they cannot take a policy decision to change the size of the cake.

Other formulae could be used to distribute resources to the devolved authorities, yet still allow the centre to retain the same high degree of political and fiscal control. Chief among these is the so-called 'needs assessment'. This mechanism operates by allocating funds to different areas based on an assessment of the different levels of resource required to provide a common standard of service across the whole country. Our research for the Leverhulme Trust suggested that such mechanisms are commonplace throughout industrialised countries. Indeed, needs assessments are used to distribute funds to local authorities in England[5] Scotland and Wales and within the National Health Service in both Scotland[6] and England.

Our research also suggested that the Barnett formula is unique in the developed world. There is no country other than the UK that allocates resources at a subnational level using a formula based on changes in spending elsewhere, rather than allocating levels of spending in relation to assessed need. We now go on to consider the three difficulties with the formula that have been highlighted recently and that were mentioned in the introduction.

Fair levels of funding

An issue that regularly recurs is the inequality in levels of public spending across the different parts of the UK, and the extent to which there is convergence in the level of spending. Thus, for example, on 27 January 2004, Sir Nicholas Winterton, MP for Macclesfield, received an answer to his question to the Secretary of State for Scotland asking if he had any plans to review the Barnett formula and when he expected spending levels per head to equalise across Scotland, England and Wales.[7] His question was motivated

5 Department of the Environment, Transport and the Regions, *Local Government Finance, SSA Background* (London: Department of the Environment, Transport and the Regions, 2000), www.local.dtlr.gov.uk/finance/ssa/ssas.htm.

6 Scottish Executive, *Fair Shares for All: Report of the National Review of Resource Allocation for the NHS in Scotland* (Edinburgh: Scottish Executive, 1999), www.scotland.gov.uk/library2/doc01/fsag-00.htm.

7 HC Deb, 27 January 2004, col. 271W.

by a widespread view in the north of England that the region is disadvantaged by the Barnett formula and that a needs-based assessment would be more appropriate. The Scottish Parliament's policies such as the abolition of tuition fees, higher salaries and better conditions for teachers and better conditions of service, and the provision of free personal care for the elderly have only increased the grievance felt in the north of England. The data in table 4.2 show that there are significant differences between and among the devolved jurisdictions and the English regions.

On a per capita basis, spending in key policy areas such as health and education in Scotland and Northern Ireland remains substantially above that in England and well above the UK average. Table 4.2 also shows that the North East and North West of England spent significantly less per capita in 2002–03 across most key programmes than did London and the devolved authorities.

The argument from the north of England is that these differences cannot be justified on the basis of need. However, the assertion that Scotland and Northern Ireland receive over-generous budget allocations is difficult to demonstrate if one considers the whole spectrum of government policies as a proper needs assessment should do. There has not been any published UK-wide needs assessment for over 25 years. However, we can conduct a very simple needs-assessment exercise, which will indicate that the grievances of northern politicians may be genuine. To do this we construct a crude indicator of relative need.[8] Rates and regulations for social security are common throughout the UK. High levels of social security payments tend to be linked with high levels of unemployment, inactivity and dependency. They are also indicative of low levels of income. Per head social security payments are thus simple, but plausible, indicators of relative need.

One way of judging the generosity of public provision in a particular region would then be to take the ratio of total identifiable expenditure to social security spending in that region. Large values of this ratio crudely indicate that overall public spending is high, given the apparent level of need and vice versa. Values for 2002–03 are shown in figure 4.1. It is immediately apparent that the regions in the north of England come out worst from this calculation. But interestingly, the highest level of provision is not in any of the devolved jurisdictions, but instead in London. One explanation in London's defence is that it is considerably more expensive to provide a common standard of service in London than elsewhere due to higher wages, property prices and the cost of living. Similarly, costs are higher in Scotland and Wales because of the low population density. High costs in London and

8 We are grateful to Peter Jones for this suggestion.

Table 4.2. UK identifiable expenditure on services by country and region (per head), 2002–03 (accruals per head)

	General public services	Public order and safety	Enterprise and economic development	Science and technology	Employ-ment policies	Agriculture, fisheries and forestry	Transport	Environ-ment protection	Housing and community amenities	Health	Recreation, culture and religion	Education and training	Social protection	Total
North East	83	387	166	14	107	87	197	101	81	1203	105	1012	2920	6463
North West	56	371	97	17	77	71	204	103	103	1181	85	953	2725	6043
Yorkshire and Humber	60	285	122	13	57	87	185	96	81	1081	93	955	2423	5538
East Midlands	67	300	86	13	37	102	147	90	49	946	79	882	2213	5011
West Midlands	63	300	91	13	47	84	169	84	61	1045	77	923	2417	5374
South West	74	263	62	15	38	148	140	98	56	999	68	797	2219	4976
Eastern	65	247	40	41	38	82	156	95	23	990	66	799	2065	4697
London	95	470	51	23	43	17	563	102	230	1282	146	1085	2416	6522
South East	62	269	48	41	26	54	174	105	61	1005	71	813	1970	4699
England	69	323	77	23	47	75	230	98	89	1085	88	911	2337	5453
Scotland	154	362	105	24	136	131	231	200	143	1262	164	1038	2629	6579
Wales	129	320	208	12	48	100	183	168	88	1186	185	970	2881	6479
Northern Ireland	146	720	328	12	26	236	191	184	166	1214	54	1215	2774	7267
UK Identifiable	81	338	93	22	54	86	226	112	96	1109	99	934	2401	5652

Source: HM Treasury, *Public Expenditure Statistical Analyses 2004*, Cm 6201 (London: HM Treasury, 2004).

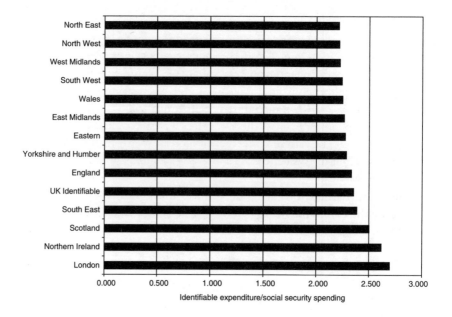

Figure 4.1 Identifiable public expenditure relative to 'need', 2002–03

rurality in Scotland and Wales are not reflected in a measure of need based solely on social security payments, but it is difficult to believe that this is sufficient justification for the substantial differences in our chosen measure between these areas and those in the north of England.

Strains on devolved government: the rate of change of funding and the Barnett squeeze

One problem with the Barnett formula has been the different levels of funding it provides for each devolved territory. This has been particularly the case for Northern Ireland, where the 2000 Spending Review for the period 2000–03 implied a smaller proportionate rise in spending in Northern Ireland than in Scotland, Wales or England.[9] The reason why the increase in Northern Ireland is smaller than in other parts of the UK has to do with the so-called 'Barnett squeeze'. One of us has explained how the mathematics of the Barnett formula implies that the process of applying population-based changes to different levels of expenditure will eventually equalise per capita

9 HM Treasury, *Spending Review 2000*, Cm 4807 (London: The Stationery Office, 2000).

public expenditure throughout the UK.[10] The formula ensures that those areas that enjoy higher levels of per capita spending receive slightly lower proportionate rises in spending than those with lower levels of per capita spending. Hence Northern Ireland, which from table 4.2 has the highest per capita spending among the constituent parts of the UK, can expect the lowest increases. HM Treasury has agreed that the formula will bring about equality in per capita expenditure across the UK. Hence it is recognised as a 'convergence formula'.[11] The rate of convergence increases with the rate of growth in public spending in those areas to which the formula applies and with the rate of inflation.

But if the Barnett formula is indeed a convergence formula, how sustainable are the commitments to additional spending that have been made by the devolved authorities? The devolved authorities very much see these as measures that deliver the differentiation from Westminster that legitimises devolution. They include higher teachers' salaries in Scotland following from the McCrone Committee's Report,[12] free prescriptions for the under-25s in Wales and the commitment to free personal care for the elderly that has been made by the Scottish Executive.

The simple answer is that these are not sustainable in the long run. The Barnett formula will eventually equalise per capita spending (irrespective of need) in England, Scotland, Wales and Northern Ireland. Hence any measures that imply higher levels of spending on one section of the community by the devolved authorities will have to be counterbalanced by measures that imply less spending on other sections of the community. So, for example, free personal care for the elderly in Scotland might be bought at the cost of poorer nursery provision in Scotland compared with England.

Even if per capita spending is not equalised, but instead adjusted for need, the same argument that additional spending commitments would not be sustainable would still apply. This is because a needs adjustment measures the spending required to deliver a *common* level of service across areas. It is implicitly based on an assumption that broadly common services will be delivered. For example, a needs adjustment would not be sustainable if there were substantively different approaches to health service funding between devolved authorities.

10 Bell, D. N. F., *The Barnett Formula* (unpublished mimeo: Department of Economics, University of Stirling, 2001).
11 Andrew Smith MP in response to Joyce Quin MP. HC Deb, 19 July 2001, col. 425.
12 Scottish Executive. *A Teaching Profession for the 21st Century: Agreement reached following recommendations made in the McCrone Report* (Edinburgh: Scottish Executive, 2000).

There is an underlying question as to whether devolution that confers significant policy-making powers to subnational governments is consistent with needs-based allocation systems that are controlled by central government. If central government is at liberty to design and amend the 'common level of service' which it is prepared to fund in the regions and which forms the basis of the needs assessment, how can subnational governments implement policies that are significantly different from those applied at the centre? Even though such policies might have wide public support in the regions, the devolved authorities will not be able to implement the policy change unless they:

1   make significant efficiency gains in other parts of public services;
2   cut back on the provision of other services; or
3   are able to find new sources of revenue to fund the desired changes.

The first option is difficult if, as is the case in the UK, there are national pay scales for a significant proportion of public service workers and legislation constrains the way in which many public services are provided. The second is likely to inflict significant costs on other groups in society. The political costs of removing services always tend to be higher than the costs of not providing them in the first instance. The final option requires a greater degree of fiscal autonomy than the UK Treasury is currently prepared to contemplate.

In reality, none of the politicians can justify their arguments for higher or lower levels of expenditure because, as we mentioned above, the Barnett formula is a convergence formula. Convergence relies on continued growth in public spending, with the rate of convergence being greater the greater the growth rate of public spending. Unlike almost all mechanisms used to allocate resources at a subnational level in other advanced nations, it does not reflect relative need. And since no attempt has been made to measure relative need for over twenty years, the arguments that we have seen for changes to Barnett-determined allocations are built on partial and incomplete evidence.

Returning to the issue of convergence, it is clear that as far as some politicians are concerned (notably those from the North East of England), it is not happening fast enough and as far as others (for example, from Northern Ireland) are concerned, it is happening too quickly. The Barnett formula is caught in a pincer movement between those who want to protect their existing spending advantages and those who wish to undermine the status quo. The Barnett formula cannot provide a valid reference point for this debate, because it is only concerned with changes and not with the relative priorities that can be attached to competing claims for resources from different parts of the UK. Until there is some intellectual basis for the discussion of relative priorities, the Barnett debate will be conducted on the basis of winners and losers.

So far, we have avoided mention of Wales. From table 4.2, it is clear that the Welsh DEL will only be modestly affected by the Barnett squeeze and from figure 4.1, it appears that Wales is reasonably well resourced given our crude indicator of need.[13] Does this imply that Wales, unlike all other parts of the UK, is reasonably content with the Barnett formula? The answer to this question is a resounding 'no', but to see why we must move on to our final section, which considers the difficulties of integrating the Barnett formula with parts of the UK fiscal structure and in particular, those parts that are designed to take account of need.

Other funding mechanisms and the fiscal structure of the UK

The legislation that set up the devolved Parliament and Assemblies has left them in a weak position to resist the imposition of funding settlements decided solely by Westminster. As is discussed in detail in chapter 5, this is particularly the case for Wales, where funds from the EU under Objective 1 have had a significant impact on the levels of spending. These were first added in the 2000 Spending Review, increasing the baseline for spending in Wales by almost £300 million between 2000–01 and 2003–04. The UK Government made further additional payments of £106 million, £128 million and £147 million for 2005–06, 2006–07 and 2007–08. Similar considerations apply to claims on the UK Reserve, and to policies (such as the Scottish one on long-term care for the elderly) that have knock-on effects on non-devolved matters (in this case, attendance allowance). The current situation, which relies on ad hoc adjustments and agreements, would be difficult to sustain if the devolved governments were of a different political hue from that in the centre.

One escape route would be to offer greater fiscal freedom to the devolved authorities: the Liberal Democrats, as well as the Scottish National Party (SNP), have supported this approach. It also gained the support of international economists gathered together to discuss Scotland's economic future through the Allander Series of lectures.[14] They advocated a move towards a greater degree of fiscal autonomy, allowing Scotland to tax and spend on its

13 A DEL is the Departmental Expenditure Limit – the level of spending set by the Treasury through the process of Spending Reviews for three-year periods. DELs account for the bulk of devolved administration spending.

14 The Allander Series brought together a number of economic experts to offer their advice on improving Scotland's prospects for economic growth. See in particular Ronald Macdonald and Paul Hallwood, *The Economic Case for Fiscal Federalism in Scotland*. Papers are available at: www.fraser.strath.ac.uk/Allander/AllanderPapers.htm.

own account. This has sometimes been termed 'fiscal federalism', largely because the term 'fiscal autonomy' has been appropriated by the SNP. However, this is largely a Scottish debate – there is little discussion in Wales or Northern Ireland about fiscal autonomy, because public spending in these parts of the UK appears to be higher than the tax revenue collected there.

There is a wide range of international examples where state (or even local) governments exert varying degrees of local control over personal income, sales, property and value added taxes. The arguments in favour of local control of taxation and spending are broadly that:

1   Devolved governments know more about the preferences of their citizens than does central government.
2   Policy differences between devolved authorities can provide valuable experiments in policy design.
3   Centrally determined rules are likely to be less flexible to meet local conditions, either due to political constraints that force equal treatment of different localities or because central government prefers simple allocation mechanisms.
4   Decentralisation protects taxpayers from excessive taxation by central government because devolved areas will compete to offer individuals and businesses lower rates of taxation.

The main arguments against devolving taxes are that:

1   There will be unwelcome 'spillover' effects from one authority to the next if they pursue different tax and spend strategies (an example might be the influx of the elderly into Scotland if its policies on long-term care are more generous than those in England).
2   There may be scale economies in the provision of some public goods, which makes their production in a devolved setting inefficient. This may be true for defence, but it is not at all obvious why it should be true for health.
3   There is an insurance argument that pooling of resources to help areas experiencing difficult economic conditions is more easily brought about if there is a central authority able to control transfers to the poorer areas.

Whatever the economic merits of the former arguments, they have not persuaded any UK Government that they offset the case against extending fiscal powers to the devolved authorities. One particular reason for this may be the Labour Party in Scotland, both because it fears a significant worsening of Scotland's funding position and because such a move would play into the hands of the Nationalists. The Treasury is fairly predictable in its resistance to any diminution of its macroeconomic control over the economy. It is unlikely that the devolved authorities will be permitted any move towards even a small extension of their fiscal powers in the short to medium term.

Conclusion

The Barnett formula is now the perennial issue in finance and resources for the devolved administrations. It has been assailed by politicians from the regions of England who think its *level* of support is too generous to the devolved authorities. From the other side it has been criticised by politicians from the devolved Parliament and Assemblies who feel that Barnett-determined *changes* in funding to their institutions are insufficient to enable them to show that devolution is making a real difference. It is also a very curious bedfellow to other forms of support to the devolved authorities, particularly those that are based on some form of needs assessment.

The Barnett formula will continue to 'squeeze' the devolved authorities. The present administration will postpone a thorough review of the Barnett formula until the costs of doing so are unsustainable, probably until the 'squeeze' has brought Scotland and Northern Ireland much closer to the levels of funding that a needs assessment might imply. By such a method they will minimise the risk of too stark a change in the funding landscape. If that is so then continuing interim arrangements for Wales will be necessary.

The mechanisms that are used to resolve differences over funding between the centre and the devolved authorities overwhelmingly favour the centre. If the issue of rebalancing these is not addressed, then the ability of the devolved bodies to deliver significantly differentiated policies will be seriously compromised. And ultimately this will only serve to devalue the process of devolution in the public perception.

5
The politics of devolution finance and the power of the Treasury

Alan Trench*

This chapter is concerned with the intergovernmental politics of devolution finance. It is not an economic or financial analysis of how the devolved institutions are funded, but rather it looks at the processes by which that funding is allocated and the way in which decisions about funding are made, and by whom. It aims to identify where financial power lies within the UK's devolved system, to discuss how that power is actually used, and to analyse the implications of the Treasury's power for the devolved institutions. The chapter therefore both examines a key structural element of the relationship between the UK Government and the devolved administrations, and serves as a case study of how they relate to each other in an area of the highest importance to each of them. Key to this relationship, of course, is the working and effects of the Barnett formula, and what that in fact means for intergovernmental relations. The easiest way to approach this question is through looking at how the processes of allocating funding to the devolved administrations operate, as these are not only important in themselves but also reflect deeper issues of power which can be hard to identify more directly.

This relationship is formed against the backdrop of increasing centralisation of power within the UK Government. This has been documented clearly in journalistic and Parliamentary accounts, if less clearly in academic ones.[1] At the same time as devolution has transferred power to the new institutions, within the UK Government the grip of both the Prime Minister and the

*   Like my other chapters in this book, this chapter draws heavily on interviews with officials in the UK Government and devolved administrations. As a condition of access, no official was to be identified publicly. I am grateful to them all for their help. I am also grateful to Robert Hazell and Scott Greer for their comments on earlier drafts. The usual disclaimer applies.
1   See House of Commons Select Committee on the Treasury, *HM Treasury*, 2000–01 Session 3rd Report, HC 73-I (London: The Stationery Office, 2001), especially chap. 2; Burch, M. and Holliday, I., 'The Blair Government and the Core Executive', *Government and Opposition*, 39:1 (2004), 1–21, especially 6–7.

Chancellor of the Exchequer over the rest of government has increased significantly. In the case of the Prime Minister, the levers appear to have been the various policy and strategy units in 10 Downing Street and the need for ministers to secure Prime Ministerial (and so advisers') approval for their plans before being able to proceed with them.[2] For the Chancellor, the instrument has been the Treasury, and its control over public spending and policy proposals of line departments in Whitehall. However, the existence of the Barnett formula and the fact that the devolved administrations are funded through block grants (with no control over the allocation of funding within that block) deprive the Treasury of some of the instruments used to extend its power across Whitehall, such as public service agreements (PSAs).[3]

As is now well known (and discussed in chapter 4 above), the Barnett formula's origins lie in the nineteenth century, and the use of the Goschen formula (originally to allocate funding for Scottish church schools). Over the twentieth century, the mechanism came to be used for an increasing number of matters, and extended from Scotland to Wales and by a parallel formula to Northern Ireland. As part of the planning for devolution in the late 1970s, the Treasury carried out a needs assessment which showed that significantly greater amounts of spending would be justified for all three territories than for England – but that that amount would be less than what Scotland or Northern Ireland already received. Implementing the needs assessment would therefore mean a significant and politically unpalatable cut in spending, particularly in Scotland. As an interim measure the scope of the formula was extended, and named after Joel Barnett, then Chief Secretary to the Treasury, to govern increases in the departmental budgets of the Scottish and Welsh Offices (and, by a parallel formula, the Northern Ireland Office). It was intended to serve as a stop-gap arrangement, though it also had the arithmetical consequence that growth in public spending would over time lead to convergence of that spending on the English level.[4] As explained in chapter 4, the formula delivers proportionate increase in spending for Scotland, Wales

2   See Kavanagh, D., 'The Blair Premiership', in Seldon, A., and Kavanagh, D. (eds), *The Blair Effect 2001–5* (Cambridge: Cambridge University Press, 2005).

3   PSAs have not, however, been as effective as the Treasury might have wished, even in Whitehall. See James, O., 'The UK Core Executive's Use of Public Service Agreements as a Tool of Governance', *Public Administration*, 82:2 (2004), 397–419. See also Adams, J., 'PSAs and Devolution; Target Setting Across the UK', *New Economy*, 9:1 (2002), 31–5.

4   For a discussion, see Heald, D., 'Territorial public expenditure in the United Kingdom', *Public Administration*, 72 (1994), 147–75. It remains unclear to what extent convergence was an intentional feature of the system, or merely a side-effect.

and Northern Ireland on a population basis, depending on increases in spending for England. The formula only relates to increases (not the baseline of spending), and only applies where there is an increase in spending for a service in England which is 'comparable' to devolved functions. The system so established was based on automaticity in calculating the size of the territorial Offices' block grants, and on freedom to vire (move money between budgetary heads) within those grants. The territorial departments therefore always had greater freedom of operation than their Whitehall counterparts.[5] Nonetheless, the formula served to protect a higher level of public spending in Scotland, although this was tempered by a number of adjustments made (to deal with Scotland's declining population, for example) during the 1990s.

One aspect of automaticity was that the formula is meant to serve as a way of braking growth in Scottish spending, by preventing Scottish Secretaries of State making special arguments to increase their budgets.[6] The claim that the formula succeeded in restraining such rounding-up (even if it failed to deliver convergence) that McLean and McMillan make is doubtful, however. Despite official claims that the Barnett formula was applied consistently it is clear that considerable bargaining went on between the Scottish Office and the Treasury about funding matters, and that the Barnett formula would be bypassed if a case could be made.[7] Evidently such deals proliferated (and were

---

5 For accounts of the relationship between the territorial departments and the Treasury, and the management of territorial finance before devolution, see Thain, C. and Wright, M., *The Treasury and Whitehall: The planning and control of public expenditure, 1976–1993* (Oxford: Clarendon Press, 1995), especially chap. 14; and Deakin, N. and Parry, R., *The Treasury and Social Policy: The contest for control of welfare strategy* (Basingstoke: Macmillan, 2000), especially chap. 8. Classic (if now dated) accounts of the working of the Treasury include Heclo, H. and Wildavsky, A., *The Private Government of Public Money: Community and policy inside British politics* (London: Macmillan, 2nd edn, 1981); and Brittan, S., *Steering the Economy: The role of the Treasury* (Harmondsworth: Pelican, 1971).

6 McLean, I. and McMillan, A., 'The Distribution of Public Expenditure across the UK Regions', *Fiscal Studies*, 24:1 (2003), 45–71 at 52.

7 Heald ('Territorial public expenditure in the United Kingdom', 168–70) identifies five different ways in which such bypasses could occur. In his memoirs, Ian Lang (Secretary of State for Scotland between 1990 and 1995) writes, 'I calculated after two years as Secretary of State that the Barnett formula had reduced the Scottish Office budget by £17 million, while separate deals with the Treasury had increased it by £340 million. The very existence of the Barnett formula, far from inhibiting me, enabled me to concentrate on special deals to augment our resources.' Lang, I., *Blue Remembered Years: A political memoir* (London: Politicos, 2002), 194. Other accounts suggest that the formula was applied more consistently and that bypassing it was difficult, however; see e.g. Deakin and Parry, *The Treasury and Social Policy*, chap. 8.

themselves part of the reason why the formula has failed to deliver convergence), to the extent that it is possible to see the Barnett formula before devolution as the starting point for calculating the size of the Scottish, Northern Irish or Welsh blocks, but not necessarily the finishing point.

Adopting the Barnett formula for devolution

Before proceeding to consider what role the Treasury plays in practice in intergovernmental relations, it is worth examining how the block grant and formula mechanism, and the use of the Barnett formula in that context, came about, and the implications of that decision. In fact, it is not clear how this decision was made. Interviewing has established that this decision was taken by Gordon Brown personally, with startling speed. It was made in May 1997, within days of Labour's election victory, before civil servants had time to prepare detailed briefs on the question and even before the new Cabinet committee on devolution policy (DSWR: Devolution to Scotland, Wales and the (English) Regions) had met for the first time. The first meeting of the DSWR committee accepted the continuation of the Barnett formula as one of the givens of devolution, not an issue for resolution during the preparation of the white papers and devolution bills. This was contrary to the expectation of at least some of the officials involved, who had foreseen this as one of the most difficult issues to be dealt with in preparing devolution. They were drawing on past experience; this had been one of the thorniest issues in preparing for devolution in the 1970s. The decision was, therefore, one that had been made in advance. It is worth considering the basis on which it was made, if it was made by the Chancellor alone and without any briefing from the civil service. While some of the pre-devolution policy analyses had touched on finance (and there is good reason to believe Brown was aware of them), none of those could be exhaustive.[8] In any case, they were academic analyses which for all their impartiality and rigour were lacking the focus or range of information available in government. The implication must be that this was a matter on which the Chancellor had made up his mind some considerable time in advance, and that as far as he was concerned it was a part of the framework of devolution, was not subject to reconsideration depending on the advice of officials, and was not for more general debate during the preparation of devolution.

8 See for example Blow, L., Hall, J. and Smith, S., *Financing Regional Government in Britain*, IFS Commentary No. 54 (London: Institute for Fiscal Studies, 2nd edn, 1996); The Constitution Unit, *Scotland's Parliament: Fundamentals for a new Scotland Act* (London: The Constitution Unit, 1996), especially chap. 5.

It is also worth considering what exactly this decision involved. In fact, it required three decisions. One was to fund the devolved administrations by a block grant; the second was to use the existing baseline of spending for that grant, and the third was to inflate that baseline subsequently by the existing Barnett formula, not some other indicator. The first meant ruling out ways of allowing the devolved institutions to raise substantial amounts of revenue for themselves (as local government in the UK does, and constituent units in many federations such as Australia do). It also meant ruling out the possibility of raising revenue centrally and then transferring assigned revenues to the devolved institutions – in other words, hypothecating some tax income to the devolved administrations.

The second decision provided that the inherited patterns of spending were to be preserved. These patterns, it is true, were only used after the Treasury had undertaken the far-reaching Comprehensive Spending Review in 1998, which was its instrument for restructuring public spending across government as a whole and indicating the areas that would be priorities for spending increases in subsequent years.[9] That resulted in significant increases in funding for Scotland and Wales (of £4.1 billion and £2.2 billion respectively, over three years) but, if that was influenced by any assessment of need, that was not conveyed in the white paper that set out the results of the review. Similarly, the use of the (population-related) Barnett formula was retained, rather than some other deflator relating to need, such as the inverse of gross domestic product, a proxy for poverty (as suggested by Iain McLean), or an index related directly to need (such as social security spending, suggested by David Bell).[10]

9 See HM Treasury, *Modern Public Services for Britain: Investing in reform. Comprehensive Spending Review: New public spending plans 1999–2002*, Cm 4011 (London: The Stationery Office, 1998). Following completion of the Comprehensive Spending Review, the Treasury published in March 1999 *Funding the Scottish Parliament, National Assembly for Wales and Northern Ireland Assembly: A statement of funding policy* (henceforth *Statement of Funding Policy*). This has been republished after each biennial Spending Review and is now in its fourth edition. It is available at www.hm-treasury.gov.uk/media/CB2/3C/Funding_the_Scottish_Parliament_National_Assembly_for_Wales(296kb).pdf (visited November 2005). The Comprehensive Spending Review also brought in the present structure of Departmental Expenditure Limits (DELs), to which broadly speaking the Barnett formula applies, and Annually Managed Expenditure (AME), to which it does not. Most AME spending is not affected by devolution, but it also applies to agriculture spending (from the Common Agricultural Policy), which is routed through the devolved administrations.

10 McLean has suggested using per capita GDP as a deflator, but only in default of agreement between the UK Government and devolved administrations about other mechanisms to adjust payments to the devolved administrations. His rationale has been that the use of so unattractive a measure would in fact impel agreement on a

Each of these was a significant decision with far-reaching and probably long-lasting implications. For them to have been taken so quickly, with so little ministerial or official consideration, was remarkable. This is not to say that the decision was in some sense wrong – indeed, it had many advantages. The use of a block grant system may have made the devolved administrations reliant on the UK Government for their revenue but it avoided potential disputes with the UK Government (which might have included a devolved challenge to the Treasury's authority), and the possibility of different tax regimes operating in different parts of the UK, with consequent diseconomies particularly for business. It significantly reduced the amount of administrative upheaval that devolution would involve for all concerned. It emphasised devolved autonomy (because it was a block grant, not allocated to particular budget heads or items) while maintaining the unity of the United Kingdom and its system of public finances.[11] The maintenance of this existing (and well-established) system also prevented a potential backlash from taxpayers in England, as it avoided opening the question of how much money went to the devolved institutions, and the relation this bore (or bears) to the amount of revenue raised in those territories. It is widely believed that the amounts spent in Scotland, Wales and Northern Ireland exceed the amount of tax revenue generated there – in other words, that the devolved administrations spend more than their taxpayers generate, and that therefore there is a substantial English subsidy to them. Data to support (or refute) this are scant, but appear to support the view in relation to Scotland. According to *GERS* for 2002–03, total Scottish spending on services was £38,595 million and total managed expenditure was £40,879 million, while total revenues were £31,620 million. Total spending therefore exceeded revenues by £6975 million, and total managed expenditure exceeded revenues by £9259 million.[12]

more sensible one. Treasury officials, by contrast, appear to regard it as a suitable measure in itself. See McLean, I., 'A Fiscal Constitution for the UK', in Chen, S. and Wright, T. (eds), *The English Question* (London: The Fabian Society, 2000). Bell and Christie have suggested social security spending as a closer proxy for need; see chapter 4 above, and Bell, D. and Christie, A., 'Finance – The Barnett Formula: Nobody's child', in Trench, A. (ed.), *The State of the Nations 2001: The second year of devolution in the United Kingdom* (Exeter: Imprint Academic, 2001).

11 See Heald, D. and McLeod, A., 'Embeddedness of UK Devolution Finance within the Public Expenditure System', *Regional Studies*, 39:4 (2005), 495–518, for an explanation of ways in which the Barnett formula does this on the technical level.

12 See Scottish Ministers, *Government Expenditure & Revenue in Scotland 2002–2003 (GERS)*, SE/2004/273 (Edinburgh: Scottish Executive, 2004), tables 6.6, 6.7 and 6.8. These figures exclude oil revenues, however. For a discussion of the problems with the data in *GERS*, see Goudie, A., '*GERS* and Fiscal Autonomy', *Scottish Affairs*, 41 (2002), 56–85.

The decision to use an adapted version of Barnett also avoided the problems that arose with financing a devolved Northern Ireland, before 1972. Northern Ireland was supposed to fund itself; the UK Government would remit to the province the tax revenue raised there, less a contribution for 'Imperial purposes'. In fact this revenue was never adequate, particularly after Northern Ireland came to adopt British standards of social welfare. Complicated and protracted negotiations between the Treasury and the devolved Ministry of Finance resulted, in attempts to resolve the problem. The solutions generally involved various forms of creative accountancy and disguised subsidy from the UK, initially relating to the Imperial contribution but then extending to further-reaching methods, bypassing in substance the formal mechanisms and principles that were intended to underpin the system. The situation was clearly an administrative and financial nightmare.[13]

The implication of using the block and formula mechanism is clear; it meant that from the outset (and quite apart from legal and political issues) the devolved administrations would remain tied into the UK Government's plans and financial structures for the indefinite future. The larger question is what impact that had on the devolved institutions.

Why and how the Barnett formula is important

The main implication of the block and formula system, and the Barnett formula, is very simple; it makes the devolved administrations important spenders of public money in their parts of the UK. As table 5.1 shows, the Scottish Executive and National Assembly for Wales spend about half of total public spending in those nations. For Northern Ireland, the proportion of public spending is rather higher, even if social security spending (routed but not in practice controlled by the Northern Ireland departments) is stripped out. But the devolved administrations do not dominate public spending, let alone monopolise it. Other parts of government account for significant amounts of spending, indicating that devolved government is only one part of the overall structure of government, even in Scotland, Wales and Northern Ireland.

Beyond this, the use of the Barnett formula has a number of consequences. First and most important, the block grant and formula system

---

13 This account owes a great deal to Mitchell, J., 'Undignified and Inefficient: Financial relations between London and Stormont', *Contemporary British History*, 20:1 (2006), 57–73. See also Lawrence, R. J., *The Government of Northern Ireland: Public finance and public services 1921–1964* (Oxford: Clarendon Press, 1965).

Table 5.1. Territorial and devolved public spending, 2003–04 (£ million)

Country	Total public spending	Percentage of identifiable UK public spending	Total spending by devolved administration	Percentage of overall identifiable UK public spending in the region spent by the devolved administration[c]
England 296131 79	n/a			
Scotland	37152	10	19916	55.6
Wales	20277	5	9820	48.4
Northern Ireland[a]	13527	4	11539	85.3
Northern Ireland excluding social security[b]	Idem	2[c]	7725[c]	57.1
UK identifiable public spending	367086	98		
Identifiable spending outside UK	8829	2		
Non-identifiable public spending	61718	n/a		
TOTAL	437633	100[d]	41275	11.2[e]

Sources:

Total public spending and percentage of identifiable UK public spending columns: from HM Treasury, *Public Expenditure Statistical Analyses 2005*, table 8.1.

Total spending by devolved administration:

For Scotland, from Scottish Executive Consolidated Resource Accounts for year ended 31 March 2004, SE/2004/267, Consolidated Summary of Outturn, p. 17 (total outturn).

For Wales: National Assembly for Wales Resource Accounts 2003–04, p. 14 (net operating cost).

For Northern Ireland: *Financial Auditing and Reporting 2003–2004: General Report by the Comptroller and Auditor-General for Northern Ireland*, HC 96 (London: The Stationery Office 2005), figure 1, p. 9, net outturn total.

Percentage of identifiable UK public spending column: own calculation.

Notes:

[a] Northern Ireland spending is that by Northern Ireland departments (which therefore corresponds with spending on functions that were devolved under the Northern Ireland Act 1998). This includes social security spending.

[b] According to PESA 2005 (see above), table 8.5a, 'social protection' spending in Northern Ireland totals £3814 million. Non-social security spending therefore totals £7725 million, or 57.1 per cent of total public spending there.

[c] Author's calculation.

[d] Total relates to identifiable UK public spending and so excludes non-identifiable spending in column above.

[e] 11.2 per cent relates to total identifiable UK public spending. For UK total public spending (identifiable and non-identifiable), it is 9.4 per cent.

makes the devolved administrations purely spending agencies, not fully functioning governments. They lack an important element of accountable and responsible government – the power to make decisions about how much revenue to raise from taxpayers, and to be held accountable for such decisions at the ballot box. That raises the question of how important that lack of accountability is; economists assume that it is fatal to the exercise of any meaningful autonomy (as David Bell and Alex Christie argue in chapter 4).

Second, however, from a political point of view the block grant offers real autonomy in spending. Within the block there are very few constraints over how the devolved administrations allocate spending; they genuinely can direct money towards their own priorities. Such constraints as exist are informal or political in nature. Because increases are tied to what the UK Government does for England, there is often pressure for the devolved administrations to use the money in similar ways. That pressure comes from their own elected Parliament or Assembly and the local media, however, not UK institutions. From a Whitehall point of view, there is little interest generally in controlling what the devolved administrations do. As Ron Watts shows in chapter 11, this contrasts with the practice in many federal systems, where much spending is targeted to particular policy areas or subject to other conditions.

Third, the devolved administrations are largely confined to that particular package of funding. The lack of revenue-raising powers makes it very hard for them to supplement their resources. They cannot use borrowing to do so, as they only have power to borrow with the consent of the Treasury, to balance cash-flow problems. One possible source, which has been used to a degree, is to reduce the amount the devolved administration contributes to local government, and require local authorities to raise the balance by increasing council tax or non-domestic rates. These can therefore serve as proxy taxes for the devolved administrations. Use of that is constrained by the *Statement of Funding Policy*, and its provisions to claw back revenue if the Treasury considers the increases to threaten public spending targets.[14] In any case, the amount this raises as a proportion of total devolved administration spending is limited, and the amount of flexibility it offers therefore even more limited.[15] Even if the Scottish Parliament were to use its tax-varying power to the full, that would raise (or reduce) public spending in Scotland by only £840

14 *Statement of Funding Policy*, section 5.
15 Scottish revenue from this source accounts for 15 per cent of Scottish Executive spending, while the amount for Wales is apparently somewhat less: see Heald, D. and McLeod, A., 'Revenue-raising by UK Devolved Administrations in the Context of an Expenditure-based Financing System', *Regional and Federal Studies*, 13:4 (2003), 67–90.

million, a small sum in the overall context of an annual budget of £37 billion or thereabouts.[16] While from a political point of view fiscal responsibility is not necessarily a pre-requisite for the existence of autonomy, the combination of no responsibility for raising revenue and the very limited flexibility in varying the amount of funding available does limit the overall autonomy of the devolved administrations.

Fourth, the key decisions about Barnett were and are taken at UK level, and often within the Treasury. The initial decision to adopt Barnett, the spending baseline from the Comprehensive Spending Review, and the details of the *Statement of Funding Policy* are all adopted, unilaterally, by the UK. The processes by which this happened were closed and not open to public scrutiny. Moreover, they have not been expressly agreed with the devolved administrations, and have not been given statutory form. There is therefore nothing formally or legally to prevent the UK Government from altering them; the restraints on the UK are political or administrative and practical in nature.

Fifth, the financial integration of the devolved administrations into the UK system stands in marked contrast to the generous legal and administrative powers given to them. These financial arrangements need to be regarded as a pillar of devolution (at least of New Labour's vision of it), and as a way of defining the parameters of devolution at the outset.

Sixth, the limited amount of deliberation about the adoption of the block grant and formula system can be related to the conservatism visible in the way government institutions have adapted to devolution generally (discussed in more detail in chapters 8 and 12). From the point of view of the Treasury, the devolved administrations are spending departments with rather eccentric arrangements and only a limited susceptibility to Treasury control. Preserving Barnett avoids challenging the fiscal framework of the United Kingdom, but does help to preserve a complicated set of financial and institutional arrangements. (This may be at the price of straining the underlying rationale of that system, as McLean and McMillan argue, but that is a separate issue from the administrative considerations.[17]) This conservatism is mirrored by a technical aspect of the working of those arrangements. Money is not paid directly to the devolved administration, but is 'voted' by the UK Parliament to the relevant Secretary of State, under the annual Appropriation

16 The effect of using the Scottish tax-varying power is given in each year's Budget statement. This figure comes from HM Treasury, *Budget 2005: Investing for our future: Fairness and opportunity for Britain's hard-working families*, Financial Statement and Budget Report, HC 372 (London: The Stationery Office, 2005), para. A.9.

17 McLean and McMillan, 'The Distribution of Public Expenditure'.

Act. The Secretaries of State, and not Parliament directly, then pay that money to the devolved institutions, after deducting the cost of running their own offices. (This also creates scope to inflate the size of those offices with little restraint, as happened when Dr John Reid was Secretary of State for Scotland.) In finance, as in many other matters, the historic inheritance has been highly important.

Seventh, circumstances (in particular significant and sustained growth in public spending) have minimised the pressures on the block grant and formula arrangement, and particularly the Barnett element of it. Shortage of funds has not been a problem for any of the governments involved since 1999.

However, and eighth, administrative (as well as fiscal) considerations will put increasing strain on these financial arrangements in the future. Tying spending allocations to the devolved administrations to spending on 'comparable functions' in England assumes that the English functions are indeed 'comparable'. As devolved policy develops and different ways of making and delivering public services emerge, that will be decreasingly the case – unless the nature of finance itself constrains the devolved administrations to keep more or less in step with England. One possible outcome is therefore to limit devolved policy divergence to the margins, and ensure that the devolved administrations continue simply to vary slightly what the UK Government does for England. The other is that the system comes under real strain, as their services bear a decreasing resemblance to those provided by the UK Government.

Dealing with the Treasury: making routine financial decisions

The great achievement of the use of the block grant and formula mechanism is that it both simplifies and puts on one side politically the question of finance in routine intergovernmental relations. Both are common sources of tension in federal systems, and can also be found in the intra-governmental bargaining that takes place within any particular government (as vividly illustrated by the 'historic' writings about the Treasury and its role).[18] So what happens when the most important questions are off the table, and intergovernmental dealings therefore concern important but essentially second-order issues or routine administrative matters? This section and the next are largely

18 See Thain and Wright, *The Treasury and Whitehall*; Heclo and Wildavsky, *The Private Government of Public Money*; Deakin and Parry, *The Treasury and Social Policy*.

concerned with what we can learn from the processes and issues that have been the subject of Treasury-devolved administration interaction since 1999. They discuss the sorts of matters that are dealt with, to show how little controversy attaches to a wide range of matters that arise – despite the importance of these in a broader context.

On one level, the process is very straightforward. For the most part, financial allocations to the devolved administrations are automatic. The allocations in the previous year or Spending Review are taken, and increased by amounts corresponding to the factors set out in the *Statement of Funding Policy*, and that is it. Sorting out what they mean is largely an arithmetical matter, taking a small number of officials (few of them senior) in both the Treasury and the devolved administrations.[19] The process as a whole requires few staff and generally operates with little fuss or dispute. For the devolved administrations, the main issue is to secure the amounts to which they are entitled, particularly when additional funds for Whitehall departments are announced in the course of a year. That requires the devolved administrations to establish whether the funds are for devolved or non-devolved functions (not always as straightforward as it may appear), to ensure that they receive any extra to which they are entitled, and that the Treasury has not made any errors in calculating the transfers due to the devolved administrations. This therefore triggers one source of low-level intergovernmental negotiation, if not bargaining. The approaches of the Scottish Executive and Welsh Assembly Government (WAG) vary here; the Executive tends to be somewhat less pushy than WAG, perhaps reflecting the greater financial pressures on the National Assembly.

Beyond this, routine interactions between the UK Government and devolved administrations on finance matters take three forms: those relating to administrative matters, those triggered by Spending Reviews, and those relating to the UK Reserve. In general, however, interviews suggest that such interactions are limited in frequency and scope, and are even less than they were before devolution (when they were already somewhat limited).

The administrative interactions of the Treasury and the devolved administrations relate to the matters of broader concern to the Treasury. Once these

---

19 The Treasury team numbers 6 or 7. The numbers engaged on Barnett-related matters for all or most of their time in each devolved administration appear to be similar or slightly larger, but still are no more than 12. Many of the staff in the devolved administrations are concerned with the mechanical aspects of the finance mechanism, the work of a devolved administration finance division being very different from the policy-driven approach of the Treasury. For a detailed discussion, see Keating, M., *The Government of Scotland: Public policy making after devolution* (Edinburgh: Edinburgh University Press, 2005), chap. 6.

would have included civil service issues, including staffing levels, but with the transfer of control over such matters to departments in the 1990s this no longer figures.[20] Since devolution, these have generally embraced a number of fairly routine and non-political matters, such as the introduction of resource accounting and budgeting (RAB) across government and its implications – which include costing for the use of office space and other government-owned capital assets. This has raised a number of difficulties, especially for Northern Ireland (both under devolution and direct rule), as a number of services provided by the Northern Ireland departments are pro-vided by local government in England (which is not subject to the regime). The problems this posed led to the granting of exemptions from RAB for Northern Ireland. A second subject has been routine issues of financial man-agement, including the handling of year-end flexibility by the devolved administrations. By and large, such matters are interesting more for the extent of UK interest in technical aspects of the working of devolved government, rather than their substantive effect.

So far as Spending Reviews are concerned, officials in all governments are cagey in interview about how much lobbying takes place during them. The main thrust of such reviews clearly concerns spending by UK departments, whether on 'English' functions or on non-devolved ones, and the assumption that the Barnett formula applies automatically to the outcome has also pre-vailed. That has not altogether stopped lobbying by the devolved administra-tions, usually by the losers under the Barnett formula (Wales and Northern Ireland) to secure enhanced funding allocations, but such lobbying has been limited in scope and is generally not something officials wish to discuss.[21] In general lobbying is limited to narrower concerns which may have the effect of increasing funding allocations. One area where this has taken place relates to the classification of functions as 'English' or 'UK', as English spending trig-gers a Barnett consequential and UK spending does not. In the 2000 Spending Review one such change did take place, with spending on public transport in London reclassed as English rather than UK spending.[22] Although spending on London transport has increased significantly since then, the amount involved for the devolved administrations will still be modest. Such a bargaining position therefore reflects a combination of a

20 See chapter 3.
21 For an example of lobbying by a devolved administration, see Page, E. C. and Jenkins, B., *Policy Bureaucracy: Government with a cast of thousands* (Oxford: Oxford University Press, 2005), p. 91.
22 These items are classed as 'LA Transport Grant' and 'LRT administration' in Annex C, the 'Schedule of Comparable Sub-programmes', to the 2000 edition of the *Statement of Funding Policy*.

desire to get all the administrations can and to establish principles about the dividing-line between English and UK functions. (By contrast, the Channel Tunnel and its high-speed rail link remains a UK not an English service, so does not trigger any Barnett consequential – even though the benefit of the tunnel and rail link to northern England, let alone Scotland, Wales or Northern Ireland, is hard to fathom.)

This process recurs whenever functions are transferred to the devolved administrations – as with local railway services in Scotland and later Wales, or fire service and support in Wales. It may take some considerable time to agree the financial terms on which such transfers of functions are made (in other words, the size of the initial extra contribution to the devolved administration's DEL) after the principle of transferring the function has been agreed. Such negotiations are of course vital – a function is worse than useless if there are no funds to support it, as it is a further draw on existing funds. Such negotiations can be trying for all involved but have been dealt with largely away from the public eye.

There are limits to what is discussed. Interviewing shows that UK Government officials (whether in the Treasury or the Scotland or Wales Offices) are clear that they cannot discuss details of internal UK Government matters (including the Budget, Spending Reviews and other spending announcements) with the devolved administrations. Thus, during Spending Reviews and annual UK budget rounds, much of the discussion takes place in the absence of the devolved administrations. Only when the Chancellor of the Exchequer sits down after making his statement in the House of Commons do Treasury officials contact their devolved counterparts to explain the significance of what has been announced for the devolved administrations. They are unable to gain advance notice of what is proposed, even confidentially, and to the extent that any representations take place they are made by the territorial Office, which in those circumstances cannot seek the views or advice of the devolved administration first.[23] This exposes the devolved administration to the risk of embarrassment, if they are unable to mask their ignorance of matters of such importance to them. The devolved administrations are therefore in an uncomfortable half-way house for financial matters, subject to UK Government decisions but unable to be heard directly in the formulation of many of those decisions.

23 This contrasts with practice in most federal systems, where the federal government will usually give some sort of advance access to its planned budget to finance officials from constituent units, informally and confidentially. In Canada, this often takes the form of locked-room access to the detailed documents on the morning of budget day.

Regarding the UK Reserve, devolution has made little difference. The devolved administrations may make claims on it through the territorial Secretaries of State, as Whitehall departments do through their own ministers.[24] Such claims are considered by Treasury ministers 'in exceptional circumstances, on a case by case basis'. This specifically applies where either a UK department is granted access to the Reserve because of 'exceptional pressures on a spending programme' and the devolved administration has a similar programme and faces similar pressures, or where the devolved territory faces 'exceptional and unforeseen domestic costs which cannot reasonably be absorbed within existing budgets without a major dislocation of existing services'.[25] Discretion therefore remains with the Treasury – and, in case of dispute, ultimately with the UK Cabinet, *not* the Joint Ministerial Committee (JMC). There have been few cases of claims by the devolved administrations to date, the main one being for some of the consequential costs of the 2001 outbreak of Foot and Mouth Disease.[26] These related to matters such as the loss of tourism revenue, not the costs of dealing with the outbreak itself, destroying slaughtered animals or compensating farmers for slaughtered animals, as these were borne from the AME budget. As similar problems affected farmers in England, the case clearly fell within the first of the two legs noted above and was relatively uncontroversial – but had the costs been greater in Scotland, Wales or Northern Ireland than in England, it is impossible to know what might have happened.

Similarly, there was intensive bargaining over the extra £50 million or so sought by the Scottish Executive to cover the costs of the July 2005 G8 summit held at Gleneagles, and the associated public demonstrations. The Executive's case was clearly stronger for the G8 summit – the UK had taken a decision about a reserved matter (foreign relations) that had serious effects for a devolved one (policing). It was successful in securing £20 million, although that sum was later said to be far less than the actual costs of policing the event.[27]

---

24 In addition, the devolved administrations maintain their own reserves (as do UK departments). Such reserves are relatively small, however, and would not enable the devolved administration to cope with any major financial shock.

25 *Statement of Funding Policy*, para. 9.2.

26 See House of Lords Select Committee on the Constitution, Session 2002–03 2nd Report, *Devolution: Inter-institutional Relations in the United Kingdom*, HL 28 (London: The Stationery Office, 2003), paras 96–101.

27 See BBC News, 'Minister Reveals G8 Costs Pledge', 22 March 2005, http://news.bbc.co.uk/1/hi/scotland/4370561.stm; First Minister's official spokesman's media briefing, 20 May 2005, transcript at www.scotland.gov.uk/News/This-Week/Media-Briefings/050520/Q/pno/1.

Deciding political questions: untrammelled authority?

If so much can be dealt with largely by officials, what falls to Treasury and devolved ministers? What matters are sufficiently controversial or important that ministerial involvement is necessary?

One issue is the general management of public services: value for money, delivery issues, and general liaison and coordination. That is important enough to claim ministers' attention, and has been organised through six-monthly meetings of finance ministers, initially convened (and chaired) by Paul Boateng when he was Chief Secretary to the Treasury.[28] Those meetings have simply been 'quadrilateral' meetings (although junior ministers from the Scotland and Wales Offices have attended, as well as devolved ministers and a junior minister from the Northern Ireland Office). They have taken place outside the Joint Ministerial Committee framework (discussed in detail in chapter 8). Use of the JMC for economic matters has been halting at best. In February 2000, the Chancellor convened a single meeting of the JMC for the Knowledge Economy, but it has not met since. Around the same time (in December 1999) the Chancellor chaired a meeting of the JMC for Poverty, which similarly ceased to meet. That was, however, revived with little notice in September 2002, and issued a communiqué indicating a strongly Brown-ite social policy agenda and an ambitious work plan, with a determination to coordinate devolved functions such as health and education with social security matters to tackle poverty. It also laid out plans for three further meetings during the first half of 2003 to develop and coordinate policy in those areas.[29] Those meetings never took place – possibly because the Chancellor's interest moved elsewhere (this was the time of planning and undertaking the war in Iraq). Interviewing suggests, however, that devolved concern about the extent to which the Treasury was seeking to direct devolved policy was also a factor, and that the quiet or passive resistance of the devolved administrations was sufficient to persuade the Treasury that this would not be a fruitful use of time and resources. And similarly, in late 2003 there were suggestions that there would shortly be a meeting of a new functional format of the JMC, for

---

28 The first such meeting took place in March 2003 and was the subject of a Treasury press notice (no. 37/03, 10 March 2003). Treasury officials have confirmed in interview that meetings have continued to take place since then roughly every six months, but press releases have not been issued for those meetings.

29 The communiqué is available at www.dca.gov.uk/constitution/devolution/ jmc/jmcp_communique_sept_2002.pdf. See also the Treasury press notice, PN 90/02, at www.hm-treasury.gov.uk/newsroom_and_speeches/press/2002/ press_90_02.cfm (both visited November 2005).

the Economy, and that the JMC for the Knowledge Economy would be rolled into that. All that was awaited was a date for the first meeting. However, that meeting did not happen during 2004 or 2005.

There have been more controversial matters in which ministerial involvement was greater. Most of the key examples arise from the conduct of Spending Reviews: the question of Objective 1 funds for Wales in 2001, the attempt by the Scottish Executive in 2001 to secure extra funds for their policy of free care for the elderly, the handling of the 2004 Spending Review and the Treasury's 2005 decision to turn the planned Spending Review for 2006 into a Comprehensive Spending Review in 2007. Despite the importance of each matter, politically and financially, the JMC framework was not invoked in dealing with any of them, and each was dealt with largely autonomously within the Treasury. In the run-up to Spending Review 2002, Northern Ireland's Department of Finance and Personnel had clearly sought considerably more than this, however, and ran a lobbying campaign which included calling on the Secretary of State for support and reworking of the 1979 needs assessment, using an updated version of the Treasury's methodology. The Department evidently thought this significantly strengthened its hand in negotiations with the Treasury, though this assessment was open to question on methodological grounds (the Department had been free to make its own assumptions in updating the process, after all) and it appears to have carried relatively little weight with the Treasury.[30] The National Assembly for Wales approached the matter in a more low-key way, challenging the Treasury rather less, and appears to have been rewarded for its tact in the form of securing matching funding for its Objective 1 status. What Northern Ireland secured was a borrowing power that formed part of the 'Reinvestment and Reform' initiative, announced some months before the Review was completed, and conditional on a wide-ranging programme of restructuring its finances including reviews of water charges and a range of other services.[31]

The story of Objective 1 for Wales is well known. Parts of Wales ('West Wales and Valleys') were granted Objective 1 status by the European Commission in 1999, recognising their poor state of economic development – having

30 Northern Ireland did not have a monopoly on this information, as apparently the Treasury's own needs assessments have been updated periodically, though never published. See Heald, D. and McLeod, A., 'Beyond Barnett? Funding devolution', in Adams, J. and Robinson, P. (eds), *Devolution in Practice: Public policy differences within the UK* (London: ippr, 2002), 163.

31 See speech by the Chancellor of the Exchequer, Gordon Brown MP, Belfast, 2 May 2002. Available at www.hm-treasury.gov.uk/newsroom_and_speeches/ speeches/chancellorexchequer/speech_cx_020502.cfm (visited November 2005).

75 per cent or less of EU average per capita GDP.[32] In the UK, however, such status can have little actual value, as the Treasury retains all inward flows from the EU and regards such funds as part of the UK's overall income from the EU. Accordingly it does not automatically provide extra funds to the areas or authorities granted Objective 1 status, which have to bid for extra monies from UK sources. At the same time, however, the European Commission expects all revenues it devotes to an Objective 1 area to be matched by additional public spending in that area (additional meaning extra to the levels that would otherwise be spent there). As local or regional authorities (in this case, the National Assembly) are the applicants for Objective 1 funds and in the eyes of the European Commission receive them, they can find themselves with an obligation to carry out activities in a designated area, including an obligation to repay monies to the Commission if they fail to do so, but without any extra funds to do so. This was the position in which the National Assembly found itself in 2001. Unsurprisingly, this led to a major political row, which triggered the resignation of the First Secretary of the Assembly Cabinet, Alun Michael, and brought to office Rhodri Morgan.[33]

Subsequently, as part of Spending Review 2002, the Treasury announced a volte-face, and found 'matching funding' to enable the Assembly to use the EU's Objective 1 funds.[34] To call such monies 'match funding' is somewhat misleading. The amount released is an amount equal to that awarded by the European Commission. While in principle it is a transfer from the Treasury to enable the National Assembly to use the Commission's funds, the Assembly never gets any extra money from the Commission or as a result of Objective 1 status, except for the 'match funding'. Moreover, the funding

---

32 For general discussions of Objective 1 in Wales, see contributions to *Contemporary Wales*, 15 (2003); McAllister, L., 'Devolution and the New Context for Public Policy-making: Lessons from the EU Structural Funds in Wales', *Public Policy and Administration*, 15:2 (2000), 38–52; and House of Commons Welsh Affairs Committee, *Objective 1 European Funding for Wales*, Session 2001–02 2nd Report, HC 520 (London: The Stationery Office, 2002).

33 It would be wrong to say that Michael's departure was caused by the Objective 1 row, as this owed a great deal also to the circumstances in which the Labour Party in London drove his nomination to lead the party in Wales after Ron Davies was forced to step down. For details, see Thomas, A. and Laffin, M., 'The First Welsh Constitutional Crisis: The Alun Michael resignation', *Public Policy and Administration*, 16:1 (2001), 18; and Osmond, J., 'A Constitutional Convention by Other Means: The first year of the National Assembly for Wales', in Hazell, R. (ed.), *The State and the Nations: The first year of devolution in the United Kingdom* (Exeter: Imprint Academic, 2000).

34 See Bristow, G., 'Bypassing Barnett: The Comprehensive Spending Review and public expenditure in Wales', *Economic Affairs*, 21:3 (2001), 44–7.

provided takes the form of 'PES Cover' in the jargon, PES meaning 'Public Expenditure Survey'. It is an authority to borrow rather than a provision of extra cash from Treasury revenue. The generosity of this concession is therefore dubious. Nonetheless, its importance to Wales has been very considerable, as over the life of the Objective 1 programme (2000–07) it is worth some £1.14 billion – compared with annual National Assembly spending of £9.8 billion (for 2003–04; see table 5.1).

The position the Treasury took is almost unprecedented. The general practice for all parts of the UK awarded Objective 1 (or for that matter Objective 2) status is for the Treasury to retain the extra funds and treat them as part of general UK revenue. The only previous exception was Northern Ireland, in respect of the 'PEACE' programme announced by the Commission in 1998 following the Belfast Agreement, to promote cross-border cooperation and help stabilise the new arrangements. That clearly was an exceptional case. What was agreed by the Treasury was plainly a bypass of the Barnett formula (though not publicly described as such), and was part of the 2002 Spending Review (although it was in fact announced separately from the outcome of that Review). The closest it is possible to come to an explanation of why the Treasury refused to supply such funds (despite the consequence for Alun Michael) then did so is that, quite simply, it changed its mind.[35] While the evidence of the ministers and officials involved explains the policy reasons for doing so, it does not address the question of how the Treasury made such a decision or why they took so long to do so. The answer appears to be that they had a discretion to use, and they chose to exercise it in this way. A further underlying factor may also have played a part, however. Given the widespread agreement that Wales is the biggest loser from the Barnett formula, Objective 1 provided a convenient justification for bypassing the formula to Wales's benefit. It was therefore an opportune way to boost the Assembly's budget without opening up a process of ad hoc demands from other devolved administrations (or indeed non-devolved parts of the UK). However, it is a relatively short-term fix. When Objective 1 ends in 2007, this justification for continuing to support Wales will end, although there will be tapering provisions for several years to cushion the blow. After that, will Wales be left to its own devices, and if not what will be done for it, and how will that affect the block grant and Barnett formula system as a whole?

---

35 See House of Commons Welsh Affairs Committee, *Objective 1 European Funding for Wales*, QQ. 63, 65 and 69–71 (evidence of Rt Hon. Paul Murphy MP, Rt Hon. Rhodri Morgan AM, and Ros Dunn). It is worth noting that although a Treasury official (Mrs Dunn) was at that evidence session, no Treasury minister was – nor did one give evidence to that inquiry.

The story of the Scottish Executive's attempt to secure extra funds for the policy of long-term care for the elderly is discussed elsewhere in this volume (see chapter 8). The funding for the policy itself came from the Scottish Executive's block grant, but as a consequence claimants of attendance allowance (a social security benefit intended to enable recipients to purchase this sort of care) in Scotland lost their entitlement to it. Consequently there was a substantial saving, of between £21 million and £70 million, to the Department of Work and Pensions. In the autumn of 2002 the Scottish Executive sought to have this money paid to them to cover the costs of the policy. Interviewing shows that after discussions with other UK departments, including the Treasury, the Department of Work and Pensions declined to transfer the money saved to the Scottish Executive. While the Scots may have been aggrieved at this, it was again left entirely as a bilateral decision matter between the Executive and the Department, with no further action taken and no interest shown in taking the matter to the JMC.[36] (Scottish quiescence may also be due to a concession by the Treasury over a different matter raised at the same time, the transfer to the Treasury from the Executive of interest charges for loans for the capital costs of council housing in Glasgow following the transfer of that housing to a housing association. Those capital costs were worth much more than the amount of attendance allowance at stake. The Scottish Executive was on stronger ground in this case, as a precedent had already been set for transferring such loan liability to the Treasury where there had been voluntary transfers of council housing in England. The Glasgow transfer was, however, far larger than any transfer that had previously taken place in England; the capital value written off was apparently £196 million).[37]

The 2004 Spending Review is interesting for the Treasury's use of it to try to shape devolved spending within the block grant. Interviewing indicates that, as part of the levels of spending it agreed with the devolved administrations then (which involved significant increases for all of them), it sought to require them to allocate significant amounts to capital spending as well as revenue, in line with the plans it had for spending in England (and which it could require Whitehall departments to adhere to). In effect, the Treasury was seeking to ensure that the devolved administrations invest in capital assets rather than blow their gains on enhanced public services (which might be popular in the short term but does not accord with longer-term Treasury priority). This was regardless of local circumstances and needs, and is not

36 See for example 'Westminster rejects McLeish case on £20m for elderly care', *The Herald* (Glasgow), 25 September 2001.
37 See *Scottish Devolution Monitoring Report* (London: The Constitution Unit, August 2003), para. 8.2.

apparent from the Spending Review white paper (which merely repeats wording about the indicated levels of capital and current spending being 'indicative', which was used in past Spending Review white papers).[38] Clearly this has a profound effect on the devolved administrations, if they indeed comply with it, which they feel obliged to do.

The decision made in the summer of 2005 about the timing and nature of the next Spending Review is even more important. By announcing that the next Spending Review would be deferred a year, and be a 'comprehensive' one, Gordon Brown made a decision of considerable significance for the devolved institutions. Devolved elections are scheduled for May 2007. The review will therefore finish shortly after the elections are held, rather than ten or eleven months before them. Instead of being a major potential issue in the election campaign – especially if, with the end of the Objective 1 programme, the outcome is harsh for Wales – the issue will be shelved. No doubt this will confer an advantage for Labour in the devolved elections, even if its extent is unclear. This was not, however, a case where the Treasury responded to (or acted despite) lobbying from the devolved administrations. Rather, it did not involve or consult them (or the territorial Offices in Whitehall) at all.[39] There is no reason to think that the decision was taken with a view to affecting the 2007 elections – but it appears to have given scant consideration to the effects of its decision on devolved matters.

The picture that emerges from this discussion shows the Treasury not simply as an automated calculating-machine when it comes to funding the devolved administrations. While the block grant and formula system distances it from the most important decisions (both about the overall funding of the devolved administrations and what they do with that funding), the Treasury is active and engaged with them regarding a range of issues, some technical, some highly political, and some a mix of both. Its engagement with the devolved administrations is overwhelmingly informal, mainly at official rather than ministerial level, and often bilateral. Despite that, however, it often acts quite autonomously in taking decisions that affect devolved matters. Simply

38 HM Treasury, *2004 Spending Review: New public spending plans 2005–08*, Cm 6237 (London: The Stationery Office, 2004).

39 The written statement to Parliament announcing the change makes no mention of the implications for the devolved administrations of the decision; HC Deb, 19 July 2005, cols 55–6 WS. That statement mentioned that the Review would 'take a zero based approach to assessing the effectiveness of departments' existing spending in delivering the outputs to which they are committed', with no indication of how the Barnett formula would relate to that. In October 2005 the Chief Secretary to the Treasury did, however, confirm in a written answer that there were no plans to change the Barnett formula: HC Deb, 18 October 2005, col. 934W.

put, it makes up its own mind. Even if the big issues are not open to discussion, it can have a powerful influence through more routine matters.

Assessing the power of the Treasury

Trying to assess the power of the Treasury is not straightforward. However, the resource-dependency framework set out in the introduction serves as a useful way of trying to find a broader structure to the relationship than is shown by a number of isolated incidents.

On one level, and very crudely, the Treasury is hugely powerful in relation to the devolved administrations. It has the money on which they depend and which they seek. Without that money they are unable to act, and for practical purposes they have no other source of funding. Thus the devolved administrations can be seen as wholly dependent on the Treasury and its pleasure. Moreover, the Treasury is responsible for the formulation of the rules (the *Statement of Funding Policy* and so forth) by which it determines the basis of allocating that money to the devolved administrations. Without directly interfering in the basis of allocations it could do so less blatantly, by the way it applies those rules. Similarly, the Treasury has complete discretion about bypassing the formula or allowing claims on the UK Reserve. It has used that discretion before, and no doubt will again. Both in terms of financial resources, and the legal resources relating to use of those resources, the Treasury is extremely powerful.

In terms of organisational resources, the Treasury has superior resources to the devolved administrations. It is true that each of the devolved administrations has more staff currently deployed on intergovernmental finance matters than does the Treasury. However, many of these are concerned either with routine aspects of financial management, and even many of those working on allocation-related matters are concerned with the more mechanical aspects (checking the calculations of sums to be transferred to the devolved administrations), and each administration has at most only two or three people working on policy aspects of Barnett. This means that the situation in Scotland and Wales is very similar to that in the UK Government. Moreover, while the Treasury allocates few staff to dealing with territorial finance, it could allocate more if it needed to, given its complement of highly skilled staff working on other issues who could be transferred to devolution matters if need arose. Such skilled staff are more common in Whitehall than in Cardiff or Edinburgh, and the devolved administrations would have difficulties finding substantial numbers of staff who were already knowledgeable about the finance issues involved.

Similarly, in relation to lobbying resources, the Treasury can outweigh the devolved administrations. There is little difficulty for the Treasury in securing access to the most senior UK Government ministers or the UK Cabinet and its committees (where any dispute would ultimately be considered) to have its concerns heard. The policy agenda (and the news agenda too) are driven by the UK Government's preoccupations, usually meaning English ones. It is very hard for the devolved administrations to put their own concerns onto the agenda as a result. By contrast, the devolved administrations would have to approach such UK bodies through the territorial Secretary of State, whom they would have to convince to bring their argument to the table and speak in favour of it. If the Secretary of State declined (a serious step but not an inconceivable one) there would be little recourse left for the devolved administration as bringing it to the JMC would probably be unhelpful.[40] Moreover, the very different interests of Scotland, Wales and Northern Ireland in spending matters mean that it would be hard for them to form alliances; 'ganging up' on financial matters is unlikely often to be an option.

But the disparity between the Treasury and the devolved administrations is perhaps greatest in relation to information.[41] There is, of course, a large amount of statistical data extant about various aspects of the allocation of UK public spending and the performance of the UK economy, and much of that is disaggregated to regional level. However, a recurrent issue is the degree to which certain sorts of information are not gathered at all, or are gathered but kept by the Treasury to itself and not disclosed to the devolved administrations (or the broader public). An example of the data not gathered is vividly illustrated by the work done by Iain McLean and others to establish actual amounts of public spending broken down across the English regions.[42] This was commissioned as a piece of outside research because the information was not collected within government, and was originally sought by the Office of the Deputy Prime Minister (concerned with regional government and consequently with differing levels of dependence on public spending), with the Treasury only joining in subsequently. The scope of the research was limited to spending in the English regions (not the devolved territories) because of

40 See chapter 8 for further discussion.
41 I am grateful to David Heald and an official who must remain anonymous for explaining to me why this issue is important and what sorts of data are lacking.
42 *Identifying the Flow of Domestic and European Expenditure into the English Regions.* Report of a research project to the Office of the Deputy Prime Minister, September 2003. Available at www.nuff.ox.ac.uk/Users/McLean. This work has affected subsequent releases of official statistics. See HM Treasury and National Statistics, *Public Expenditure Statistical Analyses 2005*, Cm 6521 (London: The Stationery Office, 2005), paras 8.2–8.4.

the political sensitivities involved, but still managed to produce striking findings. Some departments, it appeared, had calculated their 'regional' spending by simply disaggregating their total spending on a per capita basis. This meant their account showed that the most populous regions were those in which they spent most – regardless of where departmental spending actually went. The political sensitivity of some of this information – for example, about how much is spent on social security benefits by region – is plain.

Beyond this, there are serious deficiencies in the available data. Some data do not exist, or at least not in any accessible form; simply setting out what the Barnett consequentials are in a particular year is not something routinely done (or at least published) by any government.[43] In other cases, the various sets of data in the public domain do not clearly interact or overlap with each other – the Public Expenditure Statistical Analyses, for example, cover both devolved and non-devolved functions and lump all public spending together without regard for which government spends the money. Access to the Treasury's public expenditure database, in particular, appears to be tightly guarded. While the devolved administrations can be expected to have reasonable information about their own activities, when it comes to the overall position of their area (for example, its economic performance) they do not have the resources to generate much for themselves. In Scotland, *GERS* is a partial exception, but has serious limitations.[44] It is also worth noting that the overarching Concordat on Statistics first concluded in 1999 appears to be of little value in practice, that the Treasury has extensive statutory powers to require information from the devolved administrations, and that the bilateral concordats between the Treasury and the devolved administrations (which duplicate the statutory powers) similarly place heavy emphasis on the information to be supplied by the devolved administration to the Treasury rather than on what the Treasury will supply to the devolved administration.[45] They are therefore dependent on the UK Government for information about public spending – on devolved

43 A notable exception is to be found in table 10.1 on p. 153 of Heald and McLeod, 'Beyond Barnett?'. See also Heald and McLeod, 'Embeddedness of UK Devolution Finance within the Public Expenditure System' for an explanation of the difficulty of tracing Barnett-related increases from one year to another, and for an attempt to do so.

44 See Goudie, '*GERS* and Fiscal Autonomy' for a discussion.

45 *Memorandum of Understanding and Supplementary Agreements between the United Kingdom Government, Scottish Ministers, the Cabinet of the National Assembly for Wales and the Northern Ireland Executive Committee*, Cm 5240 (London: The Stationery Office, 2001) (henceforth 'Memorandum of Understanding'). Annex E: Concordat on Statistics. The statutory powers are in Scotland Act 1998, s. 96, Northern Ireland Act 1988 s. 67, and Government of Wales Act 1998, s. 123.

functions in England, and on non-devolved functions (which can profoundly affect devolved ones) across the whole of the UK, as well as about the performance of the whole UK economy, and that of their part of the UK.

This suggests that the Treasury remains enormously powerful in relation to the devolved administrations. The impression of limited actual power created by the terms of the *Statement of Funding Policy* and the use of the Barnett formula is misleading; both the overall financial framework of devolution and the way that special cases are dealt with in that overall framework give the Treasury immense scope to make decisions and deny similar power to the devolved administrations.

How the Treasury uses its power

Saying that the Treasury is powerful is not the end of the story. It leads to the questions of how conscious the Treasury is of its power (and the effect that consciousness has), and of how it uses its power in the light of that consciousness. These are not easy to answer either.

Regarding the first, Treasury officials are conscious that they have a considerable degree of power, to judge by what they say in public forums, as well as what they have said in interview. That is not surprising; within government, it is axiomatic that Treasury officials at any level are powerful, and any minister or official in a spending department would normally treat them with great respect.[46] Interviewing confirms that finance officials in the devolved administrations share the sort of respect, even deference, towards the Treasury that their Whitehall counterparts have. However, it is less clear that Treasury officials are aware of quite how powerful they are in relation to the devolved institutions, or are regarded as being. The popular view of them in Scotland, Wales or Northern Ireland, as vastly powerful creatures capable of reshaping the financial future of that part of the UK with their little fingers, is gravely at odds with their self-perception as careful, rule-bound dutiful public servants. While decisions taken by the Treasury (of which the finding of match funding for Wales's Objective 1 funding, and the moving of the time and scope of the 2006 Spending Review are the most notable examples) have had major effects on the devolved administrations, the officials in the Treasury have shown only

---

46 Thain and Wright note that Treasury officials customarily deal with counterparts in spending departments who are one rung above them in the civil service hierarchy; thus departmental expenditure controllers at the former grade 5 deal with principal finance officers, customarily (former) grade 3, and so on; *The Treasury and Whitehall*, 97 and 187–9. For the general role of expenditure controllers in the Treasury, see ibid. chapters 6, 7 and 9.

limited awareness of the significance of those actions. To the extent they have, they consider that because such actions are within the powers reserved to the Treasury under the devolution arrangements, they are entitled to do so and that criticism of those decisions is somehow improper.

To an outside observer, this is largely an issue of perspective. From a Treasury point of view, the devolved administrations are small beer. They account for a very small proportion of overall UK public spending (less than 10 per cent of all public spending, according to the data shown in table 5.1). The decisions taken by the Treasury about devolution finance matters are, by Treasury standards, of limited significance. For the devolved administrations, however, they are vital; these decisions affect a very large part of the financial resources available to the devolved administrations, and other matters of great significance. There is no sign that the implications for the devolved territories play a major role in Treasury deliberations about decisions which have a major impact on them, as with the re-timing and expansion of scope of the 2007 Comprehensive Spending Review. Rather, such decisions are taken as it seems best to the Treasury. When it comes to the 2007 Spending Review, the fact that this affects the devolved elections appears to have been a very minor consideration for the Treasury, if it was a consideration at all.

Yet the devolved administrations cannot count on being of very limited concern or significance to the Treasury to get their way. While the Treasury sometimes responds to lobbying from the devolved administrations, on other occasions it just acts on its own initiative, dispensing even with the informal bilateral channels. As an actor, it is effectively autonomous and unfettered. The devolved administrations remain dependent on it, and continue to function from a Treasury point of view in very much the same way they did as UK Government departments. However, as devolution has formalised the Barnett formula and made it more rigid, while the devolved administrations have become less closely integrated into the Whitehall machine than they were as UK departments, they can find themselves somewhat worse off. Their interests may be overlooked or marginalised, and they certainly cannot count on formal institutions to help them advance their position. From a Treasury view, devolution makes managing territorial finance much easier, as negotiations over funds occur more rarely – a negotiation with a lead department, in respect of English services, will then trigger an automatic consequential for the devolved administrations. Unlike the period before devolution, when interviewing suggests that the Scottish element of a spending round would be one of the most difficult and politically fraught of negotiations with a spending department (despite the formula and the relatively small amounts of money), devolution has indeed made spending rounds much more straightforward and non-political. Whether that sort of relative ease would survive a more disputatious environment, with governments less willing to avoid disagreement with each other, and devolved administrations determined to do things differently from the UK Government, remains a moot question. The Treasury retains a high degree of power, on both the high constitutional level and the day-to-day operational one. In more contentious conditions, the restraints on its use of that power would be the same as they presently are – political in nature, or arising from administrative practicality. The Treasury's power to reshape the *Statement of Funding Policy* unilaterally is probably unusable; such a review would need, in the real world, to involve all parties (and neutral observers).

Moreover, the inherent problems of the Barnett formula remain. Much of the criticism directed at it is justified, and even the formula's supporters (at least, those outside Scotland) do so out of a combination of a desire to avoid the massively difficult process of replacing it and a sense it does some sort of rough justice. These problems inevitably underlie the relationship between the Treasury (and the UK Government generally) and the devolved administrations, and also consume a good deal of the Treasury's attention behind the scenes. What is more important in practice are the lower-profile powers that the Treasury has, and the way it uses those. In general, the Treasury exercises that power cautiously and with restraint. While the Treasury clearly retains many compelling advantages over the devolved administrations, there is only limited evidence to suggest that it has used that power to interfere directly in devolved matters. However, there are exceptions. It has sometimes acted contrary to their interests or wishes (as it does for every part of the UK Government as well), but it has not sought to compel them to do something they did not wish to do, or to prevent them from doing something they did wish to. (The same cannot be said of every Whitehall department.[47]) When it has acted contrary to their interests this has as often been due to inadvertence, or to other considerations taking priority. In general, it has been careful not to involve itself in devolved matters, and has left these to the devolved administrations.

Perhaps the best way to characterise the effect of the block and formula system on the practice of intergovernmental relations is to compare it with an elephant in a fairly small room. The elephant is too big to ignore, but everyone is too polite to comment on its presence. From time to time, the elephant swishes its tail or trunk, and that has effects no-one can ignore; but it is debatable whether the elephant intended to cause any harm by its action, and even when it did it probably did not intend its actions to have the effect they did. But it is wrong to blame the consequences of tail-swishing just on the tail; they are a consequence of having an elephant in the room, and not an animal more suited to domestic living.

47 See further chapter 8.

6

The practical outcomes of devolution: policy-making across the UK

Alan Trench and Holly Jarman

This chapter is intended to survey the trends that have emerged regarding policy-making and policy practice across the United Kingdom since devolution. Its concern is not so much with explaining why (or even how) those trends, and the differences in policy that they reveal, have come about, but simply with establishing at least some of the main respects in which the devolved administrations have used their autonomy to depart from UK Government practice. Its aim is to establish a sort of 'outcome assessment' of the impact of devolution, by looking at what governments have actually been able to do rather than what the rules and processes of devolution suggest about their powers.[1] It therefore needs to be read in conjunction with the detailed study of health policy by Scott Greer in chapter 7.

Charting post-devolution policy differences is not straightforward. One problem is with the concept of policy *divergence* (a term the chapter avoids as far as possible). This term implies that there is a norm from which others are departing. In a UK context, this implies that the UK Government's approach remains that norm and that, by doing things differently, there is somehow a departure from that norm by the devolved institutions. The concept therefore carries with it a set of references to the UK level that devolution was supposed to have undermined. However, it is hard to think of a better term to describe the practical outcomes of policy-making in a nutshell. Related to this is the issue of whether the point of devolution is to enable devolved institutions and territories to do things differently, or simply to enable them to make their own choices (which may in fact be the same as those of the UK Government). Is devolution supposed to create a mechanism for magnifying differences, or to reflect respect for identity and territorial politics based on

---

1 For general surveys of post-devolution policy, see Adams, J. and Robinson, P. (eds), *Devolution in Practice: Public policy differences within the UK* (London: ippr, 2002); Adams, J. and Schmuecker, K., *Devolution in Practice 2006: Public policy differences within the UK* (London: ippr, 2006).

that identity?[2] Even setting aside these conceptual problems, there are practical problems – how does one identify or measure such policy differences?
Using legislative provisions as an indicator has many attractions, as legislation
is published, public and accessible.[3] However, governments use legislation for
many purposes, major policy changes can be introduced without necessarily
seeking new legislation (at least, new primary legislation) for them, which this
indicator will miss – while legislative changes may not, in fact, be brought into
effect after being passed by the legislature.[4] Moreover, understanding how
exactly a legislative provision affects practice on the ground is not straightforward – but an accurate measure of policy development needs to look at
that, even if that is a much more time-consuming and demanding exercise.

As James Mitchell shows in chapter 2, variation in government practice,
including the making and delivery of policy, has a long pedigree across the
UK. However, the extent of that variation itself varied. The traditional view
was that, before devolution, the Scottish Office would take a Whitehall policy
and 'put a kilt on it' (that is, implement substantially the same policy but tailor
it in matters of detail to local circumstances). This was also sometimes called
'tartanisation'. The Welsh Office was regarded as far less active, often simply
copying out and translating into Welsh the policy adopted in Whitehall.[5]
Northern Ireland instead tended to continue doing what it had been,
responding to major Whitehall shifts but with policy made largely by an old-
fashioned civil service machine, seldom by politicians (and certainly not ones
elected by those whom they were serving). This impression was always somewhat misleading; in Wales, for example, an array of organisations to promote
economic development (such as the Welsh Development Agency and the
Development Board for Rural Wales), able to disburse substantial amounts to
attract inward investment during the 1980s and 1990s, was in marked contrast to the restraint generally prevailing in England. Even before 1999, under
a single government, there was considerable difference across the UK.

This chapter will attempt to assess a range of policy differences as they
have developed since 1999. Inevitably these are brief treatments, as in order
to gain the perspective that breadth can give one must lose the nuance that

2 For an example of this approach, see Kay, A., 'Evaluating Devolution in Wales',
   Political Studies, 51:1 (2003), 51–66.
3 Keating, M., Stevenson, L., Cairney, P. and Taylor, K., 'Does Devolution Make a
   Difference? Legislative output and policy divergence in Scotland', *Journal of
   Legislative Studies*, 9:3 (2003), 110–39.
4 See Daintith, T., 'The Techniques of Government', in Jowell, J. and Oliver, D. (eds),
   The Changing Constitution (Oxford: Oxford University Press, 3rd edn, 1994).
5 See for example Griffith, D., 'The Welsh Office and Welsh Autonomy', *Public
   Administration*, 77:1 (1999), 703–807.

more detailed studies might unveil. However, our aim is to form a view about the overall use that devolved institutions have made of their policy-making powers, and such a sketch should give at least an indication of what the devolved institutions have done (and not done) with those powers.

Social policy

Many of the policy areas that have hit the headlines over the last few years have related to social policy. The Scottish decision, in 2001, to introduce free long-term care for the elderly was controversial and caused considerable displeasure in Whitehall.[6] The actual impact of the policy is less clear; it has been said that only about 1700 people benefit from it at any time.[7] The flow north from England of elderly people to take advantage of the Scottish policy may have been expected by headline writers but cooler heads will not be surprised that it has failed to materialise.

Wales has looked to following suit but found both legal powers and finance stopped it. Scotland has also sought to introduce a different and more inclusive approach to social exclusion, but found its limited powers (in this case, the overlap between devolved matters and the reserved field of social security) made it hard to have much of an impact.[8]

The most notable innovation has probably been the notion of a Children's Commissioner, designed to safeguard the rights of children being looked after by the public sector. Initially a response to the scandals of widespread child abuse in various children's homes in north Wales, it was an early flagship project of the National Assembly for Wales and the legislation was passed just before Westminster was dissolved for the 2001 UK general election.[9] Even at that stage there was a heated debate about the powers of the Commissioner

---

6 For a detailed discussion, see Simeon, R., 'Free Personal Care: Policy divergence and social citizenship', in Hazell, R. (ed.), *The State of the Nations 2003: The third year of devolution in the United Kingdom* (Exeter: Imprint Academic, 2003). The intergovernmental aspects of this are also discussed in chapter 8.

7 In February 2004 the First Minister claimed that over 40,000 people were already benefiting from it, presumably since its introduction in July 2002. See *Scotland Devolution Monitoring Report* (London: The Constitution Unit, May 2004), para. 11.8.

8 Fawcett, H., 'The Making of Social Justice Policy in Scotland: Devolution and social exclusion', in Trench, A. (ed.), *Has Devolution Made a Difference? The State of the Nations 2004* (Exeter: Imprint Academic, 2004).

9 See Hollingsworth, K. and Douglas, G., 'Creating a children's champion for Wales? The Care Standards Act 2000 (Part V) and the Children's Commissioner for Wales Act 2001', *Modern Law Review*, 65 (2002), 58–78 for a detailed discussion.

over non-devolved matters (young offenders' institutions, secure children's homes and other placements arising from the criminal justice system). The idea of a Children's Commissioner was also adopted in Scotland and Northern Ireland, and then picked up by the UK Government for England – at which point the debate about the powers of the Welsh Commissioner returned with teeth, as the English Commissioner's powers included children in Wales who were involved in the criminal justice system.[10] Such children are therefore within the remit of the English Commissioner, even if they live in Wales, are in an institution in Wales and share a room with someone who (being outside the criminal justice system) falls under the Welsh Commissioner's functions. One key idea of the Children's Commissioner – a single person whom children with concerns about their experiences at the hands of a system they may not understand may approach with their concerns – has therefore been undermined. Despite a failure by the minister or lead department (the Department of Health) to consult the Welsh Commissioner or to heed the views expressed by the Welsh Assembly Government, it pressed ahead – to encounter a stinging Parliamentary rebuke from the Commons Welsh Affairs Committee.[11]

Policing and criminal justice

Policing and, more broadly, criminal justice is a curious area when it comes to understanding policy differences. This is of course an area devolved only in Scotland, but it is a matter of high importance for the UK as a state. Some differences have been evident, notably a less aggressive approach to law and order during the Scottish Parliament's first session (1999–2003). This appears largely to have been due to the influence of Jim Wallace as Justice and Home Affairs Minister – one of few instances where party-political differences have had a clear effect.[12] Wallace was moved following the 2003 Scottish election and subsequent coalition negotiations, and replaced by Cathy Jamieson who

10 The Acts that established the respective Children's Commissioners are: Children Act 2004 (England, with some wider functions); Commissioner for Children and Young People (Scotland) Act 2003, Part V of the Care Standards Act 2000, and the Children's Commissioner for Wales Act 2001(Wales), and the Children's Commissioner Act (Northern Ireland) 2001.

11 House of Commons Welsh Affairs Committee, Session 2003–04 5th Report, *The Powers of the Children's Commissioner for Wales*, HC 538 (London: The Stationery Office, 2004).

12 Compare the Scottish and UK Freedom of Information Acts, or the UK Regulation of Investigatory Powers Act 2001 and the Regulation of Investigatory Powers (Scotland) Act 2000, as well as Scottish reluctance to embrace the anti-social behaviour agenda of the UK Government.

took a line that is both tougher and closer to that of the UK Government, notably over anti-social behaviour and low-level disorder. On policing, differences across the border were already palpable before devolution, if only ones which close observers noticed, and which have continued (if not developed) post-devolution.[13] Why the UK was willing to transfer control of such sensitive matters beyond its control is something of a puzzle. A small part of the reason is that direct UK interests have not been affected, and that policing for key installations relating to reserved matters (military bases by the Ministry of Defence Police, railways by the British Transport Police and nuclear installations by what are now the Civil Nuclear Police) remains in the hands of all-UK forces. (To ensure this is so, a number of Westminster bills such as the Armed Forces Act 2001, Anti-terrorism Crime and Security Act 2001 and the Energy Act 2004, have been subject to Holyrood's assent under the Sewel convention.)

Another part of the answer is that a range of cross-Britain coordination mechanisms exist for a range of practical and operational matters, and in practice the two sets of police forces are closely intertwined. One such mechanism – the National Criminal Intelligence Service – is relatively well known, and embraces a number of existing intelligence units as well as newer ones. One of its six operational bases is in Scotland and the Executive is also represented on its service authority. (By contrast, the more operationally oriented National Crime Squad functions only in England and Wales, though it has links with Scottish counterparts.) The role, and in some case the existence, of others are less well known. The Police Information Technology Organisation sets UK-wide standards and practices for IT and runs the core network, the Home Office organises purchasing arrangements for other items from the mundane (police vehicles, uniforms and 'personal protective equipment') to the specialist (such as radio systems), while the Association of Chief Police Officers (ACPO; for England and Wales) liaises extensively with its Scottish counterpart, ACPOS, over a wide range of operational procedures and protocols. Similarly, while inspection of the police is a devolved matter (carried out by HM Inspectorate of Constabulary for Scotland), the Inspectorate's annual report notes that 'close links are maintained with HMIC England and Wales', including carrying out joint inspections of police forces that operate across the border (such as the British Transport Police or the former UK Atomic Energy Authority police).[14] In addition to this, senior police officers appear to have a

13 Walker, N., *Policing in a Changing Constitutional Order* (London: Sweet & Maxwell, 2000), chap. 5.
14 HM Inspectorate of Constabulary, *Annual Report of Her Majesty's Inspectorate of Constabulary for Scotland 2004/2005*, SE/2005/206 (Edinburgh: The Stationery Office, 2005).

clear sense that they remain part of a single professional force. At the same time, both in England and Wales and in Scotland, local accountability and control of policing is very limited, emphasising the importance of police (particularly chief constables') accountability to ministers. In England and Wales, the existing tools were found inadequate while David Blunkett was Home Secretary, who sought to ensure he had the power to require a police authority to require a Chief Constable to resign.[15] This power was later used against Humberside Police Authority. No such powers have been sought, or exist, for Scotland. Similarly, the Home Office's radical ideas in 2004–5 for restructuring policing in England (with larger forces and a heavier emphasis on local activity and accountability) were not followed in Scotland.

Despite this, Scotland has followed a UK lead on a number of matters. The war on terror has been responsible for many of these (and it is worth noting that the UK's reserved powers include not just 'national security' but also 'emergency powers' and 'special powers, and other special provisions, for dealing with terrorism').[16] One notable example has been the Anti-terrorism, Crime and Security Act 2001. Others include the fight against serious crime – the Proceeds of Crime Act 2002 (which provides for the seizure of property acquired through crime, even if there has been no criminal conviction) in many ways resembles a pre-devolution statute, applying similar provisions to England and Wales, Scotland and Northern Ireland and providing for there to be a single assets recovery agency.[17] This approach was characterised as 'common sense' by officials in both governments in interview. Similar considerations apply to the Serious and Organised Crime Agency (established by the Serious and Organised Crime and Police Act 2005); both Acts mix measures relating only to England and Wales with ones extending to all of Great Britain or the United Kingdom, and relating to both devolved and non-devolved matters.

These variations reflect not only the different policy approaches and political environments in which the governments north and south of the Tweed operate, but also the way in which they deal with each other. Interviewing suggests that liaison between the Scottish Justice Department's policing officials and their counterparts in the Home Office in London is limited, low level

15 See Part 3 of the Police Reform Act 2002.
16 Scotland Act 1998, Schedule 5, Head B8.
17 It is worth noting that the agency is of course discharging cross-UK functions relating to a devolved matter – but its director is appointed by the Home Secretary acting alone, without even an obligation to consult his or her Scottish counterpart. The Home Secretary does have to consult the Scottish Ministers when appointing the chairman and director-general of the Serious and Organised Crime Agency, however.

(mid-level officials – not senior officials or ministers), largely ad hoc and largely also initiated by Scotland rather than the UK Government.

Local government

The relationship with local government has been central for the devolved administrations. Local governments in Scotland and Wales are important in a number of ways – as ways of delivering public services, as major large-scale institutions which before devolution were the only territorially based political actors in the area, and to a degree important members of the political coalitions that led to devolution, as well as training-grounds for many individuals who later became members of the Scottish Parliament or National Assembly for Wales. In both countries local government is well organised, with the Convention of Scottish Local Authorities (COSLA) and the Welsh Local Government Association (WLGA) constituting strong representative and lobbying organisations. Northern Ireland is different – even compared with the usual ways in which Northern Ireland is different. Local government there has been comparatively weak since rule from Stormont, with very limited functions (principally housing and planning) and key public services such as health, social services and education delivered through a network of quangos. Despite that, council membership has been a high priority for local politicians, even trumping membership of the Northern Ireland Assembly when that was in operation.

The variations in local government start with issues of structure and area. Reorganisation before devolution created small numbers of relatively large unitary authorities in Scotland and Wales, thanks to decisions taken by the Secretaries of State. For England, the process of reorganisation was more complicated, with the Environment Secretary making decisions on advice given to him by the Local Government Commission. That has led to a complex mixed system of two-tier councils for some rural and suburban areas, and (in effect) unitary authorities in Greater London, the areas of the former metropolitan counties and 'new counties' established in 1974, major provincial cities and some other provincial suburban areas.[18] In London, there is also now an additional layer of government in the form of the Greater London Authority.[19] By comparison with England, the systems in Scotland and Wales are simplicity exemplified. Across England, resistance to further reorganisation remains

18 For a summary, see Byrne, T., *Local Government in Britain: Everyone's guide to how it works* (Harmondsworth: Penguin, 7th edn, 2000).
19 See Sandford, M., 'The Governance of London: Strategic governance and policy divergence', in Trench (ed.), *Has Devolution Made A Difference?*.

strong, and the requirement for further reform may have been a factor in the 'no' vote in the referendum on regional government for the North East in November 2004. Despite a need for reform of local government in Northern Ireland for many years, this was not attempted under direct rule and only tentatively under devolution, with the establishment of a Review of Public Administration in 2002. In November 2004 the Northern Ireland Office published its proposals for local government reform, including a reduction in the number of authorities from 26 to 7, in education boards from 5 to 1 and the consolidation of health boards along the lines of the 7 new authorities.[20] Although divergence is rooted in these historical differences, the character of central–local relationships has changed more dramatically post-devolution as local authorities turn to face the new institutions.

Differing regional structures and distributions of power have resulted in three degrees of 'partnership'. In England, the concept of 'partnership' is exported from the centre but relations remain one-way, with a heavy emphasis on audit and inspection.[21] The Scottish Executive exercises a lighter regulatory oversight, combining informal guidance with greater local government autonomy while retaining tight control of finance. In Wales, the Assembly is more dependent upon local government to deliver services and the Assembly is also under a statutory obligation to work through a partnership council with local authorities (discussed in more detail below). The result has been the creation of comparatively close relationships and the use of less formal policy instruments.[22] Given this variety of structures, finding pre-existing policy differences, such as the distinctive Welsh and Scottish variations on 'Best Value' which emerged before devolution, is not surprising.[23] While Best Value has become a formal process-driven activity in England, reshaping a wide range of local government services and activities, and rewarding high-performing councils by loosening the regime, in Scotland a less onerous statutory framework has reduced the impact on local government without discriminating among local authorities.

20 Wilson, R., in *Northern Ireland Devolution Monitoring Report* (London: The Constitution Unit, November 2004).
21 See also Travers, T., 'Local and Central Government', in Seldon, A. and Kavanagh, D. (eds), *The Blair Effect 2001–5* (Cambridge: Cambridge University Press, 2005).
22 Rawlings, R., *Delineating Wales: Constitutional, legal and administrative aspects of national devolution* (Cardiff: University of Wales Press, 2003), chap. 10.
23 Boyne, G. A., Gould-Williams, J., Law, J. and Walker, R. M., 'Best Value in Welsh Local Government: Progress and prospects', *Local Government Studies*, 25:2 (1999), 68–86; Midwinter, A. and McGarvey, N., 'Developing Best Value in Scotland: Concepts and contradictions', *Local Government Studies*, 25:2 (1999), 87–101.

Local government in England remains characterised by hierarchy, with the centre keen to impart concepts of diverse local solutions and forms of representation to local authorities. This is, in part, influenced by the centre's vision for the public sector, with local authorities being pushed to act as commissioners of services rather than providers. Partnerships in England have been envisioned as a means of local working rather than enhancing relations with higher tiers of government, and so authorities have tended to retain the well-established pattern of central–local links in existence before devolution. Central government initiatives include Regional Development Agencies, set up in 1999–2000 to improve economic development, and Local Strategic Partnerships, established along local authority boundaries to coordinate service provision in deprived areas.[24]

Other reforms reflect this tendency to prescribe from the centre, but the UK Government has not always got its own way. Under the Local Government Act 2000, councils in England were compelled to adopt a new form of arrangements for political management, by choosing from a set of fixed options including a Cabinet system or a directly elected mayor. Despite strong promotion of elected mayors (notably by the Prime Minister) the option proved attractive to only a few authorities, none of them the major urban authorities for which it was intended. The Scottish Executive rejected these prescriptive choices, opting instead to allow each authority to conduct its own review. Only a few authorities came out in favour of English-style strong executives or elected provosts.[25] Pressure from Welsh authorities allowed them to choose a fourth rural-friendly option, but in Wales too, councils were reluctant to adopt the preferred mayoral model.[26] Plans to set up English regional assemblies have also been firmly rejected, but this failure reflects a lack of enthusiasm among local residents and party political elites alike, who saw the new bodies as an additional layer of complexity in exchange for little benefit.[27]

Central–local relations in Wales lie at the opposite end of the scale from the hierarchical approach of England. The National Assembly's powers are comparatively weak and its tradition of government much more recent – local

24 Wilson, D. and Game, C., *Local Government in the United Kingdom* (Basingstoke: Palgrave Macmillan, 3rd edn, 2002), 89; Office of the Deputy Prime Minister, *Evaluation of Local Strategic Partnerships: Report of a survey of all English LSPs* (London: Office of the Deputy Prime Minister, February 2003).
25 McGarvey, N., 'Intergovernmental Relations in Scotland Post Devolution', *Local Government Studies*, 28:3 (2002), 29–48.
26 Laffin, M., Taylor, G. and Thomas, A., *A New Partnership? The National Assembly for Wales and local government* (York: Joseph Rowntree Foundation, 2002).
27 Jeffery, C., 'Devolution and Local Government', *Publius* 36:1 (2006), 57–73; McGarvey, 'Intergovernmental Relations in Scotland Post Devolution'.

government accounts for 40 per cent of public expenditure in Wales, and so the Assembly must rely on authorities to deliver services and provide information.[28] Close links have been built upon older ties between local government, Welsh Office ministers and the Labour Party, but with new emphasis upon the distinctiveness of Wales.[29] This 'closeness' has been expressed in the 'Welsh Way' as espoused by the former Minister for Finance, Local Government and Communities, Edwina Hart – close working between local and regional government that emphasises partnership and local autonomy rather than executive coercion or formal frameworks.[30] The report *Freedom and Responsibility for Local Government*, published on St David's Day 2002, emphasised partnership with local authorities while delineating responsibilities of each sphere of government. Policy agreements have been used since November 2001 to set targets while allowing for small variation across local authorities, while the Community Strategy endowed councils with new powers of 'community leadership'. This preference for softer regulation is also visible in the abandonment of league tables and reluctance to use more formal hypothecation.[31]

The 26-member Local Government Partnership Council established by the Government of Wales Act 1998 and the work of the WLGA have proved to be key instruments in this strategy. However, meetings of the Partnership Council have tended to be formal, restrained by its openness to the public and the need to make decisions by consensus, and much of the real work of the Council is undertaken in committees. The WLGA, on the other hand, has had a considerable degree of success in influencing the Assembly by choosing to behave as a think tank.[32]

The 'Welsh Way' is time-consuming, however, involving both Assembly Members and local authorities in extensive consultation. Some councils have chosen to slim down by combining departments and functions in recent years, and their capacity to follow this path may have suffered as a result. Policy agreements have also been criticised by local representatives for remaining overly prescriptive.[33]

28 Thomas, S., 'Local Government and the National Assembly: A "Welsh Way" to public sector reform?', *Wales Law Journal*, 2:1 (2002), 41–50, at 42; Jeffery, 'Devolution and Local Government'.

29 Laffin, Taylor and Thomas, *A New Partnership?*.

30 Rawlings, *Delineating Wales*. See Welsh Assembly Government, *Freedom and Responsibility for Local Government* (Cardiff: Welsh Assembly Government, 2002). At: www.wales.gov.uk/subilocalgov/content/freeresponse-e.pdf; accessed 17 August 2005.

31 Rawlings, *Delineating Wales*, 339.

32 Laffin, M., 'Is Regional Centralism Inevitable? The case of the Welsh Assembly', *Regional Studies*, 38:2 (2004), 213–23, at 218–19.

33 Laffin, Taylor and Thomas, *A New Partnership?*.

The Scottish Parliament has become more important for local government than Westminster was, providing a more formal, codified basis for central–local relationships. The Scottish Partnership framework announced in May 2001 was the first ever written protocol between two levels of government in Scotland.[34] The level of contact between MPs and councils has decreased since devolution, as local authorities reorient themselves towards regional government and MSPs.[35] This is easily explained in light of the extent to which the paths of the Executive and local government have crossed – 350 of the 400 commitments contained in the Coalition Partnership Agreement signed in 2003 impacted upon local government.[36] Unlike the National Assembly for Wales, however, the Scottish Parliament has a greater array of formal powers – the Executive is not as reliant upon local government for the delivery of services and therefore there is less need in Scotland for the kind of partnership-building necessary for Welsh government to function.[37] As a result, the goals of local autonomy and national policy have sometimes clashed. As may be expected, it is the financing of local government that has proved to be the Achilles' heel of these new partnerships. Extensive use of ring-fencing by the Scottish Executive to enforce its priorities over local preferences has caused frustration among local government representatives, leaving Scottish councils still at least as financially dependent upon higher tiers of government as English authorities.[38]

How will these partnerships fare in the future? One fundamental question is the sustainability of informal relationships between local and regional government in Scotland and Wales under any future change in the UK administration. In Scotland, informal interpersonal relations which are based primarily on party ties link the two levels.[39] As a result, the Scottish Executive has tended to pay attention to the views of strong local government supporters within the Labour Party. The Liberal Democrats have not been a silent coalition partner, however. The McIntosh report of June 1999, and the Local Government (Scotland) Act 2003 that followed, have cleared a path for the introduction of proportional representation (using the single transferable

34 McAteer, M. and Bennett, M., 'Devolution and Local Government: Evidence from Scotland', *Local Government Studies*, 31:3 (2005), 285–306.
35 Bennett, M., Fairley, J. and McAteer, M., *Devolution in Scotland: The impact on local government* (York: Joseph Rowntree Foundation, 2002).
36 McGarvey, N., in *Scotland Devolution Monitoring Report* (London: The Constitution Unit, August 2003).
37 Thomas, 'Local Government and the National Assembly'.
38 McGarvey, 'Intergovernmental Relations in Scotland Post Devolution'.
39 Bennett, Fairley and McAteer, *Devolution in Scotland*, 11.

vote) in the 2007 local elections despite stiff opposition from the COSLA.[40] A similar recommendation from the Sunderland Commission in Wales has not been acted on by the Assembly Government. Only time will tell whether resulting changes in party representation will disrupt local–regional relations. In Wales, links between Welsh Labour and local government are also integral to the work of the Partnership Council and WLGA.[41] Given that party ties currently constitute much of the network of links between local, regional and central governments, the prospects for these relationships if a change in governing party occurs at the national level are unclear.

Education

Education policy since devolution has built on historic differences across the UK. Key to this are the tradition of Welsh-medium schools (and Welsh-language teaching in other schools in Wales), continued selection at 11 in Northern Ireland, a largely public and comprehensive Scottish system, and the influence of the private and voluntary sectors in England. In general terms, Wales, after an uncertain start involving an abortive attempt to function with two education ministers and extended disagreements over performance-related pay, has laid out a new, divergent path since the publication of *The Learning Country*, in 2001.[42] Scottish education has historically stood out from the rest of the UK in terms of its ethos and personnel and by awarding unique qualifications.[43] Under devolution, Scotland has increased its distinctiveness while attempting to reconcile national standards with local autonomy. Politicians in Northern Ireland have faced new opportunities to tackle under-achievement, but the resumption of rule from London has dampened differences. England has continued to follow a path laid down under previous administrations, but is increasingly a lone voice for diverse provision of education and centrally enforced standards. Let us examine the key areas in more detail.

40 McConnell, A., *Scottish Local Government* (Edinburgh: Edinburgh University Press, 2004).
41 Laffin, Taylor and Thomas, *A New Partnership?*.
42 National Assembly for Wales, *The Learning Country: A paving document: A comprehensive education and lifelong learning programme to 2010 in Wales* (Cardiff: National Assembly for Wales, 2001).
43 Paterson, L., 'The Three Educational Ideologies of the British Labour Party, 1997–2001', *Oxford Review of Education*, 29:2 (2003), 165–86; Raffe, D., 'Devolution and Divergence in Education Policy', ippr North Seminar Paper (2005).

In early-years education, the greatest similarities across the UK can be found, but even here there are distinctions of style.[44] In England, a new, more flexible, 'Foundation Stage' curriculum for 3–5-year-olds was introduced in 2000, including planned activities and time for play based around six 'areas of learning'.[45] The earlier Scottish 3–5 curriculum and the pilot Welsh 'Foundation Phase' have a similar emphasis. The integration of childcare, education and health services is a common theme across the UK. Sure Start Scotland emphasises 'joint working' between education, social work, health and voluntary organisations, while Wales has created integrated children's centres.[46] A review of Northern Ireland early-years provision in 2004 raised the possibility of exploring the integration of care and education as in the English model.[47] England has gone furthest in encouraging the expansion of the private sector but measures to increase provision are widespread, partly due to the previously low level of services across the board.[48] From 1997, the Northern Ireland Department of Education supplemented increased public investment in early-years provision with voluntary and private sector places for the first time. The Executive extended this goal, aiming to provide a free pre-school year place for all children whose parents request one.[49] In Scotland, a new statutory duty was placed on local authorities to provide a pre-school place to the parents of all three- and four-year-olds on demand.[50]

Greater variation can be seen in the form and function of schools. English education policy under New Labour shows continuity with ideas pursued by previous Conservative administrations but initiatives to promote specialisation

44 See Wincott, D., 'Devolution, Social Democracy and Policy Diversity in Britain: The case of early-childhood education and care', in Adams and Schmuecker, *Devolution in Practice 2006*.

45 See Qualifications and Curriculum Authority, *Curriculum Guidance for the Foundation Stage* (London: Qualifications and Curriculum Authority, 2000).

46 See Cunningham-Burley, S., Jamieson, L., Morton, S., Adam, R. and McFarlane, V., *Mapping Sure Start Scotland* (Edinburgh: Centre for Research on Families and Relationships, University of Edinburgh, May 2002).

47 Department of Education, Northern Ireland, *Review of Pre-school Education in Northern Ireland* (June 2004). At: www.deni.gov.uk/about/consultation/ pre_school_review/ConsultationPaper.pdf; accessed 18 August 2005.

48 Watt, J., 'The Under-Fives: From "pre-school education" to "early years services"', in Clark, M. and Munn, P. (eds), *Education in Scotland: Policy and practice from pre-school to secondary* (London: Routledge, 1997), 19–34.

49 Department of Education, Northern Ireland, *Review of Pre-school Education in Northern Ireland*.

50 *Scotland Devolution Monitoring Report* (London: The Constitution Unit, August 2000).

among schools have multiplied.[51] Schools can become specialists in one or several subject areas in order to attract funding from the private sector, and the UK Government has encouraged additional faith-based schools, introduced privately sponsored City Academies (now spreading to other areas as just 'Academies'), Beacon Schools and the Leading Edge Partnership Programme to spread best practice, and proposed 'Foundation Status' to give schools greater financial autonomy and cut out the local education authority. Local authorities now have a duty to advertise requirements for new schools to voluntary and private sector providers, who can step in to run failing schools on short-term contracts.[52]

These centralising initiatives are a stark contrast with stronger local partnerships in Wales and Scotland, however.[53] Wales has most fiercely resisted the English model, pledging no new private sector schools and no specialist schools.[54] There are no plans to introduce specialist schools in Scotland although the 'Schools of Ambition' programme may produce a Scottish variation.[55]

The English model of testing and standards has also been rejected by the devolved administrations. England is now the only part of the UK to retain statutory testing at ages 7, 11 and 14 and school league tables, combining these with a strong focus upon literacy and numeracy. Wales has replaced tests at 7, 11 and 14 with more flexible teacher assessments and focused instead on the reduction of junior class sizes; Scotland has encouraged primary schools to set their own targets, emphasising local accountability through inspection. The first education legislation to pass through the Scottish Parliament placed new duties upon local government to raise standards.[56] Statutory testing for 7-year-olds was abolished under the Northern Ireland Executive[57] but

---

51 See Patterson, 'The Three Educational Ideologies'; Raffe, 'Devolution and Divergence in Education Policy'.
52 Chitty, C., *Education Policy in Great Britain* (Basingstoke: Palgrave, 2004), 75.
53 Bennett, Fairley and McAteer, *Devolution in Scotland*; Reynolds, D. 'Education: Building on difference', in Osmond, J. (ed.), *Second Term Challenge: Can the Welsh Assembly government hold its course?* (Cardiff and London: Institute for Welsh Affairs, November 2005), 43–51. 2005.
54 *Wales Devolution Monitoring Report* (London: The Constitution Unit, November 2001), 17.
55 See Scottish Executive, *Ambitious, Excellent Schools, Our Agenda for Action* (Edinburgh: Scottish Executive, November 2004). At: www.scotland.gov.uk/library5/education/aesaa.pdf; accessed 17 August 2005.
56 *Scotland Devolution Monitoring Report* (London: The Constitution Unit, November 1999).
57 Northern Ireland Executive press release, 'School Performance Tables Not to be Published – McGuinness' (10th January 2001). At www.nics.gov.uk/press/edu/010110e-edu.htm; accessed 3 August 2005.

replacing selection tests at age 11 has proved more difficult. From the start of his term as Education Minister, Martin McGuinness made the abolition of selection his priority – so much so that when a survey of households he commissioned showed widespread support for selection he de-emphasised the results, and announced abolition only on the eve of suspension of the devolved institutions.[58] The UK Government has upheld this decision since the imposition of direct rule, and selection is to be phased out after 2008. After criticism of the rushed modularisation of A Levels, England is moving towards a 14–19 continuum by 2008, when A Levels and GCSEs will be supplemented by vocational diplomas.[59] A similar Welsh 14–19 programme aims to provide pupils with a wider range of options, but Wales has gone further than England in developing a new Welsh Baccalaureate. Pilot studies are underway – although this move has been widely criticised for failing to link the Welsh qualification to the gold standard of the International Baccalaureate, and it runs alongside (not instead of) A Levels.

The strategy pursued in England by the UK Government stresses the needs of parents but puts additional pressure on teachers to raise standards, and on schools to provide out of hours services. This is a strong contrast with events in Scotland, where the McCrone review of pay and conditions attempted to get teaching unions on board by offering them higher pay, longer hours and additional staff support.[60]

The white paper released in October 2005 only emphasises this distinctiveness. It contains plans to allow every school to become a self-governing 'Trust' school, bringing the benefit of the 'enormous energy, drive and expertise' attributed to the private and voluntary sectors into schools – a measure reminiscent of Grant Maintained status.[61] Other features absent from Education in other regions include a renewed focus on English and Maths, and a pledge to promote 'fair admissions' policies that already exist in some schools. The report emphasises tougher treatment for poorly performing schools; schools in special measures will only have one year to improve before they are deemed to have failed and are replaced by a voluntary, faith or trust

58 *Northern Ireland Devolution Monitoring Report* (London: The Constitution Unit, November 2002), 42–3.
59 Department for Education and Skills, *Delivering Results: A strategy to 2006* (London: Department for Education and Skills, 2002). At: www.dfes.gov.uk/aboutus/strategy/pdf/DfES-Strategic%20Framework.pdf; accessed 17 August 2005.
60 *Scotland Devolution Monitoring Report* (London: The Constitution Unit, February 2001), 62.
61 Department for Education and Skills, *Higher Standards, Better Schools for All: More choice for parents and pupils*, Cm 6677 (London: The Stationery Office, 2005), 24.

school. Inspections will be more frequent, and occur with less notice. The UK Government's intentions are clear: '[Choice and diversity of provision] can only be achieved in a system that is dynamic, with weak schools replaced quickly by new ones, coasting schools pushed to improve and opportunities for the best schools to expand and spread their ethos and success throughout the system.'[62] England is increasingly following this path alone.

University funding has provided a high-profile example of divergence. In a mistake that bolstered the case for devolution, the UK-wide introduction of tuition fees failed to acknowledge that Scottish degrees last for four years and not three. A waiver for fourth-year students was negotiated, but the point was made. In 2000, up-front fees were abolished via a ministerial directive and replaced by an endowment payment after graduation, with maintenance costs subsidised by loans and income-contingent bursaries.[63] Northern Ireland sought to follow this example, and in 2001 a report by the Assembly's Higher Education Committee favoured an end to fees. Despite this support, the Executive defied the Assembly and opposed its 'no fees' stance, proposing instead a package of access measures including bursaries and childcare grants.[64] In Wales, a broad review of higher education in 2002 resulted in a ten-year strategy emphasising collaboration, 'reconfiguration' and widening access. Assembly Learning Grants were introduced to provide up to £1500 per person per year for home students in higher and further education.[65]

A further storm occurred over variable tuition fees. The Higher Education Act 2004 allowed universities to charge variable fees for the first time, in return for negotiating 'Access Agreements' aimed at widening participation through bursaries for low-income students. In England, from September 2006, students will repay fees after graduation, based on their income. Under direct rule, Northern Ireland has converged on this model. In October 2004, the UK Government announced its intention to introduce variable fees in Northern Ireland by 2006–07, despite previous opposition from all the main parties there.[66] In contrast, Wales and Scotland have no plans to introduce

---

62 *Ibid.* 20.
63 *Scotland Devolution Monitoring Report* (London: The Constitution Unit, November 2000), 52.
64 *Northern Ireland Devolution Monitoring Report* (London: The Constitution Unit, February 2001), 58.
65 *Wales Devolution Monitoring Report* (London: The Constitution Unit, November 2002), 8.
66 Northern Ireland Department of Employment and Learning press release, 'The Future of Higher Education in Northern Ireland' (29 October 2004). At www.delni.gov.uk/whatsnew/index.cfm/page/details/key/869/month/10/ year/2004; accessed 3 August 2005.

variable fees. After months of dispute, Wales successfully lobbied Westminster for powers to control student support in addition to its existing powers over higher education spending. The Higher Education Act 2004 devolved responsibility for the tuition fee regime and student support in Wales to the Assembly, and the Assembly Government subsequently announced that there would be no top-up fees in Wales until at least 2007 – leaving the UK with four distinct systems of higher education funding. Choosing not to impose top-up fees comes at a price, however, and funding this decision in the long term may prove to be more difficult than winning the power to make it.

Agriculture

While agriculture is devolved in Scotland, Wales and Northern Ireland, it is also an area heavily influenced by the European Union. There has been a tendency to assume that devolution can therefore only relate to the implementation of decisions taken in Brussels, with the European Commission exercising a strong influence. This is somewhat misleading, partly because devolution has given the devolved administrations the opportunity to influence the line taken by the UK Government in intergovernmental negotiations in the EU (discussed in more detail by Charlie Jeffery and Rosanne Palmer in chapter 10, and see Alan Trench in chapter 8), but also because the decisions to be taken at national and 'devolved' level are still significant. Once again, devolution has built on a complex relationship that existed before devolution between the Ministry of Agriculture, Fisheries and Food (MAFF) in Whitehall, the Department of Agriculture Northern Ireland, and the appropriate parts of the Scottish and Welsh Offices.[67] One early and symbolic change was the incorporation of the expression 'rural affairs' or 'rural development' into the names of the ministerial portfolios in each of the devolved administrations, to indicate a broader range of concerns than the Whitehall department had.[68] (The UK Government itself followed this lead after the 2001 Foot and Mouth crisis, when MAFF was itself abolished and became part of the new Department of the Environment, Food and Rural Affairs.) MAFF was, however, one of the less devolution-sensitive departments within Whitehall – something indicated

67 See Lowe, P. and Ward, N., 'Devolution and the Governance of Rural Affairs in the UK', in Adams and Robinson (eds), *Devolution in Practice*.
68 Thus the Scottish minister was the Minister for the Environment and Rural Development; the Welsh one, the Minister for Rural Affairs, and in Northern Ireland the department was the Department for Agriculture and Rural Development.

by the promotion of the all-UK Food Standards Agency at almost the same time as devolution took effect. The establishment of the FSA involved undoing formal transfers of responsibility to the devolved institutions over most aspects of food safety, which had been part of the preparation for devolution as they were functions of the territorial offices before 1997.[69] (The Curry report, with a remit extending only to England but recommendations affecting a range of devolved matters, suggests that such habits of mind have not ended with the restructuring of the department.[70])

The extent to which EU constraints dictate agriculture policy is variable.[71] On one issue, modulation (essentially, payments that a member state can direct away from supporting farmers directly to broader objectives of rural development), it has been a source of difficulty. Modulation was introduced as part of the 'Agenda 2000' reforms to the Common Agricultural Policy, and the devolved administrations have reportedly been keen to secure higher rates of modulation payments than the UK Government (in keeping with their concern in rural development more generally). However, that has not been possible thanks to the requirement that there only be a single rate of modulation within a member state – so the wishes of the devolved administrations were overwhelmed by the UK Government's concerns, themselves driven by the very different concerns of farming in England (where it is a less important part of the economy but dominated by larger holdings with higher levels of output than the devolved territories). A similar problem has arisen with schemes to support calf processing (Wales) or for culling ewes (Scotland), both incompatible with requirements that such schemes operate across the member state.[72] However, the rural development plans the Commission requires each member state to draw up have, in the UK, been for each constituent part. The plans reflect significantly different priorities for the different parts of the UK,

---

69 The Food Safety Act 1999, which established the FSA, was one of the first bills to be subject to a Sewel motion in the Scottish Parliament.

70 Policy Commission on the Future of Food and Farming, *Farming and Food: A sustainable future* (London: The Cabinet Office, 2002).

71 See Greer, A., *Agricultural Policy in Europe* (Manchester: Manchester University Press, 2005).

72 The former case is particularly interesting. Some in Wales believe that the scheme was possible but foundered for lack of support from MAFF. Interviewing suggests that it is also a case where the obligation to comply with EU law set out in the *Memorandum of Understanding* (and discussed in chapter 3) was used to persuade the devolved administration not to act, as the UK Government suggested that the scheme might be in breach of EU law, and that if so any fine would be calculated on the basis of the UK's population as a whole, not just that of Wales. The sanction would therefore have been gravely disproportionate to the benefit the scheme would have provided.

with the plans for Scotland and Wales emphasising the viability of agriculture and the development of rural areas more generally (in Scotland's case, with a strong emphasis on sustainable development). The Northern Ireland and England plans emphasise environmental measures more heavily. Forestry plays more of a role in the plans for Wales and Northern Ireland.[73]

More diversity was apparent during the 2001 crisis following the outbreak of Foot and Mouth Disease. Not surprisingly, the outbreak produced a welter of reports and investigations.[74] The scale and spread of the disease clearly took MAFF officials by surprise.[75] Once its scale (and the loss of control over it) became clear, the emergency mechanisms at the centre of government took over; the 'COBR' arrangements for coordination from 10 Downing Street were invoked, and subsequently the Army called in to provide manpower and practical coordination on the ground.[76] The devolved administrations were closely involved in all those arrangements, including attending some COBR meetings (and being represented by the Whitehall territorial offices when they could not). While grave in its implications for all devolved territories, only in Wales did the outbreak itself constitute a crisis: prompt and effective action in Scotland and Northern Ireland succeeded in halting its progress at a relatively early stage.[77] In the case of Northern Ireland, the cross-border dimensions were to the fore, the issue discussed (and action taken) through the machinery of the North South Ministerial Conference, and a ban on animal movements across the Irish Sea introduced by the Northern Ireland Department at an early stage. Although Ian Paisley

73 The plans were approved in October and December 2000 for the period 2000–06. They are available at http://europa.eu.int/comm/dg06/rur/ index_en.htm.
74 *Foot and Mouth Disease 2001: Lessons to be learned inquiry report*, HC 888 (London: The Stationery Office, 2002); National Audit Office, *The 2001 Outbreak of Foot and Mouth Disease: Report by the Comptroller and Auditor General*, HC 939 (London: The Stationery Office, 2002); House of Commons Public Accounts Committee, *The 2001 Outbreak of Foot and Mouth Disease*, Fifth Report Session 2002–03, HC 487 (London: The Stationery Office, 2003).
75 In ' "Carnage by Computer": The blackboard economics of the 2001 Foot and Mouth epidemic', *Social and Legal Studies*, 12:4 (2003), 425–59, David Campbell and Robert Lee go so far as to blame MAFF for the epidemic.
76 COBR (or COBRA, as it is sometimes called) stands for "Cabinet Office Briefing Room A" and is where cross-UK Government meetings of ministers and officials are held to respond to a crisis. The term has come to be used for the UK Government's crisis management machinery more generally.
77 Lowe and Ward suggest that the Scottish outbreak be compared with that in Cumbria, of which it was part epidemiologically, and note that while the outbreak lasted 3 months in Scotland it lasted 7 months in Cumbria, and that there were 5 times as many confirmed cases in Cumbria as in Scotland. 'Devolution and the Governance of Rural Affairs', 134.

sought to exploit the disease by blaming it on a cow from the Republic of Ireland, other politicians, including ones from the Democratic Unionist Party, took a more pragmatic line on cross-border cooperation in this instance (and regarding animal health more generally).

In Wales, there were clearly grave practical problems caused by the relationship between manpower and perceived responsibilities on the one hand (transferred to the National Assembly) and most of the legal powers to deal with the crisis (retained by MAFF, as a result of the bargaining process that preceded devolution, discussed in chapter 3). The result was a severe lack of coordination between the two Governments that contributed to the spread of the disease, at least initially.[78] There were also reported problems with information reaching the National Assembly from London.[79] That appears to have improved as the Assembly and MAFF developed a better working relationship, which involved closer involvement of the Assembly in making as well as implementing decisions.

By and large the devolved administrations were regarded as having handled the Foot and Mouth crisis well, in contrast to MAFF. Part of the reason is clear; they were much closer to those involved and also more aware of how their agricultural sectors worked. (Part of the problem was that MAFF had, apparently, little understanding of the cross-UK market in livestock and the extent to which animals moved around the country, which accelerated the spread of the disease. In that sense devolution delivered what it was supposed to – without drawing clear, hard and fast lines in the competences of governments, it enabled policy to be implemented and delivered better by those units closest to the problem.

Policy development after devolution

A survey as brief as this cannot hope to draw any definitive conclusions about policy development or divergence after devolution. All it can do is identify some general trends in what is happening and assess the implications of those trends.

One trend is that the devolved administrations have sought to do things differently – both from the UK Government and from the previous

78 The clearest statement of this was in the evidence of the National Assembly's Minister for Rural Affairs to the Lords Constitution Committee. See House of Lords Select Committee on the Constitution, *Devolution: Inter-institutional Relations in the United Kingdom: Minutes of evidence*, HL 147 (London: The Stationery Office, 2002), evidence of Carwyn Jones (28 May 2002), Q. 960. See also Jones, C., 'Responsibility Without Power', *IWA Agenda* (Autumn 2001, 41–3).
79 *Lessons to be Learned* report, para. 7.11.

territorial departments. Sometimes they have conspicuously done so; one (UK) official remarked in interview that Wales seeks to do things differently for the sake of it, while in Scotland they only did so if they could see a good reason for it. Part of the attraction of the 'free long-term care' policy in Scotland was that it was something that the UK Government had refused to do, and so illustrated the Scottish Executive's desire to depart from the UK approach when it wished, particularly on matters that had such symbolic value (notably universality).

A second trend is for the devolved administrations to learn from each other. In many cases, the UK Government then learns from them. The most notable case of this has been the children's commissioner, finally adopted for England after Wales, Scotland and Northern Ireland had established one. There are many others: for example, Wales considered a policy of free long-term care for the elderly after its adoption in Scotland, only to dismiss it on grounds of legal and political practicality and cost. After Scotland decided to amalgamate the various public sector audit bodies to create Audit Scotland, covering the Executive, local government and the health service, Wales followed suit to establish the Wales Audit Office. A ban on smoking in public places was on the agenda in Scotland (following Ireland's lead) before the UK Government looked at it seriously – and Wales announced its commitment before the Department of Health in Whitehall did. Sometimes the devolved institutions can simply act more quickly (Scotland legislated for a ban on fox hunting two years before Westminster did so for England and Wales), but often ideas developed in one part of the UK are picked up in other parts.

However, that tendency to 'develop differently' is shaped by two factors. One is the existing approach to policy of the pre-devolution territorial offices. Where they had already developed a different substantive approach to policy or a different way of working, that has been accentuated by devolution. This should be little surprise, given the heavy shadow policy inheritances tend to cast.[80] Where there was no such distinctive approach, it has taken longer and been harder for such an approach to develop. That has been particularly the case in Wales, given the limited policy capacity the Welsh Office had before devolution and the amount of work and time it has taken ministers, Assembly Members and officials to develop the necessary skills and interests. Such differences are developing, however, and appear to be increasing in both number and significance.

The second factor at work is the actions of the UK Government. These continue to have a profound significance. This is somewhat the case in relation

80 Rose, R. and Davies, P. L., *Inheritance in Public Policy: Change without choice in Britain* (New Haven: Yale University Press, 1994).

to reserved or non-devolved functions, but more so regarding what the UK Government does as the government for England. While the principle of measuring divergence from an English 'norm' may be questionable, it remains a sensible description of what actually happens. Diverging from that norm presents a number of challenges, practically, financially and politically. Perhaps the best area to see this at work has been higher education funding and tuition fees, where maintaining a different policy from England when students are able to move relatively freely around the UK to study presents serious challenges to both Scotland and Wales.

It is interesting that the question of formal powers to act differently appears to play only a limited part in policy distinctiveness. Wales has been able to secure such legal powers as it has needed for most of its policy initiatives, usually by piggy-backing its provisions in other departments' bills at Westminster (see further chapter 8). Scotland's attempt to develop a different approach to social exclusion has, it is true, been thwarted by the fact that social security is reserved to the UK, but that is perhaps an exception that proves the rule. What is necessary to develop a distinctive approach in terms of powers is enough powers (or other resources, as shown by Wales's experience with Foot and Mouth Disease) to get one a seat at the table and start meaningful negotiations – not enough to dictate the outcome. What Scotland had on social exclusion was not enough; what Wales (and Scotland) have for the settlement of asylum-seekers has been enough.

What has braked policy differentiation has not been legal powers, but the impact of England (discussed above) and the question of finance. Even generously funded Scotland has struggled to deliver its package of home-grown policies. None have been hugely expensive in absolute terms, but the combination of the McCrone package on teachers' pay and long-term care for the elderly have effectively eaten up the 'Barnett bonus'. It is admittedly hard to point to cases where the lack of money has meant that policy options have been considered and rejected – but probably because that lack has meant those options were not considered in the first place. All politics is about making choices, usually about the allocation of resources; but when there is no control of the amount of resources available, the nature of the choice is different.

But what seems both to drive differences in policy, and to shape successful policies, is the difference in scale between the single government before devolution and the small scale of the devolved territories. This makes for a degree of knowledge of local conditions, and an immediacy of impact of the problems that arise, which is quite different from that in the UK before devolution, or England now. Rawlings has described this as 'the closeness of Wales', and finds it a fundamentally important factor in shaping a range of relationships between the National Assembly and other bodies (notably local government, but also the health service, the Welsh Development Agency and the Environment Agency).[81] In Wales, it is similarly common for the Assembly to incorporate into itself functions that in England are given to some sort of quango, particularly in health and social services; thus incorporating the Welsh Development Agency or Education and Learning Wales, as will happen in 2006, is a continuation of a trend apparent since devolution. The relationships devolution has fostered are different in nature from those with the UK Government, and affect equally policy-making, the content of policy and the mechanisms used to deliver it. This may be seen as devolution living up to its promise; certainly it is a marked change since 1999.

81 Rawlings, *Delineating Wales*, chapters 10 and 11

7

The fragile divergence machine: citizenship, policy divergence and devolution in health policy

Scott L. Greer

We scarcely know what devolution has done to the UK as a whole. 'Devolution', writes Charlie Jeffery, 'is a project of the parts, not the whole'.[1] Vernon Bogdanor marvels at Labour's silence about the constitutional revolution it has enacted.[2] While devolution has addressed all manner of problems to do with peace in Northern Ireland, policy in Scotland, bad governance in London, and so forth, there has been remarkably little discussion of the interplay between constitutional change, public policy and citizenship rights. This silence is all the more surprising given the documented and impressive extent of policy divergence since devolution.[3] This chapter tries to unpick the relationship between constitutional change, intergovernmental relations and public policy with a focus on health. It argues that the UK, more or less by accident, has created a system which maximises policy divergence within tight sectoral limits, that policy divergence will change citizenship rights, and that the change will rebound on the politics of the constitution and devolution.

1 Jeffery, C., 'Equity and Diversity: Devolution, social citizenship, and territorial culture in the UK', Manuscript (Birmingham: University of Birmingham Institute for German Studies, 2003), 1.
2 Bogdanor, V., 'Constitutional Reform', in Seldon, A. (ed.), *The Blair Effect: The Blair Government 1997–2001* (London: Little, Brown, 2001), 139–58.
3 Exworthy, M., 'Primary Care in the UK: Understanding the dynamics of devolution', *Health and Social Care in the Community*, 9:5 (2001), 266–78; Adams, J. and Robinson, P. (eds), *Devolution in Practice: Public policy differences within the UK* (London: ippr, 2002); Greer, S. L., *Territorial Politics and Health Policy: The United Kingdom in comparative perspective* (Manchester: Manchester University Press, 2004); Keating, M. and McEwen, N. (eds), *Devolution and Public Policy: A comparative perspective*, special issue of *Regional and Federal Studies*, 15:4 (2005); Schmuecker, K. and Adams, J. (eds), *Devolution in Practice 2006: Public policy differences within the UK* (Newcastle: ippr, 2005); Greer, S. L. and Jarman, H., *Devolution and Policy Styles in the United Kingdom*, Manuscript (London: Constitution Unit, 2005); *Publius: The Journal of Federalism*, special issue on devolution in the United Kingdom (2006); and chapter 6 in this volume.

Analysis of the current financial and institutional structure of the United Kingdom shows how it gives remarkably free rein to the natural tendency of political systems to diverge – a tendency that is particularly strong in the UK, with its differentiated party systems and policy communities.[4] The devolution legislation (particularly in Scotland), the present practices of the Labour Party and the civil services, and the Barnett formula combine to insulate the devolved governments from most economic consequences of their actions, from direct central intervention and from central use of the power of the purse. The nature of most policy decisions – which deal with administration, budgets and priorities – means that this impressive de facto autonomy is what matters.

The fragility of this system is discussed throughout this book. Partisan conflict and arguments about finance are especially likely to undermine the stability of the current system. This chapter argues, however, that the great-est impact of devolution, its generation of policy divergence, is also creating divergence in social citizenship that will have important consequences for both the peoples of the UK and their political systems. As the different policy decisions cumulate in each devolved jurisdiction we are seeing the progressive construction of different models of the public sector and the public services. This entails different formal citizenship rights as the different systems retune their welfare states in different ways (as seen with services such as long-term personal care, bus passes for the elderly, prescription charges and eye tests, the availability of which varies due to devolution). It entails different judgements about means and ends in each system. It will also entail different real citizen-ship rights, since it is unlikely that all four health or education systems will improve equally under the very different policy regimes being constructed for them. England, Scotland and Wales have placed very different bets on what will improve their health services or educational systems, with England generally the most radical.[5] Such policy divergence is already one of the most marked consequences of devolution. On one hand, this means that the UK might be a model for others seeking full and meaningful policy autonomy within a state. On the other, it might mean that divergent citizenship rights provoke a backlash that leads to an ill-considered, envenomed debate about the structure of devolution and the UK.

The chapter first identifies the motors of policy divergence and the impetus for divergence, stressing that the natural operations of political

4 Greer, S. L., 'The Politics of Divergent Policy', in Greer, S. L. (ed.), *Territory, Democracy and Justice: Regionalism and federalism in Western democracies* (Basingstoke: Palgrave Macmillan, 2005), 157–74.
5 Greer, *Territorial Politics and Health Policy*; Greer and Jarman, *Devolution and Policy Styles in the United Kingdom*.

systems will produce policy divergence and that the fragmented party systems and policy communities of the UK will do so particularly quickly. It will happen because politicians and policy advocates will identify different issues at different times and select different solutions. The second section then examines the policy divergence that has taken place in one area, namely health policy. In health, we see the impact of different inherited policy communities and different party systems, spread across the many small and large decisions that cumulate into a policy trajectory. The third section identifies the institutional framework of devolution that permits considerable latitude to the pressures for divergence and the possible strains it puts on the structure of devolution.

The UK, with devolution, has built a fragile divergence machine. The divergence it produces might undermine it – or might further justify it.

Why policy *will* diverge

A problem with politics is that there is usually no correct answer to any particular question. A bigger problem with politics is that there is no correct question, either. A new minister entering office will be besieged by advocates of all manner of issue, beset by a regular series of uproars in the media, and tied down by a series of policy proposals already in the works. It is very difficult to make coherent, thought-out policy, if nothing else because the decision-makers are usually too busy (and often disinclined) to think out policy alternatives. Rather, when a problem intrudes into a politician's world, or the politician sees an opportunity to make a mark, the first policy to hand is apt to be the policy adopted. Do politicians in the different parts of the UK see the same in-trays, face the same problems and hear the same suggestions? Probably not. From that understanding of policy emerges a secular tendency to divergence between jurisdictions that is particularly marked in the case of the UK.

Policy-making

The chancy dynamic of matching problem, politician and policy is the basis of the multiple-streams approach in public policy.[6] It begins with the

6   The origins of the model are in Cohen, M., March, J. G. and Olsen, J. P., 'A Garbage Can Model of Rational Choice', *Administrative Science Quarterly*, 1:1 (1972), 1–25; Kingdon, J. W., *Agendas, Alternatives, and Public Policies* (New York: HarperCollins, 1995); Baumgartner, F. R. and Jones, B. D., *Agendas and Instability in American Politics* (Chicago: University of Chicago Press, 1993); and, for the UK, Zahariadis, N., *Markets, States, and Public Policy: Privatization in Britain and France* (Ann Arbor: University of Michigan Press, 1995), esp. 27–45.

ingredients of a policy. The most basic formula for a policy outcome is a combination of a problem (something that seems to demand a response), a politician (who can and might actually do something) and a policy (something to do). If one of the three is absent, it is unlikely anything will happen. When the three come together, a 'window of opportunity' opens in which something happens, and a policy is likely to be the result. Looking at systematic differences in the sources of problems, policies and politics gives us a rough gauge of the likelihood of divergence of the policies that ensue.

Politics is, in the UK, the ideology and strategy of governing parties, which at present means Labour in England and Wales, and Labour and the Liberal Democrats in Scotland.[7] It also incorporates an important factor, namely the individual ministers' need to 'make a mark' at something. It is the extent to which a party sees a reason to address a problem or proffer a solution. *Problems* justify the policies and the political activity. A problem is something that demands a solution; a condition is something that we must live with. Poverty is a condition – the poor are always with us – but child poverty or malnutrition are often redefined as problems. Issues travel back and forth between the two categories. Advocates constantly hope to accomplish this psychological legerdemain by trying to draw press and public attention to the issues they want to solve. The *policies*, then, also have lives of their own. Rather than being devised as solutions to problems already identified, they exist relatively independently, sustained by a support structure of professionals, academics and adherents in the civil service and interest groups that is called a policy community. From within this community, policy 'entrepreneurs' sell their ideas, proposing their chosen policies as the responses to any number of problems. With luck, they are in the right place with a plausible policy just when a politician needs a solution to a problem. All their years of lobbying, preparation, analysis and argumentation have served to make their solution seem feasible and acceptable and give it a better chance of being the outcome of this fundamentally indeterminate process.

The policy, problem and politicians all flow in their interdependent streams, but occasionally flow together. When they do, a policy decision can emerge. Plausible ideas ardently proposed (and a few implausible ones) couple with a problem, often media-generated or noticed because of a well-timed press release, a politician who must make a mark to thrive and survive enters – and a policy hits the streets of Ballymena, Pontypridd or Goole.

---

7 Zahariadis, *Markets, States, and Public Policy*, 34.

Divergence

The key to understanding policies, and the key to understanding the likelihood of policy variation over time, is to look at the systemic regularities in problems, politics and policy in each country. To the extent that these differ between two polities, we should expect that the policy outcomes will differ. And in the United Kingdom, they do differ. With or without knowing it, the four governments, as they go about solving their problems, systematically piece together problem, policy and politics in different ways. The two most visible differences are in their politics and policy communities.

Politics: party systems

UK party systems press for divergence. The United Kingdom does not have a single, state-wide, party system. Northern Irish parties are wholly separate and different, and compete to represent most vociferously either Unionists or Nationalists rather than over policy. Even in Great Britain, where there are three island-wide parties, the party systems differ markedly. Different governments face different problems and opportunities, fighting on one flank in England and different ones in Scotland and Wales. The Conservatives, Labour and the third-place Liberal Democrats vie for power in England. Scotland and Wales have marginal Conservative parties and strong nationalist parties to the left of Labour committed to loosening or eliminating the bond with the UK. Scotland also has left and libertarian parties that challenge both the nationalist SNP and Labour from their left flank. More proportional electoral systems in Scotland and Wales strengthen all the small parties, greatly strengthening Plaid Cymru and the SNP and making possible the rise of the Scottish Greens and the Scottish Socialist Party while keeping the unpopular Conservatives alive. The result is that Labour and the Liberal Democrats face very different strategic challenges in the three different parts of Great Britain. In England, the political opposition is to the right and only grumbling and backbench rebellion lies on the left. There is an incentive for Labour to choose policies attractive to voters in the centre and on the centre-right. In Scotland and Wales, by contrast, there are few Conservative votes to be won and Labour's main opposition is to its left. The voters in play are between Labour and the SNP – to Labour's left. Both Labour and the SNP then face potential damage from the Scottish Socialists and Greens if they appear to be unresponsive to the more disaffected, broadly left parts of the Scottish electorate.

In addition to the problems that Labour and the Liberal Democrats face on the left–right axis, Scottish and Welsh politics incorporate important national questions as a second political axis.[8] Labour and the Liberal Democrats' Scottishness and Welshness is invariably questionable since a unionist party must be less obviously national than a nationalist one.[9] This gives them both a positive incentive to play up divergence on key issues in order to avoid the taunt that they are London's poodles.[10] Welsh First Minister Rhodri Morgan, in his 2003 re-election bid, cleverly made great play of the 'clear red water' between left Wales and English New Labour.[11] Morgan has good reason to armour himself against Plaid Cymru by stressing his distinctive Welsh leftism, just as Tony Blair has good reason to speak tough words about the public services he wishes to reinforce and defend. The party systems of the devolved UK encourage divergence.

Policy: policy communities

If the politicians are then very different, the policy communities are as well. Fully analysing policy communities requires historical and institutional data presented elsewhere,[12] but the broadbrush outlines are visible. The English health policy community has an entrenched bias towards the use of markets and New Public Management, with its focus on contractual relationships, quasi-market relationships, independent regulation and 'strategic' governments backed up by an imposing and expensive infrastructure of market or quasi-market think tanks, newspapers, journals and academic analysts. The result is that progressive English students of social policy whose left-leaning credentials cannot be easily questioned will still speak the language of free-marketeers and advocates of the New Public Management. It is almost impossible to find, for

8 The logic is explained in Molas, I. and Bartomeus, O., *Estructura de la competencia política a Catalunya* (Barcelona: ICPS, 1998).
9 Journalist Neal Ascherson illustrates this graphically when he tells of the discomfort of Labour devolutionist George Robertson, when asked what his second choice after devolution would be – separation or total integration into the UK. The SNP and his own more anti-SNP activists would never let him forget it if he opted for the former, but the latter would be politically disastrous in a party system that demands Scottishness as a condition of entry. He failed to give an intelligible response (Ascherson, N., *Stone Voices: The search for Scotland* (London: Granta, 2002), 122).
10 Seawright, D., 'The Scottish Conservative and Unionist Party: "The lesser spotted Tory?"', in Hassan, G. and Warhurst, C. (eds), *Tomorrow's Scotland* (London: Lawrence & Wishart, 2002).
11 Constitution Unit and Institute of Welsh Affairs, *Wales Devolution Monitoring Report February 2003* (London/Cardiff: Constitution Unit and Institute of Welsh Affairs, 2003).
12 Greer, *Territorial Politics and Health Policy*.

example, English policy analysts who seriously argue for the abolition of NHS trusts, which are the basis of market mechanisms and managerial power in the health service. Market reformers dominate the English policy community.

The Scottish health policy community, by contrast, developed in the epoch of rule by the territorial Scottish Office, when a small and dependent but distinctively Scottish administration called upon a powerful, impressive and high-status set of medical elites to help it make and operate policy and administration.[13] Scotland's medical elites, organised into three Scottish Royal Colleges and four major academic medical centres and long connected into policy circles, make up for the small capacity of the Scottish Executive. The price of this added capacity and connection is that they have considerable influence over policy agendas and decisions as they shape the available problems and policies. The influence of professionals shifts the Scottish agenda towards professionalism. It gives more prominence to issues of quality improvement, partnership within health services, traditional public health and organisational forms in keeping with developing medicine rather than the managerial and consumer issues discussed in England.

The Welsh health policy community demonstrates that politics abhors a vacuum. The sources of 'insider' medical advice – managers and market reformers as in England, professional elites as in Scotland – are both weaker in Wales. There has been little institutional infrastructure for market reformers and professional elites are small in numbers and traditionally oriented to London. The infrastructure of market reformer and professional organisation, such as the London-based Royal Colleges, is weak in Wales. As a result, the Welsh health policy community includes groups that are relatively marginal elsewhere, particularly public health, local government and public sector trades unions. This has given the Welsh policy community a strong bias towards direct public provision and localism. That means integration with local government, and a focus on reducing inequality and changing the wider determinants of population health.

The Northern Irish health policy community creates a climate of permissive managerialism. The Northern Ireland Civil Service and direct rule ministers, like their Scottish equivalents, relied upon insiders in the health service to operate the system (the Welsh had alternated between reliance on London and developing their own, distinctive and valuable, capacity). The difference is that the Northern Irish policy circuits could not plug into an existing set of organised, competent elites with an agenda such as the Scottish medical leaders; Northern Ireland was too small and turbulent to sustain an independent group

<hr>

13 Woods, K. and Carter, D., *Scotland's Health and Health Services* (London: The Stationery Office/The Nuffield Trust, 2003).

of such elites. Rather, faced with the problems of public administration in a civil war, Northern Ireland's policy-makers opted even before devolution for a policy community built around existing stakeholders, above all the management of major hospitals and boards. Such status-quo-oriented groups did not provide new agendas, and neither direct rule nor devolved ministers were especially interested in policy-making. The result is an empty space in the places where other systems have high-profile policies, but at the same time considerable freedom to experiment and diverge at the lower levels. So long as the system continues to function, Northern Irish managers have had considerable autonomy (the devolved government changed this and tightened its control to a sometimes absurd extent, reflecting popular suspicion of quangos, but as one official put it in November 2003, 'normal service has resumed'). The result has been permissive managerialism: so long as the system is adequately managed, there is little push for an overall direction.

Consequences

The result, in each system, is that the problems, politics and policies all differ. As time passes and different combinations of the three emerge and join up, health (and other) policies of the UK will diverge. Natural differences in policy communities mean that we should expect policy divergence in every decentralised state; the United Kingdom's strikingly different party systems and policy communities mean that its component jurisdictions should show particularly strong tendencies to diverge. If the natural tendency of politics is to diverge then the system of intergovernmental relations becomes crucial to explaining the fate of citizenship rights. Left alone, jurisdictions will vary, possibly as much as independent states, so what keeps them from doing so? The effects of globalisation, ideas and so forth are diffused and have patchy or much-lagged effects[14] while budgets and laws, the stuff of intergovernmental politics, are hard, immediate constraints on the allocation and use of resources.

Health policy divergence

Health policy is one of the largest parts of any UK government budget, and one of the most complex. Fundamentally, health policy involves trying to manage fundamental incompatibilities. It is about providing necessary health services while coping with the fact that the potential use of resources for

14 Schmidt, V. A., *The Futures of European Capitalism* (Oxford: Oxford University Press, 2002), 13–58.

health is potentially unlimited (and heartily desired by many of the sick). It is about rationing treatment and, in public systems, trying to expand excluded populations' access to treatment. It is about managing uncertainty in matters of life and death, on levels from the individual doctor or nurse up to the allocation of acute hospitals. Health services traditionally manage all of these conflicts by entrusting diagnoses, treatments and the important and ethically charged decisions they entail to professionals trained to manage the uncertainty. But that does not make the life of a minister of health any easier. Rather, it means that the work of any health system depends on the professionals, who are articulate, difficult to control and who, when they change their understanding of their jobs, are capable of driving changes as far reaching as any that governments can force. Meanwhile, the high profile, importance and sheer human interest of the health services, coupled with their potential for entertaining tales of woe, horror and self-improvement, make them an eternal attraction for editors seeking to fill their pages and programmes.

Size, complexity and a set of fundamental contradictions mean that health services anywhere furnish a more or less endless series of problems, policies and potential political gain or loss. The odds that any one problem will be identified at the same time (or ever) in all four health systems, that it will be understood in the same way, and that the same policies will be adopted are small simply because of size and complexity, even before we consider policy communities and party systems.

In health services, this has led to pronounced divergence since 1999, best seen in organisation and public health focus.[15] Organisation is the structure that governs financial flows and the allocation of responsibility for decisions and problems. In the context of UK health politics, it involves a number of decisions: the relative balance of central and local; the relative balance of professionals and managers; and the relative balance of market against professionals and planners in resource allocations. Each UK system has chosen a different permutation that reflects its politics and makes the functioning of its health service increasingly distinct in a way that matters to the people working in it (more than a million people, across the UK), and that increasingly will define priorities for treatment and shape the patient experience.

Each has had to work with the legacy of Conservative policies introduced between 1979 and 1997, including the creation of professional management on a corporate model and the introduction of an 'internal market' that separates provision and purchasing of hospital services. The Conservative legacy was the use of management and market mechanisms, above all the formation of trusts,

15 For the details of policy decisions and trajectories in this and more fields, see Greer, *Territorial Politics and Health Policy*.

or firm-like organisations built around hospitals or other services, and the use of market logics (commissioning) in order to discipline them by letting others 'purchase' or 'commission' their services. This was implemented differently by the different territorial offices.[16] Scotland resisted the internal market and pursued different agendas within its margin of error.[17] Wales introduced management, but until John Redwood's tenure as Secretary of State the management cadre focused on overall strategy and implemented its vision of 'adding life to years, and years to life' rather than simple market-based efficiencies.[18] Northern Ireland ignored as much of the internal market as it could; there was enough for Northern Irish health policy-makers, managers and direct rule ministers to do without pursuing major policy changes. The UK was still a unified state before devolution, and the headline policies were all UK – the white paper introducing the internal market was signed by the Secretaries of State for Health, Wales, Northern Ireland, and Scotland together.[19] It was implementation that differed, and it differed because the policy communities charged with implementation varied with their histories. Since devolution they have been more able to diverge, England tending to markets, Scotland to professionalism, Wales to localism and Northern Ireland to a tradition of permissive managerialism.

What they did

There are a nearly infinite number of discrete policy fields within and around health policy, from pharmacy policy and occupational health to high-technology acute care allocation and stem cell policy, and they are all complicated and boast larger or smaller groups of animated policy advocates. This chapter briefly examines the divergence in three areas since devolution. The

16 Hunter, D., 'The Lure of the Organisational Fix', in McCrone, D. (ed.), *Scottish Government Yearbook* (Edinburgh: Unit for the Study of Government in Scotland, 1984), 230–57; Cairney, P., 'New Public Management and the Thatcher Healthcare Legacy: Enough of the theory, what about the implementation?', *British Journal of Politics and International Relations* 4:3 (2002), 375–98; Greer, *Territorial Politics and Health Policy*.

17 Hunter, D. and Wistow, G., 'The Paradox of Policy Diversity in a Unitary State: Community care in Britain', *Public Administration*, 65:1 (1987), 3–24.

18 Welsh Office, and Welsh Health Planning Forum, *Strategic Intent and Direction for the NHS in Wales* (Cardiff: Welsh Office, 1989); Longley, M. and Warner, M., 'Health and Health Delivery in Wales', in Dunkerly, D. and Thompson, A. (eds), *Wales Today* (Cardiff: University of Wales Press, 1999), 199–212; Wyn Owen, J., 'Change the Welsh Way: Health and the NHS 1984–1994', Talk at the University of Wales, Bangor (March 2000).

19 Secretaries of State for Health, Wales, Northern Ireland, and Scotland, *Working for Patients* (London: The Stationery Office, 2002).

first area is health services organisation. This is the mainstream history of the NHS systems – the lines of authority in management and the distribution of power between different units of the health services. The second is new public health (also, increasingly better, known by different tags such as the 'population health', 'wider determinants of health' or 'health and well-being' agenda, or one of several others). This is essentially an effort to improve public health on the demand side, reducing population morbidity and mortality by reducing known risk factors such as obesity, smoking, accidents and such. Given that these problems generally come with poverty, unemployment and other forms of social exclusion, as well as broader problems stemming from inequality and anomie,[20] the result is a potentially wide-ranging agenda that attacks multiple social pathologies in the name of health.[21] The third is the medical quality agenda, which attempts to infuse medical practice with more science and consistency in order to reduce variability and waste and improve outcomes. This agenda subsumes issues known as 'clinical governance' (the management of practice), 'technology assessment' and 'evidence-based medicine'. The stakes in this debate are the extent to which there are such efforts to change medical practice in the interests of the system's evidence base, quality and efficiency, and who controls it – whether it is medical elites (trying to upgrade their colleagues in practice) or managers (attempting to gain a foothold in the management of real medical work).

Scotland has opted in organisation for professionalism and, to a limited extent, planning as against managers and markets. This means that the Scottish health white paper *Partnership for Care* eliminated the firm-like trusts that are the basis of the internal market inherited from Thatcher (they were formally shut down in April–May 2004).[22] Rather, it shifts to management through Scotland's fourteen large health boards and asks them to organise treatment through 'managed clinical networks' that will integrate professionals and their concerns. This wipes out the bases of the market model inherited from the Conservatives. The civil service inherited by the Scottish Executive is, like other devolved civil services, strained, but it is still a sophisticated organisation and it works closely with the articulate, organised leaders of Scotland's profession to define and respond to policy challenges. This is Scotland's professionalism.

The focus on professionalism, born of the importance of professional (medical) leaders in Scottish health policy, also shapes Scotland's policies in

20 Wilkinson, R. G., *Unhealthy Societies* (London: Routledge, 1996).
21 Hunter, D. J., *Public Health Policy* (Cambridge: Polity, 2003).
22 Scottish Executive Health Department, *Partnership for Care: Scotland's health White Paper* (Edinburgh: The Stationery Office, 2003).

quality improvement and public health. In quality improvement, Scotland led the way before devolution through voluntary networks of physicians supported by the Scottish Office that attempted to identify and diffuse good practice. Since 1997 this has left Scotland with its own, independent, agencies for quality improvement and assessment, and has also meant that Scotland's medical leaders largely control the organisations, playing a prominent role as individuals and as participants in their work programmes and priorities. Public health usually suffers in systems with prominent medical leaders; big hospitals monopolise publicity, affection, status and money to the detriment of public health, and the prominence of Scotland's acute care sector could suggest that would happen in Scotland as well. The reason it has not happened is in large part due to the greater inherited strength and public role of public health specialists in Scottish medicine and health policy; they have substantial history, status and a role in policy debates,[23] and their solutions (such as free fruit in schools) appeal to a political system where the competition is on Labour's left.

England is the other country that is pursuing a marked, distinctive model and implementing it in organisation. It is also a model that is almost the opposite of Scotland's. If Scotland has been rolling back the 1980s and 1990s policies involving ever-closer management control over professionals and market-based resource allocation, England has been pushing them forward. England has a very high rate of policy change driven in good part by its government's media strategy, but behind it there is considerable consistency. England's government, uniquely in the UK, has focused on furthering market mechanisms (such as by establishing national tariffs for procedures commissioned), in trying to liberate trusts (by making them foundation hospitals), in promoting 'patient choice' that allows patients to select where they will receive services; and in promoting a 'diversity' agenda that encourages provision by multiple providers including the private sector; in hybrids of traditional NHS and private sector input such as Public–Private Partnerships; or a largely failed 'franchising' policy that brings in successful managers to run trusts deemed poor. Fearful of the consequences of giving market mechanisms real power, however, the Department of Health has largely locked primary care commissioners and acute trusts into legally binding contracts in pursuit of centrally specified goals,[24] so there should not be much real

23 Bhopal, R. and Last, J. (eds), *Public Health: Past, present and future: Celebrating academic public health in Edinburgh, 1902–2002* (London: The Stationery Office/The Nuffield Trust, 2004).

24 Greer, S. L., 'A Very English Institution: Central and local in the English NHS', in Hazell, R. (ed.), *The English Question* (Manchester: Manchester University Press, 2005), 194–219.

competition – and anyway the whole UK lacks the overcapacity that a properly functioning market needs if it is to work by weeding out poor providers.

For some time this focus on health services markets meant that England neglected public health. The NHS was laboriously reconstructed along market lines, which in good Smithian logic means that each part of the system focused on its part in the division of labour. The ensuing high degree of functional specialisation combined with the relentless central focus on health services (waiting lists for discrete acute treatments such as hip replacements) to sideline public health from the NHS. There is some chance this will change as a result of new work commissioned by the Government suggesting that the sustainability of public health systems depends on improving the public's health; that also reflects a sense among English policy-makers that they are resolving problems in health services.[25] Meanwhile, quality improvement in England is as geared to the requirements of a market model as Scotland's is to the dominance of professionalism in organisation. Markets (particularly markets politicians will not allow to produce negative outcomes) require regulation, and the English NHS enjoys the attention of a substantial regulatory apparatus led by the Healthcare Commission – an apparatus that was hastily shrunk through mergers after it emerged that the NHS was being regulated by more than 30 different organisations. The logic is regulatory and the agencies, while technically proficient, have their priorities and work programmes set by the centre.[26]

Wales has a different agenda, one that focuses on local population health and tries to provide it by integrating local government more closely into health service commissioning. The Welsh health services agenda has, remarkably, been partly subsumed into its new public health agenda. This involved a tremendously disruptive reorganisation that broke its 5 commissioning health authorities into 22 Local Health Boards (LHBs) that are coterminous with local government and that have substantial local government representation. Their goal is to integrate local social services with health services and promote a focus on prevention and population health rather than separate services cleaning up the problems that emerge; as an added benefit, integration with local government should make services better provided and more responsive. The Welsh health plan is a nice example of this thinking, which has a highly respectable intellectual pedigree

25 Wanless, D., *Securing Good Health for the Entire Population: Final report* (London: The Stationery Office, 2004).

26 For a valuable discussion of the ancestor of the Healthcare Commission, the Commission for Health Improvement, see Day, P. and Klein, R., *The Quality Improvers: A study of the Commission for Health Improvement* (London: King's Fund, 2004).

and which is becoming increasingly popular around the world.[27] It simply, and in statistical terms accurately, points out that the health services are one of many tools available to a government to improve population health, and that in many cases it is not the most important one. The solution, therefore, should be integration with local government – the organisational strategy – combined with 'healthy' public policies in other areas.

Wales has significant problems with this agenda, due to major capacity problems in the central administration and the 22 new LHBs, but it also suffers from a bad press. Not only are the 'losers' in Welsh health policy articulate groups such as hospital specialists and managers, who are accustomed to being central, but there has also been a series of major problems during the reorganisation that have damaged not just morale, waiting lists and administration but also the organisation of medical care. This means that the failings that come with a badly executed reorganisation accompany a lack of attention to core health services and managerial problems to put the direction of policy under severe strain. It also means that there is little pushing Wales to its own quality improvement. After devolution it continued to use England's quality apparatus (and the chief agency, the Healthcare Commission, was headed by a former Chief Medical Officer of Wales), but Welsh policy-makers perceived English auditors as out of step with their policies and administrative mechanisms and opted to create a separate Welsh audit organisation in 2004. It is doubtful whether it will be as aggressive about medical quality improvement as the (English) Healthcare Commission or the Scots equivalent, since its purpose was in good part defensive and it is part of a much larger audit structure not focused on health, while Wales still lacks a strong medical elite to push such quality policies.

Northern Ireland's health policy remains much the same in and out of devolution. Politics in Northern Ireland is not about public policy; at best it is about preserving local hospitals. Under devolution, the Sinn Fein Health Minister avoided taking decisions whenever possible (her party wins few voters for its policy stances, as against its views on nationality and high politics). Out of devolution, direct rule junior ministers with multiple portfolios are generally uninterested in rocking the boat.[28] The result is relatively little policy as understood elsewhere – not necessarily a bad thing. It is also a climate that promotes a health service preoccupied with keeping complex organisations running in complex circumstances and permits considerable

---

27 National Assembly for Wales, *Improving Health in Wales: A plan for the NHS with its partners* (Cardiff: National Assembly for Wales, 2001).

28 As seen in the commotion produced by an exception that proves the rule – a direct rule Minister, Shaun Woodward, who did take an interest in executive decisions in 2005 and proceeded to restructure health care in the south west after approximately fifteen years of debate had failed to do so.

local divergence in the absence of effective central control (central control became tight under Sinn Fein but that did not mean it was effective). This also means that there is effectively no Northern Irish quality policy (despite some organisations' work on the subject), but that there is abundant scope for local-area public health policies, aided by the long recognition of Northern Ireland's distinctiveness. For decades policy-makers have seen some of the roots of the Troubles as lying in multiple, reinforcing inequalities and have supported policies that promise to attack interlocking structures that create both violent sectarianism and ill-health.

Intergovernmental relations and policy divergence in the UK

The four parts of the UK have different policy communities and party systems, which is why they are already diverging in myriad policy decisions and why they are likely to continue to diverge. Political systems logically ought to diverge; the UK systems logically ought to diverge a great deal. So long as the problems and opportunities politicians face differ, and the policy communities posing questions and offering solutions differ, we should expect the policies to differ. This throws the question into a different light: what enables or constrains them?

Banting and Corbett, in their analysis of health politics and policy in federalism, identify two key axes of variance in the territorial politics of health policy.[29] One is the normative framework. This is the explicit code and set of regulatory or enforcement mechanisms that allow one order of government to constrain or empower another. The other is the financial system, the key resource base of a government. What constraints does it impose?

In both cases, the UK has a system that abets divergence. The normative framework is nowhere near as constraining as that faced by most meso-level governments and the financing formula, for all its quirks, leaves considerable autonomy for the devolved government.[30] It is the paradox of small changes: the way the United Kingdom created devolution left most administrative arrangements undisturbed, but the ensuing loose bonds between devolved bodies and the UK means it will produce more divergence.

29 Banting, K. G. and Corbett, S., 'Health Policy and Federalism: An introduction', in Banting, K. G. and Corbett, S. (eds), *Health Policy and Federalism: A comparative perspective on multi-level governance* (Montreal and Kingston: McGill-Queens University Press, 2002), 1–37.

30 Meso-level government means a level of government intermediate between the central or national government and the local or communal one; see Sharpe, L. J., 'The European Meso: An appraisal', in Sharpe, L. J. (ed.), *The Rise of Meso Government in Europe* (London: Sage, 1993).

Normative power

Normative power is the application of another level of government's coercive or legal resources to constrain what a government does with its authority and resources. Poirier identifies four basic forms of normative control that constrain divergence in social rights in decentralised countries,[31] in addition to the new constraints imposed by European integration (which are still to be fully felt in health policy[32]). These are constitutional norms, framework legislation, intergovernmental agreement and executive decentralisation, in which one order of government implements another's legislation. Each, in the case of the United Kingdom, is extremely weak. Without a written constitution there is no obvious set of requirements and the closest thing we have to constitutional law on devolution is silent about whether, for example, Scotland or Northern Ireland should have a universal health service at all. Framework legislation is legislation by the central/federal government to set a floor beneath which decentralised governments must not operate. In the UK, there is no such clear legislation specifying, for example, what kinds of health services Scotland must operate or to what standards. Intergovernmental negotiations, as other authors in this book and the House of Lords Constitution Committee note, are very informal and conducted partly among Labour Party politicians and partly among civil servants. The concordats that purport to regulate policy are certainly rather vague and, 'when we actually had a conflict, over long-term personal care, we looked in the concordat and found that it didn't say anything at all about our situation', as a Scottish official put it in a 2002 interview.[33]

The question of whether parts of the UK have something akin to executive decentralisation is less clear cut. Wales and Northern Ireland each have a form of constraint stemming from the fact that the UK is a devolved, rather than a federal, state. In both Northern Ireland and Wales the UK Government, in the person of the territorial Secretary of State, can exercise a powerful and somewhat capricious constraining influence. In Northern Ireland, the goal of London's policy is peace rather than good, or any, government. This means that when the Executive has seemed likely to collapse

---

31 Poirier, J., 'Pouvoir normatif et protection sociale dans les fédérations multinationales', *Canadian Journal of Law and Society/Révue Canadiénne de Droit et Societé*, 16:2 (2001), 137–71, at 147–52.

32 Greer, S. L., 'Becoming European: Devolution, Europe and health policymaking', in Trench, A. (ed.), *The Dynamics of Devolution: The State of the Nations 2005* (Exeter: Imprint Academic, 2005), 201–24.

33 See Simeon, R., 'Free Personal Care: Policy divergence and social citizenship', in Hazell, R. (ed.), *The State of the Nations 2003: The third year of devolution in the United Kingdom* (Exeter: Imprint Academic, 2003), 215–32; and chapter 8, this volume.

for one reason or another and/or when elections have appeared likely to be won by the 'wrong' parties (the Democratic Unionist Party above all, and Sinn Fein), London can use its self-granted legislative powers to suspend the workings of Northern Irish devolution. In Wales, the problem is the curious division of powers, deeply rooted in the structure of UK legislation and therefore neither visibly functional nor easy to explain. The National Assembly for Wales inherited the powers of the Welsh Office, which were in secondary legislation (a category that roughly corresponds to implementing legislation). In practice this is not really executive devolution since in health at least much of the important power is in secondary legislation. Furthermore, there is a difference between having secondary legislative powers and having implementation delegated in executive decentralisation; Wales faces not so much a coherent legal framework that it must implement as a series of rocks around which its policies must navigate or which it must ask Westminster to remove.

The point is that this is not normative power and need not have dramatic consequences on policy. Suspension of the whole Northern Ireland Assembly is hardly a tool to be used in a policy disagreement (and it also requires that there be a functioning Northern Ireland Assembly to suspend). Wales not only has considerable capacity to make policy without primary legislation but also could cause considerable trouble for Westminster in a clash – controlling a recalcitrant Wales would require absurdly tight Westminster legislation that could easily create chaos in both Wales and Westminster. While Welsh primary legislative powers as recommended by the Richard Commission or the white paper *Better Governance for Wales* would certainly simplify matters, it is easy to overstate the real impact they would have on key policy areas such as the organisation or goals of the health services. The reason is that policy is as often about management, priorities, resource allocation and 'steers' handed downward as legislation, and the resources of Wales are sufficient to do most of that without Westminster's permission (no executive decentralisation would otherwise have much point as a policy measure).

The distribution of competencies in devolution is further solidified by its basis in the pre-existing administrative structures of the state. Devolution in Northern Ireland, Scotland and Wales is not the creation of new organisations. Rather, devolution is a dramatic change in the governance of the old Northern Ireland Office, Scottish Office and Welsh Office.[34] For most purposes save

34 Milne, S. D., *The Scottish Office* (London: Allen & Unwin, 1957); Rose, R. (ed.), *Ministers and Ministries: A functional analysis* (Oxford: Clarendon, 1987); Deacon, R. M., *The Governance of Wales: The Welsh Office and the policy process, 1964–1999* (Cardiff: Welsh Academic Press, 2002); Mitchell, J., *Governing Scotland* (Basingstoke: Palgrave Macmillan, 2003).

London Cabinet representation and liaison, it replaces the old Secretaries of State with the new elected bodies. The administration remains more or less intact as it evolved when it was part of a territorially divided but politically united country. Inter-departmental battles within a single organ of government might be interesting and entertaining, but they are not like intergovernmental battles and are markedly less likely to produce concurrent competencies or flat-out conflicts over core responsibilities. This means that the Scottish Office and Department of Health each reigned supreme in their part of the UK and had very little ability to interfere directly (Cabinet government, rather than inter-departmental relations, was the fundamental guarantee of UK-wide consistency). The result is that the UK devolved governments inherited relatively clearly defined competencies reinforced by bureaucratic entrenchment and detailed allocations of competencies between the old departments.

Finance (including shielding)

Intergovernmental finance, or the provision of resources, has two faces. One is the extent to which it allows one order or level of government to intervene in the affairs of another, particularly through use of a spending power – the extent to which a government can use its resources to enact policy in an area claimed by another or use its resources as incentives for the meso-level government to adopt certain policies. The second is the extent to which the structure of intergovernmental finance exposes the meso-level government to outside economic forces – the extent to which its politics will be constrained by economic and fiscal feedback processes. It is extremely hazardous to pay attention to only one side of this coin. Full fiscal freedom sounds desirable but hardly helps a polity with a weak tax base or politics uncongenial to tax-raising (such as many American states, which pursue extreme low-tax politics because they accord with entrenched elites and supposedly represent a surer way to get jobs than the alternative 'high road' strategy of investment in human capital, infrastructure and services).

The UK financial system shields the devolved governments from both central intervention and any economic consequences of their policies. It does this because it is formula based and relatively transparent, based on the much-maligned but little-understood Barnett formula. While it is intricate, Barnett is not complex.[35] The formula, explained elsewhere in this volume, distributes

35 Good presentations are in Bell, D. and Christie, A., 'Finance – The Barnett Formula: Nobody's child', in Trench, A. (ed.), *The State of the Nations 2001: The second year of devolution in the United Kingdom* (Exeter: Imprint Academic, 2001); Heald, D. and McLeod, A., 'Beyond Barnett? Funding devolution', in

changes in spending on a strict per capita basis and thereby drives the whole UK towards equal per capita expenditure over time. It therefore gives everybody in the United Kingdom cause to feel aggrieved: England receives less per capita and will continue to do so for some time, while Northern Ireland, Scotland and Wales are all getting their budgets cut at least in terms of their rate of growth compared with England. For this reason alone, it is politically vulnerable. In addition, the calculation itself is keyed entirely to the expenditure decisions for England of the UK Government – first the UK Government decides changes in England's expenditures, then it uses population-based ratios to give Scotland and Wales their equivalent changes, and then it uses a Great Britain: Northern Ireland ratio to give Northern Ireland its share. If England unilaterally goes backwards (by, for example, abolishing the NHS), the consequence would be a corresponding cut in devolved budgets that the devolved governments could not, in theory, prevent.[36] Such dependence on England is something of an insult to the autonomy of the devolved countries. Finally, Barnett has nothing to say about the actual needs of the various parts of the UK. The historically greater funding of Scotland relative to Northeast England is not being re-evaluated; rather it is simply being eliminated over time. If Scottish sparseness or Northeast English poverty actually demand different levels of public expenditure, Barnett will not supply that.[37]

Despite all these faults, the Barnett formula does provide relatively transparent formula-based financing. This means that it deprives the UK Government of many tools used by other central governments to constrain

Footnote 35 *(cont.)*

   Adams, J. and Robinson, P. (eds), *Devolution in Practice: Public policy differences within the UK* (London: ippr, 2002); Heald, D., *Funding the Northern Ireland Assembly: Assessing the options* (Belfast: Northern Ireland Economic Council, 2003); and House of Lords Select Committee on the Constitution, Session 2002–03 2nd Report, *Devolution: Inter-institutional Relations in the United Kingdom*, HL 28 (London: The Stationery Office, 2003).

36 For confirmation that Barnett means that allocations to the devolved administrations can be reduced as well as increased, see House of Lords Select Committee on the Constitution, *Devolution: Inter-institutional Relations in the United Kingdom: Minutes of evidence*, HL 147 (London: The Stationery Office, 2002), Q. 357.

37 The 1970s Treasury needs assessment found Scotland 'overfunded' and Wales proportionately 'underfunded', even though both got more than the UK average per capita (McLean, I., 'The Purse Strings Tighten', in Osmond, J. (ed.), *Second Term Challenge: Can the Welsh Assembly Government hold its course?* (Cardiff: Institute of Welsh Affairs, 2003), 85.). RAWP (Resource Analysis Working Party) work for the Department of Health in the 1970s found the same (author's interviews). Such old calculations must be treated with caution since techniques have advanced considerably but are very suggestive – and if Wales needed more than it got in the 1970s, it is surely worse off today.

other levels of government. For example, the UK Government cannot use conditional transfers in a systematic way. Conditional transfers are subventions from the central government to another jurisdiction in support of a given policy and with strings attached. They can be enormously important.[38] The American federal government controls close to a third of 'state' spending and can attach conditions that constrain the states, often with highly dysfunctional effects. Such large amounts of money give the federal governments great power over other jurisdictions: the United States federal government has used conditional transfers for social purposes as contentious as enforcing racial desegregation in higher education or, in Canada, creating a universal public health insurance scheme.

If the UK Government does not have the power to use serious conditional transfers as a policy tool, neither does it have much ability to spend directly, as happens in other countries where the central government can go ahead and establish its own programmes. If it is to intervene, it must be via a 'UK' competency left to it and somehow relevant to the policy that attracts it. There are not many of them and the UK Government has so far not used its competencies (such as the research councils) to make showy interventions. The spending power of the centre is therefore dramatically reduced as a constraint on the devolved governments. The vast bulk of devolved funding simply does not depend on agreeing with Whitehall on policy issues, as Scotland has shown by spending its Barnett funds on policies London rejected.[39]

Barnett does not just shield the devolved countries from Whitehall. It also shields them from the economy. There is a long tradition in economics of modelling governments as firms that try to maximise revenue from taxes and calibrate their mixture of services and taxes accordingly.[40] A jurisdiction that imposes high taxes but does not provide the services that buyers (mobile capital) want will see an outflow of capital until it faces fiscal crisis and lowers taxes and services to a level that staunches the outflow. This is exactly the same process, in theory, as a new restaurant undergoes when it is initially too ornate for its market; it lowers prices and service deteriorates until it finds an equilibrium. A different jurisdiction might sell better services and charge

38 Watts, R. L., *The Spending Power in Federal Systems: A comparative analysis* (Kingston, Ontario: Queens University Institute of Intergovernmental Relations, 2000), 56–9.
39 Simeon, 'Free Personal Care'.
40 Tiebout, C. M., 'A Pure Theory of Local Expenditures', *Journal of Political Economy*, 64:5 (1956), 416–24; Oates, W. E., 'An Essay on Fiscal Federalism', *Journal of Economic Literature*, 37:3 (1999), 1120–49; see also Peterson, P., *City Limits* (Chicago: University of Chicago Press, 1981); and Peterson, P., *The Price of Federalism* (Washington: Brookings Institution, 1994).

more; the infrastructure, quality of life and developmental investment will attract capital even if it does cost more in taxes to locate there. Total dependence on a predictable funding formula such as Barnett eliminates this form of consequence. The financing of the Scottish Parliament is dependent on the English budget, not in any direct sense the Scottish economy. This leaves only feedback from the electoral consequences of economic policies, and that might be attenuated. The fact that the fiscal base of the devolved governments is separated from their fiscal capacity or fiscal policies shields them from the effects of the world economy or their own economic policies.

Intergovernmental relations and finance are two kinds of constraints on politicians beyond the ones supplied by their own democratic polity. There is no such thing as a constraint-free system; in intergovernmental finance, particularly, reduction in constraints (and money) from the centre tends to come with increased exposure to constraints from the economy. The United Kingdom's model of devolution creates few such constraints. Instead, it maximises autonomy within defined fields by leaving the devolved governments with budgetary flexibility, no overarching normative regulation and protection against economic change. The structure of UK intergovernmental relations produces a divergence machine powered by the natural drive to diverge of politics and assembled out of inherited institutional mechanisms that give it considerable effect.

Fragility

The machine might be impressive and has already delivered quite a lot of divergence. But it is also fragile, a device likely to work well only in certain climates. The first reason for its fragility is its financial basis. The Barnett formula, with its remarkable ability to distribute grievance across the political classes of the whole UK and its tenuous basis in Treasury spreadsheets, is probably the most vulnerable part. The second part is the development of the European Union. Devolved powers are focused on welfare state policy – health, education, local government and social care. Those are exactly the areas that the EU is entering. The UK Government is firmly in charge of the UK's policy in the EU, and coordination between the devolved governments and the UK Government might not be adequate to cope with the divergent interests and complex technical issues that come with the Europeanisation of social policy.[41]

41 Greer, 'Becoming European'; Jeffery, C., 'Devolution and Social Citizenship: Which society, whose citizenship?', in Greer (ed.), *Territory, Democracy and Justice*, 67–91; Jeffery, C. and Palmer, R., 'The European Union, Devolution and Power', chapter 10 in this volume.

The final, crucial reason it is fragile is that it does not build intergovernmental conflict into the structure. The vulnerability of current arrangements will emerge when determined, clever, politicians in some part of the UK turn their attention to fomenting conflict rather than dampening it down. Right now, Great Britain's three governments are partially or wholly Labour and when they speak they speak 'among friends' in the words of former Scottish Secretary Helen Liddell.[42] That will not always be the case, and we can expect that when there is real partisan divergence there will be real intergovernmental conflict (the link between state-wide party systems and stable decentralisation most famously made by Riker[43]). Then, governments will really be able to probe for ways to damage or embarrass each other, to steal credit and deliver blame, and we will probably see modifications to that system, if not wholesale reconstruction.

Living with policy divergence

This model of devolution in health, best represented by Scotland, operative in Northern Ireland when Northern Ireland is self-governing and likely to be imitated by Wales, provides a remarkable degree of autonomy to the component units. The combination of formula funding and cleanly divided competencies allows for considerable experimentation and divergence within clearly delineated policy areas that are further reinforced by their alignment with well-established bureaucratic demarcations. Catalans, forced to hew their government out of a truculent jacobin state and debate every point of endless normative legislation, are in this author's experience rightly impressed by what Scotland got.[44]

The great virtue of the UK model is precisely this degree of potential divergence, especially as seen in Scotland. There is little limitation on Scotland's experimentation in health policy, and even its sharply limited financial freedom is to some extent offset by the consequent liberation from

---

42 House of Lords Select Committee on the Constitution, *Devolution: Interinstitutional Relations in the United Kingdom: Minutes of evidence*, 10 April 2002, Q. 157.

43 Riker, W., *Federalism: Origins, operation, significance* (Boston: Little, Brown, 1964).

44 Or, more impressionistically, 'I show my children Braveheart – they love it – and my colleagues and I look at what Scotland has won in policy and in finances in such a short time and think they are ahead of us.' Author's interview with a provincial party head for the Catalan nationalist party Convergencia Democratica de Calalunya, March 2001.

economic consequences of social policies. The alternatives all build in different balances of power and judgements about the nature of citizenship. Countries such as Spain that nominate the central state as the judge and police of standards and citizenship rights might have more consistent welfare states but also encode a normative judgement (that the central state is the locus of real citizenship) and give the centre a powerful weapon to intervene in decentralised politics for more political, less weighty reasons than the preservation of citizenship rights. Canada's efforts to have provinces and territories join the federation in shaping its welfare state – the Social Union Framework Agreement – show promise but can always fall victim to intergovernmental wrangling (and indeed, the Agreement fell victim to it immediately when Quebec refused to join).[45]

But this means there is also no safety net. On the most minimal level, there is no real mechanism in the health policy system of the UK for any other government to intervene if a devolved health system enters a crisis. And the UK Government, equipped both with a vital role in intergovernmental relations and a health system that dwarfs the others, can create serious administrative problems without noticing or resolving them.

And it means that if there is an underlying sense of common citizenship rights and values across the UK, the divergence that the machine creates could eventually collide with these deep-seated expectations. There probably is such a sense of common rights – there is such a sense, with political force behind it, in other countries – that could mean that in the not-too-distant future UK-wide standards could enter politics as a value in their own right.[46]

There is no way to argue definitively that the United Kingdom is a good or bad model, that constraints should be imported from other systems, or that devolution is either perfect or flawed. Conversi points out that the distribution of powers between different levels is inherently part of a political game.[47] State elites judge the success of the state by its maintaining the integrity of the state within its borders, whereas 'peripheral nationalists' view success as the level of self-government. The success of federalism is in the process of negotiation, and a crisis occurs when somebody 'unilaterally changes the game's basic rules'.[48]

45 Trench, A., *Intergovernmental Relations in Canada: Lessons for the UK?* (London: The Constitution Unit, 2003).
46 Jeffery, 'Devolution and Social Citizenship'; Banting, K. G., 'Social Citizenship and Federalism: Is a federal welfare state a contradiction in terms?', in Greer (ed.), *Territory, Democracy and Justice*, 44–66.
47 Conversi, D., 'Autonomous Communities and the Ethnic Settlement in Spain', in Ghai, Y. (ed.), *Autonomy and Ethnicity: Negotiating competing claims in multi-ethnic states* (Cambridge: Cambridge University Press, 2000), 122–44.
48 *Ibid.*, 137

To try to argue for or against the politics of devolution in the UK would be to join in Conversi's game between state and peripheral nationalists, which is not my intent. Rather, it is to argue that the institutional structure of the UK gives remarkably free rein to policy divergence in important areas such as health and that the natural working of politics in a country with such diverse social institutions and party systems quickly produces thoroughgoing divergence. That means devolution has already had an impact on the meaning and rights associated with citizenship in the UK, and that it should continue to do so. Such divergence might justify devolution as an improvement short of independence, or by the old argument that policy divergence is what Scots want and devolution gives it to them without the disruption of independence. But so long as there is no clear sense of what UK citizenship might mean, divergence in citizenship rights will likely rebound on the whole structure of devolution. And so long as there is no clear sense of how the UK institutions interact to produce the fragile divergence machine, it is unlikely that anybody will be able to know how to repair it, steer it, turn it up, or turn it off.

8

Washing dirty linen in private: the processes of intergovernmental relations and the resolution of disputes

Alan Trench

This chapter considers how relations between the UK Government and the devolved administrations work in practice.[1] It is concerned with what issues arise, in what context, how they are handled when they do arise, and especially if they become disputatious. This involves looking at the organisational arrangements made within each government for dealing with intergovernmental relations (IGR); in this context, the machinery of government matters. While (as shown in chapter 3) the formal framework for intergovernmental relations is relatively limited and informal in comparison, this chapter will suggest that the practice of intergovernmental relations is less formal than even that framework would suggest; relations are highly cooperative and consensual in practice, with few disagreements even entering into the public domain.[2]

This can be largely attributed to two factors: political consensus across governments and the dominance of the UK Government. The substantial

---

1 An earlier version of this chapter was presented at the Political Studies Association conference, Leeds, April 2005. I am grateful to a number of officials who attended a private seminar at Dover House in June 2004 (as well as the other contributors to this book) for their comments. The usual disclaimer applies. Like my other chapters in this volume, this draws heavily on interviews with civil servants and others on terms of anonymity.

2 For general discussions of the practice of intergovernmental relations, see Trench, A., 'The More Things Change the More They Stay the Same: Intergovernmental relations four years on', in Trench, A. (ed.), *Has Devolution Made a Difference? The State of the Nations 2004* (Exeter: Imprint Academic, 2004); House of Lords Select Committee on the Constitution, Session 2002–03 2nd Report, *Devolution: Inter-institutional Relations in the United Kingdom*, HL 28 (London: The Stationery Office, 2003), chapters 1 and 2; Rawlings, R., *Delineating Wales: Constitutional, legal and administrative aspects of national devolution* (Cardiff: University of Wales Press, 2003), particularly chapters 9 and 12; Keating, M., *The Government of Scotland: Public policy making after devolution* (Edinburgh: Edinburgh University Press, 2005), especially chapter 5.

political consensus between the UK Government and devolved administrations results in absence of the sort of tension that would force each administration (and its Parliament or Assembly) to insist on the right to exercise its powers as it alone sees fit, but leads instead to a desire to cooperate and to agree so far as possible. The implications of this are explored further below, as well as in chapter 9. In its early stages, devolution has been characterised, rather paradoxically, by a desire for all the governments involved generally to follow the same path rather than different ones. The clear pre-eminence of the UK Government has made the devolved administrations averse to provoking any sort of open disagreement or dispute with the UK Government, for fear that by insisting on using those formal mechanisms they would lose the influence they can exercise in private. In other words, the devolved administrations have come to the conclusion that they can gain more by behind-the-scenes influence than by insisting on their maximal formal rights.

This chapter will seek to answer three questions. First, what explains the fact that there are relatively few intergovernmental disputes? What are the factors that mean such issues arise relatively rarely? Second, what happens to the intergovernmental disputes that do arise? What role do the formal mechanisms and processes play in resolving or defusing such issues, and why is their role so limited? Do other mechanisms exist for dealing with disputes and differences if the formal machinery does not do this? Related to this is the issue of why such disputes are conducted so largely in private and behind the scenes. Why is this considered necessary or desirable, and how is it practicable? Third, what does the practical working of intergovernmental relations suggest for a more general argument that the devolved administrations are at a significant disadvantage in the resources which they have for the conduct of intergovernmental relations, but that this does not in fact impede their exercise of autonomy?

In answering these questions, this chapter will examine the stresses and tensions that have arisen in the UK's experience of devolution to date. This emphasis may be misleading. The practice of intergovernmental relations in the UK to date has been highly consensual and cooperative. The structure of the devolution settlements means that the various governments of the United Kingdom need to cooperate with each other to deliver policy in most areas, even those that appear to be wholly devolved. Contacts for such matters are frequent and routine, even if they are ad hoc and essentially unstructured. Looking at disputes rather than cooperation is like looking at the hole of a Polo mint, not the mint itself. More importantly, how disputes are resolved and their outcomes are the litmus-test of where power lies in a system. The power of the respective parties in the devolved UK can only be properly assessed if it can be seen in the light of such a test.

The formal machinery: dealing with disputes and disagreements between governments

The Joint Ministerial Committee

The JMC was created by the Memorandum of Understanding and in its plenary form resembles meetings of first ministers in federal systems (such as the First Ministers Meeting in Canada or the Conference of Australian Governments in Australia). But a meeting of just the UK Prime Minister and the devolved first ministers would be a strange (and small) gathering, and membership, so membership also includes on the UK side the Chancellor of the Exchequer, the Deputy Prime Minister and the Secretaries of State for Scotland, Wales and Northern Ireland, and on the devolved side the deputy first ministers.[3]

According to the Memorandum of Understanding, the purpose of the JMC is 'to take stock of relations generally and to address particular issues or problems', and its functions are stated to be:

- considering non-devolved matters impinging on devolved responsibilities and devolved matters impinging on non-devolved responsibilities;
- considering devolved matters where the parties agree and where discussion of their respective treatment in different parts of the UK would be beneficial;
- keeping under review arrangements for liaison between the UK Government and devolved administrations, and also the operation of the devolution settlements generally;
- considering disputes between administrations.[4]

The JMC is to meet annually, to have a joint secretariat composed of the UK Government and the devolved administrations, and to have its

---

3 *Memorandum of Understanding and Supplementary Agreements between the United Kingdom Government, Scottish Ministers, the Cabinet of the National Assembly for Wales and the Northern Ireland Executive Committee*, Cm 5240 (London: The Stationery Office, 2001) (henceforth 'Memorandum of Understanding), paras 22–25 and 29 (and Agreement on the Joint Ministerial Committee, para. A1.2). This also avoids the problem that 'Deputy First Minister' in Scotland or Wales is merely a title, used for the leader of the junior party in the coalition and in Wales dispensed with when Labour governs alone, while in Northern Ireland the First and Deputy First Ministers have to be elected and thereafter to act together, forming in effect a single office at the peak of government.

4 *Memorandum of Understanding*, para. 23 (summarised).

deliberations kept confidential.[5] It is a consultative not an executive body, reaching agreements not decisions. Consequently, it cannot bind the parties but they are expected to support the positions it has agreed.[6] However, the JMC is the forum of last (or third) resort for resolving disputes; these should be discussed bilaterally in the first instance, and only if they cannot be resolved directly between the UK Government and devolved administration, or directly using the 'good offices' of the territorial Secretary of State, should the matter be considered by the JMC.[7] The JMC's existence therefore does not alter the fundamentally bilateral framework for intergovernmental relations discussed in chapter 3.

The dispute resolution role is, however, one that the JMC has never been called on to discharge. Although there have been a number of contentious issues to be resolved, this has not been the place to do it; as those issues have, moreover, been bilateral ones (concerning the UK Government and only one devolved administration), they have been resolved bilaterally. For the first three years after devolution (until 2002), the formal requirement of an annual meeting was kept, even though there was something of an air of a meeting for the sake of a meeting about its plenary sessions. The communiqués issued after the annual meetings suggest that the meetings were limited to 'exchanges of information about best practice' and the like, rather than addressing genuinely controversial issues in relations between the governments.[8] After meetings in the autumn of 2000, 2001 and 2002, there was no meeting in 2003 and as of November 2005 it had still not met – a gap of over three years. This may have been partly due to congested diaries, particularly on the part of the UK Prime Minister (at least one meeting was scheduled then cancelled), but it also indicates a clear lack of eagerness to use the JMC. Evidently it is simply not a matter of high priority, especially for the UK Government, which has the task of convening them. It suggests there is no desire to ensure that the machinery works effectively at times of relative quiet so it can adapt to more difficult circumstances, when there might be substantive issues to deal with.[9]

5 Ibid., Agreement on the JMC, paras A1.10 (obligation for annual meetings), A.114 and Annex A2 (joint secretariat and its functions) and A1.11 (confidentiality).
6 *Memorandum of Understanding*, Agreement on the JMC, paras. A1.6, A1.10 and A1.3
7 *Ibid.*, para. 25 and Agreement on the JMC, para. A1.7.
8 Communiqués from JMC meetings are available at: www.dca.gov.uk/constitution/devolution/jmc.htm.
9 See House of Lords Select Committee on the Constitution, 2003–04 16th Report, *Meeting with the Lord Chancellor*, Session, HL 193 (London: The Stationery Office, 2004), QQ 91–3. See also Trench, A., 'Devolution: The withering-away of the

Disuse of the JMC for dispute resolution is not simply due to the absence of problems in relations between the UK Government and devolved administrations. Rather, it happens because the initiative for resolving such disputes through the JMC would have to come from devolved administrations not the UK Government (as the UK Government can largely shape a policy to suit its needs, in a way the devolved administrations cannot), and the devolved administrations do not regard the JMC as a useful forum for resolving them. If they were to refer a matter to the JMC, it would indicate three things. First, other ways of resolving a dispute had been tried but had failed, with the efforts of the Secretary of State to use his or her 'good offices' bearing no fruit and other forums providing no help either. Second, it was appropriate to raise the issue and seek to find a solution jointly with the other devolved administrations. This would require the existence of substantial common ground between the devolved administrations. With three widely varying devolution settlements, and different policy concerns of each administration (as well as different party politics in the future), that is unlikely to occur often. Third, it would reflect a willingness, if not a positive desire, to raise the matter formally and air it in public, with an open discussion of the issue and the constitutional position of the parties, rather than to deal with it on the political level and behind the scenes.[10] In other words, it would mean airing dirty linen in public rather than private. A mechanism that appears to serve an essential role in the structure of devolution therefore in fact can be seen as serving a limited and marginal one.

An example of the lack of use of the JMC can be found in the first stage of the row between the Scottish Executive and UK Government over the Scottish policy of providing free personal care for the elderly, in autumn 2001. The Scottish policy implemented recommendations of the Royal Commission on Long Term Care chaired by Sir Stewart Sutherland that all long-term care should be provided free of charge to the user, when the UK Government had decided not to implement that in England or Wales, but to continue providing free nursing care while charging for personal care.[11] (The

---

Footnote 9 *(cont.)*

JMC?', *Public Law* (2004), 513–17. This informality was a major concern of the House of Lords Select Committee on the Constitution in its report on *Devolution: Inter-institutional Relations in the United Kingdom*. In its response to the Select Committee's report, the UK Government indicated it did not share the Committee's concern.

10 Technically, JMC meetings are confidential, but it is hard to imagine that the fact that a dispute was to be considered at one would not become public knowledge.

11 Royal Commission on Long Term Care, *With Respect to Old Age: Long term care – rights and responsibilities*, Cm 4192-I (London: The Stationery Office, 1999); Department of Health, *The NHS Plan: The Government's response to the*

inherent problem with this approach is that the distinction between nursing and personal care is hard to draw and causes many anomalies.) The Scottish policy therefore appeared more generous than the UK one, appealed to the left because it provided for a benefit to be universal not means-tested, and had already been adopted by the Liberal Democrats. However, it was a potentially expensive commitment, and also regressive in its effect because it was universal but many recipients were well-off. The combination of cost and embarrassment led to considerable opposition to the Scottish policy from the UK Government – a concern rooted in political considerations, not legal competence to enact the policy, which the UK accepted Scotland had. Discussion of such opposition took place mainly in private (and brutally direct) meetings between the politicians directly concerned, with limited involvement of civil servants or official channels, and certainly not the JMC. (It resulted in a stand-off: the UK Government would not interfere if Scotland wished to adopt the policy, even if the UK Government thought it misconceived.[12])

The JMC is not the only formal setting in which the UK's first ministers meet each other. A further explanation for the limited role of the JMC is that some of its work has in fact been exercised through the British–Irish Council (BIC), established as part of the Belfast Agreement.[13] Somewhat curiously, the BIC has continued to meet despite suspension of devolution to Northern Ireland, with Northern Ireland being represented by the direct-rule UK Government ministers from the Northern Ireland Office.[14] The BIC has taken on the function of acting as the symbolic meeting of governments of the British Isles, as well as some discussions of particular policy matters (such as the drugs or the knowledge economy). However, it has no role in resolving disputes, whether formally or informally, nor is it concerned with the relationship between devolved and non-devolved functions, nor in overseeing the

Royal Commission on Long Term Care, Cm 4818-II (London: The Stationery Office, 2000).

12 Author's interviews. See also Simeon, R., 'Free Personal Care: Policy divergence and social citizenship', in Hazell, R. (ed.), *The State of the Nations 2003: The third year of devolution in the United Kingdom* (Exeter: Imprint Academic, 2003). The sequel to this stand-off is discussed at p. 105 above.

13 *An Agreement Reached at the Multi-Party Talks on Northern Ireland*, Cm 3883 (London: The Stationery Office, 1998), Strand Three. See also Northern Ireland Act 1998, s. 52. Membership of the BIC is much broader than that of the JMC, encompassing representatives of the UK Government and UK devolved administrations, but also those from the Republic of Ireland, the Channel Islands and the Isle of Man.

14 Northern Ireland Act 2000, s. 1(5).

UK's devolution arrangements. Its work is confined to information- and experience-sharing.[15]

It is perhaps an error to assume that the JMC's primary purpose was to resolve disputes. Interviewing suggests that was not, in fact, where the idea of having such a meeting started. Rather, its origin was reportedly a concern of Donald Dewar's, that the arrangements for devolution would significantly harm Scotland because it would mean that devolved Scottish ministers were excluded from discussions of areas of UK Government policy that affected Scotland. In other words, Dewar was concerned about the impact of reserved matters on the devolved administration, and wished to ensure that the Scottish ministers could sit on the relevant UK Cabinet committees to protect Scottish interests, as they had done before devolution. Unsurprisingly, this was unacceptable to the UK Government (not least because the idea of having ministers who were not bound by UK Cabinet collective responsibility attend Cabinet committees was unthinkable to UK officials). The idea of the JMC in its plenary and functional forms was formulated instead, as a substitute for such Cabinet committees.

Other ministerial meetings

The plenary JMC is not the only way UK and devolved ministers meet. 'Functional' forms of the JMC have been established for Health, the Knowledge Economy, Poverty and Europe, and regular meetings of other ministers have taken place outside the JMC framework as well.

Some of the functional formats are concerned with social and economic development matters. The Knowledge Economy and Health formats (both areas of particular interest to Tony Blair) met several times between 1999 and 2001, then simply stopped – even though health, as an area devolved in all three territories, is an area where there is much scope for ministers and officials to learn from each other, and much need for coordination of policy as well. As discussed in chapter 5, the Poverty format (of special concern to Gordon Brown) also met several times in 1999–2000 then stopped, only to meet again in October 2002, announce an ambitious work programme for

---

15 The communiqué from its May 2005 summit meeting identifies the topics discussed as telemedicine; misuse of drugs; environment; tourism; knowledge economy; transport; indigenous, minority and lesser-used languages; and social inclusion. Although the Irish Government was represented by the Taoiseach and Welsh Assembly Government by the First Minister, the UK Government was represented by the Deputy Prime Minister and the Scottish Executive by the Deputy First Minister. See www.britishirishcouncil.org/documents/iom_summit.asp (accessed November 2005).

the coming year, and then not meet again. In late 2002 there were plans, behind the scenes, for a format of the JMC for the Economy – but this has never met either. This pattern suggests that the chief factors behind such meetings are the concerns and priorities of senior UK ministers. If they can embrace the JMC in the service of one of their initiatives, well and good; if it does not serve that purpose, they will not use it.

The situation has been rather different for the JMC (Europe), however.[16] The JMC (Europe) has met regularly, usually five times a year, since it was established. Its main role was as a way of consulting the devolved administrations about EU policy generally and particularly (during 2002–03) about the Giscard Convention on the European Constitution and subsequent intergovernmental conference. Despite meeting frequently, it seldom issues a press statement (or even announces publicly the fact of its meeting). Its most interesting aspect is that its meetings have largely superseded those of the Cabinet committee on EU matters. The European Policy (EP) committee has remained in existence, strictly speaking, but no longer meets as the JMC (Europe) includes similar members from the UK Government as well as the devolved representatives. This is reportedly a matter of time-saving; having these discussions in the presence of the devolved administrations has saved the need to consult them subsequently and avoided any concern on their part that they were being asked to agree to decisions already taken in substance, but to achieve this the UK has been willing to open its deliberations to the devolved administrations too. Officials involved report that its meetings are very valuable, although the lack of openness about its dealings means that there is no way that can be assessed objectively. In this field, though (but only this one), Donald Dewar's original vision of the role of the JMC has been fulfilled.

It is striking to the outside observer how limited are the policy areas which are dealt with by functional JMC meetings. Agriculture is one area devolved in all three territories, and is a sector in which cooperation is particularly important because of the Common Agricultural Policy, especially during its reform process in 2001–03. The failure of the devolved administrations to cooperate with the UK Government would risk the UK taking a position in EU negotiations that it could not deliver in practice. This cooperation has been organised through a regular sequence of ministerial meetings, taking place most months and tied to the agenda for forthcoming EU Council of Ministers meetings. However, these are simply quadrilateral meetings of ministers and take place outside the JMC framework, in order (officials say in

16 The role of the JMC (Europe) is also discussed by Charlie Jeffery and Rosanne Palmer in chapter 10.

interviews) to avoid the formality associated with the JMC.[17] It is unclear what role such meetings played in some of the crises in the agriculture field that have arisen, such as the outbreak of Foot and Mouth Disease in 2001 or following the UK Government's decision to authorise genetically modified seeds in early 2004 (which Wales opposed). As discussed in chapter 5, similar if less frequent quadrilateral meetings of finance ministers were started in 2003, led by the Chief Secretary to the Treasury.

However, the network of such meetings is patchy, and ministerial meetings are wholly lacking in other areas where one might expect them. These include education, an area devolved in all three jurisdictions, where there are obvious areas of overlap between devolved and retained functions such as higher education (devolved) and research funding through the research councils (still a UK matter), and where different policies are pursued by each government. There are similarly no regular discussions of environmental and planning policy, or transport matters. No ministerial meetings have taken place for health since the last JMC meeting in October 2000, nor do regular meetings take place between Scotland and the UK Government over home affairs, despite the obvious importance of coordination on a range of matters including policing, criminal law, anti-terrorism and EU matters. Instead, cooperation in all these areas is bilateral and ad hoc, reflecting the minimal adjustments made to the UK as a result of devolution.

Financial issues

Financial disputes are to be dealt with in the first instance bilaterally between the UK Treasury and the devolved administration. A first 'appeal' lies to Treasury ministers, and if the devolved administration remains dissatisfied, the matter may be referred to the UK Cabinet.[18] While the devolved administration can raise the matter at the JMC as well, it is for the UK Cabinet to make a 'final decision', so raising it at the JMC would simply be a way of indicating concern or annoyance and not a direct means to a resolution. These arrangements keep all power in the hands of the UK Government, in a situation where the devolved administrations have no alternative source of funding. They also exclude the devolved administrations from direct participation in

---

17 In fact, five ministers attend: the Rural Affairs Ministers from Scotland and Wales, either the Rural Development Minister from Northern Ireland or the Northern Ireland Office Minister responsible for rural affairs, the Minister of State to speak for English concerns, with the Secretary of State chairing the meeting.

18 HM Treasury, *Funding the Scottish Parliament, National Assembly for Wales and Northern Ireland Assembly: A statement of funding policy* (London: HM Treasury, 3rd edn, 2002), paras 11.1–11.2.

the process altogether, as it is internal to the UK Government. The devolved administrations can only be heard through the voice of the territorial Secretary of State, who at best is a proxy for them and may take a quite different view of the merits of their case. Similarly, they rely on the Secretary of State (and his or her office) to keep them informed of what is happening. For such matters, the lack of resources is profound, and such arrangements are likely to deter the devolved administrations from raising an issue formally unless their case is utterly compelling.

In chapter 5 there was a discussion of some of the consequences – notably the strains caused in Wales by the UK's initial refusal to provide 'matching funding' for the West Wales and Valleys Objective 1 area (triggering the fall of Alun Michael), only for money to be subsequently found during the discussions before the 2002 Spending Review. Similarly, in the case of the compensation to the Scottish Executive for the saving to the Exchequer on attendance allowance paid to recipients of free long-term care, the Executive accepted its rebuff gracefully and did not pursue the matter; in particular, it did not seek to take it to the JMC.

Legal disputes: the Judicial Committee of the Privy Council

The Judicial Committee of the Privy Council was given jurisdiction over devolution disputes of a legal character. In the run-up to devolution, the expectation appears to have been that there would be a substantial number of these.[19] Quite why this jurisdiction was given to the JCPC remains unclear, but desire not to cause offence in Scotland (by appearing to undermine the independence of the Scottish judicial system and the restricted routes of appeal to UK courts) was a major part.[20] Each of the devolution statutes contains provisions for cases to be referred to the Judicial Committee if they concern a 'devolution issue', and for determination of those issues without necessarily determining the case as a whole.[21] These provisions take account of the fact that important questions relating to devolution might arise in the

19 For a general discussion of such devolution-related litigation as there has been, see Gee, G., 'Devolution and the Courts', in Hazell, R. and Rawlings, R. (eds), *Devolution, Law Making and the Constitution* (Exeter: Imprint Academic, 2005).
20 The obvious alternative was the House of Lords in its judicial capacity. However, that is part of the UK Parliament and there were concerns that this might cause offence in Scotland, or even infringe the Treaty of Union of 1707. However, the difference between the Appellate Committee and the JCPC is largely cosmetic so this hardly seems compelling.
21 Scotland Act 1998, Schedule 6; Government of Wales Act 1998, Schedule 11; Northern Ireland Act 1998, Schedule 10.

course of litigation between private parties or between a private party and a devolved institution (so-called 'third-party litigation'), as well as directly between governments, and provided for the governments (through their law officers, in the case of the UK Government and Scottish Executive) to be notified of such proceedings and to be heard in them, even if they were not directly involved in the legal dispute before the courts.[22] This sort of power to intervene resembles the working of federal systems and procedure before the European Court of Justice under Article 234 of the EC Treaty, but is most unusual for the UK courts.

The definition of a 'devolution issue' is central to establishing what the jurisdiction of the JCPC is. Such an issue is essentially one of its powers or legal competence: whether an Act of the relevant parliament or assembly, or secondary legislation or an action of the relevant executive, is within the bounds of devolved competence of that body. This includes failures to act as well as actions taken, the question of whether a reserved or (in Northern Ireland) excepted matter is affected, and the question of whether human rights (meaning Convention rights as defined by the Human Rights Act 1998) or EU law have been infringed. It therefore does not include the proper conduct of proceedings by the Scottish Parliament or Northern Ireland Assembly (indeed, they are granted by statute a similar immunity to that of the Westminster Parliament under the 1688 Bill of Rights).[23] It also does not include issues relating to the running of the devolved executives, although relations among the parties holding ministerial posts in the Northern Ireland Executive have proved highly controversial and have been taken to litigation on several occasions.[24]

In practice, however, the use of the 'devolution issues' jurisdiction of the Privy Council has been limited. Between 1999 and 2004 only one Act of the Scottish Parliament was challenged, because it was alleged to infringe the European Convention on Human Rights.[25] Fourteen other cases were heard,

22 The devolution jurisdiction of the JCPC will transfer to the new UK Supreme Court, following passage of the Constitutional Reform Act 2005; see s. 40 and Schedule 9. See also section 41.

23 Scotland Act 1998, s. 28(5); Northern Ireland Act 1998, s. 5(5). In *Whaley v. Watson* [2000] SC 340, Scottish Parliamentary proceedings were challenged in the Inner House of the Court of Session on the ground that an MSP promoting private member's legislation had received practical assistance from an outside organisation interested in the subject matter, but without declaring that assistance in the register of members' interests. The challenge was dismissed and the court did not even consider whether a devolution issue arose.

24 For full citations and a discussion see Anthony, G., 'Public Law Litigation and the Belfast Agreement', *European Public Law*, 8:3 (2002), 401–22.

25 The first case, *Anderson, Reid & Doherty v. Scottish Ministers* [2003] 2 AC 602, was a challenge to the Mental Health (Public Safety and Appeals) (Scotland) Act

all involving criminal prosecutions where the offence charged or procedure followed was similarly alleged to breach human rights.[26] No case involved an intergovernmental dispute, none raised issues of whether a devolved institution had breached its powers as set out in the relevant legislation (other than in relation to the European Convention), and in the only case where the JCPC was invited to use judicial interpretation to deal with a supposed gap in the devolution legislation it declined even to consider the issue.[27] This is not because the parties to litigation consider that devolution issues are rare – between 600 and 1000 a year are notified to the UK Government, mostly from Scotland – but the law officers involved seldom decide to intervene (and those cases are seldom appealed to the higher courts).[28] The courts have therefore not used their power to modify the devolution settlements by judicial interpretation, and have in fact had only limited opportunity to consider devolution at all.

Perhaps the most striking aspect of the role of the courts in the devolution settlement was the UK's unilateral decision to change this. During what became known as the 'botched reshuffle' in June 2003, 10 Downing Street announced that a new UK Supreme Court would be established. There had been no prior consideration of the implications of this for the devolved administrations, nor any consultation of them. At the time it was not even clear how this would affect the jurisdiction of the Judicial Committee,

1999, which provided for the continued imprisonment of those who were mentally ill but adjudged incapable of improving through treatment, where they posed a continuing threat to the public. In *Whaley and Friend v. Lord Advocate*, there was a challenge to the Protection of Wild Mammals (Scotland) Act 2002. The case was dismissed on appeal to the Inner House of the Court of Session, and not appealed to the Judicial Committee.

26 The first cases are discussed in O'Neill, A., 'Judicial Politics and the Judicial Committee: The devolution jurisprudence of the Privy Council', *Modern Law Review*, 64 (2001), 603–17. Judgments in all 'devolution issue' cases are available on the internet at: www.privy-council.org.uk/output/Page31.asp.

27 *Mills v. Lord Advocate* [2004] 1 AC 441, a criminal case regarding alleged infringement of human rights because of the prosecutor's delay. The lacuna was that such issues could be raised as a devolution issue, in which case the UK Government's Scottish Law Officer, the Advocate-General for Scotland, would be notified of the case, or straightforwardly under the Human Rights Act 1998, in which case the Lord Advocate as prosecutor would be notified but not the Advocate-General. The Advocate-General sought to have all such cases treated as raising a devolution issue, so she would be notified of them. The JCPC simply dealt with the substantive case not the issue of the procedural lacuna. See also Jamieson, I., 'Relationship between the Scotland Act and the Human Rights Act', *Scottish Law Times* (News), 43 (2001).

28 Author's interviews.

although with publication subsequently of the consultation paper about the Supreme Court it became clear what was planned.[29] While the devolved administrations had no particular objections (and the proposal was subsequently given effect by the Constitutional Reform Act 2005), the fact that such a change could be contemplated without consultation of those so directly affected suggests once again that devolution matters are not a high priority for the Prime Minister.

The UK's arrangements in perspective

The UK's arrangements are characteristic in a number of respects. It makes little use of formal meetings, whether to coordinate governments' policies or to resolve disagreements or disputes between them. In the UK, whether meetings happen at all (let alone what happens at them) is a matter requiring a political decision – even for relatively routine interministerial meetings. Moreover, a driving factor in meetings of BIC and JMC, whether in plenary or functional formats, is the overlap between devolved responsibilities and the UK Government's similar responsibilities for England – a function of the UK's asymmetrical arrangements.

Similarly, the courts play a marginal role in the practice of devolution. Part of the reason for this is structural; as discussed in chapter 3, the various devolution statutes include numerous powers for adjustment of the devolution settlements at the margin, where there is or appears to be a lack of legal powers.[30] For Scotland and Northern Ireland these include powers to extend devolved competence retrospectively, in order to save an action or piece of legislation that was otherwise invalid; to extend devolved competence into reserved matters; and to transfer back functions (by amending Schedule 5 to the Scotland Act or Schedule 3 to the Northern Ireland Act) which would in fact be better exercised by the UK Government. There are also powers to vary the scope of executive devolution, either by appointing the devolved administration to act on the UK Government's behalf or by outright transfer of functions. All such transfers require consent of both governments involved and of the devolved legislature or assembly as well as of the Westminster Parliament. If the governments involved can agree on how to deal with a matter, they can reshape the boundaries of the devolution settlement without needing to refer it to the courts, and this happens with sufficient frequency (about five such instruments are made each year) that space in the Westminster legislative

---

29 Department for Constitutional Affairs, *Constitutional Reform: A Supreme Court for the United Kingdom*, Consultation Paper CP 11/03 (London, 2003).
30 See chapter 3.

programme is usually reserved in advance for such legislation.[31] This means that matters which could otherwise be considered by the courts can instead be resolved by agreement – if conditions for agreement exist. Consequently, it has been possible for litigation to be treated as a matter of last resort. While some government lawyers consider it would also be a means of resolving difficult technical legal issues where there is no political interest, that view has not yet had any tangible result.

Administrative arrangements in Whitehall

The limited scope of JMC meetings and coordination through ministerial meetings relate to what happens at official level. It both reflects the importance of coordination at official level and increases the importance of that coordination and of the way that each administration organises itself to deal with IGR. In other words, the lack of formal and ministerial mechanisms drives matters further 'downstream', to official-level liaison and working practices. This gives a broader importance to those official arrangements; in the UK context, if the administrative and bilateral machinery deals effectively with intergovernmental issues, governments will avoid any arguments or differences emerging, and it will also simplify the issues needing to be dealt with.

The UK Government's arrangements have been largely a continuation of those from before devolution. No single minister has responsibility for devolution. Rather, separate Secretaries of State (and offices) have dealt with relations with Scotland, Wales and Northern Ireland. Each of those is supported not just by civil servants and special advisors, but also by junior ministers who (for Scotland and Wales) undertake much routine work including leading on legislation in Parliament.[32] There has also been a Cabinet minister responsible for devolution (or constitutional change) as a whole – a role initially

31 This is a marked exception to practice in federal systems; even if the governments involved agreed in principle on a transfer arrangement or something similar, there would be a question over the constitutionality of such an agreement. One rare exception, in Australia, is the possibility of a referral of legislative power from states to the Commonwealth Parliament under s. 106 of the Constitution.

32 For an official account of the machinery of intergovernmental affairs, see the Memorandum by the Cabinet Office in House of Lords Select Committee on the Constitution, *Devolution: Inter-institutional Relations in the United Kingdom: Minutes of evidence*, HL 147 (London: The Stationery Office, 2002), 14–24, also available at www.dca.gov.uk/constitution/devolution/pubs/odpm_dev_609019.pdf. See also the discussion in Hazell, R., 'Intergovernmental Relations: Whitehall rules OK?', in Hazell, R. (ed.), *The State and the Nations: The first year of devolution in the United Kingdom* (Exeter: Imprint Academic, 2000).

played by the Lord Chancellor, Lord Irvine to 2001, later by the Deputy Prime Minister, John Prescott, then from June 2003 by the Secretary of State for Constitutional Affairs, Lord Falconer. After 1999 the jobs of Scottish and Welsh Secretary increasingly came to be less than full time, and from June 2003 have been combined with other portfolios.[33] On the official side, the Constitution Secretariat of the Cabinet Office was wound up as part of the 2001 reshuffle, and in June 2003 the Scotland and Wales Offices lost their independence to become parts of the Department for Constitutional Affairs, although questions of which minister they were accountable to and for what remained open, as did the exact nature of their autonomy.[34] Following the 2005 UK general election, the specialist Cabinet committee for devolution (which had last met in 2002 to consider the white paper on English regional government, *Your Region Your Choice*) was formally wound up, and responsibility for devolution transferred to the Constitutional Affairs (CA) committee. Complaints about the 'missing centre' therefore have a good deal of merit on the institutional level.[35] There is an absence of control of devolution at the centre of UK Government, whether in the form of an individual minister in charge or a strong coordination mechanism to bring together the various actors and establish overall direction.

The roles of the offices vary a good deal, however. While each has general responsibility for relations with Scotland, Wales or Northern Ireland, for advising on the devolution settlement and for non-devolved matters affecting that territory, the programme responsibilities of each office vary. For Scotland and Wales, they are limited to devolved Parliament or Assembly elections (UK elections being reserved but dealt with by the Office of the Deputy Prime

33 When Peter Hain became Secretary of State for Wales in November 2002, he effectively was part time as he retained the role of UK Government representative on the Giscard Convention considering a European Constitution. For discussion of the 2003 changes, see Hazell, R., 'Merger: What merger? Scotland, Wales, and the new Department for Constitutional Affairs', *Public Law* (2003), 650–5.

34 Their connection with the Department for Constitutional Affairs was said to be for 'pay and rations' purposes, although what that means is unclear, especially as the costs of running the offices are in fact deducted from funds allocated to the devolved administrations by the Treasury. See House of Commons Welsh Affairs Committee, *Minutes of Evidence for Wednesday 25 June 2003: The Wales Office departmental report 2003*, HC 883 (London: The Stationery Office, 2003); House of Commons Scottish Affairs Committee, *Minutes of Evidence for Tuesday 17 June 2003*, HC 815 (London: The Stationery Office, 2003).

35 For an attempt at a graphic representation of the working of the various networks after devolution, and the absence of such a centre, see Trench, A., 'Whitehall and the Process of Legislation after Devolution', in Hazell and Rawlings (eds), *Devolution, Law Making and the Constitution*, 211.

Minister), while for Northern Ireland they have included law and order, policing, prisons and criminal justice, even when devolution has been in force. However, the Wales Office has had the complicated business of dealing with Westminster legislation affecting Wales, meaning not just Wales-only bills and other Westminster legislation sought by the National Assembly, but also the effects for Wales of most UK Government bills intended primarily to deal with policy for England.[36] Paradoxically, despite having more complicated responsibilities, it has been smaller for much of the period since 1999 than the Scotland Office – in 2002, it had about 41 staff, excluding lawyers, while the Scotland Office had about 85 non-legal staff.[37] Following the 2003 reshuffle this has changed, however. According to their 2005 annual reports, the two offices have become nearly the same size, the Wales Office having 52 non-legal staff and the Scotland Office 57 non-legal staff. (The Wales Office has 2 lawyers and the Scotland Office 29, most of them in the Office of the Solicitor to the Advocate-General.[38])

Although the jobs of the territorial Secretaries of State are not now time-consuming, they are the central point of contact and liaison for the UK Government with the devolved administrations. They have an important behind-the-scenes role in meshing the two governments together at the highest level. The role is partly one of political liaison – the ministers involved all belong, of course, to one party – and partly one of pre-empting disputes and resolving them behind the scenes. They meet or speak to the devolved First Minister often; the Secretary of State for Wales and the First Minister reportedly meet each week and speak by telephone several times a week, although contact between the Scottish Secretary and First Minister appears

---

36 To facilitate this (and unlike the other territorial offices) the Wales Office signed a bilateral concordat in January 2001. The Secretary of State for Wales also has designated responsibilities to attend the National Assembly and present the UK Government's legislative programme to it, and to receive all papers for Assembly plenary sessions (though not Committee meetings): Government of Wales Act 1998, s. 31 and s. 76. No functions are conferred on the Secretary of State for Scotland by name.

37 House of Lords Select Committee on the Constitution, *Devolution: Inter-institutional Relations in the United Kingdom*, 24. As the Scotland Office at that time housed about 30 lawyers in the Office of the Solicitor to the Advocate-General for Scotland, who carried out a wide range of general Scottish legal work for UK Government departments as well as work arising specifically from devolution, it is hard to calculate the number of legal staff working directly on devolution matters.

38 See *Scotland Office and Office of the Solicitor to the Advocate General for Scotland Annual Report 2005*, Cm 6544 (Edinburgh: The Stationery Office, 2004), figures 3 and 7; *Wales Office Annual Report 2005*, Cm 6545 (London: The Stationery Office, 2005), para. 4.

somewhat less frequent. They are copied most correspondence between Whitehall departments and the devolved administrations, and 'speak for' Scotland or Wales at a large number of Cabinet committees concerned with domestic policy. (This is largely a watching brief, but would potentially be a time-consuming one if the ministers involved were not already on such committees because of their other portfolios.) From interviewing it appears that by 2004 the Scottish work of the Secretary of State for Scotland amounted to about 20 per cent of his workload, and less by 2005, while Wales has consistently taken about 20 per cent of Peter Hain's time. Their role is particularly important when it comes to issues of the devolved constitution, with the question of the number of Scottish MPs important for Helen Liddell in 2001–02, and the powers and arrangements of the National Assembly taking centre stage for Wales and the Wales Office in 2004–05. More generally, this indirect connection with the UK Government is valued by many devolved officials, who spoke warmly in interview of the value of having such representation within the UK Government and of being able to ensure that their territory's concerns are heard through that channel.

There are nonetheless ambiguities about the role of the Secretary of State. One is whether she or he is there to represent the territory to or in the UK Government, or to represent the UK Government in or to the territory. Another is what his or her obligations are to the devolved administration. As Secretary of State for Wales, Paul Murphy was keen to emphasise that he presented the views of the National Assembly, but did not represent it, and that his presentation of its views did not necessarily mean he shared them.[39] He saw himself as an advocate, not a delegate. His successor was happy to describe his role as 'negotiating and representing the Assembly', starting with the presumption that he wished to see the Assembly's wishes carried into practice but subject to the interests, objectives and policies of Whitehall departments.[40] That implies a stronger need for the Secretary of State to share the Assembly's views to be able to communicate them effectively.

Beside the 'territorial' offices there has also been a small team at the centre of government, with about half a dozen staff taking on a general role of coordinating policy on devolution, including acting as the UK part of the joint secretariat for JMCs. That team has moved from the Constitution

---

39 House of Lords Select Committee on the Constitution, *Devolution: Interinstitutional Relations in the United Kingdom: Minutes of evidence*, Evidence of Mr Murphy, 10 April 2002, Q. 175.
40 See Commission on the Powers and Electoral Arrangements of the National Assembly for Wales, *Report of the Richard Commission* (Cardiff: National Assembly for Wales, 2004), chap. 7, paras 14–15.

Secretariat in the Cabinet Office to the Office of the Deputy Prime Minister to the Department for Constitutional Affairs (DCA), but has retained its identity and responsibilities throughout. (In June 2003 it also acquired responsibility for the Crown Dependencies, meaning the Channel Islands and the Isle of Man.) This team takes a broader view of the devolution settlements, but its size and the many demands on it mean that it is unable to provide a strong central lead on policy towards the devolved institutions.

In Whitehall departments dealing with policy areas (sometimes called 'line departments'), responsibility for devolution has been less clear.[41] Most departments established posts or sections to deal with devolution questions in the early days of devolution, but these were dissolved in 2000–01 as responsibility was 'mainstreamed'. Although a nominal list of devolution contacts in each UK Government department has continued to exist, few policy officials in line departments have a specialist role in dealing with devolution. There are none, for example, in the Department of Health, Department for Education and Skills, the Department for the Environment, Food and Rural Affairs, or (now) in the Home Office. Where specialist devolution desk officers do exist, they are generally in departments such as the Ministry of Defence or the Foreign and Commonwealth Office, where there is a question of liaison with the devolved administrations but no sharing or overlap of functions. Unsurprisingly, the result is that organisation for devolution in other departments remains haphazard, depending on the awareness of devolution on the part of individual officials and the extent to which they follow procedures designed to identify and resolve such questions. Guidance for UK Government departments regarding how they should deal with the devolved administrations exists, in the form of the Devolution Guidance Notes first prepared by the Cabinet Office in 1999, and still regularly updated.[42] These are probably the most used devolution documents, and are certainly consulted more than the Memorandum of Understanding or bilateral concordats. Even with these, however, compliance is patchy and the only overall pattern remains one of inconsistency. The best indicator of whether an individual official is 'devolution aware' remains whether they have dealt with devolution issues in a previous post. Better coordination exists between government lawyers, whose network remains more active. The overall picture is one that replicates the established pattern of UK Government – one of fragmented responsibility

---

41 For a discussion of how Whitehall has responded to devolution, with an emphasis on legislative matters, see Trench, 'Whitehall and the Process of Legislation after Devolution'.

42 Now available on the internet at www.dca.gov.uk/constitution/devolution/guidance.htm#part2.

with a lack of strong coordination from the centre, in which each department is largely free to pursue its own course subject to the requirements of Cabinet approval and collective responsibility, and the coordination that necessitates.[43]

In the absence of routinised and systematic means for managing relations with the devolved administrations, much depends on frequent but ad hoc interaction. This is largely driven by whatever happens to be on the agenda of the respective governments at any time – and that often means the UK Government's agenda, given how much larger and broader its responsibilities are. At this level, the devolved administrations are very closely integrated into the administrative machinery of the UK Government. This may arise in a crisis: devolved administration officials took part in the 'COBR' emergency management machinery based at 10 Downing Street during the 2001 Foot and Mouth Disease outbreak, for example. However, the bulk of this is driven by UK Government legislation, and the devolved administrations are closely involved in UK Government department bill teams planning for or handling legislation in Parliament, occasionally by secondment but more often by telephone and email contact. For provisions that apply specifically to Wales in Westminster legislation, Welsh Assembly Government officials will brief the junior minister from the Wales Office who handles them in Parliament. For EU business, officials from the Scottish Executive and Welsh Assembly Government attend the weekly strategy and planning meetings held in London, alongside Whitehall departments.

Like much business of UK Government, such contact is driven by the concerns of the moment. It does not plan ahead for different sorts of eventualities or different political relations between the governments involved. It can also be erratic – while the norm is for the devolved administrations to be consulted or involved in UK initiatives, devolution aspects of an issue may well be overlooked in the pressure of dealing with urgent business. Consultation may take place so late that it is hard for the devolved administrations to respond in a meaningful way. It may, occasionally, not take place at all.[44] In rare cases, the devolved administrations are not involved directly because of the interests of confidentiality within UK Government, so the

43 Daintith, T. and Page, A., *The Executive in the Constitution: Structure, autonomy, and internal control* (Oxford: Oxford University Press, 1999), chapters 2 and 10.
44 This appears to have been the case with the white paper on higher education in England: Department for Education and Skills, *The Future of Higher Education*, Cm 5735 (London: The Stationery Office, 2003). This recommended 'top-up' tuition fees, with significant financial and policy implications for the devolved administrations. The content of the white paper was hotly debated within UK Government (chiefly within 10 Downing Street and between Number 10, the Treasury and the office of the Secretary of State for Education and Skills), and only finalised late in

territorial Secretaries of State and their offices must speak for the devolved administration and express their likely concerns without being able to establish what the views of the devolved administration actually are.

Part of the reason why the UK Government can afford to take such an approach is that there are few occasions when the devolved administrations can cause serious inconvenience to the UK Government. With the 2003 Higher Education white paper, the problems arising from the very late and limited consultation have simply been ignored, or left to be resolved subsequently. From a UK point of view they are trivial, however significant they may be for the devolved administrations. Similar considerations apply to two cases where consultation with Wales was late, poor and ineffective, both of which led to critical reports from the Commons Welsh Affairs Committee.[45] The refusal of the Welsh Assembly Government to sign legislation to enable the UK Government to authorise the growing of genetically modified wheat led to irritation at the UK department concerned (and the making of heavy-handed threats). One solution the UK Government offered was to 'undevolve' the power to make the regulations, so the Assembly did not have to consent to the proposed UK Government policy (which would still apply in Wales), while another was to require the Welsh Assembly Government to give its consent as what was at issue was implementation of an EU obligation.[46]

Moreover, key to the success of this approach is the fact that all the politicians involved belong to the Labour Party. There can be differences between different parts of the party, but common membership creates a set of incentives to improve the party's electoral prospects generally (a point that Martin Laffin and his colleagues develop further in chapter 9). Indeed, Labour politicians have on occasion referred to the importance of having Labour governments elected at both levels, to ensure that there is an effective 'partnership' between them. In one of his rare statements about devolution, in a newspaper interview just before the 2003 Scottish election, the UK Prime Minister said,

the day. The normal processes of the Department for Education and Skills were bypassed, and so there was no prior consultation with the devolved administrations. See also McLean, I., 'The National Question', in Seldon, A. and Kavanagh, D. (eds), *The Blair Effect 2001–05* (Cambridge: Cambridge University Press, 2005), 354.

45 See House of Commons Welsh Affairs Committee, Session 2003–04 5th Report, *The Powers of the Children's Commissioner for Wales*, HC 538 (London: The Stationery Office, 2004); House of Commons Welsh Affairs Committee, Session 2004–05 4th Report, *Police Service, Crime and Anti-Social Behaviour in Wales*, HC 46-I (London: The Stationery Office, 2005). The latter led to a revision and recirculation of Devolution Guidance Note 9 on Post-Devolution Primary Legislation Affecting Wales.

46 See 'Scotland and Wales "Bullied" over GM Crop Veto', *Independent on Sunday* (14 March 2004); author's interviews.

'It is important that the Scottish Executive works in partnership with the British Executive. There is a very clear choice, the SNP I think are actually saying that their desire is to get into wrangles with London and Westminster. This is disastrous, it will mess up the economy or stop it functioning in the way it should.'[47] The clear implication is that it would be very hard for a devolved Scottish or Welsh government to work if a different party were in office in London. There have also been rumours on a number of occasions of reluctance within the UK Government to consult devolved administrations because of the involvement of Liberal Democrats in coalition governments – particularly, but not only, when the devolved minister involved was a Liberal Democrat. In similar vein, Peter Hain and Rhodri Morgan wrote in a newspaper article at the start of the 2005 UK general election campaign that:

> A Tory victory would end the strong partnership we have been able to forge between Governments at Westminster and the Assembly. An Assembly Labour Government and a Tory UK Government at constant loggerheads, with megaphone diplomacy conducted through the media, would be a paradise for headline writers and journalists, but it would be a disaster for our schools, hospitals and hard-working communities.[48]

Party links also work in a different way, by easing communication between governments because of a shared view of the world as well as a desire to avoid conflict. As the then Scottish Secretary put it in 2002, her good relations with the Scottish First Minister were greatly helped by the fact that when they spoke to each other they knew they were 'among friends'.[49]

This approach can be characterised, then, as not merely unstructured and ad hoc but also assuming a high degree of intimacy in relations between governments. Unsurprisingly, the result of such an approach is that the substantive outcomes vary hugely.

Administrative arrangements in Edinburgh, Cardiff and Belfast

The devolved administrations each have somewhat similar arrangements for handling intergovernmental relations. They are handled by the first minister in each case (the first and deputy first ministers in Northern Ireland), with the support of a small number of officials at the centre. These often share

47 'Scotland Can Be Proud Of Us', *The Herald* (Glasgow) (17 April 2003).
48 Hain, P. and Morgan, R., 'Our Strategy for Taking Devolution to a New Level', *Western Mail* (9 April 2005).
49 House of Lords Select Committee on the Constitution, *Devolution: Inter-institutional Relations in the United Kingdom: Minutes of evidence*, Evidence of Mrs Liddell, 10 April 2002, Q. 157.

their functions with other tasks; in Scotland there is a distinction between 'policy' matters and 'constitutional' ones, each allocated to separate teams of 5–6 officials. Those officials also have other responsibilities, but are located at the centre of bureaucratic organisation within the Office of the Permanent Secretary. Those dealing with Scotland Act matters also deal with Parliamentary matters and the Holyrood legislative programme. In Wales, the central team has since the spring of 2004 (following publication of the Richard Report) been concerned principally with constitutional matters rather than managing relations from day to day. The chief point of liaison at the political level is with the territorial Secretary of State; the officials involved directly have frequent contacts with their opposite numbers in Whitehall and the other devolved administrations (both in the Scotland and Wales Offices and the DCA team).

Most interaction, however, takes place between officials in departments with policy responsibility and their counterparts in the UK Government. That occurs as and when needed. Devolved administration officials are less prone to overlooking the UK dimension of an initiative than the UK Government is of the devolved implications, partly because this is a more pressing political concern for the devolved ministers (and so is a point that needs to be addressed in any submission and in its presentation to the public) and partly because such issues are more significant in policy terms and need to be dealt with for a proposal to be workable. While the worst a devolved administration can inflict on the UK Government is inconvenience which is limited in scale and usually soluble, the devolved administrations can be seriously affected if the UK Government should be unaware of what they plan let alone if they wish to inconvenience it. Even during the Foot and Mouth Disease outbreak, the National Assembly for Wales required UK Government assistance to deal with the crisis, especially in passing legislation; although the staff responsible for animal health had transferred to the Assembly, many of the legislative functions remained in Whitehall.[50]

Northern Ireland has been something of an exception to the ways of working of the UK Government, Scottish Executive and Welsh Assembly Government, and further undermines an attempt to understand the working of the UK as a partly federal system. The most obvious difference derives from the peace process. Even under devolution the Northern Ireland Office

---

50 See House of Lords Select Committee on the Constitution, *Devolution: Inter-institutional Relations in the United Kingdom: Minutes of evidence*, Evidence of Mr Carwyn Jones, 28 May 2002, Q. 959; 41–3; *Foot and Mouth Disease 2001: Lessons to be Learned inquiry report*, HC 888 (London: The Stationery Office, 2002), para. 9.10.

retained control of a number of significant programme areas, mostly relating to law and order, giving it direct responsibility for prisoner releases or the restructuring of policing. It also has responsibility for the peace process as a whole, meaning it takes a prominent role in chairing and coordinating negotiations about a range of matters, including arms decommissioning or the review of the Belfast Agreement (which started in February 2004). The NIO's role led it to take steps it considered necessary politically, whether or not they accorded with the terms of the Belfast Agreement. That includes the assumption of the controversial power to suspend devolution and to re-start it, to continue operation of the implementation bodies for North–South cooperation, or to establish the monitoring commission to determine whether arms decommissioning has taken place.[51]

The importance of the Northern Ireland Office is not the only distinctive feature of the arrangements for Northern Ireland. One source of difference derives from relations with the Republic of Ireland which constitute Strand 2 of the Belfast Agreement, and the areas of cooperation identified in the Agreement were subsequently extended. While the nationalist parties have had a strong interest in promoting these, the inherent geographic logic of a single island also propels cooperation on many practical matters, from maritime navigation to animal health. A second factor is the history of distinct administration in Northern Ireland, which continued even under direct rule between 1972 and 2000, as well as since 2002. Consequently, Northern Ireland has an administrative apparatus and an administrative tradition that have equipped it to act for itself in circumstances where the other devolved administrations would look to the UK Government for guidance or legislation. A further one has been party political; as none of the UK parties has been elected to the Northern Ireland Assembly, the direct party links that are a feature of relations between the UK Government and British devolved administrations are absent. There can be no sense in dealings with the Northern Ireland parties that a Labour Secretary of State is 'among friends', but rather she or he has to treat all the parties involved even-handedly because such impartiality is a necessary consequence of the peace process. Equally, no UK party can seek to claim credit for actions of the Northern Ireland Executive or draw party advantage from attacking its deficiencies. One consequence of these factors has been a greater degree of formality in Northern Ireland–UK relations under devolution than has been evident for Wales or Scotland, given the greater administrative and political difference between administrations and the political imperative for the UK appearing even-handed in its dealings with Northern Ireland.

51 Northern Ireland Act 2000; Northern Ireland (Monitoring Commission etc.) Act 2003.

Relations between the devolved administrations among themselves remain limited as well as informal. Ministers from each territory have relatively little contact with each other; the visit by the Northern Ireland First and Deputy First Ministers to meet their counterparts in Scotland in June 2002 was a very rare exception.[52] Otherwise, ministers (and officials) obviously meet, but usually at meetings with the UK Government such as the JMC or BIC (or in the fringes of such meetings), or at major events such as royal weddings, state funerals or party conferences. Except for the small number of officials directly concerned with intergovernmental relations, there is little routine interaction at political or official level. Even the contact between IGR specialists is for the purpose of dealing with process issues rather than coordinating substantive positions.

The practice of routine intergovernmental relations and the role of legislation

Looked at from the point of view of someone working in government, devolution has had a curious effect. On the one hand, as discussed above, there are strong forces that mean that the various governments in the United Kingdom have a great deal to do with each other. For civil servants there is still a high degree of integration. The permanent secretaries of the Scottish Executive and National Assembly remain members of the group of permanent secretaries, and sometimes still attend the Wednesday afternoon meetings of permanent secretaries.[53] On the other hand, there is substantial disengagement. The present permanent secretaries attend those Wednesday meetings only occasionally (unlike the Executive's first Permanent Secretary, who made a point of attending). While interaction between officials at lower levels remains easy and routine, and appears to be facilitated by the recognition of staff from other administrations that common membership of the Home Civil Service underpins, that only occurs when there is a reason for it. (One significant case where there was such a need arose from the blocking by Rhodri Morgan of the appointment of Gerald Elias QC as Counsel-General to the National Assembly for Wales in 2003, which led to criticism from the Civil Service Commission.[54] In the event, no appointment was made and the office

---

52 BBC News, 'Devolved Executives Boost Links', 20 June 2002. Available at http://news.bbc.co.uk/1/hi/scotland/2054744.stm; accessed November 2005.
53 The Head of the Northern Ireland Civil Service is also invited to attend as an observer, but appears to do so only occasionally.
54 Civil Service Commissioners, *Annual Report 2003–2004* (London: Office of the Civil Service Commissioners, 2004), 21.

was abolished.) Often, there is no such reason. Officials engaged in policy development in Scotland or Wales may need to be aware of what the UK Government is doing, but in interview report that they have very limited involvement with colleagues in the UK Government and with current issues in Whitehall. Instead, their concerns are in Scotland or Wales.

However, one of the major immediate causes of intergovernmental relations on the day to day level is legislation at Westminster. The preparation and Parliamentary consideration of legislation (and its post-enactment implementation, to a much lesser degree) are a major activity of government in its own right, as well as giving government the legal resources with which to make policy.[55] Legislation therefore drives a large amount of government business, triggering many of the routine interactions of governments (and disagreements between them).[56] It is therefore worth closer consideration, for showing how the border between devolved and non-devolved matters is negotiated from day to day.[57] It also shows how the complexities and interdependencies of the devolution arrangements manifest themselves by further complicating something that was already complex enough.[58]

One immediate consequence of the different sets of devolution arrangements is that the ways Westminster is important, and the extent to which it is important, vary radically. Thus Westminster has only secondary importance for Northern Ireland on the day-to-day level, even under direct rule, as routine legislation is usually made using orders in council rather than an Act of Parliament. An Act is only normally sought where the legislation for Northern Ireland needs to follow, and be enacted at the same time as UK legislation – or where what is at issue are reserved or excepted matters, not ones within the competence of the Northern Ireland departments. A further quirk has been the peculiar application of the Sewel convention there even under

---

55 See Daintith and Page, *The Executive in the Constitution*, particularly chapter 8.
56 For recent, vividly illustrated examples of such routine interaction within the UK Government, see Page, E. C., 'The Civil Servant as Legislator: Law making in British administration', *Public Administration*, 81:4 (2003), 651–79; and Page, E. C. and Jenkins, B., *Policy Bureaucracy: Government with a cast of thousands* (Oxford: Oxford University Press, 2005).
57 For detailed consideration of legislative issues, see generally Hazell, R. and Rawlings, R. (eds), *Devolution, Law Making and the Constitution* (Exeter: Imprint Academic, 2005). This discussion owes a good deal to my own contribution to that volume.
58 See Himsworth, C., 'The General Effects of Devolution upon the Practice of Legislation at Westminster', Appendix 1 to House of Lords Select Committee on the Constitution, Session 2003–04 15th Report, *Devolution: Its effect on the practice of legislation at Westminster*, HL 192 (London: The Stationery Office, 2004).

devolution, with consent being normally signalled by the Executive Committee, not the Assembly.[59]

For Scotland, there are two areas of concern. One is Holyrood legislation. This is subject to various checks to ensure that the Parliament only legislates for matters within its legislative competence. These include certificates from the Parliament's Presiding Officer and (for Executive bills) the Executive that the bill is within competence.[60] However, there are also provisions (in sections 33 and 35 of the Scotland Act 1998) that empower the UK Government to intervene to prevent royal assent being given to a bill, and to refer a bill to the Judicial Committee, if it considers it to be beyond the Parliament's legislative competence. To ensure that no bill exceeds that competence, the UK Government's Scottish lawyers (in the Office of the Solicitor to the Advocate-General) examine each bill in detail, and check across Whitehall by what is known as a 'section 33 trawl' to ensure that the UK Government is satisfied that the Parliament has not exceeded its competence – even though this job is highly laborious and time-consuming, and to a degree duplicates checks already carried out for the devolved institutions. So far no bill has been challenged by any of these procedures (although there has been early consultation about the contents of bills to ensure that no problem arises), but this close scrutiny of legislation by another government indicates a surveillance of autonomy that is not to be found in many other areas of devolved government.

However, Sewel motions rather than UK scrutiny of devolved legislation have been the over-riding concern.[61] Although the Sewel motion mechanism was expected before devolution only to be used on rare occasions, it has in fact been widely used – for 38 Westminster bills (and 39 resolutions) in the Scottish Parliament's first session (1999–2003).[62] In the second session to December 2005, there were 26 motions (and a further 2 under consideration). According

59 See Anthony, G. and Morison, J., 'Here, There and (Maybe) Here Again: The story of law making for post-1998 Northern Ireland', in Hazell and Rawlings (eds), *Devolution, Law Making and the Constitution*.

60 See Scotland Act 1998, s. 31.

61 See generally Winetrobe, B., 'A Partnership of the Parliaments? Scottish law making under the Sewel Convention at Westminster and Holyrood', in Hazell and Rawlings (eds), *Devolution, Law Making and the Constitution*; Page, A. and Batey, A. 'Scotland's other Parliament: Westminster legislation about devolved matters in Scotland since devolution', *Public Law* (2002), 501–23; Winetrobe, B., 'Counter-Devolution? The Sewel Convention on devolved legislation at Westminster', *Scottish Law & Practice Quarterly*, 6 (2001), 286–92; and Cairney, P. and Keating, M., 'Sewel Motions in the Scottish Parliament', *Scottish Affairs*, 47 (2004), 115–34.

62 Winetrobe, 'A Partnership of the Parliaments?', 41.

to internal government guidance, there are three categories of bills for the purposes of the Sewel convention. Bills which do not affect devolved matters, or only do so incidentally and consequentially, do not need Holyrood's consent under the convention. Bills which affect devolved matters or the functions of the Scottish Executive do require consent.[63] Sometimes this dividing line is treated as clear-cut and applied in a consistent and logical manner. However, interviewing and a consideration of the Westminster statute book suggest a more fluid picture in which it is hard to explain why some bills are subject to Sewel motions and others are not.[64] (Interviewees would admit that errors were made in the early days of devolution and claimed that practice had become better, and more consistent, subsequently.) Nonetheless, an impression of variation and inconsistency persists.

In any case, it is easy to become too pre-occupied with the formal requirement of Holyrood's consent under the Sewel convention, which is subject to intergovernmental negotiation and agreement. A Sewel motion is equally triggered by a small number of clauses which happen to deal with a devolved matter in a generally non-devolved context (for example, the provisions relating to personal bankruptcy in the Limited Liability Partnerships Act 2000) as by a comprehensive code dealing with substantive devolved matters (such as the provisions for recovering criminally acquired property in the Proceeds of Crime Act 2002). By a clear if tacit agreement between governments, some legislative provisions do not need Sewel consent despite affecting devolved matters; no Sewel motions have been submitted at Holyrood for cases where criminal offences in Scotland have been created in connection with reserved matters.[65] None of the internal guidance makes any reference to such cases. Assuming that the initiative comes from Westminster, the decision that Westminster should legislate but subject to Holyrood's consent is only one of a number of possible outcomes to such negotiation. Others include omitting relevant provisions from the Westminster statute altogether, or omitting them on the basis that separate Scottish legislation will follow in due course (as happened with the provision banning incitement to religious hatred, originally included in the 2001 Anti-terrorism, Crime and Security bill but dropped because of opposition at Westminster). In some

---

63 See the Cabinet Office's *Guide to Legislative Procedures* (London: Cabinet Office, September 2003), available at www.cabinet-office.gov.uk/legislation/legguide/index.asp; accessed November 2005; and Devolution Guidance Note 10, *Post-Devolution Primary Legislation Affecting Scotland*.

64 Trench, A., *Devolution in Practice? Scottish and Welsh devolution and the Westminster statute book* (mimeo, London: The Constitution Unit, 2002).

65 See for example the Postal Services Act 2000, Part V, or the Social Security Fraud Act 2001.

cases, the initiative comes from Scotland, with the Executive deciding to sign up to a UK Government initiative with which it agrees (as with the provisions of the Adoption and Children Act 2002 relating to the adoption register). On rare occasions, there are reasons to believe that matters have been considered at Westminster under the Sewel convention because of concerns that they might fall foul of the European Convention on Human Rights and, if enacted at Holyrood, risk being void and so ineffective (though this has been denied in interview). If passed at Westminster, the worst that could happen would be the embarrassment of a declaration of incompatibility from the courts. (It should be emphasised that these suggestions have been denied by officials interviewed, but the suspicion persists.) Even when there is no direct impact on Scotland, there may be an indirect one; when fur farms were banned in England and Wales, Scotland rapidly passed similar legislation to prevent fur farms (of which there were none in Scotland at the time) from relocating north of the Tweed.

While legislation for Scotland varies a good deal, that for Wales has varied even more.[66] Westminster remains Wales's sole legislature, and the National Assembly and its powers are therefore entirely dependent on what happens at Westminster. The Welsh Assembly Government noted of Westminster legislation:

> This is one of the most fundamental aspects of the Welsh settlement, and one of the most fluid. The Assembly can neither pass primary legislation of its own, nor simply and passively accept, administer and implement UK Government policy as reflected in new primary legislation: that would be a denial of its separate democratic mandate. . . . The Assembly must therefore seek to influence primary legislation so that it reflects its own policy agenda.[67]

It can be hard to identify why some Acts of Parliament are comparatively generous to Wales and others are not. Problems with a range of issues have persisted; attempts to secure greater consistency in both the form of legislation affecting the National Assembly's functions and the substance of its powers have been largely ineffective. To a limited extent, the National

---

66 For discussions, see Patchett, K., 'The Central Relationship: The Assembly's engagement with Westminster and Whitehall', in Jones, J. B. and Osmond, J. (eds), *Building a Civic Culture: Institutional change, policy development and political dynamics in the National Assembly for Wales* (Cardiff: Institute of Welsh Affairs and Welsh Governance Centre, 2002); Rawlings, *Delineating Wales*, chap. 9; and Patchett, K., 'Principle or Pragmatism', in Hazell and Rawlings, *Devolution, Law Making and the Constitution*.

67 Memorandum by the Welsh Assembly Government in House of Lords Select Committee on the Constitution Session, *Devolution: Inter-institutional Relations in the United Kingdom: Minutes of Evidence*, 231, paras 14–15.

Assembly has been the author of its own problems, as it has failed to take an active approach to promoting consistency in Westminster legislation. The most notable case relates to the so-called 'Rawlings principles' adopted by the Assembly Review of Procedure in January 2002, and designed to codify existing principles applied by civil servants to Westminster legislation.[68] Yet in this case the principles were not communicated directly to the UK Government, awareness of them in Whitehall was very limited until the House of Lords Select Committee on the Constitution included discussion of them in its report on *Devolution: Inter-institutional Relations*, and the UK Government only set out its views on them when responding to a report by the Commons Welsh Affairs Committee on *The Primary Legislative Process as It Affects Wales* in March 2003.[69] They have not been included in subsequent revisions of the UK Government's internal guidance on *Post-Devolution Primary Legislation for Wales*, Devolution Guidance Note 9. Even so, the Assembly has failed to audit compliance with them (at least in any public form). Whether the Assembly will fare any better with the UK Government's proposals to use framework legislation for Wales in future, and subsequently to extend the Assembly's powers by orders in council, remains to be seen.[70]

This is not to suggest that the National Assembly has not generally done well in securing legislation at Westminster. Although it has seldom secured more than one Wales-only Westminster bill in any Parliamentary session, measures it has sought to promote have often been incorporated into other bills when a convenient opportunity has arisen – see for example Part 6 of the Planning and Compulsory Purchase Act 2004, relating to planning procedures in Wales. In that way, the bulk of the measures sought by the Assembly in its annual resolution have generally been achieved. This has, however, been at the price of a degree of fragmentation and

68 National Assembly for Wales, *Assembly Review of Procedure Final Report* (January 2002), Annex 4, and interview with National Assembly official, April 2002. The report appears no longer to be available from the Assembly's website and was never published in hard copy.

69 Author's interviews; House of Lords Select Committee on the Constitution, *Devolution: Inter-institutional Relations in the United Kingdom*, 35–38; House of Commons Welsh Affairs Committee, Session 2002–03 4th Report, *The Primary Legislative Process as It Affects Wales*, HC 73 (London: The Stationery Office, 2003); House of Commons Welsh Affairs Committee, Session 2002–03 3rd Special Report, *The Government Response to the Fourth Report of the Committee: The primary legislative process as it affects Wales*, HC 989 (London: The Stationery Office, 2003).

70 These proposals are set out in Wales Office, *Better Governance for Wales*, Cm 6582 (London: The Stationery Office, 2005), paras 3.8–3.21.

inaccessibility.[71] Legislation to provide for the Children's Commissioner for Wales was passed sooner than the Assembly expected, as the office was created by Part V of the Care Standards Act 2000 – but the functions were only defined in the Children's Commissioner for Wales Act 2001, and the problems of overlap with the functions of the Children's Commissioner for England when that post was legislated for in 2004 (particularly in relation to young offender's institutions and other establishments forming part of the criminal justice system) were both the subject of ongoing debate while the bill was still in Parliament, and later the subject of scathing criticism from the Commons Welsh Affairs Committee.[72]

There seem to be three factors at work in explaining these sorts of variations. One is that the devolved administrations seem to be reactive rather than active in dealing with Whitehall and Westminster. They do not wish to challenge the UK Government too much and undermine the generally benign climate in which they operate. Thus they appear to have no plan for dealing with such matters, in order to promote better or at least more consistent treatment at the hands of the UK Government. Problems with staff resources might underlie this, but that is unlikely; rather, this does not seem to have become a major issue of concern for them. The devolved administrations can, moreover, sometimes benefit from it – the combination of ignorance on the part of a Whitehall department and time pressures sometimes seem to have enabled the devolved administrations to secure a more advantageous deal from Whitehall than might otherwise have been the case.

Second, there is a wide degree of variation in how particular departments regard the devolved administrations. Some have been seen as 'devolution-hostile'. This list includes the Department for Trade and Industry (where officials seem positively to relish such a reputation); the Department for the Environment, Transport and the Regions/Department for Transport, Local Government and the Regions, until about 2002 (although this always related more to some parts of that department than others and were said to stem from one individual official who then moved to a different post); and the Ministry of Agriculture, Fisheries and Food/Department for the Environment, Food and Rural Affairs (on the agriculture side). The Home Office has also been

---

71 The only way to make sense of this is to use an online database run from Cardiff Law School: see Lambert, D. and Miers, D., 'Law-making in Wales: Wales-legislation online', *Public Law* (2002), 663–9.

72 See House of Commons Welsh Affairs Committee, *The Powers of the Children's Commissioner for Wales*. On the creation of the office of Children's Commissioner, see Hollingsworth, K. and Douglas, G., 'Creating a children's champion for Wales? The Care Standards Act 2000 (Part V) and the Children's Commissioner for Wales Act 2001', *Modern Law Review*, 65 (2000), 58–78.

the target of complaints from both administrations (and criticism from the Welsh Affairs Committee).[73] Other departments have been praised for being helpful – most notably the Foreign and Commonwealth Office (not a department with a large legislative programme, however) and the Department for Education and Skills. All this can change according to individual officials or divisions as well as overall departmental attitudes, so generalisations are hard to make.[74]

Its importance is increased, however, by the third factor: the lack of any sort of central control over devolution standards in general and over how devolution issues are dealt with in legislation in particular. As noted above, there is a 'missing centre' for devolution within UK Government. Consequently, no single actor in the UK Government scrutinises UK legislation for its compliance with the principles of devolution (indeed, except at the most general level there seems to be doubt within the UK Government that devolution has principles, rather than being a set of complicated rules). None of the important figures in the legislative process – Parliamentary Counsel (the UK Government's legislative drafters), other Government lawyers, the Cabinet Office or the Attorney General – take on such a role. The closest there is to such a scrutiniser is the Cabinet LP (Legislative Policy) committee, which needs to approve both the principle of each bill and approve its submission for drafting to Parliamentary Counsel, and then authorise its introduction into Parliament.[75] That scrutiny is at a relatively general level, does not require resolution of problems at the earlier stages but only their identification, and is not designed to establish any sort of consistency. The prospect

73 See House of Commons Welsh Affairs Committee, *Police Service, Crime and Anti-Social Behaviour in Wales*.
74 Such variation is no surprise, given the wide autonomy Whitehall departments are able to exercise. See Daintith and Page, *The Executive in the Constitution*, chapters 2 and 10. Such variation has a considerable pedigree: see Rhodes, R. A. W., *Beyond Westminster and Whitehall: The sub-central governments of Britain* (London: Unwin Hyman, 1988), 82–3.
75 Somewhat tighter procedures exist for legislation than for other governmental business. The most important such procedure is a requirement that all submissions to the UK Cabinet seeking approval for the preparation of legislation confirm that there has been consultation with the devolved administrations affected, identify any devolution questions and show how they will be dealt with. Even so, this has not always been followed and bills have been referred back when such consultation has not taken place. See the Cabinet Office's *Guide to Legislative Procedures*, and Devolution Guidance Note 9, *Post-Devolution Primary Legislation Affecting Wales* and Devolution Guidance Note 10, *Post-Devolution Primary Legislation Affecting Scotland*. See also Trench, 'Whitehall and the Process of Legislation after Devolution'.

of Parliamentary debate about such matters is hardly daunting and concerns about scrutiny in Parliament do not seem to be a major factor; Parliamentary scrutiny of aspects specifically relating to devolution is not common and even then is rarely searching.[76] The worst that can happen, in the most egregious of cases, is the sort of critical report that the Commons Welsh Affairs Committee has produced in two instances. All this is in marked contrast to the sort of scrutiny that the Human Rights Act 1998 has triggered, with thorough and informed scrutiny by a dedicated Joint Committee of both Houses of Parliament, and certification by the minister in charge on the introduction of each bill that it complies with the Convention Rights, which has engendered a much more careful approach within government as well.

Legislation therefore lets us lift the lid on how devolution has affected the actual workings of government. Both in terms of process and outcome, the overall picture is one of huge variation, shaped by a number of minimal, incremental and often ad hoc adjustments of existing mechanisms, practices and procedures to cope with institutional change. There has been little attempt to structure or formalise devolution-related procedures. The outcome has avoided both conflict and internal chaos, but at the price of huge amounts of work by those directly involved, and an increasingly convoluted, even unwieldy, set of legislation which requires specialist skills to comprehend or even find.

The role of parliaments and assemblies

A further characteristic feature of intergovernmental relations in the UK has been the interest in it shown by legislators. Although the UK's form of intergovernmental relations is highly executive-oriented, there has been much interest in it from outside the executive. This has been particularly the case at Westminster, but the Scottish Parliament and National Assembly for Wales have also been engaged. At Westminster, the territorial Secretaries of State (and in the case of Scotland the Advocate General) hold regular, if low-key, question time sessions. Debates on major issues occur from time to time.[77] However, particularly important has been the work of various committees.

76 See Hazell, R., 'Westminster as a "Three-in-One" Legislature of the UK and its Devolved Territories', in Hazell and Rawlings (eds), *Devolution, Law Making and the Constitution*.
77 For example the debates in the Lords on the Barnett formula in 2001, initiated by Lord Barnett, HL Deb 7 November 2001, cols 225–64, and the Constitution Committee's report on *Devolution: Inter-institutional Relations in the United Kingdom*, HL Deb 20 June 2003, cols 1066–96.

The outcome of their work has been a number of important reports, which have served both to help members of the various parliaments and assemblies become aware of the nature of devolution, but also to seek to change various aspects of its workings. Many of these reports have been cited in the notes to this chapter, or other chapters in the book, but it is worth noting the more important. These are set out in figure 8.1.

This indicates a degree of serious interest in the working of devolution from a range of politicians, particularly elected ones from Wales (in both Cardiff Bay and Westminster) and non-elected ones in the House of Lords. This interest has usually taken a relatively non-partisan and disinterested point of view. Most of this, however, relates to administrative issues or legislation; structural issues, and particularly finance, have been less successful in securing legislative attention.

Avoiding and resolving disagreements

What this account should have made clear is that in fact low-level intergovernmental differences or disagreements occur frequently. They arise in the course of routine contacts between governments, a consequence of the UK's model of cooperative intergovernmental relations rather than an indication of it breaking down. They are also, officials are keen to point out, a routine part of dealings between different parts of a single government as well as part of intergovernmental relations.[78] The distinctive feature of the UK system is that these disagreements are commonly resolved in much the same way as they arise – in private, behind the scenes, often by what appear to be agreements to disagree – and that they are also resolved in much the same way as inter-departmental disagreements were before devolution.

Many such disagreements are resolved directly between officials, as are many lower-level issues perhaps better characterised as 'differences' than disputes. Other 'differences' are resolved between ministers, sometimes directly and sometimes involving the 'good offices' of the Scottish or Welsh Secretary. Such agreements reflect an emergent but largely unpublished and tacit set of understandings about what 'the principles of devolution' are and what they require in a particular situation. These principles reflect the view that the devolved administrations should be free to act within their devolved competence. They acquire greater weight within government generally as

78 One official from a devolved administration said that the intergovernmental disagreements he had seen were as nothing when compared with disputes between Whitehall departments in which he was involved in the early 1990s.

Table 8.1 Major Parliamentary or Assembly committee inquiries affecting intergovernmental relations, 1999–2005

- The Commons Welsh Affairs Committee has been particularly active. Its reports include *The Primary Legislative Process as it Affects Wales* (2002–03), *The Powers of the Children's Commissioner for Wales* (2003–04), and *Police Service, Crime and Anti-Social Behaviour in Wales* (2004–05) and on the white paper *Better Governance for Wales.*[a]
- The Lords Select Committee on the Constitution carried out a major inquiry into *Devolution: Inter-institutional Relations in the United Kingdom* in 2002–03, and followed this by looking at *Devolution: Its effect on the practice of legislation at Westminster* in the context of its broader inquiry into legislation in 2003–04. As part of its remit to consider the constitutional implications of all government bills before the House of Lords, it regularly comments on the implications of proposed legislation for the devolved administrations in its periodic progress reports.[b]
- The National Assembly for Wales set up an ad hoc committee chaired by the Presiding Officer to consider the white paper *Better Governance for Wales* during the summer of 2005. Its Assembly Review of Procedure committee had made recommendations about legislative matters in 2001.
- The Scottish Parliament's Procedures Committee carried out a large inquiry into *The Sewel Convention* in 2004–5.[c]
- In response, in October 2005 the Commons Scottish Affairs Select Committee (which otherwise has shown little interest in devolution matters) announced an inquiry into *The Sewel Convention: The Westminster perspective.*

[a] House of Commons Welsh Affairs Committee, The Government White Paper: Better Governance for Wales, Session 2005–06 1st Report, HC 551 (London: The Stationery Office, 2005)

[b] Committee on the Better Governance for Wales White Paper, Report (Cardiff: National Assembly for Wales, 2005), available at:
www.wales.gov.uk/keypubassembettergov/content/bgw-report.pdf.

[c] Scottish Parliament Procedures Committee, 7th Report 2005 (session 2), The Sewel Convention, SP Paper 428 (Edinburgh: Scottish Parliamentary Corporate Body, 2005).

time goes by, the corpus of them increases and they start to become 'precedents' for official behaviour. As one official put it in interview in the summer of 2001, 'we know that we are setting the precedents at the moment. The thing is to make sure the right precedents get set.' As government in the UK is highly driven by such precedents, they have considerable importance, although they remain no more than guidelines for conduct and not rigidly binding rules. Despite the importance of such precedents, they remain wholly private and are hard to identify or confirm.

Such accommodations are themselves generally pragmatic. They are shaped by what can be agreed at the time they arise. This means that they are partly governed by precedent, partly by the issues at stake for the parties involved, and partly also by timing and the urgency of finding a solution. This process takes place against the backdrop of established precedents for dealing with such matters, and the principles of devolution as understood in government. One of those principles is that the devolved administrations should be left to deal with devolved matters – that, once devolved, a function is no longer the UK Government's responsibility. However, the ways in which devolved and reserved functions intermingle (discussed in chapter 3) mean that negotiation of the boundary between devolved and non-devolved matters is a constant task for the civil servants directly involved. For these small numbers of central officials the task is to oil the wheels not just of inter-governmental relations, but of the conduct of a wide range of governmental business where the actions of one government affect others. This demanding task is one that they manage with sufficient skill to mean that relatively few UK policy issues are said to cause problems, if the officials have been properly involved. (The instances of problems cited above are almost all cases where a lead department failed to take the advice of the territorial offices or DCA devolution team.) In such cases, there is usually an opportunity to find a solution that will at least satisfy both sides. The ability to do so is fundamentally dependent on the shared desire to find such a solution. If that desire were absent (as might very well be the case if governments of different parties were dealing with each other), the outcome might be rather different.

Where the issue stems from a devolved initiative rather than a UK Government one, there are a number of possible solutions. In such cases, the issue is likely to take rather a different form, raising the question of whether the proposed action is within devolved competence or not. If it is not (or there are real doubts about whether it is), one hypothetical solution would be to establish what the law was, according to the courts. The 'devolution issues' schedules give the courts jurisdiction (unusually) to consider the lawfulness of legislation between completing its Parliamentary passage and enactment, before it has had any actual effect.[79] This option has not been taken so far (although it has been suggested in interview that there were a small number of cases where it might have been possible). This would establish legal certainty, but at the risk of airing the issue in public and having it regarded as a 'dispute'. Its lack of use so far means that the first time an issue is dealt with in this way, it will create an air of crisis, even if the issue is a purely technical one.

In any case, it has been possible to avoid litigation because of two sets of arrangements, one expressly established under the devolution legislation and one a practice that has developed since 1999. The former has been discussed above – the various powers that exist under the devolution Acts to extend and adjust the boundaries of devolved legislative (and executive) competence.

79 See footnote 21 above.

Such powers can be, and have been, used to deal with problems that have arisen.

For matters where legislation is not the solution, alternative means of legal adjudication have arisen. This draws on the unique status of the Law Officers within the UK Government. The advice of the UK Law Officers – the Attorney-General, Solicitor-General and the Advocate-General for Scotland – carries great weight; it is regarded as binding on all parts of the UK Government until different advice is given or a court gives a contrary judgment.[80] Advice from the Scottish Executive's law officer, the Lord Advocate, appears to have similar authority within the Executive.[81] The issues on which the UK Law Officers have given opinions are, therefore, subject to advice which is so authoritative as to be binding. However, advice from the Law Officers is confidential and may not be divulged outside government without the consent of both the person seeking the advice and the Law Officers themselves. There are a substantial number of such opinions arising from devolution (interviewing suggests that these are largely on the legislative powers of the Scottish Parliament, and the implications of matters being reserved or not), which are now available across the UK Government and indeed to lawyers in the devolved administrations through an on-line database.[82] These rulings may have great effect on government, but they are emphatically private. Their importance is further increased by a practice followed on at least a few occasions in the early days of devolution, where the UK and Scottish Law Officers consulted each other and gave joint opinions. While this practice did not continue for long, each government's law officers continue to consult those of the other over the advice they propose to give. Consequently there is a body of material that constitutes a corpus of authoritative and known legal rulings to which lawyers and officials across the UK Government can (and do) have regular recourse. However, this is outside the public domain, and constitutes in effect a sort of private public law.

A further difference is the desire in the UK to reach agreement and operate by consensus rather than confrontation. This affects all those involved in intergovernmental relations, but leads to a problem for those seeking to

---

80 Author's interviews with UK Government lawyers, winter and spring 2002 and spring 2004. See also Daintith and Page, *The Executive in the Constitution*, 297–315; and Edwards, J. L., *The Attorney-General: Politics and the public interest* (London: Sweet & Maxwell, 1984).

81 Wales and Northern Ireland have been partial exceptions, as neither had law officers of their own under devolution.

82 The Law Officers only advise on matters of law – that is, whether government can lawfully do something. If it can confer power on itself by legislation to do that, the question is not a legal one so not one on which the Law Officers will advise.

understand it. Is what happens a breakdown of formal mechanisms, because these are unused, or a measure of success for a system designed to avoid use of such mechanisms?

Conclusion: power, autonomy and the practice of intergovernmental relations

Three questions were posed at the start of this chapter. They were (in essence) why are there so few intergovernmental disputes? What happens to the intergovernmental disputes that do arise, and how are those resolved? And what does the practical working of intergovernmental relations suggest about the supposed disadvantage of the devolved administrations in intergovernmental relations, given that this does not in fact impede their exercise of autonomy?

Key to answering the first, and affecting the others, is the overall political climate. This has two sets of consequences. One is the desire to make devolution appear to be a success – which politicians (and, following their lead, officials) regard as being indicated by the absence of disputes. Arranging matters so that disputes are minimised and kept private is therefore an important goal for officials, and creates a powerful impetus to find an agreement for its own sake. Related to that is the sense of a common view of the world and a common political interest that comes with the dominance of the Labour Party in all three British governments. This creates both the need for relations to be based on 'goodwill' (which was much criticised by the Lords Constitution Committee in its 2003 report) and the conditions in which they can be. Consequently, to answer the second question, the formal framework for dispute resolution is not used, and disagreements or differences are defused before they might reach that stage, by officials or by ministers. Thus the Secretaries of State for Scotland and Wales are important, if their real roles are low key and behind the scenes, and extensive work by officials is essential to pre-empt problems. The apparatus of JMC meetings and concordats plays a minimal role in this, however.

That leads to the third question, about resources. This chapter has suggested that there are three sorts of key resources for the conduct of IGR. One is the material and practical resources (mainly organisation resources, in the terminology used in the introduction, but also informational resources). On this measure, it is clear that the UK Government has far greater resources than the devolved administrations. It has more officials available to it in total, more working on IGR matters, greater time and resources to coordinate them, and more (and more senior) politicians to give direction to them than do the devolved administrations. However, in reality these officials and their ministers are not well coordinated. For all the smooth efficiency of the Whitehall machine, the absence of strong leadership from the centre (which is under-pinned by the sense that devolution no longer requires attention from the UK Prime Minister or the highest reaches of Government) means that the UK's tangible advantages are not decisive. In some cases, it would appear that a devolved administration able to organise itself so as to take a consistent approach and to argue its position with tenacity and skill has been able to out-manoeuvre the rather lumbering and uncoordinated giant of Whitehall. The staffing and practical resources available to Whitehall are more accurately viewed as potential sources of power usable in different conditions from those prevailing now, not actual ones effective at present.

A second category of resources is the opportunities afforded by the formal institutional arrangements for managing IGR – the Joint Ministerial Committee and the Judicial Committee of the Privy Council. These consti-tute constitutional resources in the terms of the introduction. While the Judicial Committee may be even-handed in its effect, this is rather irrelevant in the absence of litigation. In any case, the same cannot be said of the JMC. The way the JMC operates serves to reinforce the existing advantages of the UK Government, including reinforcing the bilateralism that runs through the structure of devolution. Even potential use of the Judicial Committee is of relatively little help, because of the sheer unpredictability of the outcome of any litigation and because using the court itself implies having lost by the existing rules of the game. The fact that the UK's command of constitutional resources enables it to change many of these institutions to suit itself only strengthens the point.

While the devolved administrations are in a weaker position than the UK Government, they still have access to many resources which they have not used in practice. These sources of power therefore similarly remain potential rather than actual. The devolved administrations have not sought to make the most of the resources they have readily to hand, let alone require the UK Government to exert itself. Part of the reason for this is the desire to avoid anything smacking of confrontation. The devolved administrations think that, whatever the short-term consequences, they would be the losers in the medium or longer term if they were to cause significant differences to become apparent between themselves and the UK Government. That includes making more use of formal mechanisms for IGR, even if privately they may consider that would be desirable. As a consequence, intergovernmental relations are not merely informal, but also take place almost entirely in private.

9

The parties and intergovernmental relations

Martin Laffin, Eric Shaw and Gerald Taylor

Introduction[1]

Devolution has meant that the politics of territory has grown in importance in Britain, but has it done so at the expense of the traditionally strong party loyalties characteristic of British politics? Has devolution weakened the role of the Britain-wide political parties or opened up new arenas of inter-party competition? The aim of this chapter is to consider these questions in relation to the Labour and the Liberal Democrat parties – Labour as the party currently in power in Westminster and the dominant party in both Scotland and Wales and the Liberal Democrats as the third party which has come to play a significant role in Scottish and Welsh public policy.

Historically, the Britain-wide political party organisations – primarily the Labour and Conservative parties – have over-ridden territorial interests and 'nationalised the electorate',[2] as they have across Western Europe.[3] British subnational politics at the local government level came to be dominated by the two main parties and, more recently, the Liberal Democrats have become a significant third party wresting control of some major local authorities from both the Conservatives and Labour. Devolution has now brought a new territorial dimension into party politics and the potential to 'de-nationalise' party politics. Two new regional-level party systems have emerged with their own distinctive party systems, different from that prevailing at the UK level. These

1 The research for this chapter was supported by a grant under the ESRC's Devolution and Constitutional Change Programme: Grant No. L219252116 (D279). This chapter draws on extensive interviews with MPs, MSPs, AMs and Labour Party officials in Scotland and Wales conducted in 2002–04 as well as documentary sources. More detailed accounts of our findings are available in a series of papers which at the time of writing were being prepared for publication.
2 Rose, R., *The Problem of Party Government* (Harmondsworth: Penguin, 1976), 16.
3 Caramani, D., *The Nationalization of Politics: The formation of national electorates and party systems in Western Europe* (Cambridge: Cambridge University Press, 2004).

new systems are characterised by Labour dominance, with the nationalist parties (the Scottish Nationalist Party and Plaid Cymru) as the main opposition parties, a Conservative party now marginalised in the two nations and, not least, a new politics of coalition with Labour and the Liberal Democrats forming coalition governments. These new, regional-level party systems introduce a rather different pattern of electoral incentives for the Britain-wide parties compared with those confronting their colleagues at the UK level. The intriguing question is how far these incentives are having a 'de-nationalising' impact on the Scottish and Welsh Labour-dominated governments, drawing them away from Labour at the centre and testing the resilience of the New Labour brand across Britain. The other key question is whether the regional–level branches of Labour and the Liberal Democrats enjoy the autonomy from their Britain-wide organisation and the capacity to develop their own policies.

The changing role of the parties must be understood within the structural constraints of the Scottish and Welsh devolution settlements. These settlements have been described elsewhere in this book, but two features are particularly salient in considering the political parties and intergovernmental relations. First, pre-devolution the collective responsibility of the Scottish and Welsh Secretaries of State in the UK Cabinet was the main mechanism of control over policy in those two nations. Devolution removed this mechanism yet failed to substitute formal intergovernmental controls. Rather, the assumption was that Labour hegemony in the two nations would continue and, therefore, party discipline and cohesion would substitute for collective responsibility. Thus from the very start devolution hinged on assumptions about the role of the political parties. Second, the system of financial support through a single block grant, fixed through the Barnett formula, has both a decentralising and a centralising potential. Its decentralising potential is that it does not involve specific policy requirements and gives the centre no mechanisms whereby it can spend money directly in Scotland or Wales where the latter have their own powers; its centralising potential is that the formula communicates the expenditure implications of policy decisions at the centre directly onto the peripheries. Consequently, the expenditure implications of any English policy changes are automatically passed on to the three devolved administrations – an important constraint on Scottish and Welsh autonomy and thus an important reassurance for those at the centre of government and in the ruling party anxious over issues of policy divergence from central policies.

This chapter considers how the Labour and Liberal Democrat parties have responded to post-devolution challenges and, in turn, how devolution has led to changes in the structures and processes of the parties. Two broad scenarios are possible. First, as many commentators have suggested is likely in the British case, the national parties may adapt to the electoral threat of regional–nationalist parties and territorial interests by 'denationalising' their electoral and governing strategies to respond to local interests and values.[4] Second, and alternatively, the national political parties may continue to have a 'nationalising' impact on politics and policy across Britain as they did on territorial politics during the twentieth century, counterbalancing the tendencies towards policy divergence made possible by devolution. 'Nationalisation' here refers to how a nation-wide party, based on the representation of functional interests and values, comes to over-ride territorial interests and values and produces policy similarities across territorial boundaries.[5] This process of nationalisation is usually associated with the centralisation of power within a state and the national political parties but, as will be seen, this is not always the case.

In this context the role that the Labour Party has come to play is of particular significance as it has been in power in Westminster and in Edinburgh and Cardiff since devolution. But the Liberal Democrats too, as Labour's coalition partners, have exercised a notable influence over the policies of both the Scottish and Welsh administrations. Northern Ireland is not considered here as it has its own distinctive party system in which the major Westminster parties do not play a direct role. Similarly, this chapter does not deal with the Conservative Party as that party currently does not hold power in Westminster nor in either Scotland or Wales.

The Scottish and Welsh Labour parties: from one-partyism to pluralism

The struggle for devolution took place mostly within the Labour Party and did not remain uncoloured by considerations of party advantage as well as nationalistic aspirations. Certainly the wide-ranging powers and spending discretion given to Scotland and even Wales reflect a remarkable shift in attitudes and policy within the party since the late 1970s when internal divisions, within what was then the party of government, defeated the first attempt to devolve power to Scotland and Wales. In the eighteen years of opposition (1979–97) the party commitment to devolution was driven, especially in Scotland but also (to a much lesser extent) in Wales, by a resurgent nationalism and, even more, by a reaction to the years of right-wing Conservative rule

---

4 Mitchell, J. and Seyd, B., 'Fragmentation in the Party and Political Systems', in Hazell, R. (ed), *Constitutional Futures* (Oxford: Oxford University Press, 1999), 93; Hopkin, J., 'Political Decentralization, Electoral Change and Party Organizational Adaptation', *European Urban and Regional Studies*, 10:3 (2003), 227–37.
5 Caramani, *The Nationalization of Politics*, 2, 5.

from London. In both nations the minds of at least some once devolution-sceptic Labour politicians were powerfully influenced by the realisation that devolved governments could provide a bulwark against a recurrence of Conservative control from London. Thus the content of the present settlement originates as much in the politics of party competitive advantage as in the resurgence of nationalism.

To succeed politically in Scotland and Wales Labour has to compete in subnational party systems, operating under their own electoral rules which differ from those at UK level. The different electoral and party systems and the politics of coalition government confront Scottish and Welsh Labour with a different set of pressures and strategic choices compared with those facing the party nationally. Thus new forces for the de-nationalisation or disaggregation of politics in Britain have been set in train and created new tensions within the Labour Party. The need, too, for the Scottish and Welsh parties to respond to their own electoral imperatives and specific circumstances could be expected to generate demands from within those parties for greater formal autonomy from the party centrally.

The Scottish and Welsh parties have limited formal autonomy from the centre of the party, but in practice they enjoy considerable freedom to determine their own policies and manage their own affairs, and considerable freedom over matters of candidate and leadership selection (discussed in more detail below). The existing tier of party organisation in Scotland and Wales (executive committees, conferences, regional administrative offices) has been supplemented by new ones, notably the Scottish and Welsh policy forums and Parliamentary and Assembly groups. Yet, at the same time the National Executive Committee (NEC) at the centre of the party retains formal responsibility for devising, amending and interpreting the rules, and for party administration and finance in both nations. The national rule book stipulates that 'the general provisions of these rules shall apply to all units of the party', including the Scottish and Welsh Executives[6] and, while power to amend the Scottish and Welsh party rules is vested in their Conferences, these amendments must be approved by the NEC.[7] However, in practice, both the Scottish and Welsh parties enjoy greater autonomy than the formal arrangements imply, for example the Scottish and Welsh general secretaries are no longer appointed centrally but jointly by the Scottish or Welsh Executive respectively plus, in the minority, members of the NEC.

In policy terms, the Scottish and Welsh parties enjoy significant freedom against a background of little pressure from the party centrally over devolved

6 Labour Party Rules (London: Labour Party, 2003), clause X (1).
7 Scottish Labour Party Rules (Glasgow: Scottish Labour Party, 2003), clause 18.

matters. There are no formal requirements for their own party policies on devolved matters to adhere to 'English' Labour policies, although some departures from central Labour policies have created tensions (see below), and as devolution has settled down those tensions have diminished. The national policy forums in each of the two nations, another reform introduced into the Labour Party in the late 1990s to replace party policy-making by Conference, are the formal channels for developing policy and they feed into the Scottish and Welsh Conferences which confirm the broad content of the manifestoes.[8] The Scottish and Welsh policy forums, too, have widened the range of people involved in the formal making of policy for the party manifestoes (including interested pressure groups as well as party members). The policy development process in the two Labour Party branches, leading to the manifestoes for the 2003 elections, proceeded with no direct interference from the party centrally. However, there are conflicting views as to whether, unofficially, influence is exerted and whether somewhat different patterns exist in Wales and Scotland. In the former case, those involved strongly reject the suggestion that the centre has steered regional-level policy-making processes (both in interviews and in their responses to earlier reports of this research).

The Scottish and Welsh parties have undergone much greater change than the Britain-wide Labour Party since devolution. Prior to devolution both parties were elitist or 'one-partyist' in their structures and attitudes – with strongly developed centralised and hierarchical structures and traditional party cultures.[9] They have now moved towards being pluralist parties with less hierarchical organisations, characterised by competing centres of power – in the form of the Labour ministry, the backbench party in the Scottish Parliament and National Assembly, Labour local government, the affiliated unions and the wider party membership. Of course, devolution could simply have reinforced one-partyism, summed up in Wales by the fears that devolution would simply create a 'Glamorgan County Council on stilts'. In reality two key factors prevented this scenario occurring. First, the new electoral systems, based on proportional representation, have ensured that Labour will not become the perpetual majority government of Scotland and Wales. Second, the centrally driven changes within the party, unrelated to devolution but intended to marginalise the left, have significantly shifted power away from party activists and towards the rank-and-file membership – not least through the introduction of candidate selection by one-member-one-vote for both devolved and general

8　Taylor, G., 'Power in the Party', in Taylor, G. (ed.), *The Impact of New Labour* (Basingstoke: Macmillan, 1999).

9　McAllister, I., 'The Labour Party in Wales: The dynamics of one-partyism', *Llafur: The Journal of Welsh Labour History*, 3:2 (1981), 79–89.

elections.[10] These reforms plus Labour's introduction of 'twinning' in the first devolved elections (whereby twinned constituencies were required to each select male and female candidates) significantly widened the pool of candidates and forced a generational shift in Scottish and Welsh politics. The Parliament and Assembly are now populated by gender-balanced, well-educated and relatively youthful Labour groups of members.

Even so, the new pluralism of the Scottish and Welsh parties has not prevented ministerial domination of policy-making. Labour ministers in both nations have been able to get their policy agenda accepted within their parties, though some concessions have been made to union pressure, for example in Scotland over employment rights to workers transferred to the private sector under Private Finance Initiative (PFI) projects. Ministers dominate the internal Labour policy processes, yet this dominance is based on consent, reflecting extensive policy consensus within the party and the absence of the conflicts which have, in the past at the British level, characterised relations between (Westminster) parliamentarians and the wider party. This consensus, too, reflects how ideological cleavages have virtually evaporated, especially within the Scottish party, which was dominated by the left–right struggle in the 1980s and 1990s. Similarly, the constituency parties no longer form platforms for left-wing insurgents, in part because of how grassroots activism has declined. Meanwhile, party discipline at Holyrood and Cardiff Bay is more relaxed and consensual than is the case at Westminster. Again the small size of the legislatures and very personal quality of relationships within them, as well as the absence of ideological polarisation, contribute to this limited emphasis on party discipline.

Labour in power in Scotland and Wales: a force for policy convergence or divergence?

Some commentators have argued that there is a significant ideological, 'right–left' difference between a Blairite centre and the Scottish/Welsh Labour ruling elites, illustrated by the latter's *apparent* rejection of market-driven solutions (such as foundation hospitals) and stress on issues of social justice and equality. As we note below, some of the most significant policy differences reflect the dynamics of coalition government rather than centre–periphery policy differences within the Labour Party. Indeed on some

10 Seyd, P., 'New Parties/New Politics? A case study of the British Labour Party', *Party Politics*, 5:3 (1999), 383–406; Shaw, E., 'New Labour – New Democratic Centralism?', *West European Politics*, 25:3 (2002), 147–70.

issues, like higher education tuition fees and free personal care for the elderly, most Labour ministers in the two nations were forced down the path of policy divergence against their better judgment given the large price tags attached to these policies. Nonetheless, there are some signs of intra-party differences within British Labour. Interestingly, these signs are more pronounced in Wales than in Scotland, despite the fact that historically the Scottish party has demonstrated more ideological divergence from the party at the centre than the Welsh party, which remained unaffected by the ideological foment of the 1980s. Certainly, First Minister Rhodri Morgan's clear 'red water' speech opening the campaign for the 2003 Assembly elections has been much touted as evidence of a Welsh 'leftward' lurch away from the Westminster party.[11]

It is very tempting to see policy differences or divergences between Labour at Westminster and in Scotland and Wales in 'left–right' terms or as indicative of party disunity. Inter-party competitive electoral pressures, at least in principle, tilt Welsh and Scottish Labour towards the left rather than to the right (as in England where the Conservatives are the main opposition). This is because in both nations the main electoral threat is from nationalist parties occupying the same social democratic ground as that of Labour and (in Scotland) from parties further to the left – the Greens and the Scottish Socialist Party, which increased their combined representation from two to thirteen at the 2003 election. The two nations' historical legacy has also left them dominated by public sector institutions and given a certain in-built policy bias towards collectivism in the form of direct public service provision rather than towards policies to marketise the public sector – the take-up of PFI projects is influenced by the willingness of local councillors and health trust members as well as by ministerial attitudes.

Closer inspection of current policy and recent policy announcements indicates that centre–periphery policy differences do not follow left–right lines. If anything the Scottish party is moving closer to the Westminster party. On law and order, in particular, it has followed a similar approach to that of the UK Government, for example pursuing anti-social behaviour orders to the discomfort of its Liberal Democrat coalition partners. Accordingly, Labour took control of the Justice portfolio after the 2003 elections. In local government and the health service, Labour ministers are seeking greater controls over the delivery of education and health services. Similarly, recent policy papers tabled before the Scottish Policy Forum in preparation for the 2007 Scottish Parliament elections propose following the Blairite emphasis on choice in public services, a greater use of the private

---

11 Morgan, R., 'Annual Lecture for National Centre for Public Policy', University of
     Wales, Swansea (December 2002).

sector and the introduction of foundation hospitals and a variation on specialist schools.[12]

In contrast, Labour in Wales has continued in its rejection of specialist schools, foundation hospitals and tests for children, and has also been more cautious than Scotland in introducing PFI projects. Wales has also reorganised its health service to make the new Local Health Boards coterminous with local government boundaries (unlike their English equivalents, the Primary Care Trusts). Note, however, that the powers to achieve this were incorporated into Westminster legislation with little controversy despite the need for Whitehall's support to do so. Yet, despite Rhodri Morgan's occasional attempts to articulate a Welsh Way, notably his 'clear red water speech' in December 2002, it is difficult to find much evidence of an ideological drive behind these Welsh policy positions. The policy papers and announcements of these positions eschew such justifications and emphasise practical policy considerations and responsiveness to expert opinion and reports. Welsh ministers, advisors and senior civil servants interviewed in the course of this research downplayed any interpretation that implied serious dissent from central party policies and pointed out that these policies reflected reasonable and pragmatic policy adaptations. Of course, Whitehall ministers themselves may well be keen to abandon the testing and target-driven policies, but simply be too committed to back down without loss of political credibility. Given that Welsh ministers simply inherited this approach, they have not felt committed to these policies and have found it, if anything, politically advantageous to change policy.

Another dimension to policy differences is the greater influence enjoyed by what those within central government have come to dub, somewhat pejoratively, 'producerist' interests – that is, local government, the public sector professions and unions. In Wales Labour local authorities have had a significant influence over Labour policy in the Assembly, partly reflected, for instance, in the reorganisation of the health service on local boundaries.[13] The Assembly has also drawn heavily on experts and professionals to devise and to consult over policies, reflecting at least in part the scarcity of countervailing organised interests and think tanks in Edinburgh and Cardiff compared with London.[14]

12 Gordon, T., 'Scottish Labour and the Politics of Choice', *Herald*, 5 July 2004; Barnes, E., 'Scots Labour U-turn over Choice', *Scotland on Sunday*, 4 July 2004.
13 Laffin, M., 'Is Regional Centralism Inevitable? The case of the Welsh Assembly', *Regional Studies*, 38:2 (2004), 213–23.
14 For discussion of the importance of experts in policy formulation, see Reynolds, D., 'Developing Differently: Educational policy in England, Wales, Northern Ireland and Scotland', in Adams, J. and Robinson, P. (eds), *Devolution in Practice: Public policy differences within the UK* (London: ippr, 2002), 93–103; and Scott Greer, chapter 7 in this volume, on health.

After devolution it seemed reasonable to predict that the Scottish and Welsh Labour parties would demand greater devolution to themselves and perhaps even a semi-federal structure for the British Labour Party. Such demands have not arisen. The new politicians have been absorbed in the challenges of government and have not seen any strong good reason, as yet, to challenge the existing structures and press for any loosening of the ties with the British party. Of course, the Labour Party policy forums do provide a devolved formal policy-making system which feeds into the processes of producing the Welsh and Scottish manifestoes. As a result, centre–periphery relations have been relatively harmonious, with the Edinburgh and Cardiff party establishments content with a division of powers and responsibilities which allows them substantial power over governmental matters even though London continues to have final responsibility for party matters. Thus with the debate about arrangements for devolution in Wales, following the Richard Commission report, the Welsh party was able to proceed without interference from London, and the position it adopted at its September 2004 special Conference largely shaped the UK Government's June 2005 white paper.

Labour Party solidarity or identity remains a force across the two nations. It is difficult to measure the strength of this force because, as yet, Scottish and Welsh Labour ministers have not felt seriously constrained by British party commitments and, indeed, have often continued to gain policy sustenance from the wider party – as is clear in Scottish Labour's law-and-order policies and new interest in choice in public services. And, as mentioned earlier, the Liberal Democrats are responsible for committing the two devolved governments to most of the policies significantly different from London.

The Labour Party in Britain – a unitary party adapts to devolution

Devolution has involved significant changes to the Scottish and Welsh Labour parties, but has Labour as a British party changed significantly? Certainly, over the last twenty years it has moved in a centralised direction, despite being the party of devolution. Since the early 1980s successive leaders have sought to position the party electorally in the middle ground of British politics and exclude the left from influence within the party.[15] The emphasis, particularly under Blair, has been on building up the 'New Labour' brand and presenting the party as unified and disciplined. Yet New Labour has not devised and enforced a devolution settlement which has put in place anything like the powers of central control and intervention which it exercises over English

15 Shaw, E., *The Labour Party since 1979* (London: Routledge, 1994).

local government or which might be expected following comparisons with federal countries.[16]

Those at the centre of the party are concerned to maintain the New Labour brand across the country and reject the notion of federalising the party or even giving the devolved areas greater constitutional independence. Their concern centres around the perceived need to preserve a common Labour identity – a brand or an ethos – across the country. Matthew Taylor worried early on that the emergence of distinct Scottish and Welsh Labour policies could threaten the presentation of a single Labour 'brand' or even the continued existence of the party.[17] The party, Taylor insisted, derived its strength and appeal from ideological unity and hence must continue to embody 'a single set of values, principles and core policies regardless of where it operates'. This concern over preserving the Labour brand has persisted. As one insider commented, the emergence of a different 'Scottish Labour brand' would 'undermine the credibility and coherence of British Labour as a whole'. Similarly, a senior party official emphasised the importance of preserving 'parameters'. He went on to say, 'We do not want a federal system within the party. We are interested in . . . how to continue to ensure that' (sic).[18]

Thus the party leadership in London remains cautious over moves towards a devolved party structure, let alone a federal party structure (as the Liberal Democrats enjoy). Too much party devolution could undermine the 'ethos' which acts as a glue within the party. Centrally the party's response to devolution has been ad hoc and piecemeal. The National Executive Committee (NEC), the governing committee of the party, remains based on functional not territorial representation, and the Scottish and Welsh parties are not formally represented (as is characteristic of state-wide parties in federal governmental systems and would be the case if the party became federalised). It has not become a mechanism for territorial representation or manage-ment within the party and has not played any role as a mechanism for inter-governmental conflict management or the exercise of party discipline in centre–periphery relations. The NEC remains a centralist body with ultimate powers of intervention and a strong English focus; this centralism is rein-forced by its de facto role as the (English) executive committee and the current Labour leadership's stress on the votes of middle England. As one NEC member observed: 'the NEC probably always has been an English Executive Committee, not only English but London'.[19]

16 Laffin, M. and Thomas, A., 'The UK: Federalism in denial?', *Publius*, 29:3 (1999), 89–108.
17 Taylor, M., 'They Have to Toe the Labour Line', *The Guardian*, 11 May 1999.
18 Interview, June 2002.
19 Interview, June 2003.

At least initially, this anxiety about avoiding the appearance of party disunity and a lingering commitment to the New Labour brand led Blair and his immediate circle to take an interest in the candidate and leadership selection processes in Scotland and Wales. Even so, these processes did not take the form of unilateral central party intervention. In Scotland, the first round of parliamentary selections was wrapped in controversy with allegations of political 'culling'. What appears to have happened, however, is that – for the most part – the London party establishment worked mainly through reliable local allies (including, some interviewees claimed, Donald Dewar) to reduce the number of left-wingers selected.[20] The two subsequent Scottish leadership contests took place with no direct attempts from those at the centre to shape the outcome. In reality, the mechanisms of party discipline are too blunt to be used by the centre to manage the affairs of the Scottish and Welsh parties. In particular, the initial candidate and leader selection processes reflected the competing forces within the local Labour elites as much as any imposition of central control. The leadership elections in Wales, in particular, illustrate the important proposition that central intervention within a political party requires at the very least cooperation from at least some members of the local party elite. The early Welsh leadership selection contests were engineered by a tacit alliance between members of the Welsh Labour Executive and the centre. Once devolution became a reality, the subsequent leadership contests, in both Scotland and Wales, took place with no direct attempts from those at the centre to shape the outcome.

The party as a channel for intergovernmental relations

What is the significance of common Labour Party membership across the two levels of government for intergovernmental relations? The formal mechanisms for such relations, particularly the Joint Ministerial Committee, have proved to be of limited significance, as Alan Trench points out in chapter 8. As noted earlier, the formal organisational channels of the Labour Party have not played a role in conflict management nor in imposing formal party discipline on the Scots and Welsh. Rather, party membership is significant in terms of the norms of party solidarity – common Labour Party membership and identity. One former Secretary of State for Education, Estelle Morris, stressed the 'comradely connections' with her Scottish and Welsh counterparts, connections which she felt considerably eased those relationships.[21] Helen

20 One high-profile victim was the left-wing MP Dennis Canavan, who stood successfully as an independent instead.
21 Interview, 11 June 2003.

Liddell, the former Scottish Secretary, referred to how relationships between the two levels were governed by a 'regime of no surprises'. However, relations did deteriorate under Henry McLeish's brief tenure as First Minister in Scotland. His decision to introduce free personal care for the elderly caused very considerable resentment in London.[22] Much arm-twisting took place until the UK Government belatedly realised that the opposition parties, in conjunction with the Liberal Democrats, would force through the policy regardless.[23] As one former Executive minister told us: 'People in London couldn't get their head round the idea that the whole point of devolution was about things being done differently.'[24] London was also aggrieved that it had not been properly consulted, thus infringing the 'no surprises' convention. It then itself signally failed to consult with the Scottish Executive over the 2004 white paper on Higher Education, advocating variable university fees, which clearly would have major knock-on effects on Scottish universities.

Notwithstanding these examples, overt conflicts have been subdued by common electoral interest. As one Scottish MP reflected: 'most of us recognise why we hang together and why we hang separately and there's good electoral reasons at the end of the day, if we end up attacking each other, we will lose out electorally'.[25] The convention of 'no surprises' clearly did ease relationships between ministers at the two levels of government and encouraged cooperative behaviour, not least in the run-up to the 2001 UK general election and the 2003 Scottish and Welsh elections. Certainly the party elites at both levels cooperate on the level of electoral strategies to the extent that each level takes particular care to avoid raising difficult issues for the other during the run-up to elections. First Minister Rhodri Morgan explained:

> The closer you get to a general election, and if you are Labour therefore as far as we are concerned down here as a minority Labour administration we would like to see the re-election of a Labour government with a working majority which we consider is essential to bed in devolution quite aside from any other party loyalty factors. . . . when we anticipate the elections will come, we will be not unhelpful you might say from the UK Government's point of view of being re-elected, . . . we are conscious of the political realities and the timings and trying to help Welsh MPs be re-elected in marginal seats is as key to us as it is to them up there.[26]

22 This policy was recommended by the Sutherland Royal Commission on Long-Term Care reporting to the UK Government, but was emphatically rejected by central government on the grounds of cost. See further chapter 8, pp. 164–5.
23 Shaw, E., 'Devolution and Scottish Labour: The case of free personal care for the elderly', Paper presented to the Annual Conference of the Political Studies Association, University of Leicester (April 2003).
24 Interview, October 2003.
25 Interview, May 2003.
26 Interview, 28 May 2000.

As was noted earlier, Blair and other Labour Whitehall ministers may initially have harboured anxieties over whether the devolved administrations might be captured by dissident elements within the party. Such anxieties have proved ill-founded. Instead, Westminster ministers have been content to accept the logic of the devolution settlements. For instance, Estelle Morris, the former Education Secretary, made it very clear that for her the devolution settlement meant that she had no difficulty in accepting the Welsh decision to abolish school pupil testing at the age of seven. She, too, looked back and puzzled at how little political coordination with Wales has been necessary in education.[27]

The role of the territorial Secretary of State as party fixer or broker between the party regionally and centrally is also salient. This role was certainly significant in Wales during Alun Michael's leadership crisis, with Paul Murphy, Welsh Secretary at the time, involved in the then-abortive coalition negotiations with the Liberal Democrats. However, as Scottish and Welsh ministers developed their own direct links with their Westminster counterparts, even before central government made it a part-time role, the role began to lose its significance (although the Welsh Secretary retains an important role in negotiating legislative time for Welsh primary legislation). However (at least in Wales) ministers and civil servants reported that the frequency of contact at ministerial level was significantly lower than they had anticipated, although the extent and frequency of normal contact varied. (This was discussed further in chapter 8.) The main reason for this limited contact is that both sides did not see the need for extensive contact – ministers in the two devolved administrations have generally found themselves absorbed by issues of service delivery rather than new Westminster legislation or the impact of UK policy for England. One area where it has remained central is when the debate moves to constitutional issues – as vividly illustrated by both Helen Liddell's role in the debate about the number of Scottish MPs in 2001–02, and Peter Hain's leading role in the debate about the response to the Richard Commission report in 2004–05. In the latter case, it has been telling that Hain, rather than Rhodri Morgan, has been the key figure in discussions within the Welsh and British party as well as within the UK Government.

Why has a very centralist party and government, which continues to control local government in England tightly, apparently allowed the devolved administrations considerable freedom of action? First, for the Westminster leadership electability is imperative, and the current strategic challenge is how to hold onto marginal seats in England. This approach has meant that Scottish and Welsh affairs have inevitably been seen as peripheral. Second, in most

27 Interview, 11 June 2003.

policy areas those at the centre have now accepted the logic of devolution and realised that there can be advantages in distancing themselves from the actions of the devolved administrations (a good example is over the perceived diffi-culties of the health service in Wales). Nonetheless, the Westminster leader-ship has not given away formal, constitutional power over the Scottish and Welsh parties, and has certainly not moved in a federalist direction, instead allowing those parties greater freedom through formally and informally del-egating powers. Of course, the Westminster leadership has no reason to change the party constitution. Indeed, Blair and his allies are very likely to see potential dangers in giving full party constitutional recognition to the two nations – not least that should left–right cleavages again emerge as significant, the left could use the devolved governments as a basis for challenging the central party, as happened during the 1980s with local government. Third, in practice the Scottish and Welsh administrations are not perceived to have strayed far from central Labour Party policy and certainly not demonstrated any left-leaning ideological differences of the sort espoused by many Labour local authorities during the turbulent decade of the 1980s. Tensions have arisen over only a few issues, most seriously the Scottish Executive's announcement of free personal care for the elderly mentioned earlier. Nevertheless, over issues in which no knock-on effects for England have been anticipated or for matters under Westminster jurisdiction, the attitude from the centre has been one of what we have called 'benign indifference'.

The Liberal Democrats: a force for convergence rather than divergence?

The Liberal Democrats are just as important a part of the story of devolution as the Labour Party. The electoral systems in Wales and Scotland have given them an entry to government, while the party's growing electoral strength is actually in England and especially in local government. They have had an impact on Scottish and Welsh policy disproportionate to their electoral support within the two nations – in 1999 and in 2003 their share of the vote was about 13 per cent in both nations compared with Labour at 35 per cent (Scotland) and 36 per cent (Wales) in 1999 and 32 per cent and 38 per cent in 2003.[28] They were and are the obvious coalition candidates as Labour sees itself in electoral competition primarily with the nationalist parties, which many Labour politicians continue to regard with deep suspicion. Conditions at the UK level were also auspicious in bringing the two sides together, with

28 Seyd, B., *Coalition Government in Scotland and Wales* (London: Constitution Unit, 2004), 9.

Blair establishing a joint Cabinet subcommittee, including five Liberal Democrat frontbenchers, to consider constitutional matters after the 1997 election.[29]

In Scotland, Liberal Democrats have served as members of two coalitions from 1999–2003 and from 2003. The first Partnership Agreement in Scotland was a tough negotiation for the Liberal Democrats, who found Labour, then led by an experienced and heavy-weight politician in Donald Dewar, reluctant to give ground. Many of the more expensive Liberal Democrat demands, such as free prescriptions and dental check-ups, had to be abandoned. Their main achievement was to get Labour to concede that it would not follow the Westminster government by committing itself to up-front university tuition fees. Donald Dewar and his Labour colleagues finally agreed to abandon this commitment, passing the issue on to the Cubie Commission for the time being. In addition, the Liberal Democrats gained two Cabinet seats and Jim Wallace, their Leader, became Deputy First Minister. Then in 2000 the Liberal Democrats also played an important role in holding Labour to delivering McLeish's commitment to free personal care for the elderly.[30]

In the following year the Liberal Democrats were more successful in Wales. By this time the financial climate was more favourable and the new Labour First Minister, Rhodri Morgan, began exploring the possibility of coalition almost immediately after his election; as Mike German has observed, 'Rhodri wanted stable government, we wanted to implement our policies'.[31] Mike German and his colleagues, too, had learnt from the Scottish experience and were determined to maximise their advantage. The Partnership Agreement was a major achievement for the Liberal Democrats. It included a large number of policies taken from their 1999 election manifesto – such as a freeze on prescriptions, free dental checks for the over 55s and under 25s, free school milk for infants and free personal care for the elderly for the first three weeks of being in receipt of care (none of these were in the 1999 Labour Welsh manifesto). These spending commitments were easier to win as Labour ministers were broadly sympathetic and recognised also that these policies would play back well to their supporters, plus they now had the funds to spend on these policies. But Labour ministers were less enthusiastic about

29 Joyce, P., *Realignment of the Left? A history of the relationship between the Liberal Democrat and Labour Parties* (Macmillan: Basingstoke, 1999), 278–9. The committee was wound up after the 2001 election.
30 Shaw, 'Devolution and Scottish Labour: The case of free personal care for the elderly'.
31 Interview, July 2004.

Liberal Democrat attempts to place proportional representation on the policy agenda. They did finally agree to appoint what became the Richard Commission to review the powers and the electoral basis of the Assembly and a commission on local government electoral arrangements. The Richard Commission was carefully timed to report after the May 2003 elections, and the Sutherland Commission on Local Government Electoral Arrangements reported in July 2002, recommending the introduction of the Single Transferable Vote for local elections, a recommendation which was then put out to further consultation and has not been implemented in the face of implacable Labour local government opposition.[32]

Then in 2003, the Scottish Liberal Democrats again found themselves able to negotiate a fresh Partnership Agreement. This time Labour was in a weakened position, having lost six seats while the Liberal Democrats has retained their seventeen seats. A comparison of the 2003 Liberal Democrat and Labour manifestoes reveals that they are close in content.[33] The main differences are that the Liberal Democrats stressed universal benefits (such as free prescription charges for all), whereas the Labour manifesto implied a more selective approach (such as reviewing prescription exemption categories); the Liberal Democrats committed themselves to moving away from central intervention in local government, whereas Labour stressed continued intervention (especially in maintaining educational standards); and, the greatest difference, Labour took a strong law-and-order approach (such as proposing to hold parents responsible for the behaviour of their children and the electronic tagging of child offenders), while the Liberal Democrats took a softer line. The Liberal Democrats compromised over Labour measures to tackle youth crime but refused to compromise over their holy grail of proportional representation in local government. Labour gave way, immediately facing powerful opposition from Labour local government, which feared serious losses, and many Labour MPs anxious to limit the spread of PR across the country. The Liberal Democrats also gained an extra Cabinet seat after the 2003 election.

At the start of this chapter the contention was advanced that devolution has opened up new possibilities for the de-nationalisation of politics and policy in the UK. However, what is striking about the Liberal Democrats is that they have pursued very similar policies in both their Partnership Agreements. Notably, the Welsh 'Partnership Agreement' was closely modelled on the

32 See Laffin, 'Is Regional Centralism Inevitable?'.
33 See *Scotland Devolution Monitoring Report* (London: The Constitution Unit, June 2003), 60, 64. At: www.ucl.ac.uk/constitution-unit/monrep/scotland/scotland_june_2003.pdf.

original Scottish Liberal Democrat draft for the 'Partnership Agreement' – an early version was even circulated electronically with 'delete Scotland text' still showing.

Even so there is little evidence to indicate that the party centrally orchestrated the coalition negotiations. Indeed the negotiators in both Scotland and Wales have strongly denied that they were subject to such central direction, although they have stressed the value to them of close contact between the Welsh and the Scottish parties, especially over negotiation strategies and policy specifics. Those involved saw the negotiations as consulting with rather than involving the UK leadership of the party. Paddy Ashdown, however, then leader of the Liberal Democrats, has claimed that the final compromise on university tuition fees was brokered at the national level. The Scottish Liberal Democrat Leader, Jim Wallace, has put on record his rejection of Paddy Ashdown's attempt to 'run the coalition negotiations by remote control from London', although he admitted having received an encouraging telephone call from Blair probably at Ashdown's instigation.[34] Similarly Blair attempted to intervene in February 2000 to save Alun Michael, who was then being threatened by a vote of no confidence in the Assembly.[35] Blair urged Charles Kennedy, the national (British) Leader of the Liberal Democrats, to use his influence to persuade German to enter into a coalition with Michael. Kennedy stressed that he had no power over the Welsh Liberal Democrats but would 'pass the message on'.[36]

The Liberal Democrats do have a federal constitution which allows the Scottish and Welsh branches considerable formal autonomy, although party officials in both nations mentioned how the National (i.e. British) Conferences too often became the English Conferences and passed resolutions which failed to take account of devolution. However, cross-Britain Liberal Democrat coordination is focused on the informal, inter-parliamentary level not that of party organisation. Thus, the Labour First Ministers occasionally meet with the Westminster Scottish and Welsh Parliamentary Labour Parties but not the full Parliamentary Labour Party. The Celtic Liberal Democrat leaders however have had a close relationship with the Westminster Liberal Democrat Shadow Cabinet and Leader. Jim Wallace and Mike German are frequent visitors to Liberal Democrat Parliamentary group and Shadow Cabinet meetings, while

34 Taylor, B., *Scotland's Parliament: Triumph and disaster* (Edinburgh: Edinburgh University Press, 2002), 76.
35 Thomas, A. and Laffin, M., 'The First Welsh Constitutional Crisis: The Alun Michael resignation', *Public Policy and Management*, 16:1 (2001), 18–31.
36 In a Radio Wales interview cited in Osmond, J., 'The Coalition Government', in *Wales Devolution Monitoring Report* (London, The Constitution Unit, December 2000).

Wallace kept Charles Kennedy closely informed of developments throughout the 2003 coalition negotiations.[37] In practice, then, the Liberal Democrat party is very *nationalised* but not necessarily *centralised*, as neither Kennedy nor his Westminster colleagues used these arrangements to seek explicitly to direct their Celtic colleagues. Indeed, given that the latter are, or were in power, they could point to flows of influence operating in both directions. Thus Liberal Democrat intra-party relationships are more nationalised than those of the Labour Party even though, paradoxically, it is the Liberal Democrats, not Labour, who have a federal constitution which gives Scotland and Wales considerable formal autonomy to run their own affairs.

What will be significant in the longer run is whether the Liberal Democrat parties in the two nations have the resources and will to generate their own distinctive policies. Contact with the British party helps compensate for the limited resources for policy development available to the Liberal Democrats in Scotland and (especially) Wales. It may well be that the need for policy development will, in future, continue to act as a nationalising force, if not necessarily a centralising force, on the party. The other significant question for them is whether to fight the 2007 Scottish elections as a coalition partner with Labour. Many Liberal Democrat MSPs are sceptical of the advantages for the party of remaining in coalition once the present package of policies in the 2003 Partnership Agreement is exhausted. Coalition partnership has not brought them a significant electoral dividend, yet many key figures are arguing that they could win more votes and still exercise considerable influence outside a coalition government.

Conclusion

The combination of devolution and centrally driven reforms within the Labour Party has certainly invigorated the Scottish and Welsh Labour parties – at least at the elite level, for the Labour grassroots in both nations are in poor shape, as elsewhere in Britain. The two parties now have a key role in recruiting and providing the new political elites in their nations and forming the policy programme. As yet these new elites have not asserted themselves within the wider party. Certainly the Scottish and Welsh first ministers have not emerged as major party barons or fixers within the wider party, indeed they are largely invisible at the UK level within the party. Yet potentially the Labour leaderships of the Celtic peripheries could be powerful platforms for any future

37 Interview with Mark Oaten MP (then Chair of the Liberal Democrat Parliamentary Group), 23 May 2003.

leaders keen to advocate a Labour Party destiny different from that favoured at Westminster. Provided they enjoyed strong support within Scotland and Wales, the Westminster Labour leadership would face considerable difficulties in quelling any such challenges. But such intriguing possibilities must be well in the future. The current political environment, quite apart from the person-alities involved, is of widespread ideological consensus within the party.

Questions also arise over whether Labour has the capacity in both Celtic nations to develop distinctive policies. The current and much-trumpeted policy differences between the centre and the two nations have arisen for a complex of reasons – decisions not to follow a central lead, the requirements of coalition government or a political system in the peripheries more open to producerist (especially professional) pressure groups compared with the UK Government. The Scottish and Welsh parties have only the indirect benefit of the world of left-leaning think tanks and advisors that exists for Labour in Westminster. Yet they often do take policy inspiration from Labour in Westminster; thus the Labour Party remains a nationalised party even if not an intrusively centralised one.

Meanwhile, the Labour Party's capacity and willingness as a Britain-wide party to adapt to devolution has proved greater than many commentators originally considered. Contrary to some predictions, devolution has not unfolded as a story of a Labour leadership using party discipline to claw back the power lost through governmental devolution. The Westminster Labour Party leadership quickly realised that party discipline was not a simple substi-tute for an absence of formal intergovernmental control mechanisms. Not least, once the two parties evolved from the one-partyist model in a pluralist direction, the Westminster leadership no longer had the powerful allies in the regional parties necessary for them to intervene effectively. These limitations of central intervention are neatly illustrated by Blair's awkward U-turns over Rhodri Morgan's leadership in Wales and then over Ken Livingstone's candi-dacy in London. In both cases heavy-handed and ill-considered intervention boomeranged and the Prime Minister found himself having to commend the qualities of men whom his spin-doctors had not long before so unreservedly disparaged. It is reasonable to read into events that Blair and his colleagues quickly learned that allowing the party in the two nations considerable lati-tude was electorally convenient and would not open up the much feared fault-lines of party disunity. Instead the Westminster leadership has fallen into an attitude of benign indifference towards the devolved administrations, an atti-tude shaped by the current strategic realities facing Labour's London leader-ship which sees that UK general elections are won or lost in middle England not in the Celtic peripheries. This central attitude of benign indifference reflects what we call the 'semi-detached' model of UK devolution, with

Westminster policy and politics dominated by English electoral and policy imperatives while the devolved territories remain peripheral. The relationship is not a zero-sum game, in which the two levels of government compete for control and influence over policy, because each level is largely working in its own 'policy space'. The centre leaves the devolved governments to make their own policies. Within this model the dominant political party retains a vital function as it reassures those at the centre of the loyalties of the political elites in the periphery, provided that the territorial units do not become platforms for ideological differences internal to the party (as occurred in Labour Party central–local relations during the 1980s).

Finally, the Liberal Democrats have been the great beneficiaries of devolution. They have been able to gain office and to get large parts of their party programme implemented. Ironically for a party which espouses proportional representation, they have enjoyed an influence in the two nations disproportionate to their own share of the vote. A further irony is how their policy achievements have often been held up as instances of policy 'divergence' from the centre, yet those policies themselves are remarkably similar across Britain and have been well coordinated. The Liberal Democrats have acted as a force for the nationalisation of policy across Britain despite having a more decentralised formal structure and a less historically rooted ethos than Labour.

10

The European Union, devolution and power

Charlie Jeffery and Rosanne Palmer

Introduction: Europe as a problem for the regions

As Alan Trench makes clear in the opening chapter of this volume, it is challenging enough to identify 'power' and 'autonomy' conceptually and measure them empirically in a two-level scenario of central and devolved government. Adding in Europe to produce a three-level scenario inevitably heightens the challenge. There are a number of contradictory dynamics at play:

- The UK central state has (asymmetrically) devolved significant competences to new institutions in Scotland, Wales and Northern Ireland.
- Responsibility for aspects of many of those competences – for example in agriculture, economic development, environment, transport – has already been transferred to the EU level.
- So the devolved institutions can only exercise 'their' competences if they can contribute to EU decision-making processes in those fields.
- But the UK centre regards the EU as an aspect of foreign policy, for which it has exclusive responsibility.
- And the EU is constituted by member states as represented by central governments and recognises regions only in an advisory role.

An initial assessment on this basis would be that the dice are loaded against the devolved institutions. Intra-state devolution may have given them significant autonomous powers, but European integration takes many of them away again.

This loading of the dice is not, of course, a phenomenon observable only in the UK. All regionalised and federal states in the EU have had to confront the same set of contradictory dynamics. Regions have always been at threat of marginalisation by an integration process founded on the interplay of member states and the European institutions.[1] In the last two decades – as the scope of European competence has widened into fields for which regions are responsible domestically – that potential for marginalisation has been articulated as a political problem. It has led to repeated attempts by some regional governments to access EU decision-making:

- The first politically significant regional responses to this problem came with the Single European Act in the mid-1980s, when the German Länder tried to boost their capacity to control and shape the European policy of the German member state government.
- The Länder were joined by (and helped to organise) a wider coalition of regions in the debates on the Intergovernmental Conferences (IGCs) that led to the Maastricht Treaty of 1991, including other 'strong' regions from Belgium, Italy and Spain, but also bodies with a broader regional and local membership like the Assembly of European Regions. The Maastricht Treaty gave for the first time (limited) recognition at the EU level of the problems European integration causes for regions by establishing the Committee of the Regions, by opening up the possibility for regional ministers to join or lead member state delegations in the Council of Ministers (subject to arrangements within member states), and by introducing the principle of subsidiarity to the Treaty (though not yet in a form that recognised regional concerns).
- Regions have since mobilised both at the domestic and European levels (notably at subsequent IGCs) to win fuller recognition and compensation for the 'problem' European integration causes them. Indeed the current constitutional debate resulted in part from regional demands at the Nice IGC. Throughout the concern has been to retain or regain (at least some) control over the spheres of competence allocated to regions under domestic law.

An initial analysis of the purpose and effect of this regional mobilisation elsewhere in the EU should help unpack the three-level relationships devolution has established in EU politics in the UK, and identify how to approach questions of who holds how much power in the UK's new multi-level governance.

---

1 Consistent with comparative practice 'region' is used here as a shorthand for all 'intermediate' democratic authorities in the EU (Länder, regions, communities, autonomous communities and 'nations' like Scotland and Wales).

Europe and the regions

One thing is clear enough: notwithstanding the (wishful) optimism of some in the late 1980s and early 1990s we are not approaching a situation in which member states and their central governments will be supplanted by a 'Europe of the Regions' acting outside the framework of established state structures. The member states remain the building blocks of the EU. The Constitutional Treaty agreed at the Intergovernmental Conference that followed the European Convention codified that status more clearly than ever before. But this does not mean that the central government institutions of the member states have been able to maintain a tight monopoly over EU policy, as it were 'gate-keeping' access to Europe.

Indeed, that monopoly has been challenged and breached as regions have mobilised to maintain and/or reassert some right of co-decision over matters for which they are domestically responsible. The extent to which the central state monopoly has been breached varies widely. The most radical breach has been in Belgium, where regional and central governments in principle now have constitutional equality of status in the external representation of the Belgian member state. The breach has been at its most limited in member states which have traditionally had weak sub-central governments, like Greece and Ireland. But even there local/regional governments' roles in implementing EU legislation, and in particular structural funding, have drawn them into the process of formulating member state policy positions in those fields. There of course exists a wide spectrum of intermediate cases between these two extremes, but there are two useful rules of thumb which apply across the spectrum:

1 Regions across the EU have sought to influence European decision-making processes to the extent that those processes impinge on their domestic policy functions, however broad, narrow, extensive or inconsequential those functions might be.[2]
2 They have done so within the framework of the member state, establishing EU decision-making as an interdependent enterprise of central and regional governments acting in some form of combination.

This line of argument has a number of implications for questions of power and autonomy:

---

2 Cf. Marks, G. *et al.*, 'Competencies, Cracks and Conflicts: Regional mobilization in the European Union', in Marks, G. *et al.* (eds), *Governance in the European Union* (London: Sage, 1996), 58–9.

- Member states remain the building blocks of the EU; in recognition of this regions have by and large accepted the logic of the member state as their vehicle of choice for access to Europe;
- But the way member states work has changed; central governments have had to accept some level of co-decision-making by regional governments in EU matters.
- Therefore, although European integration has led to the transfer of regional competences to the European level, regions have been able to 'strike back' by working alongside central governments to shape the way those competences are exercised at the European level.[3]
- Regions have in effect exchanged their original autonomy in those fields of competences for a share of the external power of the central state . . .
- . . . meaning that the central state has also had to accept a loss of its traditional autonomy in external affairs.

How much power in European decision-making?

The comments above go some way in addressing the conceptual challenge of thinking through questions of power and autonomy in a three-level scenario. There remains, however, the empirical challenge. *How much* power to co-determine the member state's EU policy do regional governments have? How much of its once monopoly role in EU affairs has the central state lost? Why do some regions have more power to co-determine the member state's EU policy than others? What explains variations in the levels of power regions have both within and between member states?

There are a number of variables which affect the answers to these questions.[4] The first and most important concerns constitutional factors. If regions mobilise in Europe because Europe impinges on their domestic competences, then those that possess the most domestic competences will be affected most by Europe and will respond most comprehensively. The impact of constitutional factors is suggested in figure 10.1, where the line A–B plots the relationship between constitutional status and influence over a member state's EU policy. Using the examples mentioned earlier, the Belgian regions might be close to point B, and those in Greece or Ireland at point A. Regions in

3 Jeffery, C., 'The Länder Strike Back: Structures and processes of European integration policy-making in the German federal system', *University of Leicester Discussion Papers in Federal Studies*, No. FS94/4 (1994).
4 This section draws on the argument set out in Jeffery, C., 'Sub-National Mobilization and European Integration', *Journal of Common Market Studies*, 38:1 (2000), 11–18.

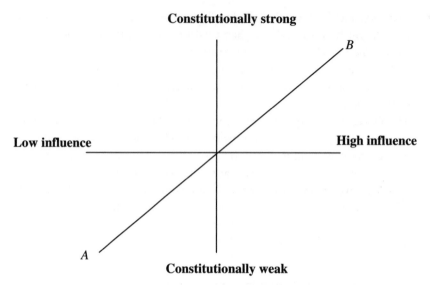

Figure 10.1 Constitutional situation and policy influence

states with asymmetric decentralisation – like Spain or the UK – might be scattered at different points along line A–B.

However, it is clear that constitutional factors are not the sole variable at play. Constitutionally stronger regions in one member state may have less impact on EU policy than constitutionally weaker regions in another member state (e.g. the city-state of Bremen in Germany as compared with Catalonia). Equally, regions with equal constitutional status in the same member state may have different levels of impact (e.g. Bremen as compared with Bavaria). So variables other than constitutional status play an intervening role to produce more differentiated outcomes:

- Among these supplementary variables is the structure of intergovernmental relations between regional and central governments. This may be formal/codified or informal and contingent, and may be uniform for all regions or vary from region to region. The particular form of organisation of intergovernmental relations may facilitate or constrain the impact of any region(s) on member state policy formulation.
- Another set of variables may be combined under the heading of entrepreneurship and reflects the differing levels of commitment and skill regions have in making the most of constitutional position and intergovernmental relations. Examples would include the administrative investment regions make in EU policy-making, the effectiveness of their political leadership, or their effectiveness in building coalitions with other actors with shared aims.

- A final variable – and the most diffuse – might be termed 'legitimacy'. A regional government's 'clout' is likely to be bigger the more it is seen to reflect a distinctive community or identity. In those circumstances its claim to play a role in EU affairs may simply be more credible than claims from other regions. An example would be the vigour of the 'stateless nationhood' of Catalonia as compared with a region like Castilla-la-Mancha in Spain which lacks a pronounced social identity.

Application to the UK

We now move on to explore a) whether the post-devolution UK reveals the same kind of pattern of central-devolved interdependence in EU decision-making and b) whether differences of impact are discernible between different UK devolved governments. Our focus is largely on Scotland and Wales given the long periods of suspension that the devolved institutions in Northern Ireland have undergone.

Constitutional status

UK devolution is asymmetrical. The Scottish Parliament has exclusive legislative competences in most fields of domestic policy, including education, health, economic development, agriculture, environment and policing. There is by and large a neat separation of its fields of activity from those of the UK Parliament in Westminster. A similar situation applies in principle in Northern Ireland, though with a slightly different set of functions and the prospect of fuller devolution of functions should the political situation there stabilise. The National Assembly for Wales is active in broadly the same set of policy fields, but has only 'secondary' legislative powers in a form of executive devolution highly dependent on the content and timetable of legislation at Westminster. The expectation generated from figure 10.1 would be that Scotland and Northern Ireland would be closer to point B than Wales. As a Scottish official put it: 'Scotland of course will have the larger agenda . . . because they have a greater range of powers over a greater range of subjects.'[5] Nonetheless that expectation might stand to be modified when the other variables noted above are explored.

Intergovernmental relations

Mostly, regions in EU member states have had to fight to break the centre's monopoly over EU policy and gain access to EU decision-making processes.

5 Interview, December 2000.

In Germany, Belgium, Austria and, most recently, Italy, the result has been a codification in constitutional law of how central and regional governments should cooperate in defining the positions of the member state. The UK provides a twofold contrast. First, its central government recognised from the outset that internal devolution brings with it external implications, and that the devolved governments therefore needed to be able to act outside the traditional domestic context. There was no fight. Second, the empowerment for devolved bodies to act externally has no legally codified, let alone constitutional, foundation.

The early recognition of the need for external engagement was explicitly acknowledged in the white papers on Scottish and Welsh devolution which shaped the subsequent devolution legislation.[6] The Welsh white paper was especially forthright:

> Foreign policy, including issues arising from the membership of the European Union will remain the responsibility of the United Kingdom Government which must continue to ensure the UK meets its obligations and exercises its rights . . . But European issues also impact on wide areas of domestic policy which will be within the remit of the Assembly. This means that the Assembly will need to be involved as closely as possible in developing UK policy on European matters.[7]

It is interesting to note the way in which these commitments in principle by the UK Government have been carried out in practice. There is little discussion of European Union issues in the Scotland Act 1998, Government of Wales Act 1998 or Northern Ireland Act 1998. Instead guidelines have been established in the form of agreements between the UK and devolved governments: the Memorandum of Understanding sets out general principles of cooperation with a number of supplementary agreements, known as concordats, setting out more detailed procedures for specific issues including EU coordination, as well as an institutional framework – the Joint Ministerial Committee, in both its plenary form and its functional one for European Union matters – for devolved–UK liaison and coordination.[8] None of these documents are legally binding. This lack of legal underpinning is (so far) unimportant in the sense that policy-makers at both levels rarely refer to the

---

6 Welsh Office, *A Voice for Wales: The government's proposals for a Welsh Assembly*, Cm 3718 (London: The Stationery Office, 1997a); Scottish Office, *Scotland's Parliament*, Cm 3658 (London: The Stationery Office, 1997).
7 Welsh Office, *A Voice for Wales*, 21–2.
8 Now *Memorandum of Understanding and Supplementary Agreements between the United Kingdom Government, Scottish Ministers, the Cabinet of the National Assembly for Wales and the Northern Ireland Executive Committee*, CM 3240 (London: The Stationery Office, 2001). The first version of the Memorandum of Understanding was Cm 4444, published in 1999.

content of the Memorandum or concordats.[9] Intergovernmental relations on Europe are typically conducted instead on a much more ad hoc basis.

The UK position in areas which touch on devolved competence is established through informal and primarily bilateral relationships between civil servants, with the European Secretariat of the Cabinet Office charged with ensuring overall coordination. In most respects current working relationships reflect those that were in place prior to devolution. Devolution has added little new to these relationships beyond a European ministers' formation of the Joint Ministerial Committee. Even this met infrequently and without much clear purpose until the European Convention revealed a need for a forum for strategic discussion on the future of the EU. Beyond this, though, the pre-devolution *intra*-governmental coordination of Scottish (or Welsh, or Northern Ireland) Office positions with those of other UK ministries has metamorphosed with minimal changes to machinery or personnel into post-devolution *inter*-governmental coordination of Scottish/Welsh/Northern Ireland devolved government positions with those of the UK Government.

The existence of a well-tried set of working practices for the inclusion of territorial priorities into the UK's EU policy positions is the most important explanation for the creation overnight of something German or Italian regions had to fight for decades for, and the Spanish regions still do not have: a practice of central–regional EU policy coordination extending from systematic information-sharing, through cooperative policy formulation to the attendance of Scottish (and less so Welsh and even less Northern Irish) ministers in UK delegations to the Council of Ministers.

Three other reasons help explain the UK central Government's positive attitude towards the inclusion of devolved governments. The first concerns the Foreign and Commonwealth Office (FCO). There is some evidence that some of the sectoral departments at UK level (like Environment at DEFRA, or the Home Office) have experienced difficulties adjusting to the changed circumstances of devolution. However, this was not the case with the FCO, which has drawn on its experience of brokering a common line, and adopted a generally positive attitude towards the devolved executives. As one Welsh official expressed it:

> The FCO have been very good. They couldn't have been more helpful. We have had problems with other departments but the FCO itself, you would expect to

9 This situation may change at the point when election outcomes establish governments of different party-political colours at UK and devolved levels. The fact that the Labour Party is the leading party of government in Westminster and in Scotland and Wales shuts out partisan conflict from 'multi-level governance'. Once partisan conflict does play a role then the respective governments may seek more fully to formalise and codify their working relations.

be the bastion of the British establishment, but it hasn't been at all you know. It has been very positive, it has welcomed devolution, it has embraced us, it has worked with us to try and help us establish links.[10]

There is a related point here which provides a benign context for the FCO to facilitate devolved government access to the EU: the post-1997 Blair governments have had a notably more positive attitude towards European cooperation than their predecessors. As part of this positive approach the UK Government has sought to deepen exchange and networking between UK officials and their counterparts elsewhere in the EU – including at the regional level. According to one Scottish civil servant: 'This present regime has said that . . . we must have more contact with partners and this will be beneficial, and so we are encouraged to do so.'[11] There may be a sub-text here: there is some anecdotal evidence that the FCO has encouraged inter-regional networking in order to exploit the intelligence the devolved administrations might be able to deliver about EU policy formulation in other regionalised member states.[12] There is certainly a stronger sense in the UK than in other member states that the FCO sees the devolved administrations as part of the same 'team' in EU affairs, as captured especially vividly in the rhetoric of the 'UKRep family' of UK-level and devolved representations in Brussels. The conclusion of the House of Lords Constitution Committee therefore seems apt: 'devolution . . . extends the reach of the external relations of the United Kingdom, by enabling governments from the UK to have relations with governments with which the UK Government itself could not'.[13]

A second additional factor that has worked in favour of a smooth adaptation of the domestic European policy formulation process to the consequences of devolution has been the partisan composition of the devolved governments in Scotland and Wales. Both have been dominated by the Labour Party, and of course the Labour Party remains in power in Westminster. This means that there have, as yet, been no partisan conflicts to complicate the intergovernmental relations of EU decision-making, as there have been periodically for example in Germany and Spain.[14]

---

10 Interview, November 2000.
11 Interview, June 2000.
12 As expressed in informal discussions with Scottish and Welsh officials.
13 House of Lords Select Committee on the Constitution, Session 2002–03 2nd Report, *Devolution: Inter-institutional Relations in the United Kingdom*, HL 28 (London: The Stationery Office, 2003), 47.
14 Cf. Bulmer, S., Jeffery, C. and Paterson, W.E. (eds), *Germany's European Diplomacy* (Manchester: Manchester University Press, 2000), 82; Börzel, T., *States and Regions in the European Union: Institutional adaptation in Germany and Spain* (Cambridge: Cambridge University Press, 2002), 98–100. The main

There is, however, thirdly, a disguised role for partisan competition, at least in Scotland. This concerns the Scottish National Party (SNP), the main opposition party in Scotland, which has a long-standing vision of exploiting the dynamics of deepening integration in Europe to loosen Scotland's bonds with the UK. The SNP has long trumpeted the slogan 'Independence in Europe', with the assumption that the open trading relations of the Single Market would limit the potential economic dislocation of secession from the UK.[15] Against this background the SNP has placed a vigorous emphasis in the Scottish Parliament on ensuring that specifically Scottish interests are expressed and represented strongly in UK positions on EU issues. The Scottish Parliament, through its plenary and its European Committee, has very quickly established itself as one of the most vigorous EU regional legislatures in holding its government to account.[16] The Labour-led governments both at UK level and in Scotland have tried to accommodate these pressures so as not to allow the SNP the potential electoral advantage of claiming that Labour does not look after Scottish interests. In this way the nationalist challenge has also helped to embed an inclusive approach to EU decision-making after devolution.

There are three interim conclusions to draw at this stage:

1   First, the UK Government has voluntarily restricted its own autonomy to allow a far-reaching practice of co-determination of EU policy with the devolved governments to be established.
2   Second, this voluntary restriction is carried out largely through bilateral channels. This means that the Scottish government, more fully responsible for a wider range of EU-relevant competences, is most intensively involved with the UK centre in EU policy co-determination (but then so was the Scottish Office before devolution). The SNP factor serves further to add to that intensity. In other words, Scotland 'scores' higher on the intergovernmental relations variable than Wales (and in the absence, for obvious reasons, of a sustained EU policy profile, than Northern Ireland).

division in Germany has been between governing and opposition parties at national level, in Spain between regional governments led by regionalist parties and the parties of central government.
15 Cf. Dardanelli, P., *The Connection between European Integration and Demands for Regional Self-Government: A rational-institutionalist comparative analysis of Scotland, 1979 and 1997*, PhD thesis, Department of Government, London School of Economics (London, 2002).
16 Heggie, G., 'The Story so Far: The role of the Scottish Parliament's European Committee in the UK–EU policy cycle', *Scottish Affairs*, 44 (2003), 114–31.

3   Third, the lack of legal underpinning for intergovernmental relations
    is both odd in comparative terms and problematic given that the benign cir-
    cumstances for intergovernmental coordination hitherto are highly contin-
    gent. There will at some point be difference in the partisan composition of
    central and devolved governments. This will complicate intergovernmental
    relations, especially if a less Euro-friendly central government is minded not
    to continue the inclusive approach established by the Blair governments
    and facilitated by the FCO. An optimistic reading would be that the weight
    of precedent on inclusion and cooperation established in the first few years
    of (party-politically congruent) devolution will be enough to contain par-
    tisan conflict. Many commentators appear, however, not to want to trust
    to precedent and would prefer to see a more formalised approach to
    intergovernmental relations that made more systematic use of formal
    mechanisms like the Joint Ministerial Committee.[17] A more formalised
    approach, such as that which exists elsewhere in the EU, would certainly
    offer a fall-back of acknowledged rules and procedures for the case that the
    'informal personal relations' between civil servants and politicians that have
    existed hitherto 'cease to be sufficient'.[18]

Entrepreneurship

The devolution of substantial constitutional powers and the inclusive
approach of the centre to intergovernmental relations create a positive opportunity structure for the devolved governments. What they make of that
opportunity is, in part at least, in their own hands. Here we can observe
notable differentiation.

The Welsh government has invested less than its Scottish counterpart in
building up the administrative capacity to engage in EU decision-making
(though this in part reflected the legacy of a weak policy capacity inherited
from the Welsh Office). As one Welsh official put it in 2000, 'it really is, at
times, a very difficult operation to engage with Whitehall because we simply

---

17 See for instance, House of Lords Select Committee on the Constitution,
    Devolution: Inter-institutional Relations in the United Kingdom, 5; Trench, A.,
    'Intergovernmental Relations: Officialdom still in control?', in Hazell, R. (ed.),
    The State of the Nations 2003: The third year of devolution in the United Kingdom
    (Exeter: Imprint Academic, 2003), 165–66; ESRC, *Devolution: What difference
    has it made? Interim findings from the ESRC research programme on devolution
    and constitutional change*, at www.devolution.ac.uk/pdfdata/Interim_Findings_
    04.pdf, p. 10; accessed November 2005.
18 House of Lords Select Committee on the Constitution, *Devolution: Inter-
    institutional Relations in the United Kingdom*, 5.

haven't got the resources and the staff to do so'.[19] One obvious example has been the respective devolved government offices in Brussels. The Welsh Brussels office was until 2003 largely a one-man show, while the Scottish government established a much better resourced operation involving a number of specialist desk officers. Scottish investment immediately created a higher profile in Brussels, but also generated a broader-based policy expertise which fed back into the capacity to argue a Scottish case vis-à-vis the UK centre.

More generally, and on the basis of this kind of administrative investment, the Scottish Executive developed what a Cabinet Office official described as an 'impressive' strategic focus quickly, learning how to maximise influence in Whitehall.[20] From a Scottish view:

> I think we've adjusted our approach in that perhaps initially we would have been sending down quite extensive comments and views on how we would like to see the line adjusted and so on, whereas now we are much more focused and we recognise that essentially we've got to have one or two clear points . . . So we have become much clearer about how we format our views, you know, what are our priorities.[21]

Scotland also stands out in terms of leadership. Jack McConnell in particular has built a high profile in the EU, first as the Scottish Minister for Europe and more recently as First Minister. McConnell has tried to shape debates, presenting thoughtful proposals to the Commission's Governance hearings,[22] to the Committee of the Regions in its debates on the European Convention,[23] and in the framework of the RegLeg grouping of Regions with Legislative Power (of which he became President in November 2003).[24] This activity has brought McConnell profile and clout which have eluded the equally committed, but arguably less focused and strategic Welsh First Minister, Rhodri Morgan.

And finally, Scotland has been more strategic in coalition-building. It has focused more on bilateral working with other 'strong' regions (Catalonia, Bavaria, North Rhine-Westphalia, Flanders), while Wales has jumped on

19 Interview, September 2000.
20 Interview, June 2003.
21 Interview, July 2000.
22 Scottish Executive and COSLA, *Joint Discussion Paper on European Governance*, March 2001, at www.europa.eu.int/comm/governance/contributions/contrib_scotcosla_en.pdf.
23 Opinion of the Committee of the Regions of 21 November 2002 on *More Democracy, Transparency and Efficiency in the European Union*, CdR 120/2002 fin.
24 McConnell, Jack, Florence Conference of Minister-Presidents of Regions with Legislative Power, 14 November 2002, speaking notes, at www.scotland.gov.uk/about/FCSD/ExtRel1/00014768/page634642154.doc.

board more diffuse multilateral networks.[25] Also, Scotland has been the UK's lead player in the RegLeg initiative, drawing on the clout and experience of powerful partner regions in a way which paid back in the UK context with Peter Hain's radical contribution to the debate on regions at the European Convention (see further below).

In all these senses, in other words, Scotland has done more of the groundwork which can make its constitutional status and opportunities in intergovernmental relations count.

Legitimacy

Both the Scottish and Welsh governments have played on national heritage as a justification for a high profile in EU matters. Again, though, Scotland has done so with more conviction and effect. To quote the late Donald Dewar:

> Devolution for me is not about Scotland's domestic affairs alone. It is and has been also about Scotland's place in a wider world, in the UK naturally enough, but also in Europe and beyond.[26]

Tellingly Dewar described this as 'being back in the mainstream':

> [Before devolution] we were losing the benefits of the real developing layer of regional politics in Europe. This was given formal expression in the EU through the creation of the Committee of the Regions. But it has a far more vivid existence through the dynamism of individual regions and the interchange between them.[27]

Scottish policy was, as Henry McLeish put it, to 'develop Scotland's devolved identity in international circles'.[28] A more populist way of expressing this is that Scotland (once again) is 'playing with the big boys', demonstrating a certain vitality and status which has to do with its character as a distinct nation within the UK. The Welsh First Minister, Rhodri Morgan, confirms this view: 'Now that we have our own elected Assembly, Wales can take its proper place among the European regions – we can look them in the eye for the first time.'[29]

---

25 Cf Jeffery, C. and Palmer, R., 'Stepping (Softly) onto the International Stage: The external relations of Scotland and Wales', in Hrbek, R. (ed.), *Außenbeziehungen von Regionen in Europa und der Welt* (Baden-Baden: Nomos, 2003), 159–72.
26 Dewar, Donald, '*Scotland and Europe: Back in the mainstream*', William & Mary Lecture, 8 December 1999.
27 *Ibid.*
28 Scottish Executive press release SE4276/2001: 'Executive's Commitment to Europe', 3 November 2001.
29 National Assembly for Wales press release W99364-Ind: 'First National Assembly Mission to Europe', 27 May 1999.

In this sense EU activity is about the status that nationhood conveys. There is a further twist in Scotland, where it is also, in part, a response to nationalist pressure. Being seen to sign RegLeg and other declarations with other 'stateless nations' such as Catalonia and Flanders, or strong regions such as Bavaria and Lombardy, gives out signals of Scottish assertion, allowing the Scottish government to ease some of the pressure created by the SNP on representing Scottish interests in Europe, or, to put it the other way: to use the SNP as an excuse to press the UK Government to meet Scottish priorities.

What difference does it all make?

The message from the above is that the UK's devolved governments (including in principle, but hardly yet in practice Northern Ireland) wield significant power alongside the central state in EU affairs. A fairly consistent message is also that Scotland wields more power than Wales by virtue of its stronger constitutional status, the advantages the SNP brings in intergovernmental relations and in emphasising the strength of Scottish national identity, and its more effective entrepreneurship. How does all this impact in more concrete policy terms?

Finding answers to that question is not straightforward. This is partly due to the dynamics of 'multi-level governance'. Multi-level governance is about multi-actor decision-making with multiple linkages between actors in the public sector and beyond at different levels of government. Identifying just who was responsible for which decision can, understandably, be extremely difficult. In addition, many of the issues in which regional governments have an interest are very technical. It may well be, for example, that in Scotland the suckler calf premium is very important or that sheepmeat is likewise in Wales, but in neither case do the issues reach the forefront of the political agenda.[30] At an everyday level EU decision-making is generally mundane, largely depoliticised and articulated in technical language. Again it is often difficult in these circumstances to identify who was responsible for a particular decision. Nonetheless we offer below a number of illustrative examples where distinctive Scottish or Welsh priorities have had an impact on UK EU policies. We also go on to explore the impact of the Scottish and Welsh governments in the 'constitutive' politics of the EU, focusing on the debates about the 'future of Europe' in the European Convention and beyond. The greater political salience of constitutive issues throws a sharper spotlight onto multi-actor decision-making and allows a rather clearer pinpointing of instances where regional governments make a difference.

---

30 House of Lords Select Committee on the Constitution, *Devolution: Interinstitutional Relations in the United Kingdom*, 50.

Everyday politics

The 'everyday' issues in which the Scottish and Welsh governments have shown they can have an impact are clustered in areas where Scottish and Welsh policy interests diverge from those in England, above all in agriculture and fisheries, or which reflect the distinctive topography of the two countries. One of the more celebrated issues was the success of the Scottish Executive in lobbying for special consideration for transport infrastructure in island communities. The issue in question was the subsidised ferry service, traditionally provided by Caledonian MacBrayne (CalMac), to connect the mainland with a number of Scottish islands. The Scottish Executive originally believed that the EU would require the ferry links to be tendered in at least three separate bundles. However, the Commission was successfully lobbied into accepting that all routes could be tendered in a single bundle.[31] A subsequent European Court of Justice ruling in the case of a bus company in Germany raised the possibility that in fact the routes would not need to be tendered at all if they could be understood as essential public services, leading the Executive to seek further clarification from the Commission on changes to regulations governing maritime transport. In this case the Executive was, with some success, exploiting an agenda opened up by the German Länder about removing state aid controls from regional government support for certain types of public service.[32]

The highest profile issue for the Scottish Executive has been fisheries policy, an area in which Scottish officials have been intensely involved both before and after devolution. Scottish Office officials and ministers regularly formed part of UK delegations for fisheries discussions prior to 1999, an arrangement that has been continued in practice since devolution, with Scottish Executive officials regularly involved in working groups, and with close cooperation between the UK Fisheries Minister and his counterpart with responsibility for fisheries, the Scottish Executive's Deputy Minister for Rural Affairs. The two ministers are constant companions during major negotiations and liaise intensively before each Fisheries Council. All this makes sense given that some 70 per cent of the North Sea catch is landed at Scottish ports. Scottish ministers therefore have a strong interest in shaping UK-wide policy insofar as the EU requires a uniform policy framework, and where relevant – for example, for the decommissioning of trawlers – in tailoring policy to the specific circumstances of Scottish fishing communities.[33]

31 'CalMac on Course to Abandon Tendering Red Tape', *The Herald* (6 October 2003).
32 Hrbek, R. and Nettesheim, M. (eds), *Europäische Union und mitgliedstaatliche Daseinsvorsorge* (Baden-Baden: Nomos, 2002).
33 Interview, Department for Environment and Rural Affairs, May 2003.

Scottish ministers have also gone to some lengths to stress their input, as part of the UK delegation, in negotiations in the Council,[34] though this is probably more for domestic consumption, and to placate the SNP, than indicative of any great negotiating clout. Any Scottish minister in the UK delegation can only follow a line agreed beforehand; it is the prior Scottish–UK negotiations that set the agenda. And there, as one Scottish Executive official put it, 'at the UK level, we are very much co-partners in developing fisheries policy'.[35] Even if – or precisely because – this is regarded as a 'nuisance' in the UK Department for Environment and Rural Affairs (DEFRA),[36] it is clear that in fisheries policy at least not much can be done in the UK's name without having the Scottish Executive on board.

There are fewer examples of the National Assembly co-determining UK policy or of lobbying to have specifically Welsh priorities addressed. One example of the latter, however, concerns the repeated closure of cockle beds in the Burry Inlet in Wales by the Food Standards Agency due to pollution. This affected the commercial earnings of cockle pickers, but the National Assembly recognised that it was not in a position to make direct compensation payments as a consequence of EU regulations on state aids. Before making a formal application, Assembly officials spoke directly to the Commission, as well as working with the Commission through DEFRA and UKRep, sounding out the probable Commission response before making a formal state aid application.[37] Compensation payments were then paid through the existing Objective 1 funding programme in Wales when it was clear that this would not contravene Commission regulations.[38]

More generally, it is increasingly clear that all the devolved administrations have been able to follow up distinctive regional priorities as the traditional framework for the Common Agricultural Policy opens out into a more fluid definition of 'rural affairs', including a new emphasis on rural development programmes focused also on environmental protection. These programmes have become increasingly regionalised, and allow fuller possibilities for devolved administrations to introduce new priorities more tightly attuned

34 See for example, 'Finnie Caught Out Over Fish Talks', *Scotsman* (31 October 2002).
35 Interview, Scottish Executive, Edinburgh, June 2000.
36 Interview, DEFRA, May 2003.
37 Interview, Welsh Assembly Government, Cardiff, April 2003.
38 Aid was sought under Article 16 of EU Regulation 2792/1999 (the Financial Instrument for Fisheries Guidance scheme, FIFG) which provides for the member state to pay compensation to fishermen for the temporary cessation of activities in certain circumstances. National Assembly Press Release, 'Financial Help for Burry Inlet Cockle Pickers Sought from Europe, Says Carwyn Jones', 24 May 2002.

to the structural needs of farming and rural communities than in any UK-wide programme which would be dominated by very different English concerns.[39] As a Scottish Executive official put it:

> And what that has led to is four separate UK regional government plans . . . submitted to the Commission separately for approval, with each of the four departments doing their own negotiations with the Commission, so we have seen four quite distinct plans emerge from the process. Different programmes to match the distinctive environments of the UK.[40]

These examples of devolved policy influence are fragmentary. But they do point to some capacity to make a difference, especially in agriculture/fisheries, one of the classic fields of Europeanised policy-making, and one in which economic structures in Scotland and Wales (and Northern Ireland) are quite distinctive as compared with England. In particular they reveal a certain capacity to lobby for exemption from EU state aid policy or, to put it more crudely, to provide public subsidies for industrial sectors significant in a devolved context but which would barely figure on the radar in a UK-wide context. These examples also point, impressionistically at least, to a greater clout for the Scottish Executive than the Welsh Assembly Government, which might be traced back to the earlier comments about capacity, leadership and purpose and the additional nuance provided by the SNP. The ability of the Scottish and Welsh governments to 'make a difference' does indeed broadly conform to the expectations set out earlier in this chapter.

Constitutive politics

A similar finding applies in constitutive politics, that is the capacity of the Welsh and Scottish governments to contribute a UK regional perspective to EU debates about the future of Europe. That has been particularly the case in the context of the European Convention, but also in other future-focused debates like that on European governance led by the European Commission from 2000 onwards. It is in this context that leadership becomes a crucial variable. Put simply, Jack McConnell has taken on a role as contributor to the future of Europe debates that Rhodri Morgan has not. Strikingly, McConnell set out an agenda at an early stage – in the Commission's Governance hearings in March 2001 – which was then pursued simultaneously in a number of forums: the Committee of the Regions, the RegLeg

---

39 Ward, N. and Lowe, P., 'Devolution and the Governance of Rural Affairs in the UK', in Adams, J. and Robinson, P. (eds), *Devolution in Practice: Public policy differences within the UK* (London: ippr, 2002), 132–4, 136–7.
40 Interview, Edinburgh, 2000.

grouping and the Joint Ministerial Committee (Europe). The key points were:[41]

- the need for some new mechanism for monitoring the application of subsidiarity ex ante (before legislation is enacted), and involving regions with legislative power;
- formalised pre-legislative consultation by the Commission of regional and local authorities; and
- greater flexibility in policy implementation so that regional and local authorities can better tailor policy to specific territorial circumstances.

Though initially set out in a somewhat ambitious way – his model for his subsidiarity watchdog was the French Constitutional Council – McConnell's agenda-setting had a perhaps unexpected outcome.[42] It may at a very general level have made a contribution to debate in the Convention via the Committee of the Regions, for which McConnell drafted one of its contributions to the Convention (including the above three points and the Constitutional Council!), and in the various declarations issued by RegLeg.[43] It had a more unexpected impact through UK channels.

In summer 2002 the UK Government decided, presumably in response to the growing profile of the regional debate, to prepare a position to feed into the Convention on regional issues. The task was delegated to Helen Liddell, then Secretary of State for Scotland, who engaged a senior civil servant, whose experience lay in different matters, to draw up a paper. The paper has never been made public. One of the present authors was, however, consulted in its preparation and can vouch that its general thrust had little in common with contributions from regional sources like RegLeg or the Committee of the Regions. Apparently it was opposed with some vigour as inadequate by the devolved administrations, at which point the UK Government asked the devolved administrations, in the framework of the JMC (Europe), to draw up an alternative paper.

The result, in lightly amended format, was the paper presented to the Convention by the UK Government representative, Peter Hain, on 'Europe and the Regions' in February 2003.[44] The paper was remarkable in many

41 Scottish Executive and COSLA, *Joint Discussion Paper on European Governance*, March 2001, Principles 5, 6 and 11.
42 McConnell, Jack, 'The Future of Europe Debate – A Scottish Perspective', Speech, 6 June 2002 at www.scotland.gov.uk/about/FCSD/ExtRel1/00014768/page1239857280.aspx; accessed November 2005.
43 Opinion of the Committee of the Regions of 21 November 2002.
44 Hain, Peter, 'Europe and the Regions', 3 February 2003, at http://register.consilium.eu.int/pdf/en/03/cv00/cv00526en03.pdf; accessed November 2005.

respects. It was officially styled as 'submitted to the European Convention on behalf of the UK Government *and* the Devolved Administrations in Scotland and Wales' [our emphasis]. Such a joint submission is rare if not more or less unprecedented in EU constitutional debates. And its content was radical, endorsing with some vigour regional demands (and, significantly, key points in the 'McConnell agenda') about improving consultation, beefing up the Committee of the Regions and improving the functioning of the subsidiarity principle. To all-round surprise it contained a commitment on the part of the UK Government to include the UK's devolved legislatures in the Convention's proposed 'early warning system' for national parliaments in the monitoring of subsidiarity (a commitment subsequently adopted by other member states including Austria and Germany). As a Welsh official aptly put it, 'the possibility that the UK could emerge as a champion of the regions was extraordinary, possibly even to itself, but certainly to observers'.[45]

The same Welsh official recalled Rhodri Morgan describing the Hain paper as Wales's 'first contribution to UK foreign policy'.[46] That would be pushing things a little too far. Though Welsh Assembly Government officials were fully involved alongside their counterparts in Scotland in drafting the Hain paper, its key thrust is clearly the agenda set out by Jack McConnell. In particular, the extension of the early warning system to regional parliaments is an adaptation of a demand that McConnell had made two years earlier in the governance hearings. The genealogy of much of the rest of the paper also traces quite directly back to McConnell. It remains unclear how some of the ideas in the Hain paper would have been translated into practice, had the Constitutional Treaty been ratified across the EU.[47] However, what is certain is that the Scottish Executive, through McConnell, has shown a real capacity to make a difference in a quite fundamental way, concerning the decision-making structures of the EU and in particular the linkages between regional and EU-level institutions.

Conclusions

In sum: the Scottish government has demonstrated a capacity to make a difference in EU policy, both in everyday politics and in constitutive politics; the

45 Clifford, Des, 'The Welsh Assembly Government, the European Convention and the Inter Governmental Conference', paper presented at the Institute of Welsh Affairs Conference on 'Wales and Europe', Cardiff, 9 February 2004.
46 *Ibid.*
47 See House of Lords Select Committee on the Constitution, Session 2002–03 9th Report, *The Draft Constitutional Treaty for the European Union*, HL 168, Memorandum by Alan Trench, 41–5.

Welsh government less so. Scotland's greater impact is explained by constitutional weight, more powerful policy capacity, more forceful leadership and the 'advantage' of a strong nationalist party committed to Scottish independence. Both the Scottish and Welsh governments have sought to exert an influence mainly within the logic of the member state (arguably networking transnationally within groupings like RegLeg has the same effect by strengthening the arguments and experience UK devolved governments can bring to bear in internal UK debates).

For reasons we have set out it is difficult to tie down many specific examples of influence, though the Hain paper to the Convention strikes us as especially notable because of the openings it has created not just in the UK but also for legislative regions in other member states. Influence in everyday politics is measured in more technical terms and may register little public impact, except on fisheries policy, where the Scottish government appears to have established a de facto grip on UK policy. Elsewhere, both devolved governments have revealed a capacity to 'tweak' policy rules, and in particular to open up the possibility of subsidy where ostensibly state aids controls do not allow it.

Does this capacity to make a difference, as we supposed, equate to a loss of autonomy on the part of central government in external affairs? The answer is a nuanced one. There does not appear to be a zero-sum game in play. If Welsh cockle farmers or CalMac can now be subsidised freely – a gain from the perspective of the Welsh or Scottish governments – it by no means follows that the UK Government has suffered a comparable 'loss'. Rather, it would seem that the diversity of economic interests across the UK can better be expressed following devolution, now that there are governments that can be more directly lobbied to express fairly narrow territorial concerns. Where the UK Government may have lost out is in its ability to control the agenda. On fisheries, and at the Convention on the regional question, it has had to prioritise devolved (largely Scottish) government priorities that would otherwise clearly not be high priorities of its own. In some fields the UK Government has to come to terms with narrowed room for manoeuvre.

Even where that is the case, the potency of the UK member state in European negotiations has not been compromised (an argument used in the more conflictual central–regional relations in Spain and Germany). On the contrary. As we have noted, the devolved administrations have not sought to work outside the logic of the member state. When a devolved government position is put with force to the UK Government, this may be an advantage for UK negotiators. Having seemingly non-negotiable domestic constraints (or presenting them as such) can be an advantage in EU negotiations.[48]

48 Bulmer and Paterson, *Germany's European Diplomacy*, 83.

Looking ahead, there may, for example, be interesting tactical possibilities for UK negotiators arising from the commitment to consult the devolved legislatures on subsidiarity questions.

But looking ahead also means reiterating the quite fundamental point that all this is highly provisional for reasons of party politics. The UK's debates about European integration are highly polarised between the government and opposition parties at UK level. The current UK opposition party, the Conservatives, take a substantially different, less pro-European, approach to EU matters. It seems unlikely that future devolved governments will share this viewpoint. Euroscepticism appears disproportionately a phenomenon of England, where the Conservatives remain strong, and from where any electoral revival seems certain to be launched. In other words there is in prospect a party-political conflict line in intergovernmental relations on Europe, underwritten by a territorial dimension. In those circumstances, the failure hitherto to codify and make justiciable devolved rights of access to EU decision-making may allow central government to cut off the possibilities for devolved governments to make a difference. This would not be a recipe for stable intergovernmental relations and could well open up ground for the kinds of central–regional conflicts over Europe seen elsewhere, but – because elsewhere there is no great central–regional divide on the desirability of European integration – at a much higher level of intensity.

11

The United Kingdom as a federalised or regionalised union

Ronald Watts*

Introduction

The overall thrust of the preceding chapters has been to advance two arguments. The first is that the United Kingdom Government remains the dominant force within the United Kingdom as a state, and that the devolved governments and legislatures remain highly dependent on the UK Government and Parliament. The second is that, nonetheless, devolution has created substantial autonomous spheres for the exercise of power by the devolved institutions within which distinctive and often divergent policies have been developed and territorial diversity asserted. Consequently, the incremental development of such distinctiveness may, over the course of time, when eventually reinforced by governments controlled by different political parties, enlarge the sphere of territorial autonomy and policy divergence so that it becomes larger and more difficult to reverse. This points to the likelihood that the tension between these two forces will be a key characteristic of the United Kingdom in the early decades of the twenty-first century.

From time to time the preceding chapters have made comparative reference to arrangements in other countries and particularly federations. This chapter will attempt to place the arguments and evidence presented in those chapters in a broader, more systematic comparative context. Comparisons will be made with similar developments and arrangements in federations, regionalised unions and unitary systems elsewhere. How these arrangements have affected the territorial distribution of power and the degree of regional autonomy will, it is hoped, contribute to an understanding of the extent to which the UK's experience is unique or resembles developments elsewhere.

*   The author would like to thank the Economic and Social Research Council's Devolution and Constitutional Change programme for enabling him to spend two months as a research visitor at the Constitution Unit at University College London, as part of the preparation of this chapter.

Among the questions that will be addressed are: Can the power structure of the devolved United Kingdom be meaningfully compared with federations? Do the power relations between the devolved territories and the United Kingdom resemble those in federal systems? Do power relations in the devolved United Kingdom resemble more those in regionalised unions or unitary political systems?

Territorial systems compared

In comparing the power structures of the devolved United Kingdom with those in other territorial political systems, some definition of categories is required in the interest of conceptual clarity. For this purpose in this chapter I follow the typology originally advanced by Daniel Elazar and now widely used with some modifications.[1] We may distinguish three terms: 'federalism' is basically not a descriptive but a normative term, and refers to the advocacy of multi-tiered government combining elements of shared rule and regional self-rule. 'Federal political systems' is a descriptive term which refers to a broad category of political systems in which, by contrast to the unambiguous single source of constitutional authority and sovereignty in unitary systems, there are two (or more) levels of territorial government, combining elements of shared rule through common institutions and of regional self-rule for the governments of the constituent units. This broad genus encompasses a whole spectrum of specific forms, ranging from devolved unions, quasi-federations and federations to confederations and beyond (see table 11.1 for the spectrum of 'federal political systems').

Within this broad genus of federal political systems 'federations' represent a particular species in which neither the federal nor the constituent units of government are constitutionally subordinate to the other; that is, each has sovereign powers derived not from another level of government but from a constitution that is not unilaterally amendable by either level of government; each is empowered to deal directly with its citizens in the exercise of its constitutionally assigned legislative, executive and taxing powers; and each is directly elected by its citizens. Examples are the United States, Switzerland, Canada (after the mid-twentieth century), Australia, Austria, Germany and Belgium.

---

1 Elazar, D. J., *Exploring Federalism* (Tuscaloosa, AL: University of Alabama Press, 1987); Elazar, D. J. (ed.), *Federal Systems of the World: A handbook of federal, confederal and autonomy arrangements* (Harlow: Longman Group Limited, 2nd edn, 1994); Watts, R. L., *Comparing Federal Systems* (Montreal and Kingston: McGill-Queen's University Press, 2nd edn, 1999), 6–14.

Some political systems are hybrids combining the characteristics of different kinds of political systems. Hybrids occur because statesmen are often more interested in pragmatic political solutions than in theoretical purity. Those polities which constitutionally are predominantly federations, but which have some over-riding federal government powers more typical of a unitary system, may be described as 'quasi-federations', a term first introduced in this sense by K. C. Wheare.[2] Examples are the Canadian Constitution of 1867 (although the unitary elements fell into disuse in the second half of the twentieth century), and the Indian, Pakistan, Malaysian and South African Constitutions which create what are predominantly federations but include some limited over-riding federal government powers. In the case of South Africa, however, the label 'federation' is not used. Recently, a second somewhat different usage of the term has been advanced in relation to the United Kingdom to refer to what is predominantly a devolved union, rather than a federation, that is moving towards more federal relationships.[3]

Regionally devolved unions represent another type of hybrid. These are territorial systems which are basically unitary in form, in the sense that ultimately constitutional authority rests with the central government, but which have devolved powers in a formally constitutional manner to territorial units of government which have a considerable measure of self-rule. Examples include Italy (since 2001), Japan, Spain (as established in 1978) and the United Kingdom (since 1998). Devolved unions are distinguished from decentralised unitary systems such as Denmark, Finland, France and Sweden. In the latter the degree of decentralisation is determined by the central government without constitutional guarantees.

In outlining such a typology, three further points need to be noted. First, in classifying individual political systems, an important distinction is that between constitutional form and operational reality. In many political systems political practice has modified the way the constitution operates. This is indicated by comparing the second and third columns in table 11.2. Among those countries where political practice has significantly transformed the character of the political system are Canada, Spain and South Africa.

A second point to note is the significance of the degree of symmetry or asymmetry among the federated or devolved entities in their relationship to the central government. In all multi-level political systems there is an unavoidable de facto asymmetry in terms of variations in territorial size, population and

2 Wheare, K. C., *Federal Government* (London: Oxford University Press, 4th edn, 1963), 17–21.
3 Bogdanor, V., *Devolution in the United Kingdom* (Oxford: Oxford University Press, 1999); Hazell, R. (ed.), *Constitutional Futures: A history of the next ten years* (Oxford: Oxford University Press, 1999).

Table 11.1. The spectrum of territorial political systems

Unitary systems	Political structures in which ultimate constitutional authority is concentrated completely in a central government. The central government may decentralise administration to regional territories but retains complete legal authority over these. Examples of decentralised unitary systems are Denmark, Finland, France and Sweden.
Unions	Polities compounded in such a way that the constituent units preserve their respective integrities primarily through the common organs of the general government rather than through dual government structures. The United Kingdom prior to devolution was an example. Other examples are Spain before 1978 and Canada before 1867.
Constitutionally devolved unions	Basically unitary in form, in the sense that ultimate authority rests with the central government, but these incorporate constitutionally protected sub-units of government which have functional autonomy. Belgium prior to becoming a federation in 1993 was an example. Other examples are Italy (since 2001), Japan and in constitutional form, Spain (as established 1978).
Quasi-federations	These are predominantly federations in their constitutions and operation, but provide the federal government with some over-riding or emergency powers more typical of a unitary system, and therefore constitute a hybrid. Examples are the Canadian Constitution of 1867 (but its unitary elements fell into disuse in the second half of the twentieth century); India, Pakistan and Malaysia which include some over-riding central emergency powers; and the South African Constitution, which has nearly all the features of a federation but did not adopt the label and gives the central government some over-riding powers
Federations	Compound polities, combining strong constituent units and a strong general government, each possessing powers delegated to it through the constitution, and each empowered to deal directly with the citizens in the exercise of its legislative, administrative and taxing powers, and each directly elected by the citizens. Examples are the United States, Switzerland, Canada (in the later twentieth century), Australia, Austria, Germany and Belgium. While it has not adopted the label, Spain in practice exhibits nearly all the features of a federation.
Confederations	These occur where several pre-existing polities join together to form a common government for certain limited purposes (for example, for foreign affairs, defence or economic purposes), but the common

government is dependent upon the constituent governments, being composed of delegates from the constituent governments, and therefore having only an indirect electoral and fiscal base. Historical examples have been Switzerland for most of the period 1291–1847 and the United States 1776–89. In the contemporary world, the European Union is primarily a confederation although it has increasingly incorporated some features of a federation and thus represents a hybrid.

Federacies

Political arrangements where a large unit is linked to a smaller unit or units, but the smaller unit retains considerable autonomy and has a minimal role in the government of the larger one, and where the relationship can be dissolved only by mutual agreement. Examples are the relationship of Puerto Rico to the United States and of the state of Jammu and Kashmir to India.

Associated states

These relationships are similar to federacies, but they can be dissolved by either of the units acting alone on prearranged terms established in the constituting document or a treaty. The relationship between New Zealand and the Cook Islands is an example.

Condominiums

Political units which function under the joint rule of two or more external states in such a way that the inhabitants have substantial internal self-rule. An example was Andorra, which functioned under the joint rule of France and Spain 1278–1993.

Leagues

Linkages of politically independent polities for specific purposes that function through a common secretariat rather than a government and from which members may unilaterally withdraw. Examples include the Arab League, the Nordic Council and the Commonwealth of Nations.

Joint functional authorities

An agency established by two or more polities for joint implementation of a particular task or tasks. The North Atlantic Fisheries Organisation (NAFO), the International Atomic Energy Agency (IAEA) and the International Labour Organisation (ILO) are three of many examples. Such joint functional authorities may also take the form of trans-border organisations established by adjoining subnational governments, e.g. the interstate grouping for economic development involving four regions in Italy, four Austrian Länder, two Yugoslav republics and one West German Land established in 1978, and the interstate Regio Basiliensis involving Swiss, German and French cooperation in the Basle area.

Source: Watts, R. L., *Comparing Federal Systems*, 2nd edn (Kingston and Montreal: McGill-Queen's University Press, 1999), 8–9.

Table 11.2. A typology of multi-tier territorial political systems

Federations and quasi-federations

1. Nominal types and examples	2. Constitutional status	3. Political practice	4. Major constituent units	5. Competency delineation	6. Constitutional amendments: role of units	7. Formal unit rep. in central policy-making	8. Asymmetries
Australia	Federation (1901)	Federation	6 states	Constitution: (large concurrent sphere)	Yes (referendums)[a]	Yes (Senate)	Symmetrical states but territories[b]
Austria	Federation (1920)	Federation	9 Länder	Constitution: leg. centralised, admin. decentralised	No (but special procedures)[c]	Yes (Bundesrat)	Symmetrical
Belgium	Federation (1993)	Federation	3 regions + 3 communities[d]	Constitution + organic laws (mostly exclusive powers)	No (but special majorities required)[e]	Partial (Senate)[f]	Asymmetry of regions and communities
Canada	Quasi-federation (1867)	Federation[h]	10 provinces	Constitution (mostly exclusive powers)	Yes (legislatures)	Appointed Senate	Asymmetry among provinces; 3 territories[g]
Germany	Federation (1949	Federation	16 Länder	Constitution (centralised leg.; decentralised admin.)	Yes (via Bundesrat)	Yes (Bundesrat)	Symmetrical
India	Quasi-federation (1950)	Quasi-federation[i]	28 states	Constitution (3 lists)	Yes (legislatures)	Yes (Rajya Sabha)	Asymmetry of states + 6 territories and federacy[j]

South Africa	Quasi-federation (1996)	Decentralised unitary[n]	9 provinces	Constitution (some central over-riding power)[p]	Yes (via NCOP)[o]	Yes[q] (NCOP)	Symmetrical
Switzerland	Federation (1848, 1999)	Federation	26 cantons	Constitution (relatively decentralised)	Yes (referendums)[a]	Yes (Council of States)	Full and half cantons
United States	Federation (1789)	Federation	50 states	Constitution (considerable conc. spheres)	Yes (legislatures)	Yes (Senate)	Symmetrical states plus federacies and territories
Devolved unions							
Italy	Devolved union with federal features (2001)	Devolved union with federal features	22 regions	Constitution + legislation after referendums[l]	Indirectly (referendum)	Yes (Senate) Consultative[m]	Asymmetrical: 17 ordinary and 5 special regions
Japan	Devolved union (1947)	Devolved union	47 prefectures	Central Diet	No (Central Diet)	Yes (House of Councillors)[k]	Symmetrical
Spain	Devolved union with federal features (1978)	Federation[r]	17 autonomous communities	Constitution[s]	No, but special requirements[t]	Partial (Senate)[u]	Asymmetrical among autonomous communities
United Kingdom	Devolved union (1998)	Devolved union (S, W, NI)	3 territories (S, W, NI)	UK Parliament	No (UK Parliament)	Consultative	Asymmetry among S, W and NI
		Decentralised unitary state (England)	1 territory (England)	UK Parliament	No (UK Parliament)	No	Unelected governments (England)

Table 11.2. (continued)

1. Nominal types and examples	2. Constitutional status	3. Political practice	4. Major constituent units	5. Competency delineation	6. Constitutional amendments: role of units	7. Formal unit rep. in central policy-making	8. Asymmetries
Decentralised unitary							
Denmark	Decentralised unitary	Decentralised unitary	Groups of Amter	Central legislation	No	No	Faroe Islands, Greenland (federacies)
Finland	Decentralised unitary	Decentralised unitary	Counties	Central legislation	No	No	Aaland Islands (federacy)
France	Decentralised unitary	Regionalised unitary	21 regions	Central legislation	No	Consultative	Corsica and overseas territories
Sweden	Decentralised unitary (1975)	Regionalised unitary	21 counties	Central legislation	No	No	Symmetrical
Centralised unitary							
Greece	Unitary	Unitary	13 development regions	Central legislation	No	No	Island regions
New Zealand	Unitary	Unitary	None	No	No	No	Cook Islands and Niue Islands (associated states)
Portugal	Unitary	Unitary	Potential planning regions	No	No	No	Azores Island and Madeira Island (federacies)

Notes:

a Referendums require federal majority and majorities in a majority of states or cantons.

b 1 territory + 1 capital territory + 7 administered territories.

c Partial amendments require 2/3 majority in federal lower house, but 1/3 of other house may request total revision followed by a referendum obtaining a majority.

d Flemish Community and Flanders Region Councils are in practice coterminous.

e Process requires a special election followed by special majorities in each house and for amendments to distribution of powers or Cour d'Arbitrage, special legislation supported by a majority of each of the two major legislative groups in Parliament.

f Senate is composed of 40 directly elected + 21 indirectly elected (by linguistic Community Councils) + 10 co-opted members.

g Considerable asymmetrical arrangements in the case of Quebec, but also some for other provinces.

h Quasi-federal constitutional features remain but have not been exercised for past half-century.

i Considerable use of emergency powers, but this has been decreasing.

j India consists of 28 states, 6 union territories, and 1 national capital territory. State of Jammu and Kashmir is a federacy relationship and Bhutan is an associated state.

k House of Councillors is elected on basis of open list proportional representation from prefectural electoral districts.

l Exclusive powers and framework powers of central government enumerated; residual powers to regions. Ordinary regions can acquire special-region status by negotiation with parliament following regional referendums.

m Senate elected on a regional basis from single member constituencies, and does not represent regional legislatures or governments.

n Predominance of African National Congress party in all levels of government undercuts constitutional structure.

o Constitutional amendments affecting provinces require support of 6 of 9 provinces in the National Council of the Provinces.

p Constitution sections 44 and 146 give national parliament broad powers to set standards in areas of provincial jurisdiction.

q Central second legislative chamber (National Council of the Provinces) consists of representatives of provincial legislatures and executives.

r Operates as a federation in all but name.

s Delineated in Constitution; provisions for negotiated transfer under Article 150.

t Amendments can be proposed by central government or autonomous community. Ratification requires 3/5 majority in each central chamber; 1/10 of either house can request a referendum; certain portions of Constitution require 2/3 majority in each house followed by a referendum.

u Senate has 44 members appointed by parliaments of autonomous communities; but 208 are directly elected.

v Scotland Act 1998, Northern Ireland Act 1998 and Government of Wales Act 1998.

economic resources. This affects their relative political influence and power. But a particular issue is whether there is de jure symmetry or asymmetry, relating to constitutional status and powers, and whether this is temporary or permanent.[4] In a number of federations, devolved unions, and even decentralised and centralised unitary systems there are elements of de jure asymmetry (see table 11.2, column 8 for examples). De jure asymmetry may be exhibited in two ways. The most common is where devolution applies to all the territories within the polity but is applied differentially among them. The second is where devolution applies only to some territories within the polity but not to others, as occurs for example in the United Kingdom or in those more centralised systems where one or a few particular units (usually islands) are in a federacy or associated state relationship.

Third, in addition to identifying differences among the categories of multi-level governance, it must be noted that within each of these categories there can be considerable variation. Among the factors producing these variations in federations, for instance, are:

- the national or multinational character of the polity; the number (from 6 states, regions or communities in Australia and Belgium to 50 states in the United States) and relative sizes (territory and population) of the constituent units;
- the form (emphasis upon exclusive powers as in Canada and Belgium or extensive areas of concurrent jurisdiction as in the United States, Australia and Germany) and scope of the particular powers assigned to each level of government (ranging from the relative centralisation in Austria and Germany to much greater decentralisation in Switzerland and Canada);
- the specific financial arrangements allocating own-source revenues and the provision for unconditional or conditional intergovernmental transfers; the constitutional symmetry or asymmetry of the federated or devolved units (symmetry in the United States, Australia and Germany but considerable asymmetry in Canada, Belgium and India);
- the executive–legislature relations within each government, which radically affect the manner in which intergovernmental relations are conducted (separation of powers in the United States and parliamentary executives in Canada, Australia, India and most European federations);
- the procedures relating to constitutional amendments, which may be ratified by state governments (Germany), legislatures (Canada and India), double-majority referendums (Switzerland and Australia) or special entrenchment procedures (Belgium);

4 Watts, R. L., 'Asymmetrical Decentralization: Functional or dysfunctional', *Indian Journal of Federal Studies*, 1 (2004), 1–42.

- the use of general supreme courts (United States, Canada and Australia) or specialised constitutional courts (Germany and Belgium);
- the representation of constituent units in the institutions of shared rule and particularly the central second legislative chamber (strong second chambers in the United States and Switzerland and weaker regional representation in Canada and Belgium);
- the character of the political parties and the relationship between the different levels within parties (distinct party systems in Canada but closely integrated party systems in the early decades of India and currently South Africa);
- and the existence or absence of a common higher public or civil service (distinct in most, but common higher public services in India).

These variations affect the character of intergovernmental processes and the power relationships between governments within federations. The resulting variations within each of the different categories identified in table 11.1 mean that at the margins the categories may shade into each other, representing a spectrum rather than being absolutely demarcated. Thus, for instance, at the margins a decentralised unitary system may shade into a devolved union, a devolved union into a quasi-federation, or a quasi-federation into a federation. For a comparison of the power relationships within the United Kingdom to those in federations and devolved unions elsewhere, these factors will be examined in the following sections of this chapter, broadly following the sequence and structure of the previous chapters in this book.

The main hypothesis that will be examined in these sections is that although the devolved United Kingdom has some features resembling those in federations and quasi-federations, it remains predominantly a devolved union in which the UK Government is clearly dominant in its relations with the devolved territories, while nevertheless creating autonomous spheres for the devolved institutions within which distinctive differentiated policies and territorial diversity have been asserted.

The constitutional and legal framework

In the previous section attention was drawn to the distinction between the formal constitutional and legal framework on the one hand, and operational practices on the other. Both affect power relationships within the polity, with the latter in some cases even transforming these. In this section we focus primarily on the former, that is the constitutional and legal framework. Chapter 2 has set out the historical basis of what James Mitchell has called 'a state of unions' upon which the formal devolution of 1998 was built, and in chapter

3 Alan Trench has analysed the formal legal framework of devolution established in the United Kingdom in that year, defining the structure of power relations.

In some respects the devolved United Kingdom shares most of the basic institutional features that mark federations. The generally accepted structural features common to federations are the following:

- a combination of common shared rule and territorial self-government requiring two territorial orders of government each acting directly on their citizens;
- a formal constitutional distribution of legislative and executive authority and allocation of revenue resources between the two orders of government ensuring some areas of genuine autonomy for each order;
- a supreme written constitution not unilaterally amendable and requiring for amendment the consent of a significant proportion of the constituent units;
- an umpire in the form of courts (or as in Switzerland provision for legislative referendums) to rule on disputes between governments;
- processes and institutions to facilitate intergovernmental collaboration for those areas where governmental responsibilities are shared or inevitably overlap;
- provision for designated representation of distinct regional views within the federal policy-making institutions, usually including specific representation in a federal second legislative chamber.

All of these except the third and to some extent the sixth are features that the devolved United Kingdom shares with federations and quasi-federations. In the case of the sixth, although the second chamber, the House of Lords, is not primarily a regional chamber, the devolved territories do have specific representation in the UK Government within the executive through their respective Secretaries of State.

But a crucial difference distinguishing the legal structure of the devolution arrangements in the United Kingdom from those in federations and quasi-federations is the absence of the third feature; that is, a supreme written constitution not unilaterally amendable by one level of government alone and requiring the formal assent, whether granted by regional governments, legislatures or referendums, of a significant proportion of the constituent units. As table 11.2, column 6, indicates, formal entrenchment of the constitutional arrangements is typical of federations and quasi-federations, and indeed even of such devolved unions as Spain and Italy. Thus, by comparison the devolved institutions in the UK have a constitutionally subordinate rather than coordinate status.

Alan Trench, in chapter 3, further identifies a number of fundamental differences from federations in terms of the limits placed on the devolved powers in the United Kingdom. To begin with, the National Assembly for Wales is limited to passing secondary legislation and exercising executive powers. In all three devolved territories, by comparison with federations, the autonomy of the devolved bodies is truncated by the requirement of the non-opposition of the UK Government, if not its active support, for a wide range of their activities; by heavy dependence upon UK Government cooperation for many other activities; by the power of Westminster to legislate in matters normally assigned to the devolved territories (even if, in the case of Scotland, under the Sewel convention this requires the assent of the Scottish Parliament); by the ease of the mechanisms to adjust legal competence at the margins, and by the procedural controls over devolved legislation (for comparisons see also table 11.2, column 5). Furthermore, contrasting with the situation in most federations and quasi-federations, the devolved territories and institutions in the United Kingdom have minimal control over their own constitutions. Thus, by comparison with federations and quasi-federations elsewhere, as Alan Trench notes in chapter 3, the ultimate maximisation of the UK Parliament's legal authority and the UK Government's dominance of inter-governmental processes mean that the formal autonomy of the devolved administrations is limited, with legal power remaining firmly in the hands of the UK Government to shape, legislate and implement policy.

Another factor which differentiates the United Kingdom from most federations, quasi-federations and regionalised unions is the impact of the radical double asymmetry that marks the devolved UK. A degree of de jure asymmetry exists in many federations, quasi-federations and regionalised unions. Notable examples are Canada, India, Malaysia, Belgium, Spain, Italy and Russia (see table 11.2, column 8 for some of these examples). But the UK exhibits a more radical asymmetry in two ways. The first is that England, which represents about 85 per cent of the UK population, has no devolution to elected regional institutions. Nor, given the result of the referendum in the North East of England in 2004, is this likely in the foreseeable future.[5] This means that devolution applies only peripherally; that is, to a minority of 15 per cent of the UK population, leaving the remainder of the country in a fundamentally unitary system. There is no equivalent to this in federations, quasi-federations or regionally devolved unions elsewhere. In those cases devolution applies throughout. The closest parallels are the federacy or associated state arrangements existing at the peripheries in a variety

5 On 4 November 2004, voters in the North East region of England rejected the proposal to set up an elected regional assembly by a margin of nearly four to one.

of decentralised and centralised unitary systems elsewhere (see table 11.2, column 8). A difference between these cases and the UK, however, is that these federacy and associate state relationships involve only a minimal role for these peripheral territories in the government of the larger state, whereas the devolved territories in the UK have full representation within the House of Commons.

A second aspect is the differential constitutional status and powers allocated to the three devolved territories. This has discouraged horizontal intergovernmental relations among them and the development of any common front among the three devolved governments in their relations with the UK Government, contrasting to what is often found in federations. The resulting predominantly bilateral intergovernmental relations have further reinforced the dominant position of the UK Government.

Another significant feature of the devolved United Kingdom is the significance of the bureaucratic linkages noted by Alan Trench in chapter 8. These have facilitated intergovernmental collaboration, but at some price to the autonomy of the devolved governments. By contrast most federations and quasi-federations have been provided with distinct public services of their own for each constituent government. Nevertheless, there are examples in India, Pakistan and South Africa of common higher public services. As in the UK, these have fostered intergovernmental accommodation. The implicit constraints upon the autonomy of devolved governments have in most of these cases been to some extent avoided by requirements ensuring that members of the common higher public services are primarily responsible to the governments to which they are attached.

While noting above the similarities and differences between the devolved UK and federations, quasi-federations and in some other regionalised unions, the question may be raised as to how the devolved United Kingdom compares with decentralised unitary systems such as those in France or Sweden. Both those countries have undergone a measure of devolution to regional units in recent years.[6] In neither are the powers of the regional units asymmetrical, except for the cases of Corsica and the overseas territories in relation to France. By comparison with the devolved territories in the UK, the functions of the 21 French regions are still mainly related to economic development. Nevertheless, they have had directly elected councils since 1986 which, despite their constitutional limitations, have 'managed to assert themselves as

---

6 Loughlin, J., *Subnational Democracy in the European Union: Challenges and opportunities* (Oxford: Oxford University Press, 2001), 185–210, 319–42; Olson, J. and Astrom, J., 'Why Regionalism in Sweden?', *Regional and Federal Studies*, 13:3 (2003), 66–89.

important actors in the French politico-administrative landscape'.[7] Sweden too has been undergoing a regional transformation, expanding the role of the 21 elected county councils.[8] One interesting feature of this development in Sweden is that rather than centrally imposing a common pattern, regions have been encouraged to develop their own models for democratic decision-making, adjusting these to specific regional priorities. In both these cases, while regional devolution has occurred, the adoption of a federal structure has clearly not been an objective. By comparison with the scope of autonomy experienced by the devolved territories within the United Kingdom, the scope of the regional units in France and Sweden has been more limited and the unitary character of their polities has remained clearly intact.

In sum, it would appear that in terms of their constitutional or legal frameworks, the devolved UK is by comparison with most federations and quasi-federations, and indeed also the devolved unions of Italy and Spain, marked by more central government dominance. In Italy a significant feder-alisation process in 2001 has been followed by further proposals in 2004 for new powers for the regions over health, education and even policing similar to some of those of the autonomous communities in Spain.[9] At the same time, the extent to which central government dominance in the United Kingdom has been exhibited in practice to date indicates that the central government has tended not to exercise its full potential powers and has left room for con-siderable autonomy for the devolved territories.

Intergovernmental financial arrangements

Intergovernmental financial relations in multi-level systems of government are particularly important because they affect the relative powers of gov-ernments in two different ways: first, these resources enable or constrain governments in the exercise of their constitutionally or legally assigned leg-islative and executive responsibilities; second, powers of taxation and expen-diture are themselves important instruments for affecting and regulating the economy. Chapters 4 and 5 of this volume, therefore, raise important finan-cial issues affecting the relative powers of the UK Government and of the gov-ernments of the devolved territories.

In this chapter comparisons with other political systems will be made in terms of the degrees of expenditure devolution, the revenue autonomy of the devolved territories and the expenditure autonomy of the devolved territo-

---

7 Loughlin, *Subnational Democracy in the European Union*, 197–8.
8 *Ibid.*, 336–7.
9 These were approved by the Italian Parliament in November 2005.

ries. These are presented in tabular form in table 11.3. In addition, comparisons of the equalisation arrangements and processes for determining financial adjustments will be considered.

The first column in table 11.3 gives some measure of the extent of expenditure devolution by tabulating the expenditures of all sub-unit governments as a percentage of total government expenditure. There, it is notable that the range of sub-unit expenditures in federations and quasi-federations generally falls between 68 per cent and 31 per cent, with Switzerland (68 per cent) and Canada and Germany (63 per cent each) the most decentralised, and Austria (31 per cent) the least decentralised. Interestingly, the devolved unions, and Sweden as a decentralised unitary system, fall within the same range. As table 5.1 showed, the UK is within a similar range, with devolved administration spending constituting 55.6 per cent of spending in Scotland, 48.4 per cent in Wales and (excluding social security spending) 57.1 per cent in Northern Ireland.

In the same table the level of revenue-raising autonomy for the federated or devolved units in different polities is indicated by the figure for own-source revenues as a percentage of their total revenues (i.e. own-source revenues plus all transfers). On this measure, as noted in chapter 4, the UK is rare, although not unique, in the low level of own-source revenues levied and collected by the devolved territories. Indeed, other than council tax, the business rates and user charges, and the as-yet-unused Scottish variable rate of income tax, the devolved territories have minimal fiscal power. In most federations and quasi-federations own-source revenues constitute a much higher proportion, between 54 per cent (India) and 80 per cent (Canada) of total sub-unit revenues (table 11.3, column 2). In a few cases such as Belgium (28 per cent for the regions and 4 per cent for the communities), Spain (23 per cent) and South Africa (4 per cent) the degree of revenue autonomy of the constituent units is significantly less than in most federations. On the other hand, it is also noteworthy that in Japan and Sweden the figures are not dissimilar to the proportion of own-source territorial revenues in most of the federations and quasi-federations. Thus, in comparative terms, the control and hence accountability of the devolved territories in the United Kingdom over the size of their total revenues is extremely limited. As a result they are almost totally dependent upon transfers from the UK Government.

While revenue autonomy provides sub-units of government with the opportunity to control the total size of their revenues, expenditure autonomy relates to the degree of discretion that they can apply to expenditures within that total revenue. In the UK, while the size of the revenues of the devolved territories is almost totally determined by Whitehall, largely through transfers based on the Barnett formula, the fact that these transfers are unconditional

Table 11.3. Financial arrangements in autonomy systems

Types and examples	Scope of expenditure*[a]	Revenue-raising autonomy**	Expenditure autonomy***
Federations and quasi-federations			
Australia	46	55	79
Austria	31	56	78
Belgium[b]			
(a) Regions (e.g. Walloon)	N/A[c]	28	82
(b) Communities (e.g. French-speaking)	N/A[c]	4	95
Canada	63	80	84
Germany	63	56	90
India	55	54	81
South Africa	50	4	89
Switzerland	68	75	83
United States	46	70	70
Devolved unions			
Japan	62	63	84
Italy[d]	N/A	Art. 119(1)[e]	Art (119) (2–6)[f]
Spain	49	23	58
United Kingdom (Scotland)[g]	56	Minimal[h]	Almost total[i]
Decentralised unitary			
Sweden	46	74	96

Sources: Watts, R. L., *Intergovernmental Fiscal Relations in Eight Countries: Final report* (Kingston: Institute of Intergovernmental Relations, Queen's University, 2004); R. L. Watts, *The Spending Power in Federal Systems: A comparative study* (Kingston: Institute of Intergovernmental Relations, 1999); Verdonck, M. and Deschouwer, K., 'Patterns and Principles of Fiscal Federalism in Belgium', *Regional and Federal Studies*, 13:4 (2003), 101-7; Heald, D. and McLeod, A., 'Revenue-raising by Devolved Administrations in the Context of an Expenditure-Based Financing System', *Regional and Federal Studies*, 13:4 (2003), 76-7; Caravita di Toritto, B., 'The Role of Local Authorities in Decentralizing Process in Italy: Institutional aspects' (unpublished paper delivered at the International Association of Centres of Federal Studies conference, Cape Town, October 2004).

Notes:
Figures are for 2000 and 2001, except those for Canada, Germany and the United States which are either 1995 or 1996, Belgium (2003) and the United Kingdom (2003–4).
* Sub-unit expenditures as per cent of total government expenditure.
** Own-source revenues as per cent of total sub-unit revenues.
*** Unconditional transfers plus own-source revenues as per cent of total sub-unit revenues.
[a] Combined state or regional and local expenditure.
[b] Single region and single community used as examples.
[c] Figure not available.
[d] Due to recency of constitutional amendment (2001), precise figures are unavailable.
[e] Under the 2001 Constitution Art. 119(1) assigns regional taxing powers subject to central government coordination, Art. 117(2 and 3).

Table 11.3. (continued)

---

^f Regions receive unconditional shares of specified federal taxes based on derivation under Art. 119(2), an unconditional equalising fund under Art. 119(3) and a borrowing power under Art. 119(5), thus having substantial expenditure autonomy. Some additional transfers (Art. 119(5)) are for specific purposes, however.

^g Because of asymmetry, among sub-units, Scotland used as example. See table 5.1 for source and comparable figures for Scotland and Wales.

^h Taxing power limited to 3 per cent of UK rate (not yet levied) plus setting local taxes, business taxes and user fees.

ⁱ Block grant based on Barnett formula comprises the majority of the funding of the devolved institutions although there are some other sources of transfers, e.g. European funding (see chapter 4).

block grants means that the devolved territories are ensured of autonomy in how they are used. Most other intergovernmental financial arrangements have relied upon a mixture of unconditional and conditional transfers to meet the gap between the own-source revenues and the expenditure needs of the constituent units. Thus, expenditure autonomy (i.e. own-source revenues plus unconditional transfers as a percentage of total revenues) in these systems has ranged generally between 70 per cent (United States) and 95 per cent (the Belgian communities), with Spain as an outlier (58 per cent). Comparatively speaking, while the devolved territories in the United Kingdom are severely constrained in terms of their revenue autonomy, within these limits there is a high degree of expenditure autonomy. Scott Greer has explained in chapter 7 that this has permitted considerable policy divergence among the devolved territories in the UK, but that the almost total dependence on unconditional transfers has shielded the governments of the devolved territories not only from Whitehall, but also from responsibility for the economic consequences of their policy decisions. In those other countries where there has been substantially more revenue autonomy, fiscal accountability has imposed a higher degree of political responsibility upon the governments of the constituent units.

In most other multi-level regimes, the financial transfer arrangements have included systematic 'equalisation' adjustments based on progressive assessments and modifications of intergovernmental transfers in order to take account of differences among territorial governments in revenue capacities and in many cases also administrative needs. Although the basis for calculating these has varied, such systematic equalisation arrangements have been established not only in all the federations and quasi-federations (except the United States), but also in Japan, Italy, Spain and Sweden.[10] The Barnett

---

10 Watts, *Comparing Federal Systems,* 50–3; Watts, R. L., *Intergovernmental Fiscal Relationships in Eight Countries: Final report* (Kingston: Institute of Intergovernmental Relations, Queen's University, 2004).

formula in the UK, by comparison, involves no periodic assessment of revenue capacity or need, and instead simply applies a formula for differential increases (unchanged from the pre-devolution formula).

Because the values of revenue resources and expenditure responsibilities inevitably change over time, most federations and quasi-federations have found it necessary to establish formal and informal processes to facilitate the correction of vertical imbalances periodically.[11] In some, adjustments are based on the advice of an independent commission or council, as in Australia, India and South Africa. In some it is the subject of extensive intergovernmental negotiation, although this takes different forms, as in Canada, Switzerland, Germany and Spain. In some, there is a formal intergovernmental negotiation process which nevertheless tends to be dominated by the central government, as in South Africa, Malaysia and Pakistan. In some, it is simply determined by federal legislation, as in the United States, Italy and Nigeria, although in the latter two cases the constitution itself stipulates the criteria to be implemented. In Japan and Sweden, ultimately it is central legislation that determines and adjusts the overall pattern of devolution in the financial arrangements, although in both countries local interests have a considerable influence on these decisions. In the case of Sweden, an Equalisation Commission has also been created to implement the equalisation arrangements. Under the UK devolution arrangements, by contrast, there is no formal process for the regular review of the financial arrangements.

In overall terms, while block funding gives a substantial degree of expenditure autonomy to the devolved administrations, these administrations remain heavily dependent on the Treasury of the UK Government for the size of their revenues. By comparison with arrangements in most federations, quasi-federations, devolved unions or even some unitary systems, the UK's financial arrangements are one of the least well developed aspects of the devolution arrangements.

Intergovernmental collaboration and conflict resolution

Within all systems of multi-level governance, the unavoidable interdependence of governments arising from areas of shared or inevitably overlapping governmental responsibilities has made mechanisms and processes for intergovernmental collaboration and conflict resolution necessary. The way these processes operate within the formal constitution and legal structure may significantly reinforce, modify or even transform the power relationships

11 Watts, *Comparing Federal Systems*, 53–5.

between the interacting governments. An understanding of how the different levels of government relate to each other is, therefore, crucial.

In chapter 8, Alan Trench has provided a nuanced analysis of the various aspects of intergovernmental relations and conflict resolution within the devolved UK. He notes that some formal mechanisms and processes have been established. These include the Joint Ministerial Committee (JMC), both in plenary and functional forms, the use of the Judicial Committee of the Privy Council to resolve legal disputes, the continued roles of the Secretaries of State for each devolved territory, and a small central team of officials within Whitehall. He observes, however, that in practice intergovernmental relations have been much less formal than the legal framework would suggest. In the first half-decade since the institutional framework of devolution was put in place, intergovernmental relations between Whitehall and the governments of the devolved territories have been 'highly cooperative and consensual in practice, with few arguments even entering into the public domain'.[12] This, he suggests, has been largely due to two factors: first, political consensus across governments, both at the party and official levels, and second, the dominance of the UK Government.

This chapter will take a broader comparative view, reviewing intergovernmental relations in a wider range of multi-level regimes and within different types of federations. One key variable that has significantly affected intergovernmental relations, not only in federations and quasi-federations but also in regionalised unions, is the executive–legislature relationship within each level of government. The character of intergovernmental relations has been significantly different in those regimes embodying the principle of the separation of powers between legislatures and executives and those involving parliamentary executives responsible to their popularly elected legislatures. In the former, exemplified by the Presidential–Congressional system in the United States, and also almost invariably replicated in the Latin American federations and quasi-federations, the dispersal of power within each tier of government has made necessary multiple channels of federal–state relations involving executives, officials, legislators and agencies interacting not only with their opposite numbers, but in a web of diffused criss-crossing relationships. Morton Grodzins has characterised this as 'marble cake federalism'.[13] Within this complex interplay of processes, Congress, and its various committees and sub-committees, has played a significant role in approving the

---

12 Trench, A., chapter 8, this volume, 160.
13 Grodzins, M., 'The Federal System', in Wildavsky, A. (ed.), *American Federalism in Perspective* (Boston: Little Brown, 1967), 257; Wright, D., *Understanding Intergovernmental Relations* (Pacific Grove, CA: Brooks/Cole, 3rd edn, 1988).

variety of specific grant programmes. As a result, lobbying of Congress's committees and members has been an important aspect of intergovernmental relations. In Switzerland, where there is also a separation of legislative and executive powers at both levels, the conduct of intergovernmental relations has some of the same features, although the unique collegial executives at both levels have played a more prominent role in intergovernmental relations.

In those other federations, quasi-federations and devolved unions where, by contrast, cabinets responsible to the parliament have operated at both levels, a prevailing characteristic has been the predominance of the executive branches in intergovernmental relations.[14] 'Executive federalism', as it has come to be called, in both formal and informal intergovernmental relations, has been most marked in Germany, Australia and Canada but has also been a major characteristic in India, Austria, Belgium, Spain and Italy. This has been a natural outcome of the existence within both levels of government of a governmental form in which dominant cabinets and strong party discipline have been induced by the requirement of continuous support by their respective legislatures. The institutions and processes of 'executive federalism' have in most cases developed pragmatically, rather than by constitutional or legal requirements. This is particularly the case, for instance, in Canada. However, in some instances – most notably the role of the Bundesrat in Germany which is composed of the instructed delegates of the state governments, and some of the intergovernmental councils and commissions in India – these have been established by the constitution. Typically in those multi-level regimes with parliamentary institutions, 'executive federalism' has taken the form of numerous meetings, ranging from those between officials to councils of ministers and to first ministers' meetings. In some, as in Canada, the structure is largely ad hoc, while others, such as in Australia, are organised more systematically. In the latter, the Council of Australian Governments oversees the collaborative processes of the variety of ministerial councils and officials' committees.

Five further characteristics typical of executive federalism should also be noted. One is that although media attention tends to focus on the meetings of ministers and first ministers, much of the most effective collaborative work is carried out at lower levels by officials with professional affinities working out differences through negotiation.[15] Second, generally there has been a preference to work out differences by negotiation and intergovernmental agreement

14 Watts, R. L., *Executive Federalism: A comparative analysis* (Kingston: Institute of Intergovernmental Relations, Queen's University, 1989); Watts, *Comparing Federal Systems*, 58, 89.
15 Dupré, J. S., 'The Workability of Executive Federalism in Canada', in Bakvis, H. and Chandler, W. M. (eds), *Federalism and the Role of the State* (Toronto: University of Toronto Press, 1987), 236–58.

rather than by litigation in the courts. Resort to judicial dispute resolution, with its winner-take-all results, has usually been considered only as a last resort (although used from time to time). Indeed, such a requirement has actually been written into the South African Constitution (Article 41(3)). Third, governments at both levels have usually established their own specialised intragovernmental organisations to ensure executive coordination of their own relations with other governments within the federation or union. Often this has taken the form of a distinct department with its own minister, although inevitably the first ministers have usually played the ultimate policy-making role in this respect. In the smaller regional units this function of intragovernmental coordination has more often usually been carried out, however, by a small section within the premier's office.[16] Fourth, where the form of the distribution of legislative and executive powers has involved the major legislative responsibility being assigned to the federal or central government, and the executive and administrative responsibility for much of this legislation has been assigned to the federated or devolved governments, as in the German and Austrian federations and in some of the devolved unions and decentralised unitary systems, the added need for coordination has strengthened the dominance of the central government. Fifth, there is a considerable range among federations in the extent and character of intergovernmental relationships, ranging from the highly intensified and interlocking relationships within the German federation to the relatively arm's-length relations in Canada, with most other federations falling somewhere between these extremes.[17]

The devolved United Kingdom with its parliamentary institutions at both levels has clearly exhibited similar characteristics in its intergovernmental relations.[18] A number of factors have given the predominantly executive interinstitutional relations within the United Kingdom a particular cast. These have included the radical asymmetry among the devolved territories which has tended to emphasise bilateral, vertical relations between these territories and Whitehall and has moderated any tendencies to horizontal, cooperative relations between them. Another has been the persistence of pre-devolution ease of inter-institutional consensus derived from the traditions of a common public service. Yet another is the relative dominance of the UK Government because of its stronger power resources, making these relations more akin to those in some other devolved unions or even decentralised unitary systems

16 Watts, *Executive Federalism: A comparative analysis*, 10–11.
17 Wachendorfer-Schmidt, U., *Federalism and Political Performance* (London: Routledge, 2000).
18 Horgan, G. W., 'Inter-institutional Relations in the Devolved Great Britain: Quiet diplomacy', *Regional and Federal Studies*, 14:1 (2004), 113–45.

where the constituent units are in a subordinate position rather than being coordinate equals in the processes of negotiating with the central government. This is illustrated by the use that has been made of the Sewel convention. Originally intended to limit intrusions by Westminster in areas of jurisdiction primarily devolved to Scotland, the Scottish Executive and Parliament have acquiesced to the regular use or misuse of the convention in order to avoid challenges to UK legislation.

Gerard Horgan has concluded, as a result, that in comparative terms four themes have marked the early development of a distinctive United Kingdom version of the executive-focused intergovernmental relations characteristic of parliamentary federations and unions: the executive dominance of these relations; a reliance upon some formal multilateral mechanisms but in practice especially bilateral processes; an increasing predominance of informal relations; and the pervasiveness of concern for confidentiality.[19]

The role of intra-party processes

Martin Laffin, Eric Shaw and Gerald Taylor in chapter 9 on the parties and intergovernmental relations, but also the authors of many other chapters, have drawn attention to the impact of the predominance of the Labour Party both in the UK Parliament and the governments of Scotland and Wales in the early years of intergovernmental relations within the devolved UK. This is particularly significant, not only because of the way in which it has facilitated consensus in intergovernmental relations during this early period following devolution, but also for the implication that when eventually the inevitable development of different parties in power in different governments occurs, the temper of intergovernmental relations is highly likely to become more conflictual.

W. H. Riker has emphasised the particularly important role of political parties in shaping and sustaining federal political systems.[20] Indeed, in many multi-level regimes, political parties have provided an important channel for resolving intergovernmental issues. The degree to which this has been the case has depended on two factors: (1) the existence of common as opposed to differentiated party systems at different levels of governments; (2) the nature of the relationships between the federal or central party organisation

---

19 *Ibid.*; see also House of Lords Select Committee on the Constitution, 2002–03, 2nd Report, *Devolution: Inter-institutional Relations in the United Kingdom*, HL 28 (London: Stationery Office, 2003).

20 Riker, W. H., 'Federalism', in Greenstein, F. I. and Polsby, N. W., (eds), *Handbook of Political Science: Governmental institutions and processes*, Vol. 5 (Reading, MA: Addison Wesley, 1975).

and the organisations of the same party within the federated or devolved units. In some federations, such as Canada for instance, there have been some parties in office at the provincial level with no counterparts in the federal Parliament. Furthermore, even those federal and provincial parties that possess the same label have tended to be quite distinct in their organisation. In such a situation it has not been unusual for the Quebec Liberal Party at times to find its closest political allies at the federal level in a Conservative government, as occurred in the Bourassa–Mulroney era, or for a Liberal federal government to find Conservative provincial governments as their closest allies, as in the constitutional deliberations of 1980–82 when the Liberal Prime Minister Pierre Trudeau's only provincial allies were the Conservative premiers of Ontario (William Davis) and New Brunswick (Richard Hatfield). Thus, in such situations intra-party relationships have not provided a major alternative to executive and bureaucratic channels for resolving intergovernmental issues. Even in Germany, where party channels between levels of government have been much more important, the recent tendency towards coalition governments at the Land level has affected the representation and operation of their governmental representatives within the Bundesrat. Indeed, the predominance of different parties in the federal government and within the Länder governments has in recent years led to counterbalancing majorities and policy blockages between the two federal legislative chambers. As a consequence, serious consideration has been given to the need for reform of the veto powers of the Bundesrat.

On the other hand, there are also clear cases where intra-party channels have largely displaced bureaucratic channels for resolving intergovernmental issues. Two extreme examples have been the cases of India during the early decades, when the Congress Party dominated most governments at both levels, and South Africa since 1996, where the African National Congress has controlled not only the central but most of the provincial governments. In both cases, the federal character of the polity was to some extent subverted by the direct controls that the central organisation of the dominant party had over the state or provincial party organisations, even to the extent of directing the choice of provincial premiers. In India, with the shattering of the dominance of the Congress Party the situation is now somewhat reversed, with the Union governments being composed of coalitions of primarily regional parties insisting upon the satisfaction within the central government of their regional interests.

Superficially, the situation in the devolved UK would appear to be somewhat akin to that in India in its early decades and in South Africa currently, with the Labour Party predominant in Westminster and in Edinburgh and Cardiff. However, the analysis in the preceding chapters indicates that party relationships have not been the primary formal channels for dealing with intergovernmental issues. Important factors have been the need for the Labour Party in Scotland and Wales to compete in the devolved party systems with nationalist rivals, and also from time to time its need to rule through coalition governments. Nevertheless, the role of the Labour Party in office at both levels has been important in setting a climate of shared objectives and in minimising and keeping out of the public arena intergovernmental disputes that might undermine its common electoral interests. It would appear that a shared common outlook within the Labour Party has at least been a major factor in inducing a spirit of non-confrontation between the different governments.

Given the conflictual impact of party differences upon intergovernmental relations elsewhere within such federations and devolved unions, for example in Canada, Australia, Germany, Spain and Italy, it is doubtful, however, whether the present spirit of intergovernmental non-confrontation within the United Kingdom will survive when eventually the different governments become marked by significant party differences.

Participation in central policy-making institutions

While not discussed in previous chapters of this volume, it should be noted that in most federations the federal second legislative chamber has played a significant role as a regionally representative body in policy-making at the federal level (see table 11.2, column 7). Among federations this role has perhaps been strongest in Germany, Switzerland and the United States, and weakest in Canada, where although the Senate's composition has a regional basis, its political legitimacy is undermined by its appointed character. In two cases, notably Germany and South Africa, the federal second chamber has in fact played a significant role as a major channel for intergovernmental relations. In the former, the Bundesrat, as an assembly composed of the instructed delegates of the Land governments, has in practice a veto on about 60 per cent of federal legislation. This has given the Länder considerable negotiating power. In the latter, despite South Africa's centralised character as a quasi-federation, the assent of the National Council of the Provinces (NCOP), an assembly composed of both provincial legislators and executives, is required for a significant portion of central legislation.

In the UK, at least as now composed, the House of Lords is not equipped to serve as a representative body for the devolved territories. On the other hand, it can serve as a source of independent reports, such as the previously cited Select Committee report on *Devolution: Inter-institutional Relations in the United Kingdom*. While the influence of the report on the UK

Government has been limited, it did draw important issues to the attention of the public.

In most effective federations and quasi-federations a representation of the major regional units within the federal executive has developed as a strong convention. In a few cases, such as Belgium (Article 99) and Switzerland (Article 175(3)), such requirements have even been incorporated in the federal constitution. The closest parallel to such arrangements in the United Kingdom has been the offices of the Secretaries of State for each of the devolved territories, as outlined by Alan Trench in chapter 8. Apparently intended to provide a voice for each devolved territory within the Cabinet at Westminster, it would appear, however, that their role in relation to devolution has yet to be clearly worked out. Whether their primary function in relation to the devolved governments is to represent their views in central policy-making or to interpret central policies to the devolved territories has yet to be fully resolved.

The impact of continental and external relations

In the nineteenth and for most of the twentieth centuries, external relations in federations were generally regarded as exclusively a matter of federal government jurisdiction, and intergovernmental relations between federal governments and the federated territories were considered a purely internal matter of only domestic concern. In the late twentieth and early twenty-first centuries two factors have changed that. One has been the increased blurring of the boundaries between external and solely domestic policy. As a result, in many federations involvement by constituent units in some aspects of international relations and the need for intergovernmental consultation on a number of issues of foreign relations have become regular practices. Furthermore, recent new federal constitutions, such as those of Belgium in 1993 (Article 167) and Switzerland in 1999 (Articles 55 and 56), recognising this situation, have made explicit the requirement for close intergovernmental consultation and collaborative action between the federal and constituent unit governments in a wide area relating to international relationships.

The second factor has been the membership of certain federations and devolved unions in wider continental supra-federal organisations such as the European Union (EU) or the North American Free Trade Area (NAFTA). The EU contains three countries that are clearly federations – Germany, Belgium and Austria – and three devolved unions – Spain and Italy, which are verging on federations in form, and the United Kingdom. Membership in the EU has affected the jurisdiction of their constituent units and led to intergovernmental consultation and participation of the constituent units in some of the EU policy-making processes. NAFTA, while a looser supra-federal organisation, is composed of three federations, the United States, Canada and Mexico, and has required adjustments in intergovernmental relations within each of these federations. In these situations the issue of how constituent units should relate to the wider supra-federal organisation and its decision-making processes has come to the fore. This has been particularly apparent in the cases of the federations and devolved unions within the EU. Indeed, Charlie Jeffery and Rosanne Palmer have noted in chapter 10 that the issues which have arisen concerning the relations of the devolved units in the UK with the EU are not unique to the UK. They parallel those in the other multi-level members of the EU. What is distinctive is the extent to which an effective *modus vivendi* for collaboration on EU issues between the UK Government and the devolved territories has been pragmatically developed, whereas the German and Italian regions had to fight for such working practices for decades and the Spanish regions have yet to achieve these. On the other hand, as with so much of intergovernmental relations in the United Kingdom, these processes are largely dependent upon the sharing of common interests, and they lack the legal and constitutional basis generally provided in fully fledged federations.

Conclusions

We can now return to the questions posed in the introduction to this chapter. First, can the power structure of the devolved UK be meaningfully compared with those in federal systems? This question can be answered at two levels. To begin with, as a multi-level polity combining shared rule for certain common purposes with self-rule of the devolved territories for specified other purposes, the devolved UK clearly belongs within the broad genus of 'federal political systems' that encompasses regionally devolved unions, federations, quasi-federations, confederations, federacies and so on as defined in table 11.1. If the question is rephrased as to whether the power structure of the devolved UK can be meaningfully compared with those in 'federations', we have noted that the United Kingdom possesses a number of essential features usually found in federations but also lacks others. Thus, a comparison with federations can be meaningful in drawing attention not only to the similarities but also to the differences and particularly to the significance of these.

Perhaps the most significant are two differences. The first is the lack of a supreme constitution as the authoritative source defining the relationships of the UK Parliament and Government with the devolved territories. A consequence is the ultimate predominance of the former and subordinacy of the latter in terms of their relative powers. The second is the double asymmetry that means that devolution in fact applies only to three territories constituting a mere 15 per cent of the total population of the UK. This form of asymmetry is not paralleled in any federation, quasi-federation or regional devolved union elsewhere.

The second question posed was whether the power relations between the devolved territories and the United Kingdom resemble those in federations. In responding to this, we must take note of a point made earlier in this chapter, that there is considerable variation in the balance of power within different existing federations. Switzerland, Canada, Belgium and increasingly India (despite some continuing quasi-federation elements in the latter) are marked predominantly by a coordinacy relationship in the power relations between central and constituent unit governments. Others, like the United States, Australia and Germany, are also marked predominately by coordinacy but with somewhat stronger federal governments. Still others, especially South Africa, are marked by the features of a quasi-federation which has led to a relatively dominant central government. There are also significant differences in the character of intergovernmental relations depending on whether their institutions at both levels are parliamentary or based on separation of powers. In relation to this spectrum of federations, although the UK's devolution arrangements exhibit some of their characteristics and share with parliamentary federations the predominance of their executives in intergovernmental relations, the UK Government is clearly dominant in its relations with the devolved territories. The latter remain highly dependent upon the UK Government and Parliament, leaving them in a subordinate rather than coordinate relationship.

Does this mean that the United Kingdom might be classified as a 'quasi-federation'? In the widely accepted usage of the term, as defined by K. C. Wheare, applying the term to polities which have virtually all the regular features of a federation except that the federal government has certain limited over-riding or emergency powers,[21] the term is not applicable to the United Kingdom because of the essential features of a federation that are missing. Vernon Bogdanor and Robert Hazell have, however, applied the term 'quasi-federation' in a more limited way to indicate a devolved structure which has some of the features of a federation and whose dynamic is likely to progress to a greater emphasis upon these features.[22] In this second, more limited sense, the United Kingdom might legitimately be referred to as a 'quasi-

---

21 Wheare, *Federal Government*.
22 Bogdanor, *Devolution in the United Kingdom*; Hazell, *Constitutional Futures*.

federation' but it is important in using the label to be clear about its limited meaning.

Third, do the power relations in the devolved UK resemble more closely those in regionalised unions or decentralised unitary systems? Here it would seem from the comparative analysis in this chapter that the devolved UK in both its legal framework and operational processes belongs essentially in the category of a regionally devolved union. Furthermore, in terms of the constitutional status of the devolved territories, the relative predominance of the UK Parliament and Government, and the limited number of regions within the union to which devolution applies, the United Kingdom is clearly less federalised than the regionally devolved unions in Spain and, after 2001, Italy. The degree of devolution is perhaps more comparable to that in Japan, although there devolution applies to all 47 prefectures and not just to some of the territories within the union.

On the other hand, the degree of autonomy of the devolved territories, and their powers to pursue divergent policies, would appear to be greater than that of the regional units in the decentralised unitary systems of Sweden and certainly France. Given that devolution in the United Kingdom applies to only a small proportion of the union's population and the unitary relationship of the UK Parliament and Government to England (a situation which the 2004 referendum in the North East of England indicates is likely to continue for the foreseeable future), in some respects the position of the devolved territories resembles the peripheral relationship of the federacies and associated states in such unitary systems as Denmark, Finland, France, New Zealand and Portugal (table 11.1). The representation and role of the United Kingdom's devolved territories within the UK Parliament suggests, however, that they are more fully integrated within the union than those other examples.

In comparing the character of intergovernmental relations in the devolved UK with those in both federations and other regionalised unions, two distinctive features clearly stand out. The United Kingdom shares with those federations and unions possessing parliamentary institutions an emphasis upon the role of the executives within each level of government in the conduct of intergovernmental relations. In parliamentary federations and regionalised unions, executive predominance has typically become the self-reinforcing prevailing mode of intergovernmental relations. The United Kingdom is already well locked into that path. But elsewhere in federations where 'executive federalism' has prevailed, there have currently been increasing concerns about the need to ensure that these processes are transparent and accountable to their legislatures and electorates. It would appear that this issue has yet to come to the fore in the UK, but it is an issue that needs to be addressed while these intergovernmental processes are still in their formative stage.

The second feature is the uniqueness of the double asymmetry within the United Kingdom, marking it off from other devolved unions and federations. The question that remains open is whether devolution will also take root in England. Present indications make that appear unlikely, at least for some time. If so, devolution within the UK will remain only partial, and this is likely to be a source of future contention, especially when, as will eventually happen, competing parties come into office in the different governments.

This comparative chapter confirms the theme of this volume. It would appear that the hypothesis is confirmed that although the United Kingdom has some features resembling those of federations and quasi-federations, it remains predominantly a devolved union. The United Kingdom Government clearly remains dominant in its relations with the devolved territories, while creating in a partial portion of its territory autonomous spheres for devolved institutions within which it has been possible for them to pursue differentiated policies and some territorial diversity.

12
Conclusion: devolution and the territorial distribution of power in the UK

Alan Trench

This conclusion will address four issues. First, it will consider the implication of the analysis presented by the various chapters in this book for the power of the devolved administrations and UK Government vis-à-vis each other, in terms of the resource-dependency framework set out in the introduction. Second, it discusses the paradox that was raised at the outset about the relationship between the centralising and decentralising aspects of devolution. Then it will use that assessment of territorial power relations to examine the United Kingdom comparatively, building on the analysis presented by Ronald Watts in chapter 11. Finally, it will examine the implications of that analysis for the future of devolution.

Power in the devolved United Kingdom

The chapters above have analysed the working of intergovernmental relations in the UK from a variety of points of view. This raises the question of what power the devolved administrations and the UK Government have in relation to each other, looked at in the round. The easiest way to show this is to revisit the headings of the components of power set out in the introduction.

1 Constitutional resources

As a starting point, all three devolved administrations are reasonably well endowed in this area. They each have significant legitimacy (if an interrupted one in the case of Northern Ireland), underpinned by their electoral mandates, and enjoy functions of sufficient breadth and importance to enable them to have power over significant areas of government. Wales obviously is least well off in this respect, but it still has enough constitutional resources to be important both within Wales and as a player in intergovernmental relations. However, as chapter 3 showed, all the devolved administrations have to cooperate with the UK Government in the exercise of many of those functions (particularly where there is an overlap between devolved and reserved or non-devolved ones). In this sense, their autonomy is limited, even if their importance in intergovernmental relations remains. They have to take account of UK Government policy in relation to England as well. They have no veto or control over actions of the UK Government which affect those functions, and the rights they do have to be informed and consulted (set out in the Memorandum of Understanding) are hard to enforce and often overlooked by the UK Government. The UK Government has, for its part, proved that it can change rules that affect the devolved administrations, unilaterally, without consultation and sometimes by oversight or at least without considering the implications of its actions for the devolved administrations. On the formal level, the UK can act unilaterally even as regards devolved matters, and may be able to pass legislation without devolved consent in matters that are devolved – but these powers are doubtful on the formal level, would be contrary to convention (of huge importance in the UK context) and if used would surely provoke a political and constitutional crisis.

In addition, the devolved territories have only minimal scope to alter their own internal constitutions. Any change to their structures or powers needs the use of various powers retained by the UK Government and Parliament. They may be able to initiate this process (as Wales did, with the Richard Commission), but all decisions about whether it goes forward and what changes are enacted lie with the UK level. The effect of this is to make constitutional issues themselves a continuing issue in intergovernmental relations, and in this respect the devolved administrations remain heavily dependent on the UK Government.

In practical terms, two other constitutional resources – the Judicial Committee of the Privy Council and the JMC – are not available to the devolved administrations. Seeking recourse to either of these to resolve a dispute would indicate a severe breakdown of political relations, so it would indicate disadvantage from the outset and involve a high level of risk for at best an uncertain chance of success (the Judicial Committee) and at worst a real likelihood of losing (the JMC).

However, the UK Government has also lost a degree of constitutional control. This is not in the formal sense of undermining the doctrine of the sovereignty of Parliament, but in the sense that it has accepted the existence of additional centres of territorial power, and has accepted the intertwining of governmental functions that the devolution arrangements entail on the legal and bureaucratic levels.

2 Legal and hierarchical resources

Wales obviously does not have the power to pass legislation to exercise its functions autonomously. While it has been largely successful in securing space in Westminster statutes when it has needed new powers, that has depended on the willingness of the UK Government to cooperate with it in doing so. As chapter 8 showed, its success in doing so has depended on supportive conditions in Westminster. While the National Assembly may have been able to make effective and imaginative use of its powers under secondary legislation to achieve many goals, the absence of proper legislative powers is a serious drawback, and is likely to remain so.

For Scotland, this is not a significant concern. However, its use of its legislative powers remains subject to a number of external constraints, such as European Union law, the European Convention on Human Rights (both of which affect the UK Parliament as well, though in a different way) and the need to demonstrate it has not legislated for reserved matters. (The same applied to Northern Ireland.)

In other respects, all three devolved administrations have the power to issue guidance or secondary legislation to implement their policies, and thanks to the structure of executive devolution are beyond UK challenge in doing so. The verdict therefore has to be that Scotland has (and Northern Ireland had) extensive power in this area, but Wales remains very dependent on the UK.

3 Financial resources

The lack of published data, in particular about need, makes it hard to assess whether the devolved governments have adequate finance for their functions. As chapters 4 and 5 showed, the general view is that the block-grant-and-formula mechanism means that Scotland does have adequate finance (indeed, is generously funded) at present, but faces greater financial limits in the future. Similarly, the general view is that Northern Ireland may be under-funded relative to need (though it receives a generous level of aggregate funding) and that Wales is under-funded. This cannot be regarded as a conclusive judgment, but is strongly indicated by the available evidence. However, the devolved administrations are not autonomous financially or fiscally; they have very limited powers to vary the overall amount of finance available to them, whether by raising revenue directly, by borrowing or in other ways.

The devolved administrations are significant spenders of public money, meaning that they are financially important in their own territories. Moreover, they do have the power to allocate funding freely in accordance with their own priorities. How useful that power is depends on whether they in fact have funds available for allocation – but they clearly are major financial players.

4 Organisational resources

All the devolved administrations possess sufficiently skilled and expert staff, and the other resources to manage their functions as they wish. The extent of control exercised through the Home Civil Service is a theoretical source of constraint on them, but its practical effect is limited and unlikely ever to be effective. What the continued existence of the Home Civil Service does is to serve as a guarantee of such principles as independence, impartiality and the principle of appointment on merit, particularly for senior posts. While this may constrain the devolved administrations, it does not give any advantage to the UK Government, which is equally subject to the same rules. The retention of a single if increasingly decentralised civil service may raise questions about accountability and loyalty of officials and autonomy of devolved administrations, but there is no evidence as yet that this weakens the devolved administrations.

On a more day-to-day level, the devolved administrations have also been able to reshape their services to their new administrative needs, reflecting new political structures and priorities. Ultimately, there are limits to the extent to which the devolved administrations can use their own organisations to promote policy goals arising from EU and some UK legislation, but these are unlikely to be major factors.

However, the resources available to the devolved administrations are not the equal of those of the UK Government; the UK simply has more people and more expertise. It is therefore likely to be a bigger source of knowledge and policy ideas, particularly for large-scale matters, than the devolved administrations can ever be. This has a knock-on effect for lobbying resources (given the broad definition used in this book); the UK Government can develop ideas and so set the agenda in a way that the devolved administrations simply cannot.

5 Lobbying resources

The devolved administrations have only limited means to be able to influence the UK Government, for all their close ties to the UK institutions. The territorial Secretaries of State are part of the UK Government not the devolved administration, and may not be willing to speak for the devolved administration or may not do so very effectively. The historic ambiguities of their role – particularly whether they were Scotland's or Wales's man in UK Government, or the UK Government's man in Scotland or Wales – have not been resolved, although the balance is now more strongly in favour of the UK aspect of their job. The disuse of the Joint Ministerial Committee means that there is no direct formal channel of communication between the devolved administrations and the UK Government collectively, or at the highest level. Informal representations may or may not receive serious consideration, and if considered may be rejected; even over the last six years, the record is variable. It is questionable whether this set of arrangements would work if there were serious political tensions in the relationship between London and Cardiff or Edinburgh.[1]

On the legislative side, suggestions made in the report of the Wakeham Royal Commission on reform of the House of Lords that a reformed house should 'play a valuable role in relation to the nations and regions of the United Kingdom' (though not become a federal chamber or take on an expressly intergovernmental role) have not borne fruit.[2] The Lords therefore has no express role as a territorial chamber, and continues to have relatively few members from Wales, Scotland or Northern Ireland. Members of the Westminster Parliament from Scotland or Wales sometimes see themselves as being in competition with their devolved counterparts (particularly over constituency casework). Even when they do not, they see their job as to refer casework to each other rather than to cooperate to promote the wider interests of their territory. Scottish or Welsh MPs therefore have not become advocates for the devolved institutions.[3] Strength in the legislature therefore cannot balance weakness in representation between executives.

A further weakness is the very limited contacts between devolved administrations, the different interests they have and the consequent difficulties they face in building alliances with each other. This enables the UK to continue to deal with them bilaterally.

So far as shaping the agenda of discussion is concerned, the devolved administrations are at a serious disadvantage. There is only limited interest in Whitehall, Westminster or from the London media in the concerns of the devolved administrations. The London policy debate is not subject to devolved influence but that debate will have an effect on the devolved administrations – as has been seen regarding the growing NHS waiting lists in Wales. Only in relatively minor matters (good policy ideas in a narrow sense, and usually ones which are cheap to implement, as identified in chapter 6) have the devolved administrations shaped the agenda.

6 Informational resources

There are considerable problems for the devolved administrations with information. At the highest level, much valuable statistical data (especially about the

1 See further Trench, A., 'Intergovernmental Relations Within the UK: The pressures yet to come', in Trench, A. (ed.), *The Dynamics of Devolution: The State of the Nations 2005* (Exeter: Imprint Academic, 2005).
2 Royal Commission on the Reform of the House of Lords, *A House for the Future*, Cm 4534 (London: The Stationery Office, 2000), chap. 6.
3 See Russell, M., 'Multilevel Politics and the Constituency Representation Role: The impact of devolution in Scotland and Wales', Paper presented to ECPR Conference, Budapest (September 2005).

Table 12.1. Resource dependency and UK intergovernmental relations: an overview

Form of resources	From devolved point of view	From UK Government point of view
Constitutional resources a) Range and scope of functions	a) Generally adequate, even for Wales (absence of policing powers controversial in N. Ireland). Overlap of devolved and non-devolved functions likely to necessitate cooperation with UK Government. UK Government also important as the government for England.	a) May need cooperation of devolved administrations to deliver initiatives affecting reserved matters. Unlikely to be affected by devolved administrations for English matters.
b) Entitlement to consultation	b) Formally entitled, though entitlement not legally enforceable. In practice, consultation can be patchy and erratic.	b) Considers itself obliged to consult and tries to enforce this, though cannot always achieve its aspiration. Continues to control UK constitution.
c) Control of constitution	c) No control of constitution. Need UK to act for major changes. UK has formal power to change unilaterally key aspects of devolved power, though would provoke major crisis if it did so without consent. UK may overlook impact on devolved bodies of changes it proposes affecting UK a whole.	c) Considers seriously devolved requests for changes to their arrangements and often grants them.
Legal and hierarchical resources a) Command of legal instruments	a) Generally adequate, though some problems for Wales.	a) UK can do what it needs in relation to England, and if need were to arise in devolved territories thanks to continued sovereignty of Parliament.
b) Powers to implement	b) Generally adequate, including for Wales.	b) No powers in devolved territories.
Financial resources a) Adequacy	a) Overall probably just about adequate – certainly for Scotland, probably for N. Ireland, probably not for Wales. But impossible to say accurately.	a) UK retains adequate resources for its purposes. Considers block-and-grant formula fair to devolved administrations.
b) Ability to allocate freely	b) Yes, though impact of UK Government decisions for England remains significant.	b) Can allocate freely for its functions.
c) Control of income		c) Has full control of its income, and determines

	c) Minimal; only council tax, and in Scotland the variable rate of income tax.	that allocated to devolved administrations.
Organisational resources a) Staff administrations b) Other resources c) Power to adjust use of resources	a) Control of staffing: yes in general, subject to financial constraints. Residual and untested accountability to UK level, especially for senior staff. b) Other resources: yes, subject to financial constraints. c) Power to adjust use of resources: yes, but limited by UK reserved matters (e.g. equal opportunities legislation).	a) Power to control civil service limited and possibly unusable. b) No formal power to shape how devolved administrations use premises etc.; some influence through co-location offices etc. c) Limited scope to influence, despite consequential effects of UK legislation
Lobbying resources a) Influencing other governments' use of its powers b) Agenda-shaping	a) Limited. Few bargaining counters. Hard to build alliances with other devolved administrations. Depends on UK desire to cooperate. Party ties may help. b) Very limited.	a) Devolved cooperation may be desirable in some areas. Impact of non-cooperation limited overall. Able to deal with administrations mostly bilaterally not collectively. b) UK dominates policy agenda, though this (and its impact) are often unintentional.
Informational resources Knowledge of other governments' initiatives	Erratic and variable.	Sometimes unaware of devolved initiatives. Only consequence is mild embarrassment.

allocation of finance and public spending) appears not to be available. If it exists at all, it is not readily available to the devolved administrations. Information about UK policy plans and developments is more readily available, but in practice this is often on an ad hoc basis and the record in this area has been patchy to date. Some information is not passed to the devolved administrations, and in practice little heed is paid to the UK's obligations under the Memorandum of Understanding or the bilateral concordats about this.

This adds up to a powerful list of disadvantages for the devolved administrations, affecting both their autonomy and their ability to be powerful actors in intergovernmental relations. Few of these disadvantages inhibit the UK Government to a comparable extent. In this context, the disuse of the JMC framework is a matter for concern. The JMC has the potential to compensate for at least some of these disadvantages that the devolved administrations face. While, as chapter 8 noted, meetings of the JMC had by 2002 come to have the air of having a meeting for the sake of a meeting, the failure to use the JMC has broader implications.

Disuse of the JMC has three effects. First, it sends a signal to the UK Government, its departments and officials, that devolution is not a high priority for government as a whole. The Prime Minister and other ministers are not involved in devolution matters and are unlikely to be embarrassed by problems that arise. These signals are followed, and devolution slips down the list of important factors as a result. While this may not directly promote a lack of awareness or sensitivity to devolution concerns in Whitehall, it certainly does nothing to remedy the ignorance and insensitivity that result. Second, disuse deprives the devolved administrations of the opportunity to raise their concerns at the highest level, in a formal way that at least guarantees attention. The UK can proceed as it wishes largely without regard to the devolved administrations, but the devolved administrations cannot reciprocate. That particularly applies to reserved matters that affect devolved functions or the devolved territories. This is all the more important given public expectations, so far disappointed, that devolution would strengthen the voice of Scotland or Wales (if not Northern Ireland) within the United Kingdom.[4] Third, disuse creates a climate in which politicians, officials, the media and the general public are unused to significant differences between the UK Government and the devolved administrations being aired and resolved in public. Instead, disagreements are resolved quietly and privately. This adds to the burdens of those who do have to resolve them (officials and politicians), while creating a

---

4 See Curtice, J., 'Public Opinion and the Future of Devolution', in Trench, *The Dynamics of Devolution*, especially pp. 118–27.

sense of crisis when normal differences between governments do creep into the public domain.

Explaining the paradox: control and restraint

Table 12.1 sets out the position regarding the resources available to both UK Government and devolved administrations for the conduct of intergovernmental relations. It can be summarised very briefly, though: there are many ways in which the UK Government can inhibit the working of the devolved administrations or trip them up, but few in which the devolved administrations can trip up the UK Government. Or, to put the point in more technical terms, devolution has not added to the number of veto players in the United Kingdom as a whole, which remains (in Stepan's terms) a single veto-player, and hence demos-enabling rather than demos-constraining, state.[5] That only applies when the UK is looked at from the centre. Looked at from the point of view of the devolved administration, however, the UK Government is at least potentially a veto player, able to obstruct their actions by a variety of means should it wish to do so. The asymmetries of the structure of devolution and the resources available to the UK Government compared with the devolved administrations have a further asymmetric effect.

At the same time, as chapters 6 and 7 showed, policy differentiation is already significant and is likely to continue. While the constraints and controls identified in chapters 3, 4 and 5 clearly exist, they are not ones that the UK Government has used. Indeed, the evidence is that the UK Government has consciously sought to avoid using them, and that when it has impinged on devolved competence or undermined devolved autonomy it has done so unthinkingly not deliberately. That lack of thought is itself indicative of the differences between the UK and federal systems, where there would be significant formal obstacles to such conduct and government practices to prevent it happening. The fact that mechanisms of constraint and control exist may have an inhibiting influence on the devolved administrations, to be sure, but there is little evidence of the UK Government acting to restrain them. The paradox identified at the start of this book remains: the devolved administrations have meaningful (if constrained) autonomy, are at significant disadvantages in intergovernmental relations, which limit their ability to exercise that

---

5   See Stepan, A., 'Electorally Generated Veto Players in Unitary and Federal Systems', in Gibson, E. L. (ed.), *Federalism and Democracy in Latin America* (Baltimore, MD: Johns Hopkins University Press, 2004), 327.

autonomy, but despite this have still been able to operate in distinctive ways compared with the UK. How, and why, is this so?

Three factors seem to be key: the generally favourable environment; the interest this creates in containing any conflict that does exist; and the UK Government's self-denying ordinance to accommodate devolution. Each of these needs examining in more detail.

The generally favourable environment

Devolution has been established in a very helpful climate. The principal helpful features are the presence of the Labour Party in office throughout the UK and the generous increases seen in public spending from 1999 to 2004. The continuing cross-Britain interests of the Labour Party (and the Liberal Democrats, to a different degree), as chapter 9 showed, mean it is not in either British party's interest to undermine its Welsh or Scottish colleagues, or vice versa. This also means that there is cooperation in getting legislation relating to devolved functions through Westminster, if that is needed, and a helpful attitude to the transfer of additional functions to the devolved administrations. Generous spending increases mean that there has been no competition for financial resources, a common source of tension in many other systems. Instead, given the financial arrangements for devolution, the UK is able to act as a source of bounty to the devolved administrations.

Containing conflict

Not only does the devolution settlement contain mechanisms for resolving actual or potential conflict quietly and away from the public gaze (discussed in chapters 3 and 8), it creates strong incentives for each party to do so. This is largely because the environment is sufficiently benign that there is little reason to escalate; if the devolved administrations lose a battle in any particular case, they are nonetheless conscious of doing pretty well overall and that alternative approaches might undermine this. Part of the calculation of doing 'pretty well overall' relates to party interest rather than territorial interest, to be sure (whether that be Labour's interest in retaining power in all three British governments, or the Liberal Democrats' in achieving some of their policy objectives and enhancing their Britain-wide status by holding office in the devolved governments). (Even for Northern Ireland, where the issue of party advantage was absent, this largely remained true – if only because the various parties there sought to secure beneficial treatment from the UK Government.) This overall calculation of interest means that each side has an interest in limiting the scope of any disagreement – to keep it low level, private, invisible (or scarcely visible) and constrained, rather than to allow it to broaden in scope or become public. As Schattschneider notes, it is the loser in a disagreement who seeks to broaden its scope. If the system creates 'wins' for both sides, there is no reason to broaden that scope.[6]

The UK's self-denying ordinance

Despite considerable ambiguity about what devolution 'means', UK Government ministers and officials seem clear that it involves handing over power for a range of functions, and then helping the devolved administrations discharge those functions while not interfering. Along with dealing with disagreements in private, this has become a central element in the new 'operating code' that has developed to deal with devolution. Equally part of that is the sense that it is not for the devolved administrations to interfere improperly in non-devolved functions, while accepting that these functions do affect devolved concerns which need to be taken into account by the UK Government in its actions. This is a profoundly difficult position, however. Because of the way devolved and non-devolved functions intertwine, complying with the general principle that devolved matters are for the devolved institutions creates huge amounts of work for officials, in working out where those boundaries lie in each particular case and in persuading ministers and perhaps colleagues in UK Government departments to accept their conclusions. For the devolved administrations, it is hard to know where the political line lies between not interfering and allowing the UK Government wholly to disregard devolved concerns. They were, after all, created to express the views of their parts of the UK, and many reserved functions are highly important to their expression of national or territorial identity. Strengthening the voice of their part of the UK is therefore an important role for the devolved administrations. Even if they wish to contain any conflict with the UK Government because of their broader interests, they have to reconcile this with the need to represent their territory.

At the same time, if the UK Government manages devolution by informal understandings like this, it needs to ensure that they are generally understood and complied with. As chapter 8 in particular showed, that is far from the case; compliance is at best variable and patchy. The worst offenders often seem to be those at the heart of government; the ignorance of the implications of devolution around the UK Prime Minister and the consequent disregard of devolved concerns on numerous occasions when Number 10 has taken the

6 Cf. Schattschneider, E. E., *The Semisovereign People: A realist's view of democracy in America* (Hinsdale, Ill: Dryden Press, 1975).

lead is striking. Sidney Low famously remarked, 'We live under a system of tacit understandings. But the understandings themselves are not always understood.'[7] Reliance on such understandings appears to be important in explaining how the devolved UK works, and ignorance or disregard of them is a key factor in explaining many of the practical problems that have arisen.

The idea of such a self-denying ordinance and other tacit understandings can be related to the idea of the 'operating code' or the 'rules of the game' as articulated by Rhodes. One example of the existence of such a code is the Memorandum of Understanding, which articulates a number of these rules and implicitly contains others. Rhodes's list of elements of a code in the context of central–local government relations in the first part of the 1980s is striking for its resemblance to the tacit understandings that underpin intergovernmental relations after devolution.[8] He identified the following items:

1 *pragmatism* in resolving doctrinal or party-political issues;
2 *consensus* preferred to imposed solutions;
3 *fairness* in hearing the views of all parties;
4 *accommodation* of all parties, to minimise antagonism, especially for losers in a debate;
5 parties respecting their *territorial or sectoral limits* and not extending their demands beyond that;
6 *secrecy* for deliberations, respected by all parties;
7 *depoliticisation* of key issues, resolving them by technical rather than political criteria;
8 *summiteering*, with decisions taken by key figures or elites dealing personally with one another;
9 respect for *local democracy*, and acceptance that some matters are out of bounds for central government;
10 respect for central government's *right to govern* on matters of national interest;
11 *trust and reliability* in the conduct of relations and in complying with these rules.

What is also striking is that many of these rules broke down, as central–local relations became more heated and politically contentious during the later 1980s

---

7 Quoted in Bulpitt, J., *Territory and Power in the United Kingdom* (Manchester: Manchester University Press, 1983), 234.
8 Rhodes, R. A. W., *Beyond Westminster and Whitehall: The sub-central governments of Britain* (London: Unwin Hyman, 1988), 91–2.

and early 1990s. Others were deliberately challenged. In the face of party-political confrontation and a difficult financial context, even relatively well-understood and generally shared rules were ineffective in mediating relations when they became difficult.[9] Bureaucratic and political mediation failed to resolve those issues. The upshot was an increasing constraint of local government by central government, including tight controls on finance (both central government grants to local government and total local government spending), and a variety of legal mechanisms through both legislation and the courts that amounted, in Loughlin's terms, to 'juridification' of central–local relations.

It is one thing to rely on the political resolution of difficult issues (rather than looking to written constitutions or judges), as the British constitution generally does. It is another to place such a heavy burden on an operating code, without institutional support or embodiment, and when the basis of that code is so vulnerable. Doing so raises difficult questions for the future of devolution.

Making sense of the UK's system of intergovernmental relations

If the UK has a set of power relations that strongly favour the UK Government rather than the devolved administrations, what does that mean for the argument that the UK has become a 'quasi-federal' system as a result of devolution? The UK has, after all, adopted a system that (in Daniel Elazar's term[10]) combines shared rule with self-rule, so by that very broad measure has moved towards a federal system – but what more can be said?

In chapter 11 Ron Watts has examined, with meticulous care, the wide range of federal and decentralised systems across the world. He notes the wide range of variation that exists among such systems, and the many ways in which power relations can vary. He carefully distinguishes between federal systems, regionalised unions and decentralised unitary states. He concludes that the UK cannot properly be said to belong to the same category as federal systems like Australia, Germany or India, let alone Canada or Belgium. In part this is

9 For further discussion, see for example Loughlin, M., *Local Government in the Modern State* (London: Sweet & Maxwell, 1986); Loughlin, M., *Legality and Locality: The role of law in central–local government relations* (Oxford: Oxford University Press, 1996); Butler, D., Adonis, A. and Travers, T., *Failure in British Government: The politics of the poll tax* (Oxford: Oxford University Press, 1994); and more generally Young, K. and Rao, N., *Local Government since 1945* (Oxford: Blackwell, 1997).
10 Elazar, D. J. (ed.), *Federal Systems of the world: A handbook of federal, confederal and autonomy arrangements* (Harlow: Longman Group Ltd, 2nd edn, 1994), 5.

due to the asymmetry of the UK's arrangements, but it is due more to the powers that the UK Government and Parliament retain in relation to the devolved institutions, both formally and in practice. At the same time, the UK is rather different from decentralised unitary states such as Sweden or France. Although the UK has certain resemblances to peculiar arrangements for peripheral regions from a number of (otherwise mostly unitary) states, he finds that the UK can best be compared to 'regionalised unions', notably Italy or Japan. These are not comparisons that have often occurred to people in the UK, perhaps partly because of ignorance of those systems.[11] They indicate, however, not just the differences between the UK and federal systems, but also the more general distinctiveness of the UK's arrangements.

Watts is not alone in reaching such a conclusion. In my own recent work on intergovernmental relations in federal systems, I considered how intergovernmental relations work in practice in federal systems generally.[12] That study found a high degree of commonality in the practice of intergovernmental relations in federal systems, with a limited range of variation caused by a number of features of such systems, mostly to do with the political system generally rather than the form of institutional arrangements that exist. (One significant variable, also identified by Ron Watts in chapter 11, is the difference between systems like that of the United States, where the doctrine of the separation of powers and the presidential system of government create a very different set of actors than in parliamentary systems like the continental European or Westminster-model systems.) Key elements of that pattern include:

- general control of the agenda by the federal or central government, and possession of greater resources overall;
- a high level of involvement for officials, with the groups of officials involved both varying according to the nature of the pattern of intergovernmental relations in that system but also shaping the pattern;
- a relatively limited role for party politics; governments relate to each other as governments and party ties are of little importance in that process;
- the importance of finance as an issue;
- varying levels of visibility or salience of intergovernmental relations, depending largely on how much mutual interdependence there is in a system;

---

11 The lack of interest is certainly not reciprocated in Italy, where many scholars interested in the Italian process of regionalisation have paid close attention to the UK and even formed a 'Devolution Club'.

12 Trench, A., 'Intergovernmental Relations: In search of a theory', in Greer, S. (ed.), *Territory, Democracy and Justice* (Houndmills: Palgrave Macmillan, 2006).

- constitutional matters and divisions of power of relatively little importance, particularly on the day-to-day level, except where constitutional
  politics have already assumed a high degree of importance – in which case
  any policy-related disagreement may become a constitutional issue too;
- a relatively limited role for the courts, which define boundaries of each
  government's functions but are not an actor in their own right.

In important respects, the UK conforms to this pattern, particularly in
the dominance of central government and the high degree of involvement of
officials. But there are also major differences. Finance has yet to emerge as a
major issue in intergovernmental relations, thanks to the relative generosity
of the mechanism used and its early adoption as a ground-rule of devolution
rather than a negotiable element of it. Party politics continues to play a major
role. So do constitutional matters, particularly where the devolution arrangements have been the least 'federal' (Wales and Northern Ireland). Salience
varies according to perspective – the importance of intergovernmental relations is seen as hugely more important in the devolved parts of the UK than
at the centre (compare coverage of the issue in the Scottish or Welsh newspapers with the London press). And the courts have yet even to play the role
of boundary-setters in the UK, partly because much of this work is done
between the governments, by agreement. Using the analysis of patterns
of intergovernmental relations adopted in that work – of 'functional' IGR
(concerned with particular policy matters narrowly defined) and 'summit-
oriented' IGR (concerned with a wide range of high-stakes political issues),
the UK is very much at the 'functional' end of the spectrum.

None of this, it should be added, takes into account the deliberate inter-
penetration of governments as part of the UK's arrangements, a consequence
of the fact that it is 'spinning out' functions of what had been a single, if territorially varied, state. (The only other federal state to attempt such a change
is Belgium. Like the UK, Belgium is seeking to transfer power away from the
centre after having built a welfare state as a unitary state. By contrast, all other
developed-world federations have built their welfare states around the institutional framework of their federal structure, and so their arrangements for
the welfare state accommodate the constitutional division of powers between
federal and constituent-unit governments.)

A further difference between the UK and 'proper' federal systems relates
to the interest shown in intergovernmental relations by parliaments and other
elected assemblies. Ron Watts notes the trend for the executive to dominate
intergovernmental relations in parliamentary federal systems, and for the role
of elected bodies to be very limited. If anything, he understates the case.
Interest in such matters from backbench legislators tends to be very limited

indeed. The subject matter does not lend itself to the sorts of activities that improve backbench careers, and indeed simply getting information can be hugely difficult. The lack of accountability and the exclusion of democratic control over intergovernmental relations amount, in some views, to the creation of a 'third level' of government, beyond the reach of either the federal/central institutions or the state/constituent-unit ones.[13] In the case of the UK, there are similar problems for elected politicians concerned about intergovernmental matters. Nonetheless, as chapter 8 showed, there has been considerable interest from elected politicians in these issues, resulting in a number of influential reports. This interest has come from two principal sources: the half-way house set of devolution arrangements for Wales, which both raise the profile of constitutional issues and give a large number of politicians an interest in taking part, and the relative calm of the House of Lords and particularly its Constitution Committee. By contrast, interest from Scottish MPs at Westminster has been limited and MSPs at Holyrood have taken their time in expressing theirs. The novelty of devolution also contributes to this, of course, but interest does not appear to be dropping off as time passes. The relative activity of legislators in the UK is in marked contrast to the lack of interest, even passivity, about such matters to be found in many other systems.

This strongly suggests that, for the time being, it is wrong to approach devolution as having established a set of quasi-federal relations in the United Kingdom. That applies on the level of the formal constitution, and on that of the working of its territorial system of government. The UK is simply, but in many important respects, fundamentally different from those systems. As noted in chapter 1, politicians and officials involved in territorial matters in the UK are often keen to emphasise that what the UK has is devolution, not federalism. They are right; as the working of the arrangements discussed throughout this book show, the UK has established something that is quite different from the sorts of relations that exist between federal governments and constituent units in federal systems.

However, it would be premature to write off the comparison between the UK and federal systems. The UK will undoubtedly change as it develops. The 'quasi-federal' model for relations between the UK and Scotland and Wales may well become more useful as that happens, not least because federal

<hr>

13 For an example of such a view in the Canadian context, see Simeon, R. and Cameron, D. A., 'Intergovernmental Relations and Democracy: An oxymoron if ever there was one?', in Bakvis, H. and Skogstad, G. (eds), *Canadian Federalism: Performance, effectiveness and legitimacy* (Toronto: Oxford University Press, 2002).

systems provide models for dealing with the complicated issues that will arise and these may well therefore commend themselves to the officials and politicians who have to deal with those problems. But at the moment that model does not adequately describe the post-devolution United Kingdom.

Instead, a better way of understanding devolution is to emphasise historical continuities. The pattern of relations that exists bears clear resemblances to the other forms of managing the 'state of unions' discussed by James Mitchell in chapter 2. The ways of managing territorial relations that have developed after devolution are closely related to those that applied before devolution; existing, often long-standing, practices found in inter-departmental relations within the UK Government, are shot through the UK's system of intergovernmental relations. Some were adopted in their entirety; in more cases, they were taken and adapted for use in changed circumstances, while retaining clear signs of their origins. This applies to the functions that were devolved, many administrative arrangements and ways of working across government, the preference for informal political mediation of differences to more formal approaches, the lack of change in internal UK procedures for matters such as legislation (and the way much legislation is still drafted), the continued use of the Barnett formula, the retention of the single Home Civil Service, the limited role of the courts and the law, the different sorts of interaction of the UK Government with the Northern Ireland departments compared with the Scottish Executive or Welsh Assembly Government, and even the distaste for having meetings of the JMC. The same also applies to the main political parties. It is startling how similar present practices are to those of ten years ago.

This is not the first time such a pattern of intergovernmental relations has developed. Something very like it can be found in relations between Northern Ireland and the UK during the period of devolution to the Stormont Parliament between 1922 and 1972, and particularly as relations developed after 1945. These similarities include an avoidance by the UK Government of intervening in devolved matters whenever possible, a permissive attitude from the UK Government to the scope of devolved functions, a determination to minimise disputes generally, a preference for informal liaison between officials with functional responsibilities with very limited coordination from the centre of government, and an avoidance of legal means of dispute resolution wherever possible. There are important differences between the two, as party politics played a much more limited role during devolution to Stormont, while finance became a much more important issue, especially as Stormont tried to keep parity with Great Britain in welfare provision. There was also relatively little engagement between governments at ministerial level and no equivalent to the JMC. These differences can be related to the environment in which devolution to Stormont took place, however, and the extent of the resemblances is striking.[14]

This approach may have made putting devolution in place much easier in the short term, and also made it much easier for devolution to 'bed in'. However, its price has been to complicate yet further what were often highly complicated forms of administration and political management. I have used elsewhere the metaphor of baroque and rococo architecture for this.[15] The structure of these arrangements was already ornate and highly detailed, but it had a clear form of distinction under which a simple, even elegant, original form was discernible. Devolution has added to the ornamentation, adding curlicue to curlicue, and creating yet more detail to the pattern. The problem is that this overwhelms the original form so it is no longer visible. What may have been elegant and even efficient once is not so any more.

Intergovernmental relations and the future of devolution

The initial phase of devolution has created a form of intergovernmental relations that is distinctive and has involved minimal change for the UK state. A significant cause of this is the continuing intertwining of devolved administrations with the UK Government, in a system that gives relatively little formal autonomy to the devolved institutions but which in practice has so far also given them a good deal of room for developing their own approaches to policy. Devolution has therefore involved a much less dramatic constitutional change than was widely expected before 1999. However, this relatively narrow scope of devolution had the great advantage that devolution could happen, and be incorporated into the UK's system of government, quickly and with much greater ease than many feared. But this does not resolve the big question – will this way of operating be adequate if, or when, it faces serious political challenge, with different parties in office at UK level and in the devolved capitals?

As so much of the present system is contingent on a particular benign set of circumstances, it is hard to conclude that this system will be robust enough to stand up under serious political pressure. There are three reasons. First, many difficult issues were shelved when devolution was put in place in 1998–99, but will come to the fore again sooner or later. Finance is the most notable such issue, but there are others. An obvious contender is the place of

14 See Birrell, D. and Murie, A., *Policy and Government in Northern Ireland: Lessons of devolution* (Dublin: Gill and Macmillan, 1980), especially chap. 1.
15 See Trench, A., *Central Government's Responses to Devolution*, Economic and Social Research Council Devolution Briefing no. 15 (January 2005).

England in a devolved United Kingdom, and the related 'West Lothian question', if the English can be persuaded to become genuinely interested in a constitutional issue. Another relates to the nature of the welfare state where devolved administrations have responsibility for some services but not others, and there has been no attempt to think through the relationship between the different levels of government in providing welfare. These issues are inherently political, and inherently contentious. When they emerge or re-emerge they will need to be dealt with – but that will happen when there are real political differences between governments, which will make resolving them all the harder.

Second, the system relies heavily on assumptions of goodwill between governments that have never been properly tested, and which may well not be able to withstand serious political differences. The implicit assumptions are either that there will be no major differences between governments, or that politicians will have such a strong interest in resolving their differences that they will never pursue a contentious issue. However, there is little consensus across territories and parties about what devolution is 'for' or how difficult issues should be dealt with. Politicians, and officials, are not used to grappling with such issues in the UK's system of government. Particularly if parties come to office which do not have a strong interest in making devolution work (and be seen to work), this system is highly vulnerable. This book has described in detail the extent to which the formal machinery of intergovernmental relations has been put out of use, and the burden left to be dealt with by individual ministers and officials in a largely unstructured and ad hoc way. It is hard to believe that this would be sustainable in the long term. What is needed are ways of helping politicians find such solutions when needed, without fuelling a sense of crisis, but despite there being real differences between them. Holding more regular and formal inter-ministerial meetings will not solve such issues in itself, but it will create a framework for dealing with such matters that is more likely to be able to cope with serious political differences than the present informal ad hoc approach.

Third, this system relies on a huge amount of work behind the scenes by officials. The UK's devolution arrangements leave so many grey areas, areas where one government's functions overlap with or affect another's, that to keep the system working requires not only care and thoughtfulness on the part of politicians but also much 'devilling' to resolve the multiplicity of technical issues that arise. That work is often not noticed by those outside government, but it is both essential to the system as it exists and hugely demanding of staff time and attention. Without a continued commitment of those civil service resources, the system will break down. Yet there is also a limit to what this sort of work can achieve. Politicians need to lead the process, not abandon it.

Over the next ten years, no doubt real political differences will emerge between the various governments in the United Kingdom. When that happens, it will test how the UK works. If devolution is to survive and succeed as a different way for the constituent parts of the UK to relate to each other, it will need an effective system of intergovernmental relations, which in turn will require a more conscious and strategic approach to the territorial management of the UK than has hitherto been shown.

Bibliography

Official documents

An Agreement Reached at the Multi-Party Talks on Northern Ireland, Cm 3883 (London: The Stationery Office, 1998).

Cabinet Office, *Guide to Legislative Procedures* (London: Cabinet Office, September 2003).

Civil Service Commissioners, *Annual Report 2003–2004* (London: Office of the Civil Service Commissioners, 2004).

Commission on the Powers and Electoral Arrangements of the National Assembly for Wales, *Report of the Richard Commission* (Cardiff: National Assembly for Wales, 2004).

Committee on the Better Governance for Wales White Paper, *Report* (Cardiff: National Assembly for Wales, 2005). At: www.wales.gov.uk/keypubassembettergov/content/bgw-report.pdf.

Council of Wales and Monmouthshire, *Third Memorandum on Its Activities*, Cm 53 (London: HMSO, 1957).

Council of Wales and Monmouthshire, *Fourth Memorandum on Government Administration in Wales*, Cmnd 631 (London: HMSO, 1959).

Department for Constitutional Affairs, *Constitutional Reform: A Supreme Court for the United Kingdom*, Consultation Paper CP 11/03 (London, 2003).

Department of Education, Northern Ireland, *Review of Pre-school Education in Northern Ireland* (Belfast, June 2004). At: www.deni.gov.uk/about/consultation/pre_school_review/ConsultationPaper.pdf.

Department for Education and Skills, *Delivering Results: A strategy to 2006* (London: Department for Education and Skills, 2002). At: www.dfes.gov.uk/aboutus/strategy/pdf/DfES-Strategic%20Framework.pdf.

Department for Education and Skills, *The Future of Higher Education*, Cm 5735 (London: The Stationery Office, 2003).

Department for Education and Skills, *Higher Standards, Better Schools for All: More choice for parents and pupils*, Cm 6677 (London: The Stationery Office, 2005). At: www.dfes.gov.uk/publications/schoolswhitepaper/pdfs/DfES-Schools%20White%20Paper.pdf.

Department of the Environment, Transport and the Regions, *Local Government Finance, SSA Background* (London: Department of the Environment, Transport and the Regions, 2000). At www.local.dtlr.gov.uk/finance/ssa/ssas.htm.

Department of Health, *The NHS Plan: The Government's response to the Royal Commission on Long Term Care*, Cm 4818-II (London: The Stationery Office, 2000).

Foot and Mouth Disease 2001: Lessons to be Learned inquiry report, HC 888 (London: The Stationery Office, 2002).

Himsworth, C., 'The General Effects of Devolution upon the Practice of Legislation at Westminster', Appendix 1 to House of Lords Select Committee on the Constitution, Session 2003–04 15th Report, *Devolution: Its effect on the practice of legislation at Westminster*, HL 192 (London: The Stationery Office, 2004).

HM Inspectorate of Constabulary, *Annual Report of Her Majesty's Inspectorate of Constabulary for Scotland 2004/2005*, SE/2005/206 (Edinburgh: The Stationery Office, 2005).

HM Treasury, *Needs Assessment Study: The report of an interdepartmental study coordinated by H.M. Treasury on the relative public expenditure needs in England, Scotland, Wales and Northern Ireland* (London: HM Treasury, 1979).

HM Treasury, *Modern Public Services for Britain: Investing in reform. Comprehensive Spending Review: New public spending plans 1999–2002*, Cm 4011 (London: The Stationery Office, 1998).

HM Treasury, *Funding the Scottish Parliament, National Assembly for Wales and Northern Ireland Assembly: A statement of funding policy* (London: The Stationery Office, 1999).

HM Treasury, *Spending Review 2000*, Cm 4807 (London: The Stationery Office, 2000).

HM Treasury, *Funding the Scottish Parliament, National Assembly for Wales and Northern Ireland Assembly: A statement of funding policy* (London: HM Treasury, 3rd edn, 2002).

HM Treasury, *Funding the Scottish Parliament, National Assembly for Wales and Northern Ireland Assembly: A statement of funding policy* (London: HM Treasury, 4th edn, 2004).

HM Treasury, *Public Expenditure Statistical Analyses 2004*, Cm 6201 (London: HM Treasury, 2004).

HM Treasury, *2004 Spending Review: New public spending plans 2005–08*, Cm 6237 (London: The Stationery Office, 2004).

HM Treasury, *Budget 2005: Investing for our future: Fairness and opportunity for Britain's hard-working families*, Financial Statement and Budget Report, HC 372 (London: The Stationery Office, 2005).

HM Treasury and National Statistics, *Public Expenditure Statistical Analyses 2005*, Cm 6521 (London: The Stationery Office, 2005).

House of Commons Public Accounts Committee, *The 2001 Outbreak of Foot and Mouth Disease*, Fifth Report Session 2002–03, HC 487 (London: The Stationery Office, 2003).

House of Commons Scottish Affairs Committee, *Minutes of Evidence for Tuesday 17 June 2003*, HC 815 (London: The Stationery Office, 2003).

House of Commons Select Committee on the Treasury, 2000–01 Session 3rd Report, *HM Treasury*, HC 73-I (London: The Stationery Office, 2001).

House of Commons Welsh Affairs Committee, 2001–02 Session 2nd Report, *Objective 1 European Funding for Wales*, HC 520 (London: The Stationery Office, 2002).

House of Commons Welsh Affairs Committee, *Minutes of Evidence for Wednesday 25 June 2003: The Wales Office departmental report 2003*, HC 883 (London: The Stationery Office, 2003).

House of Commons Welsh Affairs Committee, Session 2002–03 3rd Special Report, *The Government Response to the Fourth Report of the Committee: The primary legislative process as it affects Wales*, HC 989 (London: The Stationery Office, 2003).

House of Commons Welsh Affairs Committee, Session 2002–03 4th Report, *The Primary Legislative Process as It Affects Wales*, HC 73 (London: The Stationery Office, 2003).

House of Commons Welsh Affairs Committee, Session 2003–04 5th Report, *The Powers of the Children's Commissioner for Wales*, HC 538 (London: The Stationery Office, 2004).

House of Commons Welsh Affairs Committee, Session 2004–05 4th Report, *Police Service, Crime and Anti-Social Behaviour in Wales*, HC 46-I (London: The Stationery Office, 2005).

House of Commons Welsh Affairs Committee, Session 2005–06 1st Report, *The Government White Paper: Better Governance for Wales*, HC 551 (London: The Stationery Office, 2005).

House of Lords Select Committee on the Constitution, *Devolution: Inter-institutional Relations in the United Kingdom: Minutes of evidence*, HL 147 (London: The Stationery Office, 2002).

House of Lords Select Committee on the Constitution, Session 2002–03 9th Report, *The Draft Constitutional Treaty for the European Union*, HL 168, Memorandum by Alan Trench, 41–5.

House of Lords Select Committee on the Constitution, Session 2002–03 2nd Report, *Devolution: Inter-institutional Relations in the United Kingdom*, HL 28 (London: The Stationery Office, 2003).

House of Lords Select Committee on the Constitution, Session 2003–04 16th Report, *Meeting with the Lord Chancellor*, HL 193 (London: The Stationery Office, 2004).

Kilbrandon, Lord, *Report of the Royal Commission on the Constitution*, Cmnd 5460 (London: HMSO, 1973).

Memorandum of Understanding and Supplementary Agreements between the United Kingdom Government, Scottish Ministers, the Cabinet of the National Assembly for Wales and the Northern Ireland Executive Committee, Cm 5240 (London: The Stationery Office, 2001).

National Assembly for Wales, *Improving Health in Wales: A plan for the NHS with its partners* (Cardiff: National Assembly of Wales, 2001).

National Assembly for Wales, *The Learning Country: A paving document: A comprehensive education and lifelong learning programme to 2010 in Wales* (Cardiff: National Assembly for Wales, 2001). At: www.wales.gov.uk/subieducationtraining/content/PDF/learningcountry-e.pdf.

National Assembly for Wales, *Assembly Review of Procedure Final Report* (Cardiff: January 2002).

National Audit Office, *The 2001 Outbreak of Foot and Mouth Disease: Report by the Comptroller and Auditor General*, HC 939 (London: The Stationery Office, 2002).

Policy Commission on the Future of Food and Farming, *Farming and Food: A sustainable future* (London: The Cabinet Office, 2002).

Qualifications and Curriculum Authority, *Curriculum Guidance for the Foundation Stage* (London: Qualifications and Curriculum Authority, 2000). At: www.qca.org.uk/downloads/5585_cg_foundation_stage.pdf.

Royal Commission on Long Term Care, *With Respect to Old Age: Long term care – rights and responsibilities*, Cm 4192-I (London: The Stationery Office, 1999).

Royal Commission on the Reform of the House of Lords, *A House for the Future*, Cm 4534 (London: The Stationery Office, 2000).

Scotland Office, *The Size of the Scottish Parliament: A consultation* (London: December 2001).

Scotland Office and Office of the Solicitor to the Advocate General for Scotland Annual Report 2005, Cm 6544 (Edinburgh: The Stationery Office, 2004).

Scottish Constitutional Convention, *Scotland's Parliament, Scotland's Right* (Edinburgh: Scottish Constitutional Convention, 1995).

Scottish Consultative Council on the Curriculum, *A Curriculum Framework for Children 3 to 5* (Edinburgh: Learning and Teaching Scotland, 1999). At: www.ltscotland.org.uk/earlyyears/files/cf25.pdf.

Scottish Executive, *Fair Shares for All: Report of the National Review of Resource Allocation for the NHS in Scotland* (Edinburgh: Scottish Executive, 1999). At www.scotland.gov.uk/library2/doc01/fsag-00.htm.

Scottish Executive, *A Teaching Profession for the 21st Century: Agreement reached following recommendations made in the McCrone Report* (Edinburgh: Scottish Executive, 2000).

Scottish Executive, *Ambitious, Excellent Schools, Our Agenda for Action* (Edinburgh: Scottish Executive, November 2004). At: www.scotland.gov.uk/library5/education/aesaa.pdf.

Scottish Executive and COSLA, *Joint Discussion Paper on European Governance*, March 2001. At www.europa.eu.int/comm/governance/contributions/contrib_scotcosla_en.pdf.

Scottish Executive Health Department, *Partnership for Care: Scotland's health White Paper* (Edinburgh: The Stationery Office, 2003).

Scottish Ministers, *Government Expenditure & Revenue in Scotland 2002–2003*, SE/2004/273 (Edinburgh: Scottish Executive, 2004).

Scottish Office, *Scotland's Parliament*, Cm 3658 (London: The Stationery Office, 1997).

Scottish Office, *The Scotland Bill: A guide* (Edinburgh: Scottish Office, 1997).

Scottish Parliament, *Community Care and Health (Scotland) Bill Policy Memorandum* (Edinburgh: Scottish Parliament, 2001). At www.scottish.parliament.uk/parl_bus/bills/b34s1pm.pdf.

Scottish Parliament Procedures Committee, 7th Report 2005 (session 2), *The Sewel Convention*, SP Paper 428 (Edinburgh: Scottish Parliamentary Corporate Body, 2005).

Secretaries of State for Health; Wales; Northern Ireland; and Scotland, *Working for Patients* (London: The Stationery Office, 2002).

The Government's Response to the Second Report of the Select Committee on the Constitution, Session 2002–03 (HL Paper 28) Devolution: Inter-institutional relations in the United Kingdom, Cm 5780 (London: The Stationery Office, 2003).

Welsh Office, *A Voice for Wales: The Government's proposals for a Welsh Assembly*, Cm 3718 (London: The Stationery Office, 1997).

Wales Office, *Better Governance for Wales*, Cm 6582 (London: The Stationery Office, 2005).

Wales Office Annual Report 2005, Cm 6545 (London: The Stationery Office, 2005).

Welsh Assembly Government, *Freedom and Responsibility for Local Government* (Cardiff: Welsh Assembly Government, 2002). At: www.wales.gov.uk/ subilocalgov/content/freeresponse-e.pdf.

Welsh Office and Welsh Health Planning Forum, *Strategic Intent and Direction for the NHS in Wales* (Cardiff: Welsh Office, 1989).

Secondary literature

Adams, J., 'PSAs and Devolution; Target Setting Across the UK', *New Economy*, 9:1 (2002), 31–5.

Adams, J. and Robinson, P. (eds), *Devolution in Practice: Public policy differences within the UK* (London: ippr, 2002).

Adams, J. and Schmuecker, K., *Devolution in Practice 2006: Public policy differences within the UK* (London: ippr, 2006).

Agranoff, R., 'Autonomy, Devolution and Intergovernmental Relations', *Regional and Federal Studies*, 14:1 (2004), 26–65.

Allison, G., *Essence of Decision: Explaining the Cuban Missile Crisis* (Boston: Little, Brown and Company, 1971).

Allison, G. and Zelikov, P., *Essence of Decision* (Harlow: Longman, 1999).

Anthony, G., 'Public Law Litigation and the Belfast Agreement', *European Public Law*, 8:3 (2002), 401–22.

Anthony, G. and Morison, J., 'Here, There and (Maybe) Here Again: The story of law making for post-1998 Northern Ireland', in Hazell, R. and Rawlings, R. (eds), *Devolution, Law Making and the Constitution* (Exeter: Imprint Academic, 2005), 155–92.

Armstrong, K., 'Contesting Government, Producing Devolution: The repeal of "section 28" in Scotland', *Legal Studies*, 23:2 (2003), 205–28.

Ascherson, N., *Stone Voices: The search for Scotland* (London: Granta, 2002).

Bailey, S., *Cross on Principles of Local Government Law* (London: Sweet & Maxwell, 1992).

Banks, J. C., *Federal Britain? The case for regionalism* (London: George Harrap & Co., 1971).

Banting, K. G., 'Social Citizenship and Federalism: Is a federal welfare state a contradiction in terms?', in Greer, S. L. (ed.), *Territory, Democracy and Justice: Regionalism and federalism in Western democracies* (Basingstoke: Palgrave Macmillan, 2005), 44–66.

Banting, K. G. and Corbett, S., 'Health Policy and Federalism: An introduction', in Banting, K. G. and Corbett, S. (eds), *Health Policy and Federalism: A comparative perspective on multi-level governance* (Montreal and Kingston: McGill-Queens University Press, 2002), 1–37.

Bartlett, T., 'Ireland: From legislative independence to legislative union', in Dickinson, H. T. and Lynch, M. (eds), *The Challenge to Westminster: Sovereignty, devolution and independence* (East Linton: Tuckwell Press, 2000), 61–70.

Baumgartner, F. R. and Jones, B. D., *Agendas and Instability in American Politics* (Chicago: University of Chicago Press, 1993).

Beer, S., *Britain against Itself* (London: Faber, 1982).

Bell, D. and Christie, A., 'Finance – The Barnett Formula: Nobody's child', in Trench, A. (ed.), *The State of the Nations 2001: The second year of devolution in the United Kingdom* (Exeter: Imprint Academic, 2001), 135–51.

Bell, D. N. F., *The Barnett Formula* (unpublished mimeo: Department of Economics, University of Stirling, 2001).

Bennett, M., Fairley, J. and McAteer, M., *Devolution in Scotland: The impact on local government* (York: Joseph Rowntree Foundation, 2002).

Bhopal, R. and Last, J. (eds), *Public Health: Past, present and future: Celebrating academic public health in Edinburgh, 1902–2002* (London: The Stationery Office/The Nuffield Trust, 2004).

Birrell, D. and Murie, A., *Policy and Government in Northern Ireland: Lessons of devolution* (Dublin: Gill and Macmillan, 1980).

Blackburn, R. and Plant, R. (eds), *Constitutional Reform: The Labour Government's constitutional reform agenda* (London: Longman, 1999).

Blow, L., Hall, J. and Smith, S., *Financing Regional Government in Britain*, IFS Commentary No. 54 (London: Institute for Fiscal Studies, 2nd edn, 1996).

Bogdanor, V., *Devolution* (Oxford: Oxford University Press, 1979).

Bogdanor, V., *Devolution in the United Kingdom* (Oxford: Oxford University Press, 1999).

Bogdanor, V., 'Constitutional Reform', in Seldon, A. (ed.), *The Blair Effect: The Blair Government 1997–2001* (London: Little, Brown, 2001), 139–58.

Bogdanor, V., *Devolution in the United Kingdom* (Oxford: Oxford University Press, 2nd edn, 2001).

Börzel, T., *States and Regions in the European Union: Institutional adaptation in Germany and Spain* (Cambridge: Cambridge University Press, 2002).

Boyne, G. A., Gould-Williams, J., Law, J. and Walker, R. M., 'Best Value in Welsh Local Government: Progress and prospects', *Local Government Studies*, 25:2 (1999), 68–86.

Bristow, G., 'Bypassing Barnett: The Comprehensive Spending Review and public expenditure in Wales', *Economic Affairs*, 21:3 (2001), 44–7.

Brittan, S., *Steering the Economy: The role of the Treasury* (Harmondsworth: Pelican, 1971).

Bulmer, S., Jeffery, C. and Paterson, W. E. (eds), *Germany's European Diplomacy* (Manchester: Manchester University Press, 2000).

Bulpitt, J., *Territory and Power in the United Kingdom* (Manchester: Manchester University Press, 1983).

Burch, M. and Holliday, I., 'The Blair Government and the Core Executive', *Government and Opposition*, 39:1 (2004), 1–21.

Burgess, M., *The British Tradition of Federalism* (London: Leicester University Press, 1995).

Burrows, N., *Devolution* (London: Sweet & Maxwell, 2000).

Butler, D., Adonis, A. and Travers, T., *Failure in British Government: The politics of the poll tax* (Oxford: Oxford University Press, 1994).

Butt Philip, A., *The Welsh Question: Nationalism in Welsh politics 1945–1970* (Cardiff: University of Wales Press, 1975).

Byrne, T., *Local Government in Britain: Everyone's guide to how it works* (Harmondsworth: Penguin, 7th edn, 2000).

Cairney, P., 'New Public Management and the Thatcher Healthcare Legacy: Enough of the theory, what about the implementation?', *British Journal of Politics and International Relations* 4:3 (2002), 375–98.

Cairney, P. and Keating, M., 'Sewel Motions in the Scottish Parliament', *Scottish Affairs*, 47 (2004), 115–34.

Campbell, D. and Lee, R., '"Carnage by Computer": The blackboard economics of the 2001 Foot and Mouth epidemic', *Social and Legal Studies*, 12:4 (2003), 425–59.

Caramani, D., *The Nationalization of Politics: The formation of national electorates and party systems in Western Europe* (Cambridge: Cambridge University Press, 2004).

Carmichael, P. and Knox, C., 'Towards "a new era"? Some Developments in Governance of Northern Ireland', *International Review of Administrative Sciences*, 65:1 (1999), 103–16.

Chitty, C., *Education Policy in Great Britain* (Basingstoke: Palgrave, 2004).

Clarke, J., *The Local Government of the United Kingdom* (London: Sir Isaac Pitman & Sons Ltd, 14th edn, 1948).

Cohen, M., March, J. G. and Olsen, J. P., 'A Garbage Can Model of Rational Choice', *Administrative Science Quarterly*, 1:1 (1972), 1–25.

Constitution Unit, *An Assembly for Wales* (London: The Constitution Unit, 1996).

Constitution Unit, *Scotland's Parliament: Fundamentals for a new Scotland Act* (London: The Constitution Unit, 1996).

Constitution Unit and Institute of Welsh Affairs, *Wales Devolution Monitoring Report February 2003* (London/Cardiff: Constitution Unit and Institute of Welsh Affairs, 2003).

Conversi, D., 'Autonomous Communities and the Ethnic Settlement in Spain', in Ghai, Y. (ed.), *Autonomy and Ethnicity: Negotiating competing claims in multi-ethnic states* (Cambridge: Cambridge University Press, 2000), 122–44.

Cunningham-Burley, S., Jamieson, L., Morton, S., Adam, R. and McFarlane, V., *Mapping Sure Start Scotland* (Edinburgh: Centre for Research on Families and Relationships, University of Edinburgh, May 2002). At: www.scotland.gov.uk/library5/education/msss.pdf.

Curtice, J., 'Public Opinion and the Future of Devolution', in Trench, A. (ed.), *The Dynamics of Devolution: The State of the Nations 2005* (Exeter: Imprint Academic, 2005), 117–36.

Daintith, T., 'The Techniques of Government', in Jowell, J. and Oliver, D. (eds), *The Changing Constitution* (Oxford: Oxford University Press, 3rd edn, 1994).

Daintith, T. and Page, A., *The Executive in the Constitution: Structure, autonomy, and internal control* (Oxford: Oxford University Press, 1999).

Dalyell, T., *Devolution: The End of Britain?* (London: Jonathan Cape, 1977).

Dardanelli, P., *The Connection between European Integration and Demands for Regional Self-Government: A rational-institutionalist comparative analysis of Scotland, 1979 and 1997*, PhD thesis, Department of Government, London School of Economics (London, 2002).

Davies, J., *A History of Wales* (Harmondsworth: Penguin, 1994).

Day, P. and Klein, R., *The Quality Improvers: A study of the Commission for Health Improvement* (London: King's Fund, 2004).

Deacon, R. M., *The Governance of Wales: The Welsh Office and the policy process, 1964–1999* (Cardiff: Welsh Academic Press, 2002).

Deakin, N. and Parry, R., *The Treasury and Social Policy: The contest for control of welfare strategy* (Basingstoke: Macmillan, 2000).

Dewar, D., '*Scotland and Europe: Back in the mainstream*', William & Mary Lecture, 8 December 1999.

Di Toritto, B. C. 'The Role of Local Authorities in Decentralizing Process in Italy: Institutional aspects' (unpublished paper delivered at the International Association of Centres of Federal Studies conference, Cape Town, October 2004).

Dicey, A. V., *England's Case Against Home Rule* (London: John Murray, 1886).

Dicey, A. V., *Letters on Unionist Delusions* (Edinburgh: R&R Clark, 1887).

Dicey, A. V., 'The American Commonwealth', *Edinburgh Review*, 169 (1889), 481–518.

Dicey, A. V., *A Leap in the Dark: A criticism of the principles of home rule as illustrated by the Bill of 1893* (London: John Murray, 1893).

Dicey, A. V., *A Fool's Paradise: Being a constitutionalist's criticism on the Home Rule Bill of 1912* (London: John Murray, 1913).

Dupré, J. S., 'The Workability of Executive Federalism in Canada', in Bakvis, H. and Chandler, W. M. (eds), *Federalism and the Role of the State* (Toronto: University of Toronto Press, 1987), 236–58.

Edmonds, T., *The Barnett Formula* (House of Commons Library Research Paper 01/108) (London: House of Commons Library, 2001).

Edwards, J. L., *The Attorney-General: Politics and the public interest* (London: Sweet & Maxwell, 1984).

Elazar, D. J., *Exploring Federalism* (Tuscaloosa, AL: University of Alabama Press, 1987).

Elazar, D. J. (ed.), *Federal Systems of the World: A handbook of federal, confederal and autonomy arrangements* (Harlow: Longman Group Limited, 2nd edn, 1994).

Elwyn Jones, G. and Wynne Roderick, G., *A History of Education in Wales* (Cardiff: University of Wales Press, 2003).

ESRC, *Devolution: What difference has it made? Interim findings from the ESRC research programme on devolution and constitutional change* (Swindon: ESRC, 2004). At www.devolution.ac.uk/pdfdata/Interim_Findings_04.pdf.

Exworthy, M., 'Primary Care in the UK: Understanding the dynamics of devolution', *Health and Social Care in the Community*, 9:5 (2001), 266–78.

Fawcett, H., 'The Making of Social Justice Policy in Scotland: Devolution and social exclusion', in Trench, A. (ed.), *Has Devolution Made a Difference: The State of the Nations 2004* (Exeter: Imprint Academic, 2004), 237–54.

Featherstone, H. L., *A Century of Nationalism* (London: Thomas Nelson, 1939).

Foster, R., *Modern Ireland 1600–1972* (Harmondsworth: Penguin, 1990).

Gee, G., 'Devolution and the Courts', in Hazell, R. and Rawlings, R. (eds), *Devolution, Law Making and the Constitution* (Exeter: Imprint Academic, 2005), 252–94.

Gibson, E. L., *A Study of the Council for Wales and Monmouthshire, 1948–1966* (Unpublished LLB Thesis, University College of Wales, Aberystwyth, 1968).

Goudie, A., '*GERS* and Fiscal Autonomy', *Scottish Affairs*, 41 (2002), 56–85.

Gowan, I., *Government in Wales*, Inaugural Lecture as Professor of Political Science (University College of Wales, Aberystwyth, December 1965).

Greer, A., *Agricultural Policy in Europe* (Manchester: Manchester University Press, 2005).

Greer, S. L., *Territorial Politics and Health Policy: The United Kingdom in comparative perspective* (Manchester: Manchester University Press, 2004).

Greer, S. L., 'A Very English Institution: Central and local in the English NHS', in Hazell, R. (ed.), *The English Question* (Manchester: Manchester University Press, 2005), 194–219.

Greer, S. L., 'Becoming European: Devolution, Europe and health policy-making', in Trench, A. (ed.), *The Dynamics of Devolution: The State of the Nations 2005* (Exeter: Imprint Academic, 2005), 201–24.

Greer, S. L., 'The Politics of Divergent Policy', in Greer, S. L. (ed.), *Territory, Democracy and Justice: Regionalism and federalism in Western democracies* (Basingstoke: Palgrave Macmillan, 2005), 157–74.

Greer, S. L. and Jarman, H., *Devolution and Policy Styles in the United Kingdom*, Manuscript (London: Constitution Unit, 2005).

Grey, T., 'Do We Have an Unwritten Constitution?', *Stanford Law Review*, 27 (1975), 705–10.

Griffith, D., 'The Welsh Office and Welsh Autonomy', *Public Administration*, 77:1 (1999), 703–807.

Grodzins, M., 'The Federal System', in Wildavsky, A. (ed.), *American Federalism in Perspective* (Boston: Little Brown, 1967), 256–77.

Hadfield, B., 'Seeing it Through? The multifaceted implementation of the Belfast Agreement', in Wilford, R. (ed.), *Aspects of the Belfast Agreement* (Oxford: Oxford University Press, 2001), 84–106.

Hain, Peter, 'Europe and the Regions', 3 February 2003. At http://register.consilium .eu.int/pdf/en/03/cv00/cv00526en03.pdf.

Harvie, C., *Scotland and Nationalism* (London: George Allen & Unwin, 1977).

Hazell, R. (ed.), *Constitutional Futures: A history of the next ten years* (Oxford: Oxford University Press, 1999).

Hazell, R., 'Intergovernmental Relations: Whitehall rules OK?', in Hazell, R. (ed.), *The State and the Nations: The first year of devolution in the United Kingdom* (Exeter: Imprint Academic, 2000), 149–82.

Hazell, R., 'Merger: What merger? Scotland, Wales, and the new Department for Constitutional Affairs', *Public Law* (2003), 650–5.

Hazell, R., 'Westminster as a "Three-in-One" Legislature of the UK and its Devolved Territories', in Hazell, R. and Rawlings, R. (eds), *Devolution, Law Making and the Constitution* (Exeter: Imprint Academic, 2005), 226–51.

Hazell, R. (ed.), *The English Question* (Manchester: Manchester University Press, 2006).

Heald, D., 'Territorial public expenditure in the United Kingdom', *Public Administration*, 72 (1994), 147–75.

Heald, D., *Funding the Northern Ireland Assembly: Assessing the options* (Belfast: Northern Ireland Economic Council, 2003).

Heald, D. and McLeod, A., 'Beyond Barnett? Funding devolution', in Adams, J. and Robinson, P. (eds), *Devolution in Practice: Public policy differences within the UK* (London: ippr, 2002), 147–75.

Heald, D. and McLeod, A., 'Revenue-raising by UK Devolved Administrations in the Context of an Expenditure-based Financing System', *Regional and Federal Studies*, 13:4 (2003), 67–90.

Heald, D. and McLeod, A., 'Embeddedness of UK Devolution Finance within the Public Expenditure System', *Regional Studies*, 39:4 (2005), 495–518.

Hechter, M., *Internal Colonialism: The Celtic fringe in British national development 1536–1966* (London: Routledge & Kegan Paul, 1975).

Heclo, H. and Wildavsky, A., *The Private Government of Public Money: Community and policy inside British politics* (London: Macmillan, 2nd edn, 1981).

Heggie, G., 'The Story so Far: The role of the Scottish Parliament's European Committee in the UK–EU policy cycle', *Scottish Affairs*, 44 (2003), 114–31.

Himsworth, C. M. G. and O'Neill, C. M., *Scotland's Constitution: Law and practice* (Edinburgh and London: Lexis Nexis, 2003).

Hollingsworth, K. and Douglas, G., 'Creating a children's champion for Wales? The Care Standards Act 2000 (Part V) and the Children's Commissioner for Wales Act 2001', *Modern Law Review*, 65 (2000), 58–78.

Hopkin, J., 'Political Decentralization, Electoral Change and Party Organizational Adaptation', *European Urban and Regional Studies*, 10:3 (2003), 227–37.

Horgan, G. W., 'Inter-institutional Relations in the Devolved Great Britain: Quiet diplomacy', *Regional and Federal Studies*, 14:1 (2004), 113–45.

Hrbek, R. and Nettesheim, M. (eds), *Europäische Union und mitgliedstaatliche Daseinsvorsorge* (Baden-Baden: Nomos, 2002).

Hunter, D., 'The Lure of the Organisational Fix', in McCrone, D. (ed.), *Scottish Government Yearbook* (Edinburgh: Unit for the Study of Government in Scotland, 1984), 230–57.

Hunter, D. and Wistow, G., 'The Paradox of Policy Diversity in a Unitary State: Community care in Britain', *Public Administration*, 65:1 (1987), 3–24.

Hunter, D. J., *Public Health Policy* (Cambridge: Polity, 2003).

Institute of Public Policy Research, *A Written Constitution for the UK* (London, Mansell, 1991).

Jackson, A., *Home Rule: An Irish history, 1800–2000* (London: Weidenfeld and Nicolson, 2003).

James, O., 'The UK Core Executive's Use of Public Service Agreements as a Tool of Governance', *Public Administration*, 82:2 (2004), 397–419.

Jamieson, I., 'Relationship between the Scotland Act and the Human Rights Act', *Scottish Law Times* (News), 43 (2001).

Jeffery, C., 'The Länder Strike Back: Structures and processes of European integration policy-making in the German federal system', *University of Leicester Discussion Papers in Federal Studies*, No. FS94/4 (1994).

Jeffery, C., 'Sub-National Mobilization and European Integration', *Journal of Common Market Studies*, 38:1 (2000), 11–18.

Jeffery, C., 'Equity and Diversity: Devolution, social citizenship, and territorial culture in the UK', Manuscript (Birmingham: University of Birmingham Institute for German Studies, 2003).

Jeffery, C., 'Devolution and the European Union: Trajectories and futures', in Trench, A. (ed.), *The Dynamics of Devolution: The State of the Nations 2005* (Exeter: Imprint Academic, 2005), 179–99.

Jeffery, C., 'Devolution and Social Citizenship: Which society, whose citizenship?', in Greer, S. L. (ed.), *Territory, Democracy and Justice: Regionalism and federalism in Western democracies* (Basingstoke: Palgrave Macmillan, 2005), 67–91.

Jeffery, C., 'Devolution and Local Government', *Publius*, 36:1 (2006), 57–73.

Jeffery, C. and Palmer, R., 'Stepping (Softly) onto the International Stage: The external relations of Scotland and Wales', in Hrbek, R. (ed.), *Außenbeziehungen von Regionen in Europa und der Welt* (Baden-Baden: Nomos, 2003), 159–72.

Jones, C., 'Responsibility Without Power', *IWA Agenda* (Autumn 2001), 41–3.

Jones, J. B. and Balsom, D. (eds), *The Road to the National Assembly for Wales* (Cardiff: University of Wales Press, 2000).

Joyce, P., *Realignment of the Left? A history of the relationship between the Liberal Democrat and Labour Parties* (Macmillan: Basingstoke, 1999).

Kavanagh, D., 'The Blair Premiership', in Seldon, A. and Kavanagh, D. (eds), *The Blair Effect 2001–5* (Cambridge: Cambridge University Press, 2005), 3–19.

Kay, A., 'Evaluating Devolution in Wales', *Political Studies*, 51:1 (2003), 51–66.

Kearney, H., *The British Isles* (Cambridge: Cambridge University Press, 1989).

Keating, M., *The Government of Scotland: Public policy making after devolution* (Edinburgh: Edinburgh University Press, 2005).

Keating, M. and McEwen, N. (eds), *Devolution and Public Policy: A comparative perspective*, special issue of *Regional and Federal Studies*, 15:4 (2005).

Keating, M., Stevenson, L., Cairney, P. and Taylor, K., 'Does Devolution Make a Difference? Legislative output and policy divergence in Scotland', *Journal of Legislative Studies*, 9:3 (2003), 110–39.

Kellas, J., *The Scottish Political System* (Cambridge: Cambridge University Press, 1973).

Kellas, J., *The Scottish Political System* (Cambridge: Cambridge University Press, 3rd edn, 1984).

Kendle, J., *Federal Britain: A history* (London: Routledge, 1997).

Kingdon, J. W., *Agendas, Alternatives, and Public Policies* (New York: HarperCollins, 1995).

Kishlansky, M., *A Monarchy Transformed: Britain 1603–1714* (Harmondsworth: Penguin, 1996).

Kramnick, I., 'Introduction' to Alexis de Tocqueville, *Democracy in America* (London: Penguin, 2003), ix–lii.

Laffin, M., 'Is Regional Centralism Inevitable? The case of the Welsh Assembly', *Regional Studies*, 38:2 (2004), 213–23.

Laffin, M. and Thomas, A., 'The UK: Federalism in denial?', *Publius: The Journal of Federalism*, 29:3 (1999), 89–108.

Laffin, M., Taylor, G. and Thomas, A., *A New Partnership? The National Assembly for Wales and local government* (York: Joseph Rowntree Foundation, 2002).

Lambert, D. and Miers, D., 'Law-making in Wales: Wales-legislation online', *Public Law* (2002), 663–9.

Lang, I., *Blue Remembered Years: A political memoir* (London: Politicos, 2002).

Lawrence, R. J., *The Government of Northern Ireland: Public finance and public services 1921–1964* (Oxford: Clarendon Press, 1965).

Lessing, D., *Prisons We Choose to Live Inside* (London: HarperCollins, 1994).

Lipset, S. M. and Rokkan, S., 'Cleavage Structures, Party Systems and Voter Alignments', in Lipset, S. M. and Rokkan, S. (eds), *Party Systems and Voter Alignments: Cross-national perspectives* (New York: Free Press, 1967), 1–64.

Lipsky, M., *Street Level Bureaucrats* (New York: Russell Sage Foundation, 1980).

Lodge, G., Russell, M. and Gay, O., 'The Impact of Devolution on Westminster: If not now, when?', in Trench, A. (ed.), *Has Devolution Made a Difference? The State of the Nations 2004* (Exeter: Imprint Academic, 2004), 193–216.

Longley, M. and Warner, M., 'Health and Health Delivery in Wales', in Dunkerly, D. and Thompson, A. (eds), *Wales Today* (Cardiff: University of Wales Press, 1999), 199–212.

Loughlin, J., *Subnational Democracy in the European Union: Challenges and opportunities* (Oxford: Oxford University Press, 2001).

Loughlin, M., *Local Government in the Modern State* (London: Sweet & Maxwell, 1986).

Loughlin, M., *Legality and Locality: The role of law in central–local government relations* (Oxford: Oxford University Press, 1996).

Lowe, P. and Ward, N., 'Devolution and the Governance of Rural Affairs in the UK', in Adams, J. and Robinson, P. (eds), *Devolution in Practice: Public policy differences within the UK* (London: ippr, 2002), 117–39.

Lukes, S., *Power: A radical view* (London: Macmillan, 1974).

Lynch, M., *Scotland: A new history* (London: Pimlico, 1992).

Lynch, P., *Scottish Government and Politics: An introduction* (Edinburgh: Edinburgh University Press, 2001).

MacCormick, J., *The Flag in the Wind: The story of the national movement in Scotland* (London: Victor Gollancz, 1955).

Mackintosh, J. P., *The Devolution of Power* (London: Penguin, 1968).

Madgwick, P. and Rose, R. (eds), *The Territorial Dimension in United Kingdom Politics* (London: Macmillan, 1982).

Mansergh, N., *The Unresolved Question: The Anglo-Irish settlement and its undoing, 1912–72* (New Haven and London: Yale University Press, 1991).

Marks, G. *et al.*, 'Competencies, Cracks and Conflicts: Regional mobilization in the European Union', in Marks, G., Scharpf, F., Schmitter, P. and Streeck, W. (eds), *Governance in the European Union* (London: Sage, 1996).

McAllister, I., 'The Labour Party in Wales: The dynamics of one-partyism', *Llafur: The Journal of Welsh Labour History*, 3:2 (1981), 79–89.

McAllister, L., 'Devolution and the New Context for Public Policy-making: Lessons from the EU Structural Funds in Wales', *Public Policy and Administration*, 15:2 (2000), 38–52.

McAteer, M. and Bennett, M., 'Devolution and Local Government: Evidence from Scotland', *Local Government Studies*, 31:3 (2005), 285–306.

McConnell, A., *Scottish Local Government* (Edinburgh: Edinburgh University Press, 2004)

McConnell, J., 'The Future of Europe Debate – A Scottish Perspective', Speech, 6 June 2002. At www.scotland.gov.uk/about/FCSD/ExtRel1/00014768/page1239857280.aspx.

McEwen, N., 'State Welfare Nationalism: The territorial impact of welfare state development in Scotland', *Regional and Federal Studies*, 12:1 (2002), 66–90.

McGarvey, N., 'Intergovernmental Relations in Scotland Post Devolution', *Local Government Studies*, 28:3 (2002), 29–48.

McLean, I., 'Are Scotland and Wales Over-represented in the House of Commons?', *Political Quarterly*, 66 (1995), 250–68.

McLean, I., 'A Fiscal Constitution for the UK', in Chen, S. and Wright, T. (eds), *The English Question* (London: The Fabian Society, 2000), 80–95.

McLean, I., 'The Purse Strings Tighten', in Osmond, J. (ed.), *Second Term Challenge: Can the Welsh Assembly Government hold its course?* (Cardiff: Institute of Welsh Affairs, 2003), 82–98.

McLean, I., 'The National Question', in Seldon, A. and Kavanagh, D. (eds), *The Blair Effect: 2001–05* (Cambridge: Cambridge University Press, 2005), 339–61.

McLean, I. and McMillan, A., 'The Distribution of Public Expenditure across the UK Regions', *Fiscal Studies*, 24:1 (2003), 45–71.

Midwinter, A. and McGarvey, N., 'Developing Best Value in Scotland: Concepts and contradictions', *Local Government Studies*, 25:2 (1999), 87–101.

Milne, S. D., *The Scottish Office* (London: Allen & Unwin, 1957).

Mitchell, J., 'Conceptual Lenses and Territorial Government in Britain', in Jordan, U. and Kaiser, W. (eds), *Political Reform in Britain, 1886–1996* (Bochum: Brockmeyer, 1997), 1–64.

Mitchell, J., *Governing Scotland* (Basingstoke: Palgrave Macmillan, 2003).

Mitchell, J., 'Scotland: Expectations, policy types and devolution', in Trench, A. (ed.), *Has Devolution Made a Difference? The State of the Nations 2004* (Exeter: Imprint Academic, 2004), 11–41.

Mitchell, J., 'Re-inventing the Union: Dicey, devolution, and the Union', in Miller, W. (ed.), *Anglo-Scottish Relations from 1900 to Devolution* (Oxford: The British Academy/Oxford University Press, 2005), 35–61.

Mitchell, J., 'Undignified and Inefficient: Financial relations between London and Stormont', *Contemporary British History*, 20:1 (2006), 57–73.

Mitchell, J. and Seyd, B., 'Fragmentation in the Party and Political Systems', in Hazell, R. (ed.), *Constitutional Futures* (Oxford: Oxford University Press, 1999), 86–110.

Molas, I. and Bartomeus, O., *Estructura de la competencia política a Catalunya* (Barcelona: ICPS, 1998).

Moran, M., *The British Regulatory State: High modernism and hyper-innovation* (Oxford: Oxford University Press, 2003).

Morgan, E. S., *Inventing the People: The rise of popular sovereignty in England and America* (New York: W.W. Norton & Company, 1988).

Morgan, K. O., *Wales: Rebirth of a nation, 1880–1980* (Oxford: Oxford University Press, 1982).

Morgan, K. O., *Callaghan: A life* (Oxford: Oxford University Press, 1997).

Morgan, R., 'Annual Lecture for National Centre for Public Policy', University of Wales, Swansea (December 2002).

Mulholland, M., *Northern Ireland at the Crossroads: Ulster Unionism in the O'Neill years, 1960–9* (London: Macmillan, 2000).

Munro, R., *Looking Back: Fugitive writings and sayings* (London: Thomas Nelson, 1930).

Murdoch, A., 'Scottish Sovereignty in the Eighteenth Century', in Dickinson, H. T. and Lynch, M. (eds), *The Challenge to Westminster: Sovereignty, devolution and independence* (East Linton: Tuckwell Press, 2000), 42–9.

Musgrove, R., *The Theory of Public Finance* (New York: McGraw Hill, 1959).

Nairn, T., *The Break-Up of Britain* (London: Verso, 1981).

Nairn, T., *After Britain: New Labour and the return of Scotland* (London: Granta Books, 2000).

Newark, F. H., 'The Law and the Constitution', in Wilson, T. (ed.), *Ulster Under Home Rule: A study of the political and economic problems of Northern Ireland* (Oxford: Oxford University Press, 1955), 14–54.

Northern Ireland Devolution Monitoring Reports (London: The Constitution Unit, 1999–2005). At: www.ucl.ac.uk/constitution-unit/publications/devolution-monitoring-reports/index.html.

O'Day, A., *Irish Home Rule, 1867–1921* (Manchester: Manchester University Press, 1998).

O'Leary, B. and McGarry, J., *The Politics of Antagonism: Understanding Northern Ireland* (London: Athlone Press, 2nd edn, 1996).

O'Neill, A., 'Judicial Politics and the Judicial Committee: The devolution jurisprudence of the Privy Council', *Modern Law Review*, 64 (2001), 603–17.

Oates, W. E., 'An Essay on Fiscal Federalism', *Journal of Economic Literature*, 37:3 (1999), 1120–49.

Office of the Deputy Prime Minister, *Evaluation of Local Strategic Partnerships: Report of a survey of all English LSPs* (London: Office of the Deputy Prime Minister, February 2003). At: www.local.odpm.gov.uk/research/lsp.pdf.

Olson, J. and Astrom, J., 'Why Regionalism in Sweden?', *Regional and Federal Studies*, 13:3 (2003), 66–89.

Osmond, J., 'A Constitutional Convention by Other Means: The first year of the National Assembly for Wales', in Hazell, R. (ed.), *The State and the Nations: The first year of devolution in the United Kingdom* (Exeter: Imprint Academic, 2000), 37–77.

Osmond, J., 'The Coalition Government', in Osmond, J. (ed.), *Coalition Politics Come to Wales: Monitoring the National Assembly September to December 2000* (Cardiff: Institute of Welsh Affairs, 2000).

Page, A. and Batey, A., 'Scotland's other Parliament: Westminster legislation about devolved matters in Scotland since devolution', *Public Law* (2002), 501–23.

Page, E. C., *Governing by Numbers* (Oxford: Hart Publishing, 2002).

Page, E. C., 'The Civil Servant as Legislator: Law making in British administration', *Public Administration*, 81:4 (2003), 651–79.

Page, E. C. and Jenkins, B., *Policy Bureaucracy: Government with a cast of thousands* (Oxford: Oxford University Press, 2005).

Parris, H., *Constitutional Bureaucracy: The development of British central administration since the eighteenth century* (London: George Allen & Unwin, 1969).

Parry, R., 'Devolution, Integration and Modernisation in the United Kingdom's Civil Service', *Public Policy and Administration*, 16:3 (2001), 53–67.

Patchett, K., 'The New Welsh Constitution: The Government of Wales Act 1998', in Jones, J. B. and Balsom, D. (eds), *The Road to the National Assembly for Wales* (Cardiff: University of Wales Press, 2000), 229–64.

Patchett, K., 'The Central Relationship: The Assembly's engagement with Westminster and Whitehall', in Jones, J. B. and Osmond, J. (eds), *Building a Civic Culture: Institutional change, policy development and political dynamics in the National Assembly for Wales* (Cardiff: Institute of Welsh Affairs and Welsh Governance Centre, 2002), 17–31.

Patchett, K., 'Principle or Pragmatism: Legislation for Wales by Westminster and Whitehall', in Hazell, R. and Rawlings, R. (eds), *Devolution, Law Making and the Constitution* (Exeter: Imprint Academic, 2005), 112–54.

Paterson, L., *The Autonomy of Modern Scotland* (Edinburgh: Edinburgh University Press, 1994).

Paterson, L., 'The Three Educational Ideologies of the British Labour Party, 1997–2001', *Oxford Review of Education*, 29:2 (2003), 165–86.

Peterson, P., *City Limits* (Chicago: University of Chicago Press, 1981).

Peterson, P., *The Price of Federalism* (Washington: Brookings Institution, 1994).

Poirier, J., 'Pouvoir normatif et protection sociale dans les fédérations multinationales', *Canadian Journal of Law and Society/Révue Canadiénne de Droit et Societé*, 16:2 (2001), 137–71.

Poirier, J., 'The Functions of Intergovernmental Agreements: Post-devolution concordats in a comparative perspective', *Public Law* (2001), 134–57.

Powell, E., 'Britain and Europe', in Holmes, M. (ed.), *The Eurosceptical Reader* (Houndmills: Macmillan, 1996), 75–87.

Publius: The Journal of Federalism, 36:1, special issue on devolution in the United Kingdom (2006).

Raffe, D., 'Devolution and Divergence in Education Policy', IPPR North Seminar Paper (2005). At: www.ippr.org.uk/uploadedFiles/ipprnorth/events/2005/Sem7-Paper.pdf.

Randall, P. J., *The Development of Administrative Decentralisation in Wales from the Establishment of the Welsh Department of Education in 1907 to the Creation of the Post of Secretary of State for Wales in October 1964* (Unpublished MSc. Econ. Thesis, University of Wales, 1969).

Rawlings, R., 'Concordats of the Constitution', *Law Quarterly Review*, 116 (2000), 257–86.

Rawlings, R., 'Quasi-legislative Devolution: Powers and principles', *Northern Ireland Legal Quarterly*, 52 (2001), 54–81.

Rawlings, R., 'Towards a Parliament: Three faces of the National Assembly for Wales', *Contemporary Wales*, 15 (2003), 1–19.

Rawlings, R., *Delineating Wales: Constitutional, legal and administrative aspects of national devolution* (Cardiff: University of Wales Press, 2003).

Rawlings, R., 'Hastening Slowly: The next phase of Welsh devolution', *Public Law* (2005), 824–52.

Reynolds, D., 'Developing Differently: Educational policy in England, Wales, Northern Ireland and Scotland', in Adams, J. and Robinson, P. (eds), *Devolution in Practice: Public policy differences within the UK* (London: ippr, 2002), 93–103.

Reynolds, D., 'Education: Building on difference', in Osmond, J. (ed.), *Second Term Challenge: Can the Welsh Assembly Government hold its course?* (Cardiff and London: Institute for Welsh Affairs, November 2005), 43–51.

Rhodes, R. A. W., *Control and Power in Central–Local Government Relations* (Aldershot: Gower, 1981).

Rhodes, R. A. W., '"Power Dependence". Theories of central-local relations: A critical reassessment', in Goldsmith, M. (ed.), *New Research in Central–Local Relations* (Aldershot: Gower, 1986), 1–33.

Rhodes, R. A. W., *Beyond Westminster and Whitehall: The sub-central governments of Britain* (London: Unwin Hyman, 1988).

Rhodes, R. A. W. and Dunleavy, P. (eds), *Prime Minister, Cabinet and Core Executive* (Basingstoke: Macmillan, 1995).

Rhodes, R. A. W., Carmichael, P., McMillan, J. and Massey, A., *Decentralizing the Civil Service: From unitary state to differentiated polity in the United Kingdom* (Buckingham: Open University Press, 2003).

Riker, W. H., 'Federalism', in Greenstein, F. I. and Polsby, N. W., (eds), *Handbook of Political Science: Governmental institutions and processes*, Vol. 5 (Reading, MA: Addison Wesley, 1975), 93–172.

Riker, W., *Federalism: Origins, operation, significance* (Boston: Little, Brown, 1964).

Rokkan, S. and Urwin, D., *Economy, Territory, Identity: The politics of West European peripheries* (London: Sage, 1983).

Rose, R., *The Problem of Party Government* (Harmondsworth: Penguin, 1976).

Rose, R., *The Territorial Dimension in Government: Understanding the United Kingdom* (Chatham, NJ: Chatham, 1982).

Rose, R. (ed.), *Ministers and Ministries: A functional analysis* (Oxford: Clarendon, 1987).

Rose, R. and Davies, P. L., *Inheritance in Public Policy: Change without choice in Britain* (New Haven: Yale University Press, 1994).

Russell, M., 'Multilevel Politics and the Constituency Representation Role: The impact of devolution in Scotland and Wales', Paper presented to ECPR Conference, Budapest (September 2005).

Sandford, M., 'The Governance of London: Strategic governance and policy divergence', in Trench, A. (ed.), *Has Devolution Made A Difference? The State of the Nations 2004* (Exeter: Imprint Academic, 2004), 141–63.

Sandford, M. and Hetherington, P., 'The Regions at the Crossroads: The future for subnational government in England', in Trench, A. (ed.), *The Dynamics of Devolution: The State of the Nations 2005* (Exeter: Imprint Academic, 2005), 91–113.

Schattschneider, E. E., *The Semisovereign People: A realist's view of democracy in America* (Hinsdale, Ill: Dryden Press, 1975).

Schmidt, V. A., *The Futures of European Capitalism* (Oxford: Oxford University Press, 2002).

Schmuecker, K. and Adams, J. (eds), *Devolution in Practice II: Public policy differences around the UK* (Newcastle: ippr, 2005).

Scotland Devolution Monitoring Reports (London: The Constitution Unit, 1999–2005). At: www.ucl.ac.uk/constitution-unit/publications/devolution-monitoring-reports/index.html.

Seawright, D., 'The Scottish Conservative and Unionist Party: "The lesser spotted Tory?"', in Hassan, G. and Warhurst, C. (eds), *Tomorrow's Scotland* (London: Lawrence & Wishart, 2002), 66–82.

Seyd, B., *Coalition Government in Scotland and Wales* (London: Constitution Unit, 2004).

Seyd, P., 'New Parties/New Politics? A case study of the British Labour Party', *Party Politics*, 5:3 (1999), 383–406.

Sharland, J., *A Practical Approach to Local Government Law* (London: Blackstone Press, 1997).

Sharpe, L. J., 'The European Meso: An appraisal', in Sharpe, L. J. (ed.), *The Rise of Meso Government in Europe* (London: Sage, 1993), 1–39.

Shaw, E., *The Labour Party since 1979* (London: Routledge, 1994).

Shaw, E., 'New Labour – New Democratic Centralism?', *West European Politics*, 25:3 (2002), 147–70.

Shaw, E., 'Devolution and Scottish Labour: The case of free personal care for the elderly', Paper presented to the Annual Conference of the Political Studies Association, University of Leicester (April 2003).

Simeon, R., 'Free Personal Care: Policy divergence and social citizenship', in Hazell, R. (ed.), *The State of the Nations 2003: The third year of devolution in the United Kingdom* (Exeter: Imprint Academic, 2003), 215–35.

Simeon, R. and Cameron, D. A., 'Intergovernmental Relations and Democracy: An oxymoron if ever there was one?', in Bakvis, H. and Skogstad, G. (eds), *Canadian Federalism: Performance, effectiveness and legitimacy* (Toronto: Oxford University Press, 2002), 278–95.

Smith, B. C., *Decentralisation: The territorial dimension of the state* (London: George Allen & Unwin, 1985).

Smith, M., *The Core Executive in Britain* (Basingstoke: Macmillan, 1999).

Stepan, A., 'Electorally Generated Veto Players in Unitary and Federal Systems', in Gibson, E. L. (ed.), *Federalism and Democracy in Latin America* (Baltimore, MD: Johns Hopkins University Press, 2004), 323–61.

Stewart, A. T. Q., *The Narrow Ground: Aspects of Ulster, 1609–1969* (London: Faber and Faber, 1977).

Taylor, B., *Scotland's Parliament: Triumph and disaster* (Edinburgh: Edinburgh University Press, 2002).

Taylor, B. and Thomson, K. (eds), *Scotland and Wales: Nations again?* (Cardiff: University of Wales Press, 1999).

Taylor, G., 'Power in the Party', in Taylor, G. (ed.), *The Impact of New Labour* (Basingstoke: Macmillan, 1999), 9–25.

Thain, C. and Wright, M., *The Treasury and Whitehall: The planning and control of public expenditure, 1976–1993* (Oxford: Clarendon Press, 1995).

The Constitution Unit, *Scotland's Parliament: Fundamentals for a new Scotland Act* (London: The Constitution Unit, 1996).

Thomas, A. and Laffin, M., 'The First Welsh Constitutional Crisis: The Alun Michael resignation', *Public Policy and Administration*, 16:1 (2001), 18–31.

Thomas, S., 'Local Government and the National Assembly: A "Welsh Way" to public sector reform?', *Wales Law Journal*, 2:1 (2002), 41–50.

Tiebout, C. M., 'A Pure Theory of Local Expenditures', *Journal of Political Economy*, 64:5 (1956), 416–24.

Tocqueville, Alexis de, *Democracy in America* (London: Penguin, [1835] 2003 edn).

Travers, T., 'Local and Central Government', in Seldon, A. and Kavanagh, D. (eds), *The Blair Effect 2001–5* (Cambridge: Cambridge University Press, 2005), 68–93.

Trench, A., *Devolution in Practice? Scottish and Welsh devolution and the Westminster statute book* (mimeo, London: The Constitution Unit, 2002).

Trench, A., 'Intergovernmental Relations: Officialdom still in control?', in Hazell, R. (ed.), *The State of the Nations 2003: The third year of devolution in the United Kingdom* (Exeter: Imprint Academic, 2003), 143–67.

Trench, A., *Intergovernmental Relations in Canada: Lessons for the UK?* (London: The Constitution Unit, 2003).

Trench, A., 'Devolution: The withering-away of the JMC?', *Public Law* (2004), 513–17.

Trench, A. (ed.), *Has Devolution Made a Difference? The State of the Nations 2004* (Exeter: Imprint Academic, 2004).

Trench, A., 'The More Things Change the More They Stay the Same: Inter-governmental relations four years on', in Trench, A. (ed.), *Has Devolution Made a Difference?: The State of the Nations 2004* (Exeter: Imprint Academic, 2004), 165–92.

Trench, A., *Better Governance for Wales: An analysis of the white paper on devolution for Wales* (ESRC Devolution and Constitutional Change programme, Devolution Policy Paper, no. 13, August 2005).

Trench, A., *Central Government's Responses to Devolution*, Economic and Social Research Council Devolution Briefing no. 15 (January 2005).

Trench, A. (ed.), *The Dynamics of Devolution: The state of the nations 2005* (Exeter: Imprint Academic, 2005).

Trench, A., 'Intergovernmental Relations Within the UK: The pressures yet to come', in Trench, A. (ed.), *The Dynamics of Devolution: The State of the Nations 2005* (Exeter: Imprint Academic, 2005).

Trench, A., 'Whitehall and the Process of Legislation after Devolution', in Hazell, R. and Rawlings, R. (eds), *Devolution, Law Making and the Constitution* (Exeter: Imprint Academic, 2005), 192–225.

Trench, A., 'Intergovernmental Relations: In search of a theory', in Greer, S. (ed.), *Territory, Democracy and Justice* (Houndmills: Palgrave Macmillan, 2006), 224–56.

Trevelyan, G. M., *The English Revolution 1688–1689* (London: Oxford University Press, 1938).

Verdonck, M. and Deschouwer, K. 'Patterns and Principles of Fiscal Federalism in Belgium', *Regional and Federal Studies*, 13: 4 (2003), 101–7.

Vestri, P. and Fitzpatrick, S., 'Scotland's Councillors', *Scottish Affairs*, 33 (2000), 62–81.

Wachendorfer-Schmidt, U., *Federalism and Political Performance* (London: Routledge, 2000).

Wales Devolution Monitoring Reports (London: The Constitution Unit, 1999–2005). At: www.ucl.ac.uk/constitution-unit/publications/devolution-monitoring-reports/ index.html.

Wales Labour Party, *Better Governance for Wales: A Welsh Labour policy document* (Cardiff: Wales Labour Party, 2004).

Walker, N., *Policing in a Changing Constitutional Order* (London: Sweet & Maxwell, 2000).

Wanless, D., *Securing Good Health for the Entire Population: Final report* (London: The Stationery Office, 2004).

Watson, M., *Year Zero: An inside view of the Scottish Parliament* (Edinburgh: Polygon, 2001).

Watt, J., 'The Under-Fives: From "pre-school education" to "early years services"', in Clark, M. and Munn, P. (eds), *Education in Scotland: Policy and practice from pre-school to secondary* (London: Routledge, 1997), 19–34.

Watts, R. L., *Executive Federalism: A comparative analysis* (Kingston: Institute of Intergovernmental Relations, Queen's University, 1989).

Watts, R. L., *Comparing Federal Systems* (Montreal and Kingston: McGill-Queen's University Press, 2nd edn, 1999).

Watts, R. L., *The Spending Power in Federal Systems: A comparative study* (Kingston: Institute of Intergovernmental Relations, Queen's University, 1999).

Watts, R. L., *Intergovernmental Fiscal Relationships in Eight Countries: Final report* (Kingston: Institute of Intergovernmental Relations, Queen's University, 2004).

Watts, R. L., 'Asymmetrical Decentralization: Functional or dysfunctional', *Indian Journal of Federal Studies*, 1 (2004), 1–42.

Wheare, K. C., *Federal Government* (London: Oxford University Press, 4th edn, 1963).

Whyte, J., *Interpreting Northern Ireland* (Oxford: Clarendon, 1991).

Wilford, R. (ed.), *Aspects of the Belfast Agreement* (Oxford: Oxford University Press, 2001).

Wilkinson, R. G., *Unhealthy Societies* (London: Routledge, 1996).

Wilson, D. and Game, C., *Local Government in the United Kingdom* (Basingstoke: Palgrave Macmillan, 3rd edn, 2002).

Wincott, D., 'Devolution, Social Democracy and Policy Diversity in Britain: The case of early-childhood education and care', in Adams, J. and Schmuecker, K., *Devolution in Practice 2006: Public policy differences within the UK* (London: ippr, 2006), 76–97.

Winetrobe, B., 'Counter-Devolution? The Sewel Convention on devolved legislation at Westminster', *Scottish Law & Practice Quarterly*, 6 (2001), 286–92.

Winetrobe, B., 'Scottish Devolved Legislation and the Courts', *Public Law*, (2002), 31–8.

Winetrobe, B., 'A Partnership of the Parliaments? Scottish law making under the Sewel Convention at Westminster and Holyrood', in Hazell, R. and Rawlings, R. (eds), *Devolution, Law Making and the Constitution* (Exeter: Imprint Academic, 2005), 39–70.

Woods, K. and Carter, D., *Scotland's Health and Health Services* (London: The Stationery Office/The Nuffield Trust, 2003).

Wright, D., *Understanding Intergovernmental Relations* (Pacific Grove, CA: Brooks/Cole, 3rd edn, 1998).

Wyn Owen, J., 'Change the Welsh Way: Health and the NHS 1984–1994', Talk at the University of Wales, Bangor (March 2000).

Young, K. and Rao, N., *Local Government since 1945* (Oxford: Blackwell, 1997).

Zahariadis, N., *Markets, States, and Public Policy: Privatization in Britain and France* (Ann Arbor: University of Michigan Press, 1995).

Index